D1532958

Great American Writers

TWENTIETH CENTURY

EDITOR

R. BAIRD SHUMAN

University of Illinois

Index Volume

SCOTCH PLAINS PUBLIC LIBRARY
1927 BARTLE AVENUE
SCOTCH PLAINS, N.J. 07076

MARSHALL CAVENDISH

NEW YORK • TORONTO • LONDON • SYDNEY

Marshall Cavendish
99 White Plains Road
Tarrytown, New York 10591-9001

Website: www.marshallcavendish.com

© 2002 Marshall Cavendish Corporation

All rights reserved. No part of this book may be reproduced or uti-
lized in any form or by any means electronic or mechanical, including
photocopying, recording, or by an information storage and retrieval
system, without prior written permission from the publisher and
copyright holder.

Salem Press

Editor: R. Baird Shuman
Managing Editor: R. Kent Rasmussen

Manuscript Editors: Heather Stratton
                     Lauren M. Mitchell
Assistant Editor: Andrea Miller
Research Supervisor: Jeffry Jensen
Acquisitions Editor: Mark Rehn

Marshall Cavendish

Project Editor: Marian Armstrong
Editorial Director: Paul Bernabeo

Designer: Patrice Sheridan

Photo Research: Candlepants
                   Carousel Research
                   Linda Sykes Picture Research
                   Anne Burns Images

Indexing: AEIOU

Library of Congress Cataloging-in-Publication Data

Great American writers: twentieth century / R. Baird Shuman, editor.
     v. cm.
     Includes bibliographical references and indexes.
     Contents: v. 1. Agee-Bellow--v. 2. Benét-Cather--v. 3. Cormier-
Dylan--v. 4. Eliot-Frost--v. 5. Gaines-Hinton--v. 6. Hughes-Lewis--v. 7.
London-McNickle--v. 8. Miller-O'Connor--v. 9. O'Neill-Rich--v. 10.
Salinger-Stein--v. 11. Steinbeck-Walker--v. 12. Welty-Zindel--v. 13.
Index.
     ISBN 0-7614-7240-1 (set)—ISBN 0-7614-7253-3 (v. 13)
   1. American literature--20th century--Bio-bibliography--
Dictionaries. 2. Authors, American--20th century--Biography--
Dictionaries. 3. American literature--20th century--Dictionaries. I.
Shuman, R. Baird (Robert Baird), 1929-

PS221.G74 2002
810.9'005'03
[B]   2001028461

Printed in Malaysia; bound in the United States

07 06 05 04 03 02   6 5 4 3 2 1

Contents

Glossary

allegory: the expression of truths or generalizations about human existence by the use of symbolic fictional figures and actions

apocalyptic narrative: narrative about, relating to, or resembling an apocalypse, i.e., foreboding imminent disaster or final doom

autobiographical novel: an autobiography thinly disguised as, or transformed into, a novel

autobiography: a personal account of one's own life, especially for publication; a biography of oneself narrated by oneself

avant-garde: pioneers or innovators, especially in art and literature, who develop new or experimental concepts

ballad: a poem or song narrating a popular story; a form of short narrative folk song

Bildungsroman: a novel dealing with one person's early life and development

biography: a form of nonfiction literature of which the subject is the life of an individual

confessional poets: those who write intimately autobiographical poetry

courtly love: a late-medieval conventionalized code prescribing conduct and emotions of ladies and their lovers

dialect poetry: poetry written in a regional variety of language distinguished by features of vocabulary, grammar, and pronunciation from other regional varieties

dual narrative: a story told by two narrators

end-rhyme: in poetry, a rhyme that occurs in the last syllables of verses

first-person narrator: "I," one of the characters involved in a story, narrates the story and the story is thus seen from that character's point of view

flashback: an interruption of the chronological sequence in a story by the interjection of an event that occurred earlier in the story

free verse: poetry of any line length and any placement on the page, with no fixed measure or meter

gothic romance: European Romantic, pseudomedieval fiction having a prevailing atmosphere of mystery and terror

grotesques: a decorative style in which animal, human, and vegetative forms are interwoven and deformed to the point of absurdity; grotesques in literature are often used for comedy or satire; sometimes grotesques are presented in the form of a character that is somehow deformed or impaired (physically or psychologically) who acts in a manner not considered normal

Harlem Renaissance: a period of literary vigor and creativity, centered in the black ghetto of Harlem in New York City, that took place during the 1920s

historical fiction: a novel that has a period of history as its setting and that attempts to convey the spirit, manners, and social conditions of a past age with realistic detail and fidelity to historical fact

humanism: a devotion to human attributes or qualities

idiom: syntactical, grammatical, or structural form of language established by usage and having a meaning not deducible from the meanings of the individual words

imagery: figurative illustration, especially used for particular effects

imagist: a follower of a twentieth-century movement in poetry advocating free verse and the expression of ideas and emotions through clear precise images

impressionism: a theory or practice in painting, especially among French painters of about 1870, of depicting the natural appearances of objects by means of dabs or strokes of primary colors in order to simulate reflected light

impressionistic writing: the depiction of a scene, emotion, or character by details intended to evoke subjective and sensory impressions rather than by recreating or representing an objective reality

interior monologue: a usually extended representation in monologue of a fictional character's sequence of thought and feeling

internal rhyme: a rhyme between a word within a line and another word either at the end of the same line or within another line

irony: the use of words, often humorous or sarcastic, to express something other than, and especially the opposite of, the literal meaning

Kafkaesque: of, relating to, or suggestive of Franz Kafka or his writings, especially having a nightmarishly complex, bizarre, or illogical quality

magic realism: Latin-American literary phenomenon characterized by the incorporation of fantastic or mythical elements matter-of-factly into otherwise realistic fiction

metaphor: a figure of speech in which a word or phrase denoting one kind of object or action is used in place of another to suggest a likeness or analogy between them; an implied comparison

mock epic: form of satire that applies the elevated heroic style of the classical epic to a trivial subject

multiple-viewpoint narrative: a story told by a third-person narrator, not limited in viewpoint to any one character, and thus the narrator can comment on every aspect of the story

myth: a traditional narrative usually involving supernatural or imaginary persons and embodying popular ideas on natural or social phenomena

narrative poetry: a verse of poem that tells a story; main forms are the epic and the ballad

naturalism: realism in art or literature, specifically a theory in literature emphasizing scientific observation of life without idealization or the avoidance of the ugly

Neoplatonism: a late antiquity modification of the philosophy of Plato that stresses that actual things are copies of transcendent ideas, incorporating Aristotelian and post-Aristotelian conceptions that see the world as emanating from an ultimate indivisible being with whom the soul is capable of being reunited in trance or ecstasy

nonfiction novel: a book-length narrative of actual people and actual events written in the style of a novel

objective correlative: literary theory first set forth by T. S. Eliot in the essay "Hamlet and His Problems" and published in *The Sacred Wood* (1920). According to the theory, "the only way of expressing emotion in the form of art is by finding an 'objective correlative'; in other words, a set of objects, a situation, a chain of events that shall be the formula of that *particular* emotion; such that when the external facts, which must terminate in sensory experience, are given, the emotion is immediately evoked."

oral tradition: the knowledge and beliefs of cultures that are transmitted by word of mouth

parody: a literary work in which the style of an author is closely imitated in an exaggerated way for comic effect or in ridicule

pastoralism: a literary style dealing with the lives of shepherds or rural life in general and typically drawing a contrast between the innocence and serenity of the simple life and the misery and corruption of city life

pastoral poetry: a poem dealing with the lives of shepherds or rural life in general; many pastoral poems are remote from the realities of any life, rustic or urban

picaresque novel: an early form of the novel, with an episodic structure, usually a first-person narrative, relating the adventures of a rogue or lowborn adventurer who drifts from place to place and from one social milieu to another in an effort to survive

regionalism: emphasis on regional locale and characteristics in art and literature

rhythm: a measured flow of words and phrases in verse or prose determined by various relations of long and short or accented and unaccented

romanticism: a literary, artistic, and philosophical movement originating in Europe in the eighteenth century and lasting roughly until the mid–nineteenth century; characterized chiefly by a reaction against the Enlightenment and Neoclassicism with their stress on reason, order, balance, harmony, rationality, and intellect.

satire: the use of ridicule, irony, sarcasm, etc. to expose folly or vice or to lampoon an individual

slang: an informal nonstandard vocabulary composed typically of coinages, arbitrarily changed words, and extravagant, forced, or facetious figures of speech

Socialist Realism: the officially sanctioned theory and method of artistic, including literary, composition prevalent in the Soviet Union from 1932 to the mid-1980s

sonnet: a poem of fourteen lines (usually pentameters) using any of a number of formal rhyme schemes, in English usually having ten syllables per line

stanza: the basic metrical unit in a poem or verse, consisting of a recurring group of lines (often four lines and usually not more than twelve) that may or may not rhyme

stream-of-consciousness: narrative technique in nondramatic fiction intended to render the flow of myriad impressions—visual, auditory, physical, associative, and subliminal—that together with rational thought impinge on the consciousness of an individual

stream-of-consciousness novels: a story that uses the narrative techniques of interior monologue

street vernacular: language or dialect native to the urban street environment

stresses: accentuation; emphases laid on syllables or words; accents, especially the principal one in a word

style: a distinctive manner of expression

symbolism: the use of symbols to represent ideas; specifically, an artistic and poetic movement or style using symbols and indirect suggestions to express ideas, emotions, etc.

syntax: the way in which linguistic elements (as words) are put together to form constituents (as phrases or clauses)

tragicomic realism: a realistic drama or a situation blending tragic and comic elements

vernacular speech: a language or dialect native to a region or country rather than a literary, cultured, or foreign language

Winners of the Nobel Prize for Literature

The Nobel Prize for Literature is one of six prizes awarded annually from a fund established under the will of Alfred Bernhard Nobel (1833–1869), a Swedish chemist, engineer, and industrialist who had an abiding interest in literature. In his youth he had written poetry in English, and the beginnings of a novel were found among his papers. The Nobel Prize for literature, generally awarded to a writer for a body of work, has come to be one of the most highly regarded of international awards.

Names appearing in **boldface** indicate writers covered in this encyclopedia set.

2001	V.S. Naipaul	British
2000	Gao Xingjian	Chinese
1999	Günter Grass	German
1998	José Saramago	Portuguese
1997	Dario Fo	Italian
1996	Wislawa Szymborska	Polish
1995	Seamus Heaney	Irish
1994	Kenzaburo Oe	Japanese
1993	**Toni Morrison**	American
1992	Derek Walcott	West Indian
1991	Nadine Gordimer	South African
1990	Octavio Paz	Mexican
1989	Camilo José Cela	Spanish
1988	Naguib Mahfouz	Egyptian
1987	Joseph Brodsky	Russian–American
1986	Wole Soyinka	Nigerian
1985	Claude Simon	French
1984	Jaroslav Siefert	Czechoslovakian
1983	William Golding	British
1982	Gabriel Garcia Marquez	Colombian–Mexican
1981	Elias Canetti	Bulgarian–British
1980	Czeslaw Milosz	Polish–American
1979	Odysseus Elytis	Greek
1978	**Isaac Bashevis Singer**	American
1977	Vicente Aleixandre	Spanish
1976	**Saul Bellow**	American
1975	Eugenio Montale	Italian
1974	Eyvind Johnson	Swedish
	Harry Edmund Martinson	Swedish
1973	Patrick White	Australian
1972	Heinrich Böll	German
1971	Pablo Neruda	Chilean

1970	Aleksandr I. Solzhenitsyn	Russian
1969	Samuel Beckett	Irish
1968	Yasunari Kawabata	Japanese
1967	Miguel Angel Asturias	Guatemalan
1966	Samuel Joseph Agnon	Israeli
	Nelly Sachs	Swedish
1965	Mikhail Sholokhov	Russian
1964	declined by Jean-Paul Sartre	French
1963	Giorgios Seferis	Greek
1962	**John Steinbeck**	American
1961	Ivo Andric	Yugoslavian
1960	Saint-John Perse	French
1959	declined by Salvatore Quasimodo	Italian
1958	Boris L. Pasternak	Russian
1957	Albert Camus	French
1956	Juan Ramón Jiménez	Spanish
1955	Halidor K. Laxness	Icelander
1954	**Ernest Hemingway**	American
1953	Sir Winston Churchill	British
1952	François Mauriac	French
1951	Par F. Lagerkvist	Swedish
1950	Bertrand Russell	British
1949	**William Faulkner**	American
1948	**T. S. Eliot**	American-British
1947	André Gide	French
1946	Hermann Hesse	German–Swiss
1945	Gabriela Mistral	Chilean
1944	Johannes V. Jensen	Danish
1940–1943	(not awarded)	
1939	Frans E. Sillanpää	Finn
1938	**Pearl S. Buck**	American
1937	Roger Martin du Gard	French
1936	**Eugene O'Neill**	American
1935	(not awarded)	
1934	Luigi Pirandello	Italian
1933	Ivan A. Bunin	Russian
1932	John Galsworthy	British
1931	Erik A. Karlfeldt	Swedish
1930	**Sinclair Lewis**	American
1929	Thomas Mann	German
1928	Sigrid Undset	Norwegian
1927	Henri Bergson	French
1926	Grazia Deledda	Italian
1925	George Bernard Shaw	Irish
1924	Wladyslaw S. Reymont	Polish
1923	William Butler Yeats	Irish
1922	Jacinto Benavente	Spanish
1921	Anatole France	French
1920	Knut Hamsun	Norwegian
1919	Carl F. G. Spitteler	Swiss
1918	(not awarded)	

1917	Karl A. Gjellerup	Danish
	Henrik Pontoppidan	Danish
1916	Verner von Heidenstam	Swedish
1915	Romain Rolland	French
1914	(not awarded)	
1913	Rabindranath Tagore	Indian
1912	Gerhart Hauptmann	German
1911	Maurice Maeterlinck	Belgian
1910	Paul J. L. Heyse	German
1909	Selma Lagerlöf	Swedish
1908	Rudolf C. Eucken	German
1907	Rudyard Kipling	British
1906	Giosuè Carducci	Italian
1905	Henryk Sienkiewicz	Polish
1904	Frédéric Mistral	French
	José Echegaray	Spanish
1903	Björnsterne Björnson	Norwegian
1902	Theodor Mommsen	German
1901	René F. A. Sully Prudhomme	French

Winners of Pulitzer Prizes

The Pulitzer Prize, named after newspaper magnate Joseph Pulitzer, is any of a series of prizes awarded annually by Columbia University in New York City. These prizes recognize outstanding public service and achievement in American journalism, letters, and music. Following are recipients of prizes in fiction, drama, and poetry as well as special citations.

Names appearing in **boldface** indicate writers covered in this encyclopedia set.

FICTION

2001	Michael Chabon	*The Amazing Adventures of Kavalier and Clay*
2000	Jhumpa Lahiri	*Interpreter of Maladies*
1999	Michael Cunningham	*The Hours*
1998	Philip Roth	*American Pastoral*
1997	Steven Millhauser	*Martin Dressler: The Tale of an American Dreamer*
1996	Richard Ford	*Independence Day*
1995	Carol Shields	*The Stone Diaries*
1994	E. Annie Proulx	*The Shipping News*
1993	Robert Olen Butler	*A Good Scent From a Strange Mountain*
1992	Jane Smiley	*A Thousand Acres*
1991	John Updike	*Rabbit at Rest*
1990	Oscar Hijuelos	*The Mambo Kings Play Songs of Love*
1989	**Anne Tyler**	*Breathing Lessons*
1988	**Toni Morrison**	*Beloved*
1987	Peter Taylor	*A Summons to Memphis*
1986	Larry McMurtry	*Lonesome Dove*
1985	Alison Lurie	*Foreign Affairs*
1984	William Kennedy	*Ironweed*
1983	**Alice Walker**	*The Color Purple*
1982	John Updike	*Rabbit Is Rich*
1981	John Kennedy Toole	*A Confederacy of Dunces*
1980	Norman Mailer	*The Executioner's Song*
1979	John Cheever	*The Stories of John Cheever*
1978	James Alan McPherson	*Elbow Room*
1977	(not awarded)	
1976	**Saul Bellow**	*Humboldt's Gift*
1975	Michael Shaara	*The Killer Angels*
1974	(not awarded)	
1973	**Eudora Welty**	*The Optimist's Daughter*
1972	Wallace Stegner	*Angle of Repose*
1971	(not awarded)	
1970	Jean Stafford	*Collected Stories*
1969	N. Scott Momaday	*House Made of Dawn*

1968	**William Styron**	*The Confessions of Nat Turner*
1967	**Bernard Malamud**	*The Fixer*
1966	**Katherine Anne Porter**	*Collected Stories*
1965	Shirley Ann Grau	*The Keepers of the House*
1964	(not awarded)	
1963	**William Faulkner**	*The Reivers*
1962	Edwin O'Connor	*The Edge of Sadness*
1961	**Harper Lee**	*To Kill a Mockingbird*
1960	Allen Drury	*Advise and Consent*
1959	Robert Lewis Taylor	*The Travels of Jaimie McPheeters*
1958	**James Agee**	*A Death in the Family*
1957	(not awarded)	
1956	MacKinlay Kantor	*Andersonville*
1955	**William Faulkner**	*A Fable*
1954	(not awarded)	
1953	**Ernest Hemingway**	*The Old Man and the Sea*
1952	Herman Wouk	*The Caine Mutiny*
1951	Conrad Richter	*The Town*
1950	A.B. Guthrie Jr.	*The Way West*
1949	James Gould Cozzens	*Guard of Honor*
1948	James A. Michener	*Tales of the South Pacific*
1947	Robert Penn Warren	*All the King's Men*
1946	(not awarded)	
1945	**John Hersey**	*A Bell for Adano*
1944	Martin Flavin	*Journey in the Dark*
1943	**Upton Sinclair**	*Dragon's Teeth*
1942	Ellen Glasgow	*In This Our Life*
1941	(not awarded)	
1940	**John Steinbeck**	*The Grapes of Wrath*
1939	Marjorie Kinnan Rawlings	*The Yearling*
1938	John P. Marquand	*The Late George Apley*
1937	Margaret Mitchell	*Gone With the Wind*
1936	Harold L. Davis	*Honey in the Horn*
1935	Josephine W. Johnson	*Now in November*
1934	Caroline Miller	*Lamb in His Bosom*
1933	T.S. Stribling	*The Store*
1932	**Pearl S. Buck**	*The Good Earth*
1931	Margaret Ayer Barnes	*Years of Grace*
1930	Oliver LaFarge	*Laughing Boy*
1929	Julia M. Peterkin	*Scarlet Sister Mary*
1928	**Thornton Wilder**	*The Bridge of San Luis Rey*
1927	Louis Bromfield	*Early Autumn*
1926	**Sinclair Lewis**	*Arrowsmith* (declined)
1925	**Edna Ferber**	*So Big*
1924	Margaret Wilson	*The Able McLaughlins*
1923	**Willa Cather**	*One of Ours*
1922	Booth Tarkington	*Alice Adams*
1921	**Edith Wharton**	*The Age of Innocence*
1920	(not awarded)	
1919	Booth Tarkington	*The Magnificent Ambersons*
1918	Ernest Poole	*His Family*
1917	(not awarded)	

DRAMA

2001	David Auburn	*Proof*
2000	Donald Margulies	*Dinner With Friends*
1999	Margaret Edson	*Wit*
1998	Paula Vogel	*How I Learned to Drive*
1997	(not awarded)	
1996	Jonathan Larson	*Rent*
1995	**Horton Foote**	*The Young Man From Atlanta*
1994	Edward Albee	*Three Tall Women*
1993	Tony Kushner	*Angels in America: Millennium Approaches*
1992	Robert Schenkkan	*The Kentucky Cycle*
1991	Neil Simon	*Lost in Yonkers*
1990	August Wilson	*The Piano Lesson*
1989	Wendy Wasserstein	*The Heidi Chronicles*
1988	Alfred Uhry	*Driving Miss Daisy*
1987	August Wilson	*Fences*
1986	(not awarded)	
1985	Stephen Sondheim and James Lapine	*Sunday in the Park With George*
1984	**David Mamet**	*Glengarry Glen Ross*
1983	Marsha Norman	*'night, Mother*
1982	Charles Fuller	*A Soldier's Play*
1981	Beth Henley	*Crimes of the Heart*
1980	Lanford Wilson	*Talley's Folly*
1979	Sam Shepard	*Buried Child*
1978	Donald L. Coburn	*The Gin Game*
1977	Michael Cristofer	*The Shadow Box*
1976	Michael Bennett, James Kirkwood, Nicholas Dante, Marvin Hamlisch, and Edward Kleban	*A Chorus Line*
1975	Edward Albee	*Seascape*
1974	(not awarded)	
1973	Jason Miller	*That Championship Season*
1972	(not awarded)	
1971	**Paul Zindel**	*The Effect of Gamma Rays on Man-in-the-Moon Marigolds*
1970	Charles Gordone	*No Place to Be Somebody*
1969	Howard Sackler	*The Great White Hope*
1968	(not awarded)	
1967	Edward Albee	*A Delicate Balance*
1966	(not awarded)	
1965	Frank D. Gilroy	*The Subject Was Roses*
1964	(not awarded)	
1963	(not awarded)	
1962	Frank Loesser and Abe Burrows	*How to Succeed in Business Without Really Trying*
1961	Tad Mosel	*All the Way Home*
1960	George Abbott, Jerome Weidman,	

	Sheldon Harnick, and Jerry Bock	Fiorello!
1959	**Archibald MacLeish**	J.B.
1958	Ketti Frings	Look Homeward, Angel
1957	**Eugene O'Neill**	Long Day's Journey into Night
1956	Frances Goodrich and Albert Hackett	The Diary of Anne Frank
1955	**Tennessee Williams**	Cat on a Hot Tin Roof
1954	John Patrick	Teahouse of the August Moon
1953	William Inge	Picnic
1952	Joseph Kramm	The Shrike
1951	(not awarded)	
1950	Richard Rodgers, Oscar Hammerstein II, and Joshua Logan	South Pacific
1949	**Arthur Miller**	Death of a Salesman
1948	**Tennessee Williams**	A Streetcar Named Desire
1947	(not awarded)	
1946	Russel Crouse and Howard Lindsay	State of the Union
1945	Mary Chase	Harvey
1944	(not awarded)	
1943	**Thornton Wilder**	The Skin of Our Teeth
1942	(not awarded)	
1941	Robert E. Sherwood	There Shall Be No Night
1940	William Saroyan	The Time of Your Life
1939	Robert E. Sherwood	Abe Lincoln in Illinois
1938	**Thornton Wilder**	Our Town
1937	George S. Kaufman and Moss Hart	You Can't Take It With You
1936	Robert E. Sherwood	Idiot's Delight
1935	Zoe Akins	The Old Maid
1934	Sidney Kingsley	Men in White
1933	Maxwell Anderson	Both Your Houses
1932	George S. Kaufman, Morrie Ryskind, and Ira Gershwin	Of Thee I Sing
1931	Susan Glaspell	Alison's House
1930	Marc Connelly	The Green Pastures
1929	Elmer Rice	Street Scene
1928	**Eugene O'Neill**	Strange Interlude
1927	Paul Green	In Abraham's Bosom
1926	George Kelly	Craig's Wife
1925	Sidney Howard	They Knew What They Wanted
1924	Hatcher Hughes	Hell-Bent for Heaven
1923	Owen Davis	Icebound
1922	**Eugene O'Neill**	Anna Christie
1921	Zona Gale	Miss Lulu Bett
1920	**Eugene O'Neill**	Beyond the Horizon
1919	(not awarded)	
1918	Jesse Lynch Williams	Why Marry?
1917	(not awarded)	

POETRY

2001	Stephen Dunn	*Different Hours*
2000	C. K. Williams	*Repair*
1999	Mark Strand	*Blizzard of One*
1998	Charles Wright	*Black Zodiak*
1997	Lisel Mueller	*Alive Together: New and Selected Poems*
1996	Jorie Graham	*The Dream of the Unified Field*
1995	Philip Levine	*The Simple Truth*
1994	Yusef Komunyakaa	*Neon Vernacular*
1993	Louise Glück	*The Wild Iris*
1992	James Tate	*Selected Poems*
1991	Mona Van Duyn	*Near Changes*
1990	Charles Simic	*The World Doesn't End*
1989	Richard Wilbur	*New and Collected Poems*
1988	William Meredith	*Partial Accounts: New and Selected Poems*
1987	Rita Dove	*Thomas and Beulah*
1986	Henry Taylor	*The Flying Change*
1985	Carolyn Kizer	*Yin*
1984	Mary Oliver	*American Primitive*
1983	Galway Kinnell	*Selected Poems*
1982	**Sylvia Plath**	*The Collected Poems*
1981	James Schuyler	*The Morning of the Poem*
1980	Donald Justice	*Selected Poems*
1979	Robert Penn Warren	*Now and Then: Poems 1976–1978*
1978	Howard Nemerov	*Collected Poems*
1977	James Merrill	*Divine Comedies*
1976	John Ashbery	*Self-Portrait in a Convex Mirror*
1975	Gary Snyder	*Turtle Island*
1974	Robert Lowell	*The Dolphin*
1973	Maxine Winokur Kumin	*Up Country*
1972	James Wright	*Collected Poems*
1971	William S. Merwin	*The Carrier of Ladders*
1970	Richard Howard	*Untitled Subjects*
1969	George Oppen	*Of Being Numerous*
1968	Anthony Hecht	*The Hard Hours*
1967	**Anne Sexton**	*Live or Die*
1966	Richard Eberhart	*Selected Poems*
1965	John Berryman	*77 Dream Songs*
1964	Louis Simpson	*At the End of the Open Road*
1963	**William Carlos Williams**	*Pictures From Breughel*
1962	Alan Dugan	*Poems*
1961	Phyllis McGinley	*Times Three: Selected Verse From Three Decades*
1960	W. D. Snodgrass	*Heart's Needle*
1959	Stanley Kunitz	*Selected Poems 1928–1958*
1958	Robert Penn Warren	*Promises: Poems 1954–1956*
1957	Richard Wilbur	*Things of This World*
1956	Elizabeth Bishop	*Poems, North and South*
1955	**Wallace Stevens**	*Collected Poems*
1954	Theodore Roethke	*The Waking*
1953	**Archibald MacLeish**	*Collected Poems*
1952	**Marianne Moore**	*Collected Poems*

1951	**Carl Sandburg**	*Complete Poems*
1950	**Gwendolyn Brooks**	*Annie Allen*
1949	Peter Viereck	*Terror and Decorum*
1948	W. H. Auden	*The Age of Anxiety*
1947	Robert Lowell	*Lord Weary's Castle*
1946	(not awarded)	
1945	Karl Shapiro	*V-Letter and Other Poems*
1944	**Stephen Vincent Benét**	*Western Star*
1943	**Robert Frost**	*A Witness Tree*
1942	William Rose Benét	*The Dust Which Is God*
1941	Leonard Bacon	*Sunderland Capture*
1940	Mark Van Doren	*Collected Poems*
1939	John Gould Fletcher	*Selected Poems*
1938	Marya Zaturenska	*Cold Morning Sky*
1937	Robert Frost	*A Further Range*
1936	Robert P. Tristram Coffin	*Strange Holiness*
1935	Audrey Wurdemann	*Bright Ambush*
1934	Robert Hillyer	*Collected Verse*
1933	**Archibald MacLeish**	*Conquistador*
1932	George Dillon	*The Flowering Stone*
1931	**Robert Frost**	*Collected Poems*
1930	Conrad Aiken	*Selected Poems*
1929	**Stephen Vincent Benét**	*John Brown's Body*
1928	Edwin Arlington Robinson	*Tristram*
1927	Leonora Speyer	*Fiddler's Farewell*
1926	Amy Lowell	*What's O'Clock*
1925	Edwin Arlington Robinson	*The Man Who Died Twice*
1924	**Robert Frost**	*New Hampshire: A Poem with Notes and Grace Notes*
1923	Edna St. Vincent Millay	*The Ballad of the Harp-Weaver; A Few Figs from Thistles; other works*
1922	Edwin Arlington Robinson	*Collected Poem*
*1919	Margaret Widdemer	*Old Road to Paradise*
	Carl Sandburg	*Corn Huskers*
*1918	Sara Teasdale	*Love Songs*

The poetry prize was estabished in 1922. The 1918 and 1919 awards were made from gifts provided by the Poetry Society.

SPECIAL CITATIONS

1992	Art Spiegelman, for *Maus*
1984	Theodore Seuss Geisel (Dr. Seuss)
1978	E. B. White
1977	Alex Haley, for *Roots*
1973	*George Washington, Vols. I–IV,* by James Thomas Flexner
1961	*American Heritage Picture History of the Civil War*
1960	*The Armada,* by Garrett Mattingly
1957	Kenneth Roberts, for his historical novels
1944	Richard Rodgers and Oscar Hammerstein II, for *Oklahoma!*

Further Reading

Adam, Julie. *Versions of Heroism in Modern American Drama: Redefinitions by Miller, O'Neill, and Anderson.* New York: St. Martin's Press, 1991.

American Poetry: The Twentieth Century. New York: Library of America, 2000.

Baker, Houston A., Jr. *Modernism and the Harlem Renaissance.* Chicago: University of Chicago Press, 1987.

Bennett, Paula. *My Life, a Loaded Gun: Dickinson, Plath, Rich, and Female Creativity.* Urbana: University of Illinois Press, 1990.

Bloom, Harold, ed. *Twentieth-Century American Literature.* The Chelsea House Library of Literary Criticism. New York: Chelsea House Publishers, 1985.

Brinkmeyer, Robert H., Jr. *Three Catholic Writers of the Modern South.* Jackson: University Press of Mississippi, 1985.

Caron, Timothy Paul. *Struggles over the Word: Race and Religion in O'Connor, Faulkner, Hurston, and Wright.* Macon, GA: Mercer University Press, 2000.

Chamberlain, John. *The Turnabout Years: America's Cultural Life, 1900–1950.* Ottawa, IL: Jameson Books, 1992.

Elbert, Monika M., ed. *Separate Spheres No More: Gender Convergence in American Literature, 1830–1930.* Tuscaloosa: University of Alabama Press, 2000.

Gates, Henry Louis, and Nellie Y. McKay, eds. *The Norton Anthology of African American Literature.* New York: W.W. Norton & Company, 1997.

Gleason, William A. *The Leisure Ethic: Work and Play in American Literature, 1840–1940.* Stanford, CA: Stanford University Press, 1999.

Hart, James David, and Phillip Leininger, eds. *The Oxford Companion to American Literature,* 6th edition. New York: Oxford University Press, 1995.

Hartsock, John C. *A History of American Literary Journalism.* Amherst: University of Massachusetts Press, 2001.

Hoover, Paul, ed. *Postmodern American Poetry: A Norton Anthology.* New York: W. W. Norton & Co., 1994.

Howard, Lillie P., ed. *Alice Walker and Zora Neale Hurston: The Common Bond.* Contributions in Afro-American and African Studies. Westport, CT: Greenwood Press, 1993.

Kirschke, James J. *Willa Cather and Six Writers from the Great War.* Lanham, MD: University Press of America; Intercollegiate Studies Institute, 1990.

Lakritz, Andrew M. *Modernism and the Other in Stevens, Frost, and Moore.* Gainesville: University Press of Florida, 1996.

Merriam-Webster's Dictionary of American Writers. Springfield, Mass., 2001.

Mullen, Bill. *Popular Fronts: Chicago and African-American Cultural Politics, 1935–46.* Urbana: University of Illinois Press, 1999.

Ostwalt, Conrad Eugene. *After Eden: The Secularization of American Space in the Fiction of Willa Cather and Theodore Dreiser.* Lewisburg, PA: Bucknell University Press; London: Associated University Presses, 1990.

Robertson, Michael. *Stephen Crane, Journalism, and the Making of Modern American Literature.* New York: Columbia University Press, 1997.

Rosen, Kenneth, ed. *Voices of the Rainbow: Contemporary Poetry by Native Americans.* New York: Arcade Publishing, 1993.

Scruggs, Charles. *The Sage in Harlem: H. L. Mencken and the Black Writers of the 1920s.* Baltimore: Johns Hopkins University Press, 1984.

Sewell, Marilyn, ed. *Claiming the Spirit Within: A Sourcebook of Women's Poetry.* Boston: Beacon Press, 1996.

Sielke, Sabine. *Fashioning the Female Subject: The Intertextual Networking of Dickinson, Moore, and Rich.* Ann Arbor: University of Michigan Press, 1997.

Sims, Norman, and Mark Kramer, eds. *Literary Journalism: A New Collection of the Best American Nonfiction.* New York: Ballantine Books, 1995.

Stout Janis P. *Strategies of Reticence: Silence and Meaning in the Works of Jane Austen, Willa Cather, Katherine Anne Porter, and Joan Didion.* Charlottesville: University Press of Virginia, 1990.

Updike, John, and Katrina Kenison, eds. *The Best American Short Stories of the Century.* New York: Mariner Books, 2000.

Wall, Cheryl A. *Women of the Harlem Renaissance.* Women of Letters Series. Bloomington: Indiana University Press, 1995.

Wilson, Christopher P. *White Collar Fictions: Class and Social Representation in American Literature, 1885–1925.* Athens: University of Georgia Press, 1992.

Writers by Genre

AUTOBIOGRAPHERS

Anderson, Sherwood
Angelou, Maya
Giovanni, Nikki
Masters, Edgar Lee
Miller, Arthur
Sandburg, Carl
Sinclair, Upton
Stein, Gertrude
Welty, Eudora
Williams, Tennessee
Williams, William Carlos
Wright, Richard

CHILDREN'S BOOK AUTHORS

Alvarez, Julia
Angelou, Maya
Atwood, Margaret
Baldwin, James
Blume, Judy
Bontemps, Arna
Brooks, Gwendolyn
Buck, Pearl S.
Cormier, Robert
Davies, Robertson
Gardner, John
Giovanni, Nikki
Hinton, S. E.
Hughes, Langston
Laurence, Margaret
London, Jack
Mamet, David
Morrison, Toni
Oates, Joyce Carol
Plath, Sylvia
Potok, Chaim
Sandburg, Carl
Sexton, Anne
Sinclair, Upton
Singer, Isaac Bashevis
Stein, Gertrude
Tan, Amy

Tyler, Anne
Walker, Alice
Welty, Eudora

ESSAYISTS

Alvarez, Julia
Atwood, Margaret
Baldwin, James
Bellow, Saul
Capote, Truman
Carver, Raymond
Cather, Willa
Davies, Robertson
Didion, Joan
Eliot, T. S.
Ellison, Ralph
Gardner, John
Hersey, John
London, Jack
MacLeish, Archibald
Mamet, David
Morrison, Toni
O'Brien, Tim
Porter, Katherine Anne
Rich, Adrienne
Sexton, Anne
Singer, Isaac Bashevis
Stein, Gertrude
Stevens, Wallace
Tan, Amy
Terkel, Studs
Walker, Alice
Welty, Eudora
Wilder, Thornton
Williams, Tennessee
Williams, William Carlos
Wright, Richard

FICTION WRITERS

Agee, James
Alvarez, Julia

Anderson, Sherwood
Atwood, Margaret
Baldwin, James
Bellow, Saul
Benét, Stephen Vincent
Blume, Judy
Bontemps, Arna
Brooks, Gwendolyn
Buck, Pearl S.
Capote, Truman
Carver, Raymond
Cather, Willa
Cormier, Robert
Davies, Robertson
Didion, Joan
Dreiser, Theodore
Dunbar, Paul Laurence
Ellison, Ralph
Faulkner, William
Ferber, Edna
Fitzgerald, F. Scott
Foote, Horton
Gaines, Ernest J.
Gardner, John
Gibson, William
Hemingway, Ernest
Hersey, John
Hinton, S. E.
Hughes, Langston
Hurston, Zora Neale
Irving, John
Knowles, John
Laurence, Margaret
Lee, Harper
Lewis, Sinclair
London, Jack
Malamud, Bernard
Mamet, David
Masters, Edgar Lee
McCarthy, Cormac
Miller, Arthur
Morrison, Toni
Munro, Alice
Norris, Frank
Oates, Joyce Carol
O'Brien, Tim
O'Connor, Flannery
Ortiz Cofer, Judith
Piercy, Marge
Plath, Sylvia
Porter, Katherine Anne
Portis, Charles

Potok, Chaim
Salinger, J. D.
Sandburg, Carl
Schaefer, Jack Warner
Sinclair, Upton
Singer, Isaac Bashevis
Stein, Gertrude
Steinbeck, John
Styron, William
Tan, Amy
Tyler, Anne
Walker, Alice
Welty, Eudora
Wharton, Edith
Wilder, Thornton
Williams, Tennessee
Williams, William Carlos
Wright, Richard
Zindel, Paul

JOURNALISTS

Agee, James
Capote, Truman
Cather, Willa
Cormier, Robert
Ferber, Edna
Hersey, John
Knowles, John
Laurence, Margaret
London, Jack
Norris, Frank
Portis, Charles
Sandburg, Carl
Schaefer, Jack Warner
Sinclair, Upton
Steinbeck, John

LYRICISTS

Dylan, Bob

PLAYWRIGHTS

Anderson, Sherwood
Angelou, Maya
Baldwin, James
Bellow, Saul
Benét, Stephen Vincent

Bontemps, Arna
Capote, Truman
Cummings, E. E.
Davies, Robertson
Dreiser, Theodore
Dunbar, Paul Laurence
Eliot, T. S.
Ferber, Edna
Foote, Horton
Frost, Robert
Gardner, John
Gibson, William
Hansberry, Lorraine
Hemingway, Ernest
Hughes, Langston
Jeffers, Robinson
Lewis, Sinclair
London, Jack
MacLeish, Archibald
Mamet, David
Masters, Edgar Lee
McCarthy, Cormac
Miller, Arthur
Moore, Marianne
Morrison, Toni
Oates, Joyce Carol
O'Neill, Eugene
Ortiz Cofer, Judith
Piercy, Marge
Sexton, Anne
Sinclair, Upton
Singer, Isaac Bashevis
Stein, Gertrude
Steinbeck, John
Stevens, Wallace
Styron, William
Wilder, Thornton
Williams, Tennessee
Williams, William Carlos
Wright, Richard
Zindel, Paul

POETS

Agee, James
Alvarez, Julia

Anderson, Sherwood
Angelou, Maya
Atwood, Margaret
Baldwin, James
Benét, Stephen Vincent
Bontemps, Arna
Brooks, Gwendolyn
Carver, Raymond
Cather, Willa
Cummings, E. E.
Dreiser, Theodore
Dunbar, Paul Laurence
Eliot, T. S.
Faulkner, William
Frost, Robert
Gardner, John
Gibson, William
Giovanni, Nikki
Hughes, Langston
Jeffers, Robinson
MacLeish, Archibald
Mamet, David
Masters, Edgar Lee
Moore, Marianne
Norris, Frank
Oates, Joyce Carol
O'Neill, Eugene
Ortiz Cofer, Judith
Piercy, Marge
Plath, Sylvia
Rich, Adrienne
Sandburg, Carl
Sexton, Anne
Stein, Gertrude
Stevens, Wallace
Walker, Alice
Wharton, Edith
Williams, Tennessee
Williams, William Carlos

YOUNG ADULT AUTHORS

Blume, Judy
Bontemps, Arna
Cormier Robert
Zindel, Paul

Comprehensive Index of Writers

Page numbers in **boldface** type indicate full articles.

Abbott, George **8**:1025

Achebe, Chinua **6**:824

Adams, Franklin P. **4**:502

Addison, Joseph **3**:336, 339, 343

Aeschylus **6**:788, **9**:1167, 1179

Agee, James **1:11-24**
  African Queen, The (screenplay) **1**:11
  awards and honors **1**:14
  background and early life **1**:12-13, 19
  Death in the Family, A **1**:11, 13, 14, 15, 17, 18-20
  filmmaking **1**:11, 13, 14, 15-16
  genres and works **1**:15-23
  highlights in life **1**:14
  influences on **1**:19, 23
  journalistic career **1**:12-13
  "Knoxville: Summer of 1915" **1**:13, 15
  Let Us Now Praise Famous Men **1**:11, 13, 14, 15, 17, 19, 20-22
  Morning Watch, The **1**:13, 14, 16-17, 23
  Night of the Hunter, The (screenplay) **1**:11, 13, 14, 17
  Permit Me Voyage **1**:12-13, 15
  Quiet One, The **1**:14, 16
  themes and issues **1**:15, 18

Akins, Zoé **12**:1619

Albee, Edward **11**:1528, **12**:1713, 1717
  Ballad of the Sad Café adaptation **7**:978, 982

Aleichem, Sholom **10**:1399

Alexander, Paul **10**:1306

Alger, Horatio **8**:1086, **11**:1532

Algren, Nelson **11**:1531

Allen, Paula Gunn **12**:1683

Allende, Isabel **8**:1058

Alvarez, Julia **1:25-40**
  academic career **1**:28, 29
  "Against Cinderella" **1**:38

background and life **1**:26-29

"Bilingual Sestina" **1**:38

"Bookmaking" **1**:38

education **1**:26

"Gladys Poems, The" **1**:38

"Heroines" **1**:38

highlights in life **1**:28

Homecoming: New and Collected Poems **1**:28, 29, 32, 37-38

Homecoming: Poems **1**:28, 29, 32, 37

How the García Girls Lost Their Accents **1**:28, 29, 32, 33-34

influences on **1**:31

In the Name of Salomé **1**:32

In the Time of the Butterflies **1**:28, 29, 30, 32

In Time of Butterflies **1**:28, 32

"Joe Poems, The" **1**:38

"Making Our Beds" **1**:37-38

"Making Up the Past" **1**:38

Old Age Ain't for Sissies (ed.) **1**:28, 29, 32

Other Side, The: El Otro Lado **1**:28, 29, 32, 38

"Other Side, The": *El Otro Lado* **1**:38

"Picky Eater" **1**:39

"Redwing Sonnets" **1**:38

Secret Footprints, The **1**:28, 32

Seven Trees **1**:28, 29, 32

Something to Declare **1**:28, 29, 30, 31, 39

"Staying Up Alone" **1**:38

themes and issues **1**:30-31, 33, 34, 36, 39

!Yo! **1**:28, 29, 30, 32, 36-37

Alvarez, Ruth M. **9**:1168

Anderson, Sherwood **1:41-56**, **9**:1229, **10**:1429
  "Adventure" **1**:52
  as Faulkner influence **4**:477-78, 481, 482, 485

as influence **1**:41, 53

"Awakening, An" **1**:53

awards and honors **1**:44, 45

background and life **1**:42-45, 49

Beyond Desire **1**:46, 48

"Book of the Grotesque, The" **1**:52

business writing **1**:42-43, 44

critical commentary on **1**:46, 54

Dark Laughter **1**:45, 46, 48

"Death in the Woods" **1**:54

Death in the Woods and Other Stories **1**:44, 48, 54

"Egg, The" **1**:41, 46, 54-55

"Godliness: A Tale in Four Parts" **1**:52

"Hands" **1**:52

Hello Towns! (newspaper column) **1**:45, 48

Hemingway and **1**:41, 45, 53, **5**:661, 669

highlights in life **1**:44

Home Town **1**:45, 48

Horses and Men: Tales Long and Short **1**:45, 46, 48

influences on **1**:45, 46, 49, 55, 56

"I Want to Know Why" **1**:55, 56

Kit Brandon **1**:45, 46, 48, 55

Letters of Sherwood Anderson, The **1**:48

Letters to Bab: Sherwood Anderson to Marietta D. Finley **1**:48

"Man's Story, The" **1**:46

Many Marriages **1**:45, 46, 48, 55-56

Marching Men **1**:45, 48

Mid-American Chants **1**:44, 45, 48, 56

Modern Writer, The **1**:48

New Testament, A **1**:48

"Nobody Knows" **1**:52-53

No Swank **1**:45, 48
"Paper Pills" **1**:52
Perhaps Women **1**:45, 48
"Philosopher, The" **1**:52
Plays: Winesburg, Ohio, and Others **1**:48
plays by **1**:44, 45
Poor White **1**:41, 44, 45, 48, 49-51
Puzzled America **1**:45, 48
Sherwood Anderson: Selected Letters **1**:48
Sherwood Anderson's Memoirs **1**:44, 46, 48
Sherwood Anderson's Notebook **1**:44, 48
"Sophistication" **1**:53
Story Teller's Story, A **1**:44, 45, 48
style **1**:47-48, 49, 53-54
Tar: A Midwest Childhood **1**:44, 48
themes and issues **1**:44, 46-47, 49, 51-52, 54
Triumph of the Egg, The: A Book of Impressions from American Life in Tales and Poems **1**:44, 45, 46, 48, 54, 55
"Untold Lie, The" **1**:52
Windy McPherson's Son **1**:44, 45, 46, 48
Winesburg, Ohio **1**:41, 42, 44, 45, 46, 47, 48, 50, 51-54
Angelou, Maya **1:57-80**
  All God's Children Need Traveling Shoes **1**:60, 68, 73-74
  And Still I Rise **1**:67, 68
  as mother **1**:58, 59, 60, 61, 62, 71, 74, 75, 76, 78, 80
  awards and honors **1**:60, 61, 69, 78
  background and life **1**:58-61
  Brave and Startling Truth, A **1**:68
  Cabaret for Freedom (coauthor) **1**:59, 60, 68
  career as performer **1**:59, 60, 71, 76, 80
  character and action **1**:71, 75-76
  childhood silence of 160, **1**:58
  children's books **1**:68
  Complete Collected Poems of Maya Angelou, The **1**:68, 78
  Dunbar as influence **3**:397
  eulogy for Baldwin **1**:107
  Even the Stars Look Lonesome **1**:68
  Gather Together in My Name **1**:60, 68, 76, 78-80
  Heart of a Woman, The **1**:68, 80

highlights in life **1**:60
I Know Why the Cage Bird Sings **1**:60, 62, 68, 74-76
in Africa **1**:60, 61, 73-74, 80
influences on **1**:64, 65, 69
I Shall Not be Moved: Poems **1**:68
Just Give Me a Cool Drink of Water 'fore I Diiie **1**:60, 68, 78
Kofi and His Magic (with Courtney-Clarke) **1**:68
Life Doesn't Frighten Me (with Basquiat) **1**:68
literary legacy **1**:67
"Little Girl Speakings" **1**:78
major works **1**:73-78
My Painted House, My Friendly Chicken, and Me (with Courtney-Clarke) **1**:68
Now Sheba Sings the Song **1**:68
Oh Pray My Wings Are Gonna Fit Me Well **1**:60, 68
"On the Pulse of Morning" **1**:61, 69
On the Pulse of Morning **1**:68
Phenomenal Woman: Four Poems Celebrating Women **1**:68
Poems: Maya Angelou **1**:68
poetic style **1**:64, 66-67
racial views **1**:64
Shaker, Why Don't You Sing? **1**:68
Singin' and Swingin' and Gettin' Merry Like Christmas **1**:60, 68, 76-78
themes and issues **1**:62, 64, 67, 69, 71, 73-74, 76
universal appeal **1**:69, 71
Wouldn't Take Nothing for My Journey Now **1**:60, 68, 71
Anouilh, Jean **4**:443
Apollinaire, Guillaume **10**:1429
Aristotle **12**:1637-38
Armah, Ayi Kwei **11**:1579
Arnold, Edwin T. **7**:966-67
Arnold, Matthew
  as Angelou influence **1**:65
  as Frost influence **4**:569
Ashley, Robert **4**:486
Atelier Julien **8**:1087
Atwood, Margaret **1:81-100**
  Alias Grace **1**:84, 89, 90, 91
  Animals in the Country, The **1**:90
  Anna's Pet (with Barkhouse) **1**:90
  Atwood, Margaret **1**:83
  awards and honors **1**:83, 85
  background and life **1**:82-85
  Blind Assassin, The **1**:85, 90
  Bluebeard's Egg **1**:90

Bodily Harm **1**:90
"Bread" **1**:98, 99
Cat's Eye **1**:81, 82, 90, 97
Circle Game, The **1**:85, 90
Dancing Girls **1**:90
Double Persephone **1**:83, 85, 90
dualities **1**:87
Edible Woman, The **1**:81, 85, 90
Expeditions **1**:90
Good Bones **1**:90
Handmaid's Tale, The **1**:81, 84, 85, 91-95
"Happy Endings" **1**:99
highlights in life **1**:85
influences on **1**:82, 83, 88
Interlunar **1**:90
Journals of Susanna Moodie, The **1**:84, 89, 90, 95, 97-99
Kaleidoscopes Baroque: A Poem **1**:90
Lady Oracle **1**:85, 90, 95-96
Life Before Man **1**:90
literary criticism on **1**:85
major works **1**:89-96
Margaret Atwood: Conversations **1**:90
Morning in the Burned House **1**:90
Murder in the Dark **1**:90, 98, 99
Oxford Book of Canadian Verse in English, The (ed.) **1**:90
Poems 1965-1975 **1**:90
Poems 1976-1989 **1**:90
poetry **1**:88
Power Politics **1**:90
Princess Prunella and the Purple Peanut (with Kowalski) **1**:90
Procedures for Underground **1**:90
Robber Bride, The **1**:81, 90, 99
Second Words: Selected Critical Prose **1**:90
Selected Poems **1**:90
Selected Poems II **1**:90
Servant Girl, The (teleplay) **1**:84, 190
Snake Poems **1**:90
Snowbird (screenplay) **1**:90
Snowbird (teleplay) **1**:84
Speeches for Dr. Frankenstein **1**:90
Strange Things: the Malevolent North in Canadian Literature **1**:90
Surfacing **1**:81, 90
Survival: A Thematic Guide to Canadian Literature **1**:85, 90
Talismans for Children **1**:90
themes and issues **1**:81, 84, 86-87, 88, 89, 91, 95

Toronto settings **1**:87
True Stories **1**:90
Trumpets of Summer (with Beckwith) **1**:84
Two-Headed Poems **1**:90
Up the Tree **1**:90
victimization complicity portrayal **1**:84, 87, 88, 95
What Was in the Garden **1**:90
Wilderness Tips **1**:90
You Are Happy **1**:90
Auden, W. H. **7**:977, 985, **8**:1045
as Rich influence **9**:1279
Austen, Jane **8**:1051, 1057

Babbitt, Irving **4**:438, 441, **11**:1468
Bacon, Roger **10**:1342
Bacon, Sir Francis **8**:1039
Baker, George Pierce **9**:1160
Baldwin, James **1**:**101-22**
Amen Corner, The **1**:104, 105, 110, 111-13
Another Country **1**:104, 105, 110, 120, **11**:1492
as preacher **1**:104, 105, *106*, 108, 109, 116, 118
awards and honors **1**:104
background and life **1**:102-7, 109, 111
Blues for Mister Charlie **1**:104, 105, 110, 113-14
Conversations with James Baldwin (Standley and Pratted ed.) **1**:110
Devil Finds Work, The **1**:106, 110
Dialogue, A: James Baldwin and Nikki Giovanni **1**:106, 110, **5**:631, 635, 642
"Down at the Cross: Letter from a Region in My Mind" **1**:120-21
"Everybody's Protest Novel" **1**:105
Evidence of Things Not Seen, The **1**:106, 110
Fire Next Time, The **1**:104, 105, 110, 120-21
Giovanni and **5**:631, 635, 642
Giovanni's Room **1**:105
Going to Meet the Man **1**:110
Go Tell It on the Mountain **1**:105, 110, 115-16, **5**:642
"Harlem Ghetto, The" **1**:105
"Harlem Then and Now" **1**:105
highlights in life **1**:104
If Beale Street Could Talk **1**:106, 110, 121-22

influences on **1**:102, 105, 109
James Baldwin: Collected Essays (Morrison ed.) **1**:106, 110
Jimmy's Blues: Selected Poems **1**:106, 110
Just Above My Head **1**:106, 110
literary legacy **1**:108, 110
Little Man, Little Man: A Story of Childhood **1**:106, 110
major works **1**:115-20
"Many Thousands Gone" **1**:105
Morrison and **8**:1055
"My Dungeon Shook: Letter to My Newphew on the One Hundredth Anniversary of the Emancipation" **1**:120
Nobody Knows My Name: More Notes of a Native Son **1**:105, 110
No Name in the Street **1**:105, 110
Notes of a Native Son **1**:110, 122
Nothing Personal (with Avedon) **1**:110
One Day When I Was Lost: A Scenario Based on "The Autobiography of Malcolm X" **1**:106, 110
"Previous Condition" **1**:105, 122
Price of the Ticket, The: Collected Nonfiction, 1948-1985 **1**:106, 110
Rap on Race, A **1**:105
Rap on Race, A (with Mead) **1**:105, 110
"Sonny's Blues" **1**:117-18
"Stranger in the Village" **1**:118-20
Styron and 492, **11**:491
Tell Me How Long the Train's Been Gone **1**:105, 110
themes and issues **1**:105, 108, 115-16, 118-19
Walker and **11**:1569
Welcome Table, The (uncompleted) **1**:111, 113
Wright and **12**:1693, 1699, 1704
Balzac, Honoré de **3**:380
Bambara, Toni Cade **6**:751, **8**:1053
Baraka, Amiri **6**:744
as Brooks influence **2**:198, 202
eulogy for Baldwin **1**:107
Barnett, Whit **7**:977
Barrie, James M. **4**:505
Barry, Philip **2**:154
Barth, John **2**:261, **5**:601
Barthelme, Donald **5**:601
Beauvoir, Simone de **12**:1695, *1700*
as Piercy influence **9**:1202
as Rich influence **9**:1280

Beckett, Samuel **7**:937, **9**:1168
Bellow, Saul **1**:**123-42**
Actual, The **1**:132, 138
Adventures of Augie March, The **1**:125, 126, 132
awards and honors **1**:124, 125, 126, 127, *130*
background and life **1**:124-27
Bellarosa Connection, The **1**:132, 138-40
Dangling Man **1**:124, 126, 132
Dean's December, The **1**:127, 132, 140
Henderson the Rain King **1**:129, 130, 132, 140
Herzog **1**:125, 132, 133, 134-36
Him with His Foot in His Mouth and Other Stories **1**:132
Humboldt's Gift **1**:125, 127, 129, 130, 132, 133, 136-37
influences on **1**:129
It All Ends Up: From the Dim Past to the Uncertain Future **1**:132
Last Analysis, The **1**:132
literary legacy **1**:133
major works **1**:134-38
More Die of Heartbreak **1**:132, 140-41
Mosby's Memoir's and Other Stories **1**:132
Mr. Sammler's Planet **1**:132, 140
Ravelstein **1**:129, 132
Seize the Day **1**:124, 129, 132, 133, 137-38
"Silver Dish, A" **1**:126
Singer and **10**:1400, 1403
Something to Remember Me By: Three Tales **1**:132
Styron and **11**:1495
Theft, A **1**:132
themes and issues **1**:128, 130-31, 133, 134, 136
To Jerusalem and Back: A Personal Account **1**:130, 132
Under the Weather **1**:132
Wrecker, The **1**:132
Benchley, Robert **4**:502
Benét, Stephen Vincent **2**:**149-62**
Abraham Lincoln **2**:153, 155
All That Money Can Buy **2**:153, 155
awards and honors **2**:149, 150, 151, 152
background and life **2**:150-52
Ballad of the Duke's Mercy, The **2**:155

"Ballad of William Sycamore, 1790-1871, The" **2**:151, 160
Ballads and Poems, 1915-1930 **2**:155
Beginning of Wisdom, The **2**:151, 152, 155
Book of Americans, A (with Benét) **2**:151, 154, 155
Burning City **2**:152, 155
Cheers for Miss Bishop **2**:153, 155
Child Is Born, A: A Modern Drama of the Nativity **2**:155
"Devil and Daniel Webster, The" **2**:151, 152, 155, 157
"Doc Mellhorn and the Pearly Gates" **2**:151
"End to Dreams, An" **2**:151, 152
Fitzgerald and **2**:155, **4**:537
Five Men and Pompey **2**:150, 152, 155
"Freedom's Hard-Bought Thing" **2**:152
Headless Horseman, The **2**:155
Heavens and Earth **2**:151, 155
Hemingway and **2**:155
highlights in life **2**:152
influences on **2**:154, 156, 160
"Into Egypt" **2**:155
"Jacob and the Indians" **2**:160-61
James Shore's Daughter **2**:155
Jean Huguenot **2**:151, 155
John Brown's Body **2**:149, 151, 152, 153-54, 155, 158-59
"Johnny Pye and the Fool-Killer" **2**:151, 155
"King David" **2**:151, 155
Last Circle, The: Stories and Poems **2**:155
Lindsay and **2**:156
"Listen to the People" **2**:155
"Litany of Dictatorships" **2**:154
literary legacy of **2**:155-56
"Litter of Rose Leaves, The" **2**:155
major works **2**:157-59
"Metropolitan Nigthmare" **2**:154
"Mountain Whippoorwill, The" **2**:151
Nerves (with Farrar) **2**:155
"Nightmare at Noon" **2**:154
"Ode to the Austrian Socialists" **2**:154
Sandburg and **2**:151, 156
Selected Letters of Stephen Vincent Benét **2**:155
Selected Works of Stephen Vincent Benét **2**:155

"Silver Jemmy" **2**:154
"Song of the Woods, A" **2**:150
Spanish Bayonet **2**:151, 155, 161
Stephen Vincent Benét: Selected Poetry and Prose **2**:155
Stephen Vincent Benét on Writing: A Great Writer's Letters of Advice to a Young Beginner **2**:155
"Summons to Be Free, A" **2**:155
Tales Before Midnight **2**:155
That Awful Mrs. Eaton (with Farrar) **2**:155
themes and issues **2**:153, 154-55, 157, 158
"Thirteen O'Clock" **2**:155
Tiger Joy **2**:155
Twenty-five Short Stories **2**:155
We Stand United, and Other Radio Scripts **2**:155
Western Star **2**:149, 152, 155
Young Adventure: A Book of Poems **2**:150, 155
Young People's Pride **2**:151, 155
Benson, Robert Hugh **4**:525
Benson, Sally **12**:1647
Berneis, Peter **12**:1664
Berry, Wendell **4**:563
Bishop, John Peale **4**:517, 525
Blake, William **1**:83, 88, **3**:348, **12**:1700
Bloom, Allan **1**:129
Blotner, Joseph L. **4**:486
Blume, Judy **2**:**163-80**
Are You There God? It's Me, Margaret **2**:165, 166, 167, 168, 170, 171-73, 180
awards and honors **2**:166, 167
background and life **2**:164-67
Blubber **2**:166, 167, 170, 172, 173-74
censorship and **2**:167
controversial topics **2**:167, 169
Deenie **2**:167, 169, 170, 172, 176-78
Forever… **2**:166, 168, 172, 174-76
Freckle Juice **2**:166, 172
Fudge-a-Mania **2**:167, 172
"Fudge" series **2**:166, 167, 170
Here's to You, Rachel Robinson **2**:167, 172
highlights in life **2**:166
Iggie's House **2**:163, 165, 166, 172
influences on **2**:170
It's Not the End of the World **2**:172, 178

Judy Blume Diary, The **2**:172
Judy Blume Memory Book, The **2**:172
Just as Long as We're Together **2**:167, 172
Letters to Judy: What Your Kids Wish They Could Tell You **2**:166, 167, 172
major works **2**:171-76
One in the Middle Is the Green Kangaroo, The **2**:165, 166, 172
Otherwise Known as Sheila the Great **2**:166, 172
Pain and the Great One, The **2**:172
Places I Never Meant to Be: Original Stories by Censored Writers (ed.) **2**:167, 172
Smart Women **2**:167, 172
Starring Sally J. Freedman as Herself **2**:170, 172
Summer Sisters **2**:166, 167, 172, 178-79
Superfudge **2**:172
Tales of a Fourth Grade Nothing **2**:166, 172
themes and issues **2**:168-69
Then Again, Maybe I Won't **2**:166, 167, 169, 172, 179-80
Tiger Eyes **2**:166, 167, 172
Wifey **2**:166, 167, 172
Bogan, Louise **8**:1039, **10**:1372
Bogard, Travis **9**:1168
Bogosian, Eric **7**:934
Bone, Robert **3**:415
Bontemps, Arna **2**:**181-94**
American Negro Poetry (ed.) **2**:187
Anyplace but Here (with Conroy) **2**:184, 187
Arna Bontemps-Langston Hughes Letters, 1925-1967 (Nichols ed.) **2**:187
Autobiography of an Ex-Colored Man, The (Johnson; Bontemps ed.) **2**:187
awards and honors **2**:183, 184
background and life **2**:182-85
Black Thunder **2**:183, 184, 187, 188, 189-90, 191, 192
Book of Negro Folklore, The (ed. with Hughes) **2**:187, **6**:737
Chariot in the Sky: A Story of the Jubilee Singers **2**:187
Drums at Dusk **2**:183, 186, 187, 188, 191-93
Famous Negro Athletes **2**:187
Fast Sooner Hound, The (with Conroy) **2**:187

Father of the Blues (with Handy)
  2:187
Frederick Douglass: Slave, Fighter, Freeman **2**:187, 188, 193
Free and Easy (with Cullen)
  2:184, 187, 188
Free at Last: The Life of Frederick Douglass **2**:187, 188, 193
God Sends Sunday **2**:182, 183, 184, 187, 188, 193
Golden Slippers: An Anthology of Negro Poetry for Young Readers (ed.) **2**:187
"Golgotha Is a Mountain" **2**:184, 188, 193
Great Slave Narratives (ed.) **2**:187
Harlem Renaissance Remembered, The (ed.) **2**:187
highlights in life **2**:184
Hold Fast to Dreams: Poems Old and New (ed.) **2**:187
"Hope" **2**:184
Hughes and **6**:729, 737
influences on **2**:182, 185
"I, Too, Sing America" (with Hughes) **2**:185, **6**:728, 742
librarian career **2**:181, 182, 183, 184
Lonesome Boy **2**:187
major works **2**:189-93
Mr. Kelso's Lion **2**:187
"Nocturne at Bethesda" **2**:188
Old South, The: "A Summer Tragedy" and Other Stories of the Thirties **2**:187, 188
One Hundred Years of Negro Freedom **2**:187
Pasteboard Bandit, The **2**:187
Personals **2**:187
Poetry of the Negro, 1746-1949, The (ed. with Hughes) **2**:187, **6**:737
Poetry of the Negro, 1746-1970, The (ed.) **2**:187
Popo and Fifina: Children of Haiti (with Hughes) **2**:186, 187, 188, **6**:737
"Return, The" **2**:184, 188
Sad-Faced Boy **2**:186, 187
Sam Patch: The High, Wide, and Handsome Jumper (with Conroy) **2**:187
Slappy Hooper: The Wonderful Sign Painter (with Conroy) **2**:187
St. Louis Woman (with Cullen)
  2:184, 187, 188
Story of George Washington Carver, The **2**:187, 188

Story of the Negro, The **2**:184, 187
"Summer Tragedy, A" **2**:184, 188, 192, 193-94
themes and issues **2**:188
They Seek a City (with Conroy)
  2:187
We Have Tomorrow **2**:187, 188
You Can't Pet a Possom **2**:186, 187
Young Booker: Booker T. Washington's Early Days **2**:187, 188
Bowen, Elizabeth **9**:*1215*
Bowles, Paul **7**:977
Brach, Gerard **12**:1722
Bradstreet, Anne **1**:88
Brawley, Benjamin **3**:401, 406, 413, 415
Braxton, Joanne **3**:406, 407
Brecht, Bertolt **12**:1658
Breslin, Jimmy **9**:1247
Brodsky, Joseph **4**:563
Bromfield, Louis **4**:502, 503
Brontë, Charlotte **6**:775
Brontë, Emily **8**:1073, 1077
Brooke, Rupert **4**:525
Brooks, Gwendolyn **2**:**195-208**, **11**:1569
  "African Fragment" **2**:208
  Aloneness **2**:203
  "Anniad, The" **2**:204, 207
  Annie Allen **2**:195, 197, 199, 203, 204-5, 207
  Aurora **2**:203
  autobiographical fiction **2**:207
  awards and honors **2**:195, 197, 198, 199, 204, 205
  background and life **2**:196-99
  Bean Eaters, The **2**:197-98, 203, 206-7
  Beckonings **2**:203
  Black Love **2**:203
  Blacks **2**:203
  Black Steel: Joe Frazier and Muhammad Ali **2**:203
  Bronzeville Boys and Girls **2**:197, 203
  "Bronzeville Mother Loiters in Mississippi, A. Meanwhile, a Mississippi Mother Burns Bacon" **2**:206-7
  Capsule Course in Black Poetry Writing, A **2**:293
  career turning point **2**:198
  Children Coming Home **2**:203
  "Eventide" **2**:197
  Family Pictures **2**:203, 207
  Giovanni and **5**:630, 644

Gottschalk and the Grande Tarantelle **2**:203
Harlem Renaissance and **2**:196
highlights in life **2**:199
"II" **2**:204
"I love those little booths at Benvenuti's" **2**:205
influences on **2**:196, 197, 198, 199, 202, 204, 208
In the Mecca **2**:198, 203
Jump Bad: A New Chicago Anthology (ed.) **2**:203
"kitchenette folks" **2**:207
"Life of Lincoln West, The" **2**:207
literary legacy **2**:200, 203
major works **2**:204-6
Maud Martha **2**:197, 203, 207
"mother, the" **2**:205
Near-Johannesburg Boy, The **2**:203
"obituary for a living lady" **2**:205
"Paul Robeson" **2**:207
Primer for Blacks **2**:203
"Report from Part One" **2**:208
Report from Part One: An Autobiography **2**:198, 203, 207-8
Report from Part Two **2**:203
Riot **2**:203
Selected Poems **2**:198, 203
"Sources and Illuminations" **2**:208
Street in Bronzeville, A **2**:197, 199, 203, 205-6, 207
"Sundays of Satin Legs Smith, The" **2**:197, 205-6
themes and issues **2**:200
Tiger Who Wore White Gloves, The: Or, You Are What You Are **2**:203
To Disembark **2**:203
Very Young Poets **2**:203
Wall, The **2**:203
"We Real Cool" **2**:203, 206
Winnie **2**:203
"Womanhood, The" **2**:204
World of Gwendolyn Brooks, The **2**:198, 203
Young Poets' Primer **2**:203
Broun, Heywood **4**:*502*
Brown, Claude **8**:1051
Brown, Sterling A. **3**:397, 403
Browne, Sir Thomas **9**:1251-52, **11**:1502
Browning, Robert **4**:569, **7**:952, **10**:1338
Bryant, William Cullen **10**:1338
Bryer, Jackson R. **9**:1168

Buck, Pearl S. **2:209-32**
  All Men Are Brothers (Shih Nai-an; Buck transl.) **2:**212, 213, 218
  All Under Heaven **2:**218
  American Argument: With Eslanda Goode Robeson (with Robeson) **2:**218
  American Unity and Asia **2:**218
  Angry Wife, The (under pseud. of) **2:**218
  awards and honors **2:**209, 212, 213, *214*, 215
  background and life **2:**210-14
  Big Wave, The **2:**214, 218
  Bridge for Passing, A **2:**218
  Bright Procession (under pseud. of Sedges) **2:**218
  Children for Adoption **2:**218
  Child Who Never Grew, The **2:**218
  "China and the West" **2:**212
  China as I See It **2:**218
  China Flight **2:**218
  China in Black and White **2:**218
  China Past and Present **2:**218
  China Sky **2:**218
  Chinese experiences **2:**211, 213
  Chinese Novel, The **2:**218
  "Chinese Woman Speaks, A" **2:**212, 215
  Come, My Beloved **2:**218
  Command the Morning **2:**218
  Death in the Castle **2:**218
  Dragon Seed **2:**218
  East and West **2:**218
  East and West and the Novel **2:**218
  East Wind: West Wind **2:**213, 218
  Exile, The **2:**215, 218
  Far and Near, Stories of Japan, China, and America **2:**218
  Fighting Angel: Portrait of a Soul **2:**215, 218
  film adaptations **2:**217
  First Wife and Other Stories, The **2:**218
  "First Wife, The" **2:**215
  Fourteen Stories **2:**218
  Friend to Friend: A Candid Exchange Between Pearl S. Buck and Carlos F. Romulo (with Romulo) **2:**218
  Gifts They Bring, The: Our Debt to the Mentally Retarded **2:**218
  Goddess Abides, The **2:**218
  God's Men **2:**215, 218
  Good Deed and Other Stories, The **2:**218

  Good Earth, The **2:**23-24, 211, 212, 213, 215, 218, 227
  Hearts Come Home and Other Stories **2:**218
  Hidden Flower, The **2:**214, 215, 218
  highlights in life **2:**212
  House Divided, A **2:**218
  House of Earth **2:**218
  How it Happens: Talk About the German People, 1914-33, with Ema von Pustau (with Pustau) **2:**218
  Imperial Woman **2:**215, 217, 218, 224-26
  "In China, Too" **2:**211, 212
  influences on **2:**217
  "Is There a Case for Foreign Missions?" **2:**213
  Johnny Jack and His Beginnings **2:**218
  Joy of Children, The **2:**218
  Kennedy Women, The: A Personal Appraisal **2:**218
  Kinfolk **2:**215, 218
  Letter from Peking **2:**218
  Living Reed, The **2:**214, 218
  Long Love, The (under pseud. of Sedges) **2:**218
  Lovers and Other Stories, The **2:**218
  major works **2:**223-28
  Mandala **2:**218
  Man Who Changed China, The: The Story of Sun Yat-Sen **2:**218
  Mother, The **2:**215, 217, 218
  My Several Worlds: A Personal Record **2:**218
  New Year, The **2:**218
  Of Men and Women **2:**212, 218, 230
  Once upon a Christmas **2:**218
  One Bright Day and Other Stories for Children **2:**218
  Other Gods: An American Legend **2:**215, 218
  Patriot, The **2:**218, 229
  Pavilion of Women **2:**215, 217, 218, 229, 230
  Pearl S. Buck's America **2:**218
  Peony **2:**218
  People of Japan, The **2:**218
  Portrait of a Marriage **2:**214, 218
  Promise, The **2:**218
  Rainbow, The **2:**218
  Satan Never Sleeps **2:**218
  Secrets of the Heart **2:**218

  Sons **2:**218
  Stories for Little Children **2:**218
  Story Bible, The **2:**218
  Talk About Russia: With Masha Scott (with Scott) **2:**218
  Tell the People: Talks with James Yen About the Mass Education Movement (with Yen) **2:**218
  themes and issues **2:**213-14, 215
  This Proud Heart **2:**212, 213, 215, 218, 230-31
  Three Daughters of Madame Liang, The **2:**218, 231-32
  Time Is Noon, The **2:**218
  Today and Forever **2:**218
  To My Daughters with Love **2:**218
  Townsman, The (under pseud. of Sedges) **2:**212, 214, 215, 218, 226-28
  Twenty-seven Stories **2:**218
  Voices in the House (under pseud. of Sedges) **2:**218
  "Warning to Free Nations" **2:**214
  What America Means to Me **2:**218
  Woman Who Was Changed and Other Stories, The **2:**218
  women's issues **2:**215
  Young Revolutionist, The **2:**218
Bunyan, John **3:**325, 330, **11:**1497
Burnett, Whit **10:**1302, 1306
Burns, Robert **3:**399, **11:**1460
Burroughs, Edgar Rice **2:**256, **10:**1344
Bush, Katharine **4:**524

Cabell, James Branch **4:**525
Cain, James M. **7:**929, 935
Campbell, James **3:**399
Campbell, Joseph **12:**1632, 1646
Camus, Albert
  as Styron influence **11:**1492
  as Wright influence **12:**1700, 1709
Canby, Vincent **4:**526
Canham, Erwin **10:**1327
Capote, Truman **2:233-54**
  Answered Prayers: The Unfinished Novel **2:**237, 238, 241, 242, 245
  background and life **2:**234-38
  Beat the Devil (screenplay with Huston) **2:**235, 238, 242
  Breakfast at Tiffany's: A Short Novel and Three Stories **2:**235, 242, 244, 245
  Capote Reader, A **2:**238, 242
  Christmas Memory, A **2:**242
  cinematic techniques **2:**248-49

Dogs Bark, The: Public People and Private Places **2**:242, 251
film role in *Murder by Death* **2**:237
Foote and **4**:551
gothic elements **2**:249
Grass Harp, The **2**:240, 242, 245, 246-48, *246*
Grass Harp, The: A Play **2**:235, 238, 242
"Handcarved Coffins: A Nonfiction Account of an American Crime" **2**:238, 252
highlights in life **2**:238
House of Flowers (play with Arlen) **2**:235, 238, 242
In Cold Blood **2**:233, 237, 238, 240, 242, 244, 245, *245*, 248-50, *250*, 251, **6**:836
influences on **2**:241, *243*
Innocents, The (screenplay) **2**:237, 238, 242
"I Remember Grandpa: A Story" **2**:242
journalistic character studies **2**:244
Knowles and **6**:807
Lee and **6**:*834*, 836, 838
literary legacy **2**:242
Local Color **2**:235, 238, 242
major works **2**:246-50
Muses Are Heard, The **2**:235, 238, 242
Music for Chameleons **2**:238, 242, 251-52
Observations (with Avedon) **2**:242
"One Christmas" **2**:242
Other Voices, Other Rooms **2**:234, 238, 242, 245, 252
reportorial fiction **2**:244-45, 252
Selected Writings p. **2**:242
stylistic dualities **2**:245
surrealism and symbolism 247, **2**:252
Thanksgiving Visitor, The **2**:242
themes and issues **2**:239-40, 242, 248, 249, 252
Three by Truman Capote **2**:242
Tree of Night and Other Stories, A **2**:235, 238, 242
Trilogy: An Experiment in Multimedia (with Perry and Perry) **2**:242
Carmichael, Stokely **5**:629, *629*, **8**:1051
Carroll, Lewis **12**:1717, 1718
Carter, Keith **4**:547
Carver, Raymond **2**:255-68

"Are You a Doctor?" **2**:257
At Night the Salmon Move **2**:257, 258, 261
awards and honors **2**:257, 258
background and life **2**:256-57, 256-58, 258
"Bath, The" **2**:262-63
Cathedral **2**:257, 258, 259, 261, 262
"Cathedral" **2**:263
crucial turning point for **2**:257
Elephant and Other Stories **2**:261
"Errand" **2**:264-65
"Fires" **2**:261
Fires: Essays, Poems, Stories **2**:261
Furious Seasons and Other Stories **2**:261
highlights in life **2**:258
"Hummingbird" **2**:*260*
influences on **2**:256-57, 258, 259, 260, 261, 264
literary legacy **2**:261
major works **2**:262-66
minimalism **2**:261
Near Klamath **2**:257, 258, 261
"Neighbors" **2**:265-66
New Path to the Waterfall, A **2**:258, 261
No Heroics, Please: Uncollected Writings **2**:261
Outdoor Life as influence on **2**:256
"Put Yourself in My Shoes" **2**:257, 261
"Small, Good Thing, A" **2**:262-63
Sports Afield as influence on **2**:256
themes and issues **2**:259
This Water **2**:258, 261
Two Poems **2**:261
Ultramarine **2**:258, 261
What We Talk About When We Talk About Love **2**:255, 257, 258, 259, 261, 262
"What We Talk About When We Talk About Love" **2**:266-67
Where I'm Calling From **2**:258, 259, 261, 262
Where Water Comes Together with Other Water **2**:258, 261
"Why Don't You Dance?" **2**:266
Will You Please Be Quiet, Please? **2**:255, 257, 258, 259, 261
"Will You Please Be Quiet, Please?" **2**:257, 258, 267-68
Winter Insomnia **2**:261
Cather, Willa **2**:**269-86**, **7**:1005, **8**:1051, **12**:1596

Alexander's Bridge **2**:274, 278
April Twilights **2**:278
as Mamet influence **7**:930, 937
awards and honors **2**:273-74
background and life **2**:270-74
beauty of prose style **2**:277
Death Comes for the Archbishop **2**:269, 272, 274, 276-77, 278, 279-81
"Death in the Desert, A" **2**:275
film adaptations **2**:273
highlights in life **2**:274
influences on **2**:271, 276
journalism experience **2**:270-71
Kingdom of Art, The: Willa Cather's First Principles and Critical Statements, 1893-1896 **2**:278
literary legacy **2**:277-78
Lost Lady, A **2**:274, 278
Lucy Gayheart **2**:274, 278
major works **2**:279-84
My Antonia **2**:269, 272, 274, 275-76, 278
My Mortal Enemy **2**:278
Not Under Forty **2**:274, 278
Obscure Destinies **2**:274, 278
Old Beauty and Others, The **2**:274, 278
One of Ours **2**:273, 274, 278
O Pioneers! **2**:269, 272, 274, 275, 278, 279, 281-84
"Paul's Case" **2**:271, 275, 285-86
Professor's House, The **2**:272, 274, 277, 278
Sapphira and the Slave Girl **2**:274, 278
Shadows on the Rock **2**:269, 272-73, 274, 277, 278
Song of the Lark, The **2**:272, 274, 275, 278
teaching career **2**:271, 274, 285
themes and issues **2**:275, 275-77
Troll Garden, The **2**:271, 274, 278, 285
Uncle Valentine and Other Stories: Willa Cather's Collected Short Fiction, 1915-1929 **2**:278
Willa Cather in Europe **2**:278
Willa Cather on Writing **2**:278
Willa Cather's Collected Short Fiction, 1892-1912 **2**:278
World and the Parish, The: Willa Cather's Articles and Reviews, 1893-1902 **2**:278
Writings from Willa Cather's Campus Years **2**:278

Youth and the Bright Medusa
    2:274, 278
Chandler, Raymond **4**:479
Chaney, John Griffith. *See* London,
    Jack
Chase, Horton **11**:1454
Chaucer, Geoffrey **5**:597, 599, 602,
    11:1514
Cheever, John **2**:257
Chekhov, Anton **7**:916, **10**:1399
    as Carver influence **2**:259, 260,
        261, 264
    as Foote influence **4**:548
    as Mamet influence **7**:928, 935,
        937
    as McCullers influence **7**:976,
        985
    as Tyler influence **11**:1549
    as T. Williams influence **12**:1658
Chesnutt, Charles **3**:409-10
Chesterton, G. K.
    as Benét influence **2**:150
    as Fitzgerald influence **4**:525
Cheuse, Alan **7**:918
Chin, Frank **11**:1505
Cisneros, Sandra **1**:31
Clark, Kenneth **1**:106
Cleaver, Eldridge **1**:104, 107, **3**:371
Cliff, Michelle **9**:1280, 1281, 1291
Clurman, Harold **7**:978, **9**:1172
Codman, Ogden, Jr. **12**:1614, 1615,
    1622
Coleridge, Samuel Taylor **5**:608
Commins, Dorothy **9**:1168
Connally, Marc **4**:502
Conrad, Joseph **4**:525, **12**:1700
Conroy, Jack **2**:183, 184, 185, 187
Cooper, James Fenimore
    as Anderson influence **1**:42, 49
    as Benét influence **2**:160
Cormier, Robert **3**:293-310
    After the First Death **3**:296, 299,
        301, 307
    "And So On" **3**:294
    background and life **3**:294-96
    Beyond the Chocolate War **3**:300,
        301, 304
    Bumblebee Flies Anyway, The
        3:296, 298, 301
    career turning point **3**:296
    Chocolate War, The **3**:295-96,
        297, 298, 299, 300, 301, 302-
        4, 305, 307
    Eight Plus One **3**:297, 300, 301,
        308
    Fade **3**:300, 301, 304-5

Frenchtown Summer **3**:301
Heroes **3**:299, 301
highlights in life **3**:297
I Am the Cheese **3**:296, 297, 298,
    299, 301, 305-7
*I Have Words to Spend: Reflections
    of a Small Town Editor* **3**:297,
    301
influences on **3**:294, 295, 300
In the Middle of the Night **3**:301
Little Raw on Monday Morning, A
    3:295, 301
"Little Things That Count, The"
    3:294, 297
major works **3**:302-7
Now and at the Hour **3**:295, 297,
    301
Other Bells for Us to Ring **3**:301
style **3**:301
*Take Me Where the Good Times
    Are* **3**:295, 301
Tenderness **3**:301, 308
themes and issues **3**:298-99,
    302, 304, 305
Tunes for Bears to Dance To **3**:300,
    301, 309
We All Fall Down **3**:301, 310
Coward, Noel **4**:540
Cowley, Malcolm **4**:479, 485, 486
Cox, Hyde **4**:567
Crane, Hart **12**:1658
Crane, Stephen **1**:17, **8**:1124,
    9:1157
    as Dreiser influence **3**:380
    as Norris influence **8**:1085,
        1090, 1092
    as Potok influence **9**:1266
    as Wright influence **12**:1694,
        1698, 1700
Creeley, Robert **3**:317
Crummell, Alexander **3**:399
Cullen, Countée
    as Brooks influence **2**:196
    Baldwin and **1**:105
    Bontemps and **2**:181, 184, 185,
        187, 188
    Dunbar as influence **3**:397
    Hughes and **6**:738
Cummings, E. E. **3**:311-32
    Adventures in Value **3**:319
    "All in green went my love rid-
        ing" **3**:329
    & **3**:315, 316, 319, 330
    Anthropos: The Future of Art **3**:319
    "anyone lived in a pretty how
        town" **3**:326, 327

    as Brooks influence **2**:196
    as cultural icon **3**:315-16
    awards and honors **3**:316
    background and life **3**:312-17
    "Buffalo Bill's" **3**:319, 329-30
    "Cambridge ladies who live in
        furnished souls, the" **3**:329
    capitalization of signature 322-
        23, **3**:320
    CIOPW **3**:319
    Collected Poems **3**:315, 316, 319
    Complete Poems, 1913-1962 **3**:319
    Dos Passos and **3**:313
    *E. E. Cummings: A Selection of
        Poems* **3**:319
    Eight Harvard Poets (poems in)
        3:313, 316
    Eimi **3**:315, 316, 319, 330-31
    Enormous Room, The **3**:314, 316,
        319, 320, 324-25, 329, 330
    *Etcetera: The Unpublished Poems of
        E. E. Cummings* **3**:319
    Fifty Poems **3**:319
    "F is for foetus" **3**:327
    "floatfloafloff" **3**:327
    highlights in life **3**:316
    Him **3**:315, 316, 319
    i: six nonlectures **3**:319
    "i like my body when it is with
        your" **3**:330
    Independent Art Shows and
        3:314, 315
    "Index 1916" **3**:313
    influences on **3**:312, 313, 314,
        318, 324, 325, 330
    "in Just-spring when the world is
        mud luscious" **3**:317, 329
    Is 5 **3**:319, 331-32
    "i sing of Olaf glad and big" **3**:326
    Joy Farm and **3**:315, 316
    linguistic strategies **3**:326
    lowercase use **3**:318, 320, 322-23
    major works **3**:324-30
    "may i feel said he" **3**:326
    medieval ballads and **3**:318, 327,
        329
    "mOOn Over tOwns mOOn" **3**:327
    Moore and **8**:1038, 1040, 1045
    "my girl's tall with hard long
        eyes" **3**:330
    "my sweet old etcetera" **3**:331
    "next to of course god America i"
        3:331
    Ninety-five Poems **3**:316, 319
    No Thanks **3**:315, 319
    1 x 1 **3**:319

1/20 Poems **3**:319

"pity this busy monster,ma-
nunkind" **3**:326, 327

Poems, 1923-1954 **3**:316, 319,
325-27

poetry readings **3**:316

Pound and **3**:318

Red Front, The (translation) **3**:319

Santa Claus: A Morality **3**:319

satirical talent **3**:313, 318, 319,
330, 331

Selected Letters of E. E. Cummings
3:319

Seventy-three Poems **3**:319

"she being Brand" **3**:331, *332*

"somewhere i have never traveled
gladly beyond" **3**:326

stylistic innovations **3**:315, 317,
318, 320, 322-23, 325

themes and issues **3**:318-19,
324-26, 327

Tom: A Ballet **3**:319

Tulips and Chimneys **3**:314, 316,
319, 320, 327-30

"Tulips and Chimneys" **3**:328

typographic innovation **3**:314,
317-18, 326

work habits **3**:315

World War I service **3**:313-14

W[ViVa]: Seventy New Poems **3**:319

Xaipe **3**:319

XLI Poems **3**:315, 316, 319

Dahlberg, Edward **12**:1687

Dante Alighieri **7**:970

as Cummings influence **3**:330

as Eliot influence **4**:444

as MacLeish influence **7**:894, 898

as Stevens influence **11**:1484

Darwin, Charles

as Dreiser influence **3**:380

as London influence **7**:876, 877,
881, 887

as Norris influence **8**:1092,
1093, 1101

Davies, Robertson **3**:333-52

Animal U. **3**:344

At My Heart's Core **3**:344

At the Gates of the Righteous **3**:344

background and life **3**:334-38

Cornish trilogy **3**:337, 338

Cunning Man, The **3**:337, 344

Deptford trilogy **3**:335, 337, 338,
343, 345, 347, 350

Diary of Samuel Marchbanks, The
3:335, 344

*Enthusiams of Robertson Davies,
The* **3**:344

Eros at Breakfast **3**:344

Eurocentricity of **3**:343

Fifth Business **3**:337, 338, 344,
345-47, 350

Fortune, My Foe **3**:338, 344

*For Your Eye Alone: Robertson
Davies' Letters, 1976-1995* (ed.
Grant) **3**:344

grotesques portrayals **3**:340

*Happy Alchemy: On the Pleasures
of Music and the Theatre* (ed.
Surridge and Davies) **3**:344

highlights in life **3**:338

High Spirits **3**:344

Hope Deferred **3**:344

Hunting Stuart **3**:344

influences on **3**:335, 336, 338,
339, 340, 343, 349, 350

Jig for the Gipsy, A **3**:337, 344

journalism experience **3**:335,
337, 339, 341, 343

King Phoenix **3**:344

Leaven of Malice **3**:337, 340, 341,
344, 347-48, 351

literary legacy **3**:341, 343

*Love and Libel: Or, The Ogre of the
Provincial World* **3**:337, 341,
344, 348

Lyre of Orpheus, The **3**:337, 344

major works **3**:345-50

Manticore, The **3**:337, 344, 350

Marchbanks' Almanack **3**:344

*Merry Heart, The: Reflections on
Reading, Writing, and the World
of Books* **3**:344

Mixture of Frailties, A **3**:337, 340-
41, 344, 351

Murther and Walking Spirits **3**:*334*,
337, 338, 344

One Half of Robertson Davies **3**:344

Overlaid **3**:341, 344

*Personal Art, The: Reading to Good
Purpose* **3**:344

Question Time **3**:344

Reading and Writing **3**:344

Rebel Angels, The **3**:337, 344

*Renown at Stratford: A Record of
the Shakespeare Festival in
Canada, 1953* (with Guthrie)
3:336, 344

Salterton trilogy **3**:337, 338, 340-
41, 347, 348, 349, 351

*Shakespeare for Younger Players: A
Junior Course* **3**:335, 338, 344

Shakespeare's Boy Actors **3**:335,
338, 344

Stephen Leacock: Feast of Stephen
3:344

successes **3**:341

*Table Talk of Samuel Marchbanks,
The* **3**:335-36, 344

Tempest-Tost **3**:337, 340, 344,
347, 348, 349-50

theater and **3**:341, 348

themes and issues **3**:339, 340,
345, 347, 349

*Thrice the Brinded Cat Hath
Mew'd: A Record of the Stratford
Shakespearean Festival in
Canada, 1955* (with Guthrie)
3:336, 344

*Twice Have the Trumpets Sounded:
A Record of the Stratford
Shakespearean Festival in
Canada, 1954* (with Guthrie)
3:336, 344

Voice from the Attic, A **3**:344

Voice of the People, The **3**:344

Well-Tempered Critic, The **3**:344

What's Bred in the Bone **3**:337, 344

World of Wonders **3**:337, 344, 347

Davis, Richard Harding **8**:1090, 1092

Day, Douglas **4**:486

Day, Richard **2**:256, 260

Defoe, Daniel **2**:182, 185, **10**:1345

DeLillo, Dom **9**:1251

DeVoto, Bernard **4**:558

Dickens, Charles **6**:*770*, **10**:1315,
1378, **12**:1597

as Baldwin influence **1**:102, 109

as Bontemps influence **2**:182

as Cummings influence **3**:313

as Davies influence **3**:336

as Irving influence **6**:764, 770,
772, 775, 778, 782

as Lewis influence **6**:852

as Norris influence **8**:1086, 1092

Dickinson, Emily **8**:1045, **9**:1284

as Alvarez influence **1**:31

as Piercy influence **9**:1202

as Sandburg influence **10**:1331

Didion, Joan **3**:353-74

After Henry **3**:359, 360, 361,
363, 372

background and life **3**:353-61

Book of Common Prayer, A **3**:357,
358, 361, 363, 372

California's importance to **3**:353,
354, 356, 357, 358, 359, 360,
361-62, 364, 366, 368, 369, 371

Democracy **3**:360, 361, 362-63, 372

film adaptations **3**:357

"Goodbye to All That" **3**:355, 364, 369

highlights in life **3**:358

importance of places to **3**:359-60, 371

influences on **3**:355, 362-63, 366, 369, 371

Last Thing He Wanted, The **3**:358, 361, 363, 372-74

major works 364-71

marriage to Dunne **3**:356

New York City's importance to **3**:353, 355, 356, 357, 358, 359, 362, 366, 368, 369

Panic in Needle Park, The (screenplay with Dunne) **3**:355, 357, 358, 363

Play It as It Lays **3**:357, 358, 359, 361, 363, 364-66, 371

Play It as It Lays (screenplay with Dunne) **3**:355, 357, 358, 360, 363, *364*

politics and 361-62

Run River **3**:355, 358, 359, 360, 361, 363

Salvador **3**:357, 363, 372

Slouching Towards Bethlehem **3**:353, 355, 358, 363, 364, 366, 368-69, 371

Star Is Born, A (screenplay with Dunne and Pierson) **3**:358, 363

"Sunset" **3**:355

Telling Stories **3**:363

themes and issues **3**:364, 366, 369, 371

True Confessions (screenplay with Dunne) **3**:357, 363

Up Close and Personal (screenplay with Dunne) **3**:357, 363

White Album, The **3**:354, 358, 362, 363, 369, 371

Dinesen, Isak **7**:985, **8**:1040

Dodge, Mabel **10**:1429

Dodson, Owen **1**:113

Donne, John
    as Alvarez influence **1**:38
    as Bontemps influence **2**:182
    as Eliot influence **4**:444

Doolittle, Hilda (H.D.) **8**:1034, 1039, **12**:1675, 1676, 1679

Dos Passos, John **3**:313, **4**:537

Dostoyevsky, Fyodor **9**:1215, **10**:1408, **12**:1705

as Ellison influence **4**:460, 464

as Irving influence **6**:764

as Malamud influence **7**:916

as McCullers influence **7**:976, 985

as Miller influence **8**:1014, 1020

as Morrison influence **8**:1051

Douglass, Frederick
    as Angelou influence **1**:65, 67, 69, 71
    as Dunbar influence **3**:399, 402, *403*, 404, 405, 408, 411, 413
    as *Manassas* character **10**:1384
    Bontemps and **2**:188, 193
    Ellison and **4**:460
    Hansberry and **5**:658
    Wright and **12**:1702

Dreiser, Theodore **3**:375-96, **7**:959, **9**:1157, **10**:1326, 1402
    America Is Worth Saving **3**:381
    American Diaries, 1902-1926 **3**:381
    American Tragedy, An **3**:378, 380, 381, 384, 385-86
    as Anderson influence **1**:49
    as Fitzgerald influence **4**:525, 536
    as Mamet influence **7**:937
    as Norris influence **8**:1085, 1090, 1092
    Aspirant, The (poetry) **3**:381
    awards and honors **3**:383
    background and life **3**:376-78
    Best Short Stories (Farrell ed.) **3**:381
    Best Stories of Theodore Dreiser, The (Fast ed.) **3**:381, 384
    Book About Myself, A **3**:381
    Bulwark, The **3**:381, 384
    Carnegie Works at Pittsburgh, The **3**:381
    Chains: Lesser Novels and Stories **3**:381
    character inventions **3**:379-81
    Color of a Great City, The **3**:381
    Dawn **3**:381
    Dreiser Looks at Russia **3**:378, 381, 384, *394*
    Epitaph: A Poem **3**:381
    film adaptations **3**:383
    Financier, The **3**:378, 380, 381, 384, 392, 395
    Fine Furniture **3**:381
    Free and Other Stories **3**:381
    Gallery of Women, A **3**:381
    "*Genius*", *The* **3**:381, 384, 395

Girl in the Coffin, The (play) **3**:381

Hand of the Potter, The: A Tragedy in Four Acts **3**:381

Hey, Rub-a-Dub-Dub! **3**:381

highlights in life **3**:384

Hoosier Holiday, A **3**:381

influences on **3**:375, 376, 377, 379, 380, 389

Jennie Gerhardt **3**:378, 380, 381, 384, 386-89

journalism experience **3**:375, 377, 379

Letters of Theodore Dreiser **3**:381

Letters to Louise **3**:381

literary legacy **3**:381, 383

major works **3**:385-92

Moods: Cadenced and Declaimed (poetry) **3**:381

My City **3**:381

Newspaper Days. See *Book About Myself, A*

Notes on Life (Tjader and McAleer eds.) **3**:381

Plays of the Natural and Supernatural **3**:381

Selected Magazine Articles of Theodore Dreiser (Hakutani ed.) **3**:381

Selected Poems (Saalbach ed.) **3**:381

Sister Carrie **3**:378, 379-80, 381, 384, 386, 389-92

Stoic, The **3**:378, 381, 384, 394-95

themes and issues **3**:379, 386, 389

Titan, The **3**:378, 381, 392, 394

Tragic America **3**:381

Traveler at Forty, A **3**:378, 381

"trilogy of desire" **3**:378, 392, 393, 394

Twelve Men **3**:381

Wright and **1**:1694, **12**:1698, 1700

Dr. Seuss **2**:165

Du Bois, W. E. B. **2**:193
    Hansberry and **5**:652
    Hughes and **6**:727, 730, 742

Dumas, Alexandre, the elder **9**:1158
    as Bontemps influence **2**:185
    as Schaefer influence **10**:1344, 1350

Dunbar, Paul Laurence **3**:397-416, **6**:738, **12**:1682
    "Ante-Bellum Sermon, An" **3**:403, 407, 408

as Angelou influence **1**:65, **3**:397
as Brooks influence **2**:196
as Cullen influence **3**:397
as Giovanni influence **3**:397
"At Shaft 11" **3**:413, 415
background and life **3**:398-401
"Banjo Song, A" **3**:399, 407
*Best Stories of Paul Laurence
    Dunbar, The* (Brawley ed.)
    3:406, 413, 415
Candle-Lightin' Time **3**:406
"Choice, The" **3**:407
*Clorindy: Or, The Origin of the
    Cakewalk* **3**:401, 406
*Collected Poetry of Paul Laurence
    Dunbar, The* (Braxton ed.)
    3:406, 407
"Colored Soldiers, The" **3**:407
*Complete Poems of Paul Laurence
    Dunbar, The* **3**:402, 406, 407-9
"Corn Stalk Fiddle, The" **3**:408
"Death Song, A" **3**:401
dialect poetry **3**:403
Fanatics, The **3**:401, 402, 406
Folks from Dixie **3**:401, 402, 406,
    413
"Frederick Douglass" **3**:407
Heart of Happy Hollow, The **3**:402,
    406, 415
highlights in life **3**:402
influences on **3**:398, 399, 403,
    403, 404, 405, 407, 408, 409,
    411, 413, 415
"Ingrate, The" **3**:404, 411, 413
In Old Plantation Days **3**:401,
    402, 406, 415
"In Old Plantation Days" **3**:414
"Jimsella" **3**:413, 415
literary legacy **3**:406
Love of Landry, The **3**:401, 402, 406
Lyrics of Love and Laughter **3**:401,
    402, 406
Lyrics of Lowly Life **3**:399, 406,
    407
Lyrics of Sunshine and Shadow
    3:401, 402, 406
Lyrics of the Hearthside **3**:401,
    402, 406
Majors and Minors **3**:399, 402,
    403, 406
major works **3**:407-13
"Mess of Pottage, A" **3**:412-13
"Mr. Cornelius, Office Seeker"
    3:412
"Negro Love Song, A" **3**:405-6,
    407, 408

Oak and Ivy **3**:398-99, 402, 406
"Ode to Ethiopia" **3**:399, 407
"Ol' Tunes, The" **3**:408
"One Man's Fortune" **3**:412, 413
"Our Martyred Soldiers" **3**:402
Poems of Cabin and Field **3**:406
"Poet, The" **3**:403, 405, 407
"Song, A" **3**:408
Sport of the Gods, The **3**:401, 402,
    406, 409-10, 416
*Strength of Gideon and Other
    Stories, The* **3**:401, 402, 406,
    410-13
"Strength of Gideon, The" **3**:411,
    413
"Sympathy" **3**:405
themes and issues **3**:407, 409-11
"Tragedy at Three Forks, The"
    3:412
Uncalled, The **3**:401, 402, 406,
    415-16
Uncle Eph's Christmas **3**:401, 406
"Viney's Free Papers" **3**:411
"We Wear the Mask" **3**:403, 405,
    407
"When Malindy Sings" **3**:407
Dunne, Finley Peter **6**:734
Dylan, Bob **3:417-30**
Another Side of Bob Dylan **3**:425
At Budokan **3**:425
awards and honors **3**:421
background and life **3**:418-20
Basement Tapes, The **3**:419, 425
Before the Flood **3**:425
Biograph **3**:425
Blonde on Blonde **3**:419, 421, 425
Blood on the Tracks **3**:420, 425
"Blowin' in the Wind" **3**:419,
    425-26, 428
Bob Dylan **3**:419, 421, 425
*Bootleg Series, Vol. 1-3, The: Rare
    and Unreleased, 1961-1991*
    3:425
"Boots of Spanish Leather" **3**:422
Bringing It All Back Home **3**:419,
    421, 425
"Delia" **3**:423
Desire **3**:425
Down in the Groove **3**:425
Dylan and the Dead **3**:425
Empire Burlesque **3**:425
Freewheelin' Bob Dylan, The
    3:421, 425
"Gates of Eden" **3**:422
Good as I Been to You **3**:421, 425
"Gotta Serve Somebody" **3**:423

Hard Rain **3**:425
"Hard Rain's A-Gonna Fall, A"
    3:422
highlights in life **3**:421
Highway 61 Revisited **3**:419, 421,
    425
"I Dreamed I Saw St. Augustine"
    3:423
Infidels **3**:425
influences on **3**:418-19, 420,
    421, 424, 428, 430
"It Ain't Me Babe" **3**:423
"It's Alright Ma, I'm Only
    Bleeding" **3**:423
John Wesley Harding **3**:419-20,
    421, 425
Knocked out Loaded **3**:425
"Lay, Lady, Lay" **3**:423
"Like a Rolling Stone" **3**:423, 427
Lyrics, 1962-1985 **3**:425
Lyrics, 1962-1999 **3**:425
major works **3**:425-29
"Mister Tambourine Man" **3**:423,
    428-29
MTV Unplugged **3**:425
"My Back Pages" **3**:423
Nashville Skyline **3**:420, 421, 424,
    425
New Morning **3**:425
Oh Mercy **3**:425
Pat Garrett and Billy the Kid **3**:425
Planet Waves **3**:425
"Rainy Day Women #12 & 35"
    3:423
Real Live **3**:425
Saved **3**:425
Self Portrait **3**:425
Shot of Love **3**:425
Slow Train Coming **3**:420, 421, 425
social criticism of **3**:417
*Songs of Bob Dylan from 1966
    Through 1975, The* **3**:425
Street-Legal **3**:425
Tarantula **3**:425
themes and issues **3**:425, 427,
    428
"Things Have Changed" **3**:421
*Thirtieth Anniversary Concert
    Celebration, The* **3**:425
Time out of Mind **3**:420, 421, 425
Times They Are A-Changin', The
    3:419, 421, 425
"Tombstone Blues" **3**:423
Under the Red Sky **3**:425
World Gone Wrong **3**:420, 425
Writings and Drawings **3**:425

Edgeworth, Maria **8**:1036, 1037, 1043
Eliot, George
    as Alvarez influence **1**:31
    as Norris influence **8**:1092
Eliot, T. S. **4**:437-58, **12**:1700
    Ara Vos Prec **4**:450
    as Brooks influence **2**:196
    as Cummings influence **3**:314
    as dramatist **4**:445-48
    as Ellison influence **4**:460
    Ash Wednesday **4**:440, 450, 455-56
    as MacLeish influence **7**:897
    as modernist poet **4**:437, 443
    awards and honors **4**:437, 440, 441, 446, 448
    background and life **4**:438-40
    "Burnt Norton" **4**:449-50
    Church of England conversion **4**:437, 440, 441, 444
    Cocktail Party, The **4**:440, 446, 448, 450
    Collected Poems, 1909-1935 **4**:450
    Collected Poems, 1909-1962 **4**:450
    Complete Poems and Plays, The (1962) **4**:450
    Complete Poems and Plays, The (1969) **4**:450
    Confidential Clerk, The **4**:448, 450
    Cultivation of Christmas Trees, The **4**:450
    "Dry Salvages, The" **4**:438, 451
    Elder Statesman, The **4**:441, 445, 448, 450
    Four Quartets **4**:437, 438, 440, 441, 449-51, 456
    Frost poetic approach and **4**:555, 558, 562
    "Hamlet" **4**:442
    highlights in life **4**:441
    "Hollow Men, The" **4**:441, 456-57
    influence of **4**:443, 460, **7**:897
    influences on **4**:438, 439, 440, 442, 443, 444, 445, 446, 448
    Inventions of the March Hare: Poems, 1909-1917 **4**:441, 450
    Letters of T. S. Eliot, The: Volume 1, 1898-1922 **4**:441, 450
    literary legacy **4**:443
    literary philosophy **4**:440, 442, 445
    "Love Song of J. Alfred Prufrock, The" **4**:437, 439, 441, 442, 451, 452-53, 457
    major works **4**:449-54

Moore and **8**:1035, 1039, 1040, 1042, 1045
    Murder in the Cathedral **4**:440, 441, 442, 445, *446*, 449, 450, 457
    "objective correlative" concept **4**:442
    Old Possum's Book of Practical Cats **4**:440, 441, 443, *447*, 448, 450
    Poems **4**:450
    Poems, 1909-1925 **4**:450
    Poems Written in Early Youth **4**:450
    "Portrait of a Lady" **4**:441, 451, 453
    Pound relationship **4**:439, 441, 443, 444, 450, 555, 558, 560, 562, 567
    Prufrock and Other Observations **4**:441, 450, 451-53
    Rock, The **4**:440, 445, 450
    Sacred Wood, The **4**:441, 450
    Stein and **10**:1429
    Stevens and **11**:1475
    style and complexity **4**:437
    Sweeney Agonistes (play) **4**:445, 450
    Sweeney Agonistes (poetry) **4**:450
    themes and issues **4**:437, 440, 442-43, 449, 451, 454
    "Tradition and the Individual Talent" **4**:442, 457
    Triumphal March **4**:450
    Waste Land, The **4**:437, 439, 440, 441, 442, 450, 451, 453-55, **12**:1677, 1684
    Waste Land, The: A Facsimile and Transcript of the Original Drafts Including the Annotations of Ezra Pound **4**:441, 450
    W.C. Williams and **12**:1677, 1682, 1684, 1690, 1691
    Words for Music **4**:450
Ellison, Ralph **4**:459-74, **5**:690
    "Art of Fiction, The" **4**:473
    as Angelou influence **1**:67, 69
    awards and honors **4**:462, 463, 464, 467, 470
    background and life **4**:460-64
    "Battle Royal" **4**:469
    critical reception of **4**:467
    Dunbar and **3**:410
    "Flying Home" **4**:462, 466, 472, 473
    Flying Home and Other Stories **4**:465, 466, 472-73

Going to the Territory **4**:463, 464, 466, 473
    Hurston and **6**:751
    influences on **4**:460, 461, 462, 463, 464, 470, 473, **6**:751
    Invisible Man **1**:67, **3**:410, **4**:459, 460, 462, 463, 464, 465, 466, 467, 468-70, 471, 472, 473, **12**:1708
    Juneteenth **4**:462, 463, 465, 466, 467, 470-72
    "King of the Bingo Game" **4**:462, 466, 472-73
    King of the Bingo Game and Flying Home **4**:466
    major works **4**:468-72
    Morrison and **8**:1055
    music and **4**:460, 464, 470, **6**:731
    race relations and **4**:461
    racial identity and **4**:459, 466-67, 468, 469, 470, 472
    Shadow and Act **4**:463, 465, 466, 473
    "That Same Pain, That Same Pleasure" **4**:473
    themes and issues **4**:459, 465-67, 468-69, 470-71, 472
    "World and the Jug, The" **4**:473
    Wright and **4**:461, 462, 463, 464, 473, **12**:1693, 1699, 1708
    Writer's Experience, The **4**:466
Emerson, Ralph Waldo
    as Cummings influence **3**:312, 313, 324
    as Frost influence **4**:571
    as Masters influence **7**:952
    as Tyler influence **11**:1549
Erdrich, Louise **11**:1507, 1512, 1514
Euripides **6**:787, 788, 801, **9**:1179

Falkner, William. *See* Faulkner, William
Farrar, John Chipman (playwright) **2**:155
Farrell, James T. **3**:381, **11**:1531
Fast, Howard **3**:381, 384
Faulkner, William **4**:475-98
    Absalom, Absalom! **4**:478, 481, 482, 483, 486, 495-97
    Anderson as influence **1**:41, 53, **4**:477-78, 481, 482, 485
    as Capote influence **2**:241
    as Ellison influence **4**:470

as Gaines influence **5**:584, 587, 588

As I Lay Dying **4**:478, 481, 486, 490-92

as McCullers influence **7**:985

as Morrison influence **8**:1051, 1057, 1058

as Tyler influence **11**:1549

awards and honors **4**:475, 479-80, 481, 485

background and life **4**:476-80

"Bear, The" **4**:479, 481, *496, 497*

Big Sleep, The (screenplay) **4**:479, 486

Big Woods **4**:486, 497

Cather ranked with **2**:281

Collected Short Stories of William Faulkner **4**:486

Doctor Martino and Other Stories **4**:486

Essays, Speeches, and Public Letters **4**:486

Fable, A **4**:486

Faulkner at West Point **4**:486

Faulkner-Cowley File, The: Letters and Memories, 1944-1962 **4**:486

Faulkner in the University **4**:486

Faulkner Reader, The **4**:486

Faulkner's MGM Screenplays **4**:486

film adaptations **4**:479

Flags in the Dust **4**:478, 483, 484, 486, 489

Foote and **4**:542, 543

Gardner and **5**:598

Go Down, Moses **4**:479, 481, 486, *496, 497*

Green Bough, A **4**:486

Hamlet, The **4**:478, 483, 486

Helen: A Court Ship **4**:486

highlights in life **4**:481

influence of **4**:470, **5**:558, 584, 587, **7**:985, **8**:1051, 1057, 1058, **11**:1549

influences on **1**:41, 53, **4**:477-78, 481, 482, 484, 485, **8**:1085

Intruder in the Dust **4**:479, 484, 486

Irving compared with **6**:770

Knight's Gambit **4**:486

Land of the Pharaohs (screenplay) **4**:486

Laurence compared with **6**:827

Light in August **4**:478, 481, 484, 486, 497

Lion in the Garden: Interviews with William Faulkner, 1926-1962 **4**:486

literary reputation **4**:524

major works **4**:490-95

Mamet and **7**:924

Mansion, The **4**:480, 486

Marble Faun, The **4**:477, 486

Marionettes, The: A Play in One Act **4**:486

Mayday **4**:486

McCarthy and **7**:961, 963, 971

Mississippi Poems **4**:486

modernism and **4**:477, 484, 485

Moore and **8**:1045

Mosquitoes **4**:486

multiple narrators use **4**:484, 490, 494, *496, 497*

New Orleans Sketches (ed. Collins) **4**:486

Norris as influence on **8**:1085

obscurity of **4**:484

O'Connor compared with **8**:1135

"Odor of Verbena, An" **4**:487-89

Portable Faulkner, The **4**:479, 482, 485, 486

Pylon **4**:486

racial issues and **4**:478, 485, 497

Red and Blue Club (drawing) **4**:477

Reivers, The **4**:486

Requiem for a Nun **4**:486

Road to Glory, The (screenplay) **4**:486

Sanctuary **4**:478, 486

Sartoris **4**:478, 481, 486

Selected Letters (ed. Blotner) **4**:486

Slave Ship (screenplay) **4**:486

Snopes trilogy **4**:478, 480

Soldiers' Pay **4**:478, 481, 486

Sound and the Fury, The **4**:475, 478, 481, 483, 484, 486, 490, 492-95, **11**:1494

Southerner, The (screenplay) **4**:486

Stein and **10**:1433

stream of consciousness technique **4**:475, 493, 494

stylistic innovation **4**:475, 484, 495, 497

Styron compared with **11**:1494

themes and issues **4**:478, 483, 485, 487, 489, 490, 492-93, *496, 497*

These Thirteen **4**:486

Thinking of Home: William Faulkner's Letters to His Mother and Father, 1918-1925 (Watson ed.) **4**:486

Three Famous Novels **4**:486

Today We Live (screenplay) **4**:486

To Have and Have Not (screenplay) **4**:479, 486

Town, The **4**:480, 486

Uncollected Stories of William Faulkner (Blotner ed.) **4**:486

Vision in Spring **4**:486

Welty and **12**:1589, 1594

Wild Palms, The **4**:486

William Faulkner: Early Prose and Poetry **4**:486

Wishing Tree, The **4**:486

Wright and **12**:1700

Yoknapatawpha saga **4**:475, 478, 479, 481, 482-83, 495, 497, 548

Fauset, Jessie **6**:*750*

Ferber, Edna **4**:**499-514**

American Beauty **4**:504, 507

as pacifist **4**:504

awards and honors **4**:499, 501, 502, 503, 505, 511, 512

background and life **4**:500-503

Bravo! **4**:507

Buttered Side Down **4**:507

Cheerful—By Request **4**:507

Cimarron **4**:506-8

Come and Get It **4**:504, 505, 507, 508

Dawn O'Hara: The Girl Who Laughed **4**:501, 503, 507

Dinner at Eight **4**:507

Emma McChesney and Co. **4**:507, 513

Fanny Herself **4**:502, 507

film adaptations **4**:501

Giant **4**:503, 507, 512-13

Gigolo **4**:507

Girls, The **4**:507, 513

Great Son **4**:505, 507

Half Portions **4**:507

highlights in life **4**:503

"Homely Heroine, The" **4**:501, 503

Ice Palace **4**:505, 507

influences on **4**:508

journalism experience **4**:500, 502, 503, 508

Kind of Magic, A **4**:502, 503, 505, 507

Land Is Bright, The **4**:507

literary reputation **4**:505

major works **4**:506-12

Minick **4**:502, 507

Mother Knows Best **4**:507

Nobody's in Town **4**:507

One Basket **4**:507

Our Mrs. McChesney **4**:502, 503, 504, 507, 513

Peculiar Treasure, A **4**:507

Personality Plus **4**:507, 513

"Representing T. A. Buck" **4**:501

"Roast Beef Medium" **4**:501

Roast Beef Medium **4**:507, 513

Royal Family, The **4**:503, 504, 507, 513-14

Saratoga Trunk **4**:504, 507

Show Boat **4**:499, 507, 509-11

So Big **4**:499, 501, 503, 505, 507, 511-12

Stage Door (with Kaufman; play) **4**:507

themes and issues **4**:499, 504, 505, 506-7, 509-11, 512, 513, 514

They Brought Their Women **4**:507

Trees Die at the Top **4**:507

$1200 a Year **4**:502, 507, 514

women's issues and **4**:499, 504, 505

Fisher, Dorothy Canfield **2**:271

Fitch, John, IV (pseud.). *See* Cormier, Robert

Fitzgerald, F. Scott **4**:**515-38**, **7**:902, 1005, **10**:**1429**, **11**:**1494**, **12**:1620, 1635

Afternoon of an Author: A Selection of Uncollected Stories and Essays **4**:532

All the Sad Young Men **4**:532

Anderson and **1**:45

Apprentice Fiction of F. Scott Fitzgerald, The **4**:532

as autobiographical author **4**:525

as Didion influence **3**:362

As Ever, Scott Fitzgerald **4**:532

"At Your Age" **4**:518

Babylon Revisited and Other Stories **4**:532

background and life **4**:516-20

Basil and Josephine Stories, The **4**:532

Basil Duke Lee stories **4**:517

Beautiful and Damned, The **4**:518, 522, 525, 532, 536

Benét and **2**:155

Bits of Paradise **4**:532

Crack-Up, The **4**:524, 532

"Crack-Up, The" **4**:519

Dear Scott/Dear Max: The Fitzgerald-Perkins Correspondence **4**:532

"Diamond as Big as the Ritz, The" **4**:522

film adaptations **4**:519

Flappers and Philosophers **4**:532

F. Scott Fitzgerald on Authorship **4**:532

F. Scott Fitzgerald's Ledger **4**:532

Great Gatsby, The **4**:515, 518, 520, 521, 522, 523-24, 525, 526, 528-29, 530-33, 536

"Head and Shoulders" **4**:518

Hemingway and **5**:668, 669, 670

highlights in life **4**:522

influence of **3**:362, **5**:669

influences on **4**:517, 525, 535, 536

Last Tycoon, The **3**:362, **4**:520, 522, 523, 524, 525, 532, 536-37

Letters of F. Scott Fitzgerald, The **4**:532

Letters to His Daughter **4**:532

literary reputation **4**:524

Love of the Last Tycoon, The: A Western **4**:520, 522, 523, 524, 525, 532, 536, 537

"Mystery of the Raymond Mortgage, The" **4**:516

Notebooks of F. Scott Fitzgerald, The **4**:532

Pat Hobby stories **4**:520, 522, 532

Pat Hobby Stories, The **4**:532

Portable F. Scott Fitzgerald, The **4**:515, 524, 532

Price Was High, The: The Last Uncollected Stories of F. Scott Fitzgerald **4**:532

"Rich Boy, The" **4**:521

"Romantic Egoist, The" **4**:518, 525

"Six of One —" **4**:523

Tales of the Jazz Age **4**:532

Taps at Reveille: The Stories of F. Scott Fitzgerald **4**:532

Tender Is the Night **4**:519, 521, 522, 524, 525, 532, 533-34

themes and issues **4**:521, 528-29, 530-31, 533, 534

This Side of Paradise **4**:517, 518, 522, 523, 524, 525, 532, 534-37

Thoughtbook of Francis Scott Fitzgerald **4**:532

Three Comrades (screenplay) **4**:523, 532

Vegetable, The: Or, From President to Postman (play) **4**:532

"What Kind of Husbands Do 'Jimmies' Make" **4**:522

Fitzgerald, Robert **8**:1137

Flaubert, Gustave **8**:1051, 1057, **10**:1406

as Capote influence **2**:241, *243*

as Wright influence **12**:1700

Foote, Horton **4**:**539-54**, **6**:838

as actor **4**:540-41, 543

awards and honors **4**:539, 542, 543, 544, 550, 551, 552, 554

Baby, the Rain Must Fall (screenplay) **4**:541, 544, 547

background and life **4**:540-44

Barn Burning (teleplay) **4**:479, 547

Celebration **4**:547

character development **4**:546

Chase, The (novel) **4**:542, 543, 544, 546, 547

Chase, The (play) **4**:542, 547

Convicts (screenplay) **4**:547

Courtship (play) **4**:547, 553

Courtship (screenplay) **4**:547

Cousins **4**:547

critical commentary on **4**:547-48, 550, 551, 553, 554

Dearest of Friends, The **4**:547

Death of Papa, The **4**:547, 553, 554

Displaced Person, The (teleplay) **4**:544, 547

Dividing the Estate **4**:547

Drugstore: Sunday Noon (teleplay) **4**:547

family life as subject **4**:539, 540, 545, 546, 548, 552, 554

Farewell: A Memoir of a Texas Childhood **4**:543, 544, 547

Faulkner and **4**:542, 543

film adaptations **4**:541

Flight (teleplay) **4**:542, 547

From Uncertain to Blue **4**:547

Gambling Heart, The (teleplay) **4**:547

God's Pictures **4**:547

Gone with the Wind **4**:547

Goodbye to Richmond **4**:547

Habitation of Dragons, The (play) **4**:547

Habitation of Dragons, The (teleplay) **4**:547

highlights in life **4**:543

Homecoming **4**:547

Hurry Sundown (screenplay) **4**:544, 546-47

In a Coffin in Egypt **4**:547
influences on **4**:540, 548
In My Beginning **4**:547
Laura Dennis **4**:547
legacy of **4**:547-48
Lily Dale (play) **4**:547
Lily Dale (screenplay) **4**:547
Lonely, The **4**:547
Ludie Brooks (teleplay) **4**:547
major works **4**:550-53
Man of the House, The (screen-
    play) **4**:547
*Man Who Climbed Pecan Trees,
    The* **4**:547
Member of the Family (teleplay)
    4:547
Nightingale **4**:547
Night of the Storm, The (*Roots in a
    Parched Ground*) (teleplay)
    4:547
Night of the Storm, The (*Roots in a
    Parched Land*) (play) **4**:547, 553
Night Seasons (1977 play) **4**:547
Night Seasons (1993 play) **4**:547
1918 (play) **4**:547
1918 (screenplay) **4**:547
Of Mice and Men (screenplay) **4**:547
Old Friends, The **4**:547
Old Man (teleplay) **4**:542, 543, 547
One-Armed Man, The **4**:547
Only the Heart (play) **4**:542, 547
Only the Heart (teleplay) **4**:547
On Valentine's Day (screenplay)
    4:541, 547
Orphans' Home cycle **4**:543,
    544, 553-54
Out of My House **4**:542, 547
Pastor's Son (screenplay) **4**:547
People in the Show **4**:547
"Pinch of Salt, A" **4**:541
Prisoner's Song, The **4**:547
racism and **4**:540, 550, 551
religion and **4**:550, 552, 553
Return **4**:547
Roads to Home (teleplay) **4**:547
Roads to Home, The (play) **4**:547
Rocking Chair (teleplay) **4**:547
Shape of the River, The (teleplay)
    4:547
Spring Dance **4**:547
Stalking Moon, The (screenplay)
    4:547
Storm Fear (screenplay) **4**:542,
    543, 547
Story of a Marriage, The (teleplay)
    4:547

Talking Pictures **4**:547
Tender Mercies (screenplay)
    4:539, 541, 543, 544, 546,
    547, 549-50
Texas Town **4**:542, 547
themes and issues **4**:545, 546,
    547, 549, 550, 552, 554
To Kill a Mockingbird (screenplay)
    4:539, 542, 543, 546, 547,
    550-52
Tomorrow (play) **4**:547
Tomorrow (screenplay) **4**:547
Tomorrow (teleplay) **4**:542, 547
Travelers, The (teleplay) **4**:547
Traveling Lady, The **4**:542, 544,
    547
Trip to Bountiful, The (play) **4**:542,
    547, 554
Trip to Bountiful, The (screenplay)
    4:541, 543, 546, 547, 554
Trip to Bountiful, The (teleplay)
    4:542, 547, 554
*Two Southern Idylls: Miss Lou and
    The Girls* **4**:547
Valentine's Day **4**:547, 554
Wharton Dance, The **4**:547
Widow Claire, The **4**:547
Young Lady of Property, A **4**:547
Young Man from Atlanta, The
    4:539, 543, 544, 547, 552-53
Ford, Ford Madox **1**:45, **5**:670
Forester, C. S. **1**:16, 17
Franklin, Benjamin **4**:530, **12**:1702
    as Davies influence **3**:336, 339,
    343
Frederick, Harold **4**:525
Freud, Sigmund **4**:533, **9**:1157,
    1179, 1264, 1268
    as Anderson influence **1**:45, 46,
    49, 55
Friedman, Melvin J. **11**:1494, 1495
Friedman, Norman **3**:320, 322-23
Froissart, Jean **8**:1087, 1092
Frost, Robert **4**:555-74
    "Acceptance" **4**:571
    "Acquainted with the Night"
        4:571
    "After Apple-Picking" **4**:569
    as Berry influence **4**:563
    as Brodsky influence **4**:563
    as celebrity **4**:555, 559, 562
    as Graves influence **4**:563
    as Hall influence **4**:563
    as Heaney influence **4**:563
    as lecturer **4**:558, 565
    as Meredith influence **4**:563

    as Oliver influence **4**:563
    as Rich influence **9**:1279
    as Roethke influence **4**:563
    as Wilbur influence **4**:563
    autobiographical content **4**:567
    awards and honors **4**:555, 558,
        559, 561, 563
    "Ax-Helve, The" **4**:563
    background and life **4**:556-60
    "Birches" **4**:570, 571
    blank verse use **4**:562, 573
    "Blueberries" **4**:563
    Boy's Will, A **4**:558, 560, 566-68,
        570
    Capote and **2**:234
    "Code, The" **4**:563
    Collected Poems **4**:561, 567, 570
    competitiveness of **4**:562
    Complete Poems **4**:567, 570
    conservatism of **4**:558, 571
    critical commentary on **4**:558,
        559, 561, 563, 567, 568-69
    Cummings and **3**:312
    "Death of the Hired Man, The"
        4:563, 569
    "Desert Places" **4**:571
    "Design" **4**:571
    "Fire and Ice" **4**:571
    "For Once, Then, Something"
        4:571
    *Frost: Collected Poems, Prose, and
        Plays* **4**:571
    Further Range, A **4**:561, 567, 571
    "Gift Outright, The" **4**:555, 559,
        561, 571
    "Good Hours" **4**:569
    highlights in life **4**:560-61
    "Home Burial" **4**:563, 569
    "Housekeeper, The" **4**:563
    "Hundred Collars, A" **4**:563
    "Hyla Brook" **4**:571
    influence of **4**:563, **9**:1279
    influences on **4**:565, 569, 571
    "In Hardwood Groves" **4**:567
    In the Clearing **4**:567, 570
    *Letters of Robert Frost to Louis
        Untermeyer* **4**:567
    literary legacy **4**:524, 563-64
    "Lone Striker, A" **4**:571
    lyric poetry **4**:555, 562, 566,
        567, 571
    MacLeish and **7**:897
    major works **4**:566-71
    "Maple" **4**:563
    Masque of Mercy, A (play) **4**:567,
        572

Masque of Reason, A (play) **4:**567, 572

"Mending Wall" **4:**568, 569

Mountain Interval **4:**560, 567, 571

"Mowing" **4:**566, 567

"My Butterfly" **4:**557, 560

"My November Guest" **4:**567

"Never Again Would Birds' Song Be the Same" **4:**571

New Hampshire: A Poem with Notes and Grace Notes **4:**561, 563, 567

North of Boston **4:**558, 560, 562, 563, 567, 568-70

"Nothing Gold Can Stay" **4:**571

Now Not to Be King **4:**567

"Once by the Pacific" **4:**571

"Oven Bird, The" **4:**571

Palgrave's Golden Treasury as influence on **4:**565

"Pasture, The" **4:**569

Poetry of Robert Frost, The **4:**561, 567, 570-72

"Provide, Provide" **4:**571

"Putting in the Seed" **4:**571

"Range-Finding" **4:**571

Record of a Friendship, The **4:**567

"Reluctance" **4:**567

"Road Not Taken, The" **4:**565, 571

Sandburg and **10:**1326, 1330, 1340

Selected Letters of Robert Frost (ed. Thompson) **4:**567

Selected Poems **4:**567, 570

Selected Prose **4:**567

"Servant to Servants, A" **4:**569

"Silken Tent, The" **4:**571

Steeple Bush **4:**567

"Stopping by Woods on a Snowy Evening" **4:**571

"Subverted Flower, The" **4:**571

themes and issues **4:**562, 563, 564, 566, 568, 570-71

"Trial by Existence, The" **4:**567

"Tuft of Flowers, A" **4:**567, 568

Twilight **4:**557

"Two Tramps at Mud Time" **4:**571

vernacular use **4:**555, 562, 569

Way Out, A (play) **4:**567

West-Running Brook **4:**567, 571

Witness Tree, A **4:**561, 567

"Wood-Pile, The" **4:**569

Frye, Northrup **1:**83, 88

Gaines, Ernest J. **5:581-94**

Autobiography of Miss Jane Pittman, The **5:**585, 586, 588, 589, 590-91

awards and honors **5:**584, 585, 586, 590

background and life **5:**582-86

Bloodline **5:**585, 586, 589

Catherine Carmier **5:**584, 585, 588-89, 593-94

"Comeback" **5:**584, 585

father-son relationship portrayals **5:**581, 584, 585, 588, 589, 594

Gathering of Old Men, A **5:**585, 586, 588, 589, 591-92

highlights in life **5:**585

influences on **5:**584, 587, 588, 593

In My Father's House **5:**585, 586, 588, 589, 594

Lesson Before Dying, A **5:**585, 586, 588, 589, 592-93

Little Stream, A **5:**584

Long Day in November, A **5:**587, 589

major works **5:**590-93

Of Love and Dust **5:**585, 586, 589

themes and issues **5:**587, 588, 590, 591-92, 593-94

"Turtles, The" **5:**584

Gallagher, Tess **2:**258, 259, 260

Gallup, Donald **9:**1168

García Lorca, Federico **6:**737

García Márquez, Gabriel **8:**1058, **11:**1517, 1569

Gardner, John **5:595-610**

Alliterative "Morte d'Arthure," "The Owl and the Nightingale," and Five Other Middle English Poems, The (ed.) **5:**602

Art of Fiction, The: Notes on Craft for Young Writers **5:**602

Art of Living and Other Stories, The **5:**598, 599, 602

as Carver influence **2:**256, 258, 260

awards and honors **5:**597, 598, 599

background and life **5:**596-98

Child's Bestiary, A **5:**602

Complete Works of the Gawain-Poet, The (ed.) **5:**597, 602

Construction of Christian Poetry in Old English, The **5:**602

Construction of the Wakefield Cycle, The **5:**602

Death and the Maiden **5:**602

Dragon, Dragon and Other Tales **5:**602

Forms of Fiction, The (ed. with Dunlap) **5:**602

Frankenstein (libretto) **5:**602

Freddy's Book **5:**598, 599, 602

Gilgamesh (transl.) **5:**602

Grendel **5:**598, 599, 602, 603-4

Gudgekin the Thistle Girl and Other Tales **5:**602

highlights in life **5:**599

influences on **5:**601

In the Suicide Mountains **5:**602

Jason and Medeia **5:**598, 602

King of the Hummingbirds and Other Tales, The **5:**602

"King's Indian, The: A Tale" **5:**608

King's Indian, The: Stories and Tales **5:**598, 599, 600-601, 602, 608

Life and Times of Chaucer, The **5:**598, 602

major works **5:**603-7

Mickelsson's Ghosts **5:**598, 599, 601, 602

"Midnight Reader, The" **5:**608

Nickel Mountain: A Pastoral Novel **5:**597, 598, 601, 602, 608, 609

October Light **5:**595, 598, 599, 602, 604-6

"Old Men, The" **5:**597

On Becoming a Novelist **5:**602

On Moral Fiction **5:**595, 598, 599, 601, 602, 608-9

Papers on the Art and Age of Geoffrey Chaucer **5:**602

Poems **5:**602

Poetry of Chaucer, The **5:**598, 602

Resurrection, The **5:**597-98, 599, 601, 602, 609

Rumpelstiltskin (libretto) **5:**602

"Stillness" and "Shadows" **5:**599, 602

Sunlight Dialogues, The **5:**595, 597, 598, 599, 600, 601, 602, 606-7, 609

"Tales of Queen Louisa" **5:**608

Temptation Game, The (radio play) **5:**602

themes and issues **5:**603-5, 606, 607, 609

William Wilson (libretto) **5**:602

Wreckage of Agathon, The **5**:598, 601, 602, 609-10

Garland, Hamlin **7**:1005, **8**:1085, 1090

Garrison, Lietutenant Frederick (Sinclair pseud.) **10**:1378

Gates, Henry Louis, Jr. **1**:107, **3**:406

Gellhorn, Martha **5**:664, 665, 668

Genet, Jean **1**:59, 60, **5**:657

Gibson, William **5**:611-26

   American Primitive. See *John and Abigail*

   awards and honors **5**:613, 615

   background and life **5**:612-14

   Body and the Wheel, The: A Play Made from the Gospels **5**:614, 615, 619

   Butterfingers Angel, Mary and Joseph, Herod the Nut, and the Slaughter of Twelve Hit Carols in a Pear Tree, The **5**:614, 619, 621, 626

   Cobweb, The (novel) **5**:613, 615, 616, 619

   Cobweb, The (screenplay) **5**:615, 619

   Cry of Players, A **5**:613, 615, 616, 617, 619, 621

   Dinny and the Witches: A Frolic on Grave Matters **5**:619

   Golda **5**:614, 615, 617, 619, 621, 624-26

   Golden Boy **5**:614, 619

   Goodly Creatures **5**:614, 619

   Handy Dandy **5**:619

   highlights in life **5**:612-15

   I Lay in Zion **5**:613, 615, 619

   influences on **5**:613, 615, 620

   John and Abigail **5**:617, 619

   major works **5**:618-23

   Mass for the Dead, A **5**:615, 619, 624

   Miracle Worker, The (play) **5**:611, 612, 613, 614, 615, 616-17, 618-21, 623, 625

   Miracle Worker, The (screenplay) **5**:613, 615, 619

   Miracle Worker, The (teleplay) **5**:611, 613, 615, 619

   Monday after the Miracle **5**:614, 615, 617, 619

   Notes on How to Turn a Phoenix into Ashes: The Story of the Stage Production, with the Text, of "Golda" **5**:619, 625

Raggedy Ann and Andy **5**:619

Roman Catholicism and **5**:614, 615, 620, 624

Ruby, The **5**:616

Season in Heaven, A **5**:619

Seesaw Log, The: A Chronicle of the Stage Production, with the Text, of "Two for the Seesaw" **5**:614, 619

sentimentality in work **5**:623

Shakespeare's Game **5**:619

strong-willed women characters **5**:616, 621, 625

themes and issues **5**:616, 618, 621-22, 623

Two for the Seesaw **5**:612, 613-14, 615, 616, 619, 621-23, 624

Winter Crook **5**:615, 619

Gide, André **11**:1495

Ginsberg, Allen **10**:1375

   W. C. Williams and **12**:1678, 1682, 1683, 1687, 1688

Giovanni, Nikki **5**:627-44

   "All I Gotta Do" **5**:639

   Appalachian Elders: A Warm Hearth Sampler (ed. with Dennison) **5**:635

   as lecturer **5**:631, 632, 634

   autobiographical elements **5**:634

   awards and honors **5**:627, 629, 630, 631, 632

   Baldwin and **1**:106, 110

   "Being and Nothingness (to quote a philosopher)" **5**:639

   Black Feeling, Black Talk/Black Judgement **5**:630, 635, 636, 638

   Black Judgement **5**:630, 631, 635, 636

   black oral poetry movement and **5**:627

   Blues: For All the Changes: New Poems **5**:635

   Cincinnati Black Arts Festival and **5**:629

   Civil Rights movement and **5**:627, 629, 630, 631, 633, 642

   Cotton Candy on a Rainy Day **5**:631, 635, 638-39, 641

   "Cotton Candy on a Rainy Day" **5**:638-39

   Dialogue, A: James Baldwin and Nikki Giovanni **1**:106, 110, **5**:631, 635, 642

   Dunbar as influence on **3**:397

   "Ego-Tripping" **5**:639

Ego-Tripping and Other Poems for Young Readers **5**:635

Gemini: An Extended Autobiographical Statement on My First Twenty-five Years of Being a Black Poet **5**:631, 635, 642

Genie in the Jar, The **5**:635

Grand Fathers: Reminiscences, Poems, Recipes, and Photos of the Keepers of our Traditions (ed.) **5**:635

Grand Mothers: Poems, Reminiscences, and Short Stories About the Keepers of our Traditions (ed.) **5**:635

"Great Pax Whitie, The" **5**:636

"Harvest (for Rosa Parks)" **5**:641-42

influences on **3**:397, **5**:634

Knoxville, Tennessee **5**:635

"Knoxville, Tennessee" **5**:636

language use **5**:634

Love Poems **5**:635

"Master Charge Blues" **5**:639

"Mirrors (for Billie Jean King)" **5**:641

My House **5**:631, 635

"Nigger/Can You Kill?" **5**:630, 636

Night Comes Softly: Anthology of Black Female Voices (ed.) **5**:630, 635

"Nikki-Rosa" **5**:636

"Poem (for TW)" **5**:638

Poem of Angela Yvonne Davis **5**:635

Poetic Equation, A: Conversations Between Nikki Giovanni and Margaret Walker **5**:635, 642

poetic voice **5**:633, 636

publishing firm **5**:630, 631, 634

racial views **5**:628, 634, 636

Racism 101 **5**:635, 642, 644

Re: Creation **5**:630, 635, 639-41

Sacred Cows and Other Edibles **5**:635

Selected Poems of Nikki Giovanni **5**:635

Shimmy Shimmy Shimmy Like My Sister Kate: Looking at the Harlem Renaissance Through Poems (ed.) **5**:635, 644

Spin a Soft Black Song: Poems for Children **5**:631, 635

Sun Is So Quiet, The: Poems **5**:635

themes and issues **5**:627, 634, 635, 639, 642, *643*

"This Is Not for John Lennon" **5**:641

Those Who Ride the Night Winds **5**:635, 641-42

Truth Is on Its Way (record album) **5**:630, 631, 632

Truth (record album) **5**:632

Vacation Time: Poems for Children **5**:635

Women and the Men, The **5**:631, 635

Godwin, Gail **11**:1544

Goethe, Johann Wolfgang von **7**:952

Gogol, Nikolai **9**:1251

Gordon, Caroline **8**:1142

Gordon, Ruth **11**:1530

Gorky, Maxim **9**:1167, 1173

Graham, Sheilah **4**:520, 522

Grass, Günter **6**:780, 782

Graves, Robert **1**:83, 88, **4**:563

Green, Paul **12**:1695, 1703

Greene, Graham **3**:300

Grey, Zane **2**:256, **10**:1350

Grubb, Davis **1**:17

Guillén, Nicolás **6**:737

Haeckel, Ernst **7**:877

Hakutani, Yoshinobu **3**:381

Hall, Donald **4**:563

Hamilton, Ian **10**:1304, 1306, 1311, 1313

Hamsun, Knut **10**:1399, 1408

Hansberry, Lorraine **5**:645-58, **11**:1527

awards and honors **5**:645, 652

background and life **5**:646-49

Baldwin and **1**:106

Blancs, Les: The Collected Last Plays of Lorraine Hansberry **5**:649, 654, 657

"Crystal Stair, The." See *Raisin in the Sun, A*

Drinking Gourd, The **5**:648, 654, 657

film adaptations 651-52

highlights in life **5**:649

Hughes and **6**:741

influences on **5**:652

literary legacy **5**:652

major works **5**:653-57

Movement, The: Documentary of a Struggle for Equality **5**:654, 658

"Negro Writer and His Roots, The" **5**:658

Raisin in the Sun, A (play) **5**:645, 648, 649, 650, 651, 652, 653-55, **6**:741

Raisin in the Sun, A (screenplay) **5**:648, 649, 651-52, 654

Raisin in the Sun, A (teleplay) **5**:652

Sign in Sidney Brustein's Window, The **5**:649, 650-51, 654, 655-57

themes and issues **5**:645, 647, 650-51, 652, 653, 654, 655-66

To Be Young, Gifted, and Black: Lorraine Hansberry in Her Own Words **5**:646, 649, 654, 657, 658

What Use Are Flowers?: A Fable in One Act (Nemiroff ed.) **5**:654, 658

Hardwick, Elizabeth **9**:1216

Hardy, Thomas **3**:380, **6**:770

Harjo, Joy **9**:1293

Harper, Frances **3**:410

Harris, Joel Chandler **3**:415, **8**:1058

Harvey, Anne Gray. *See* Sexton, Anne

Hastings, Michael **4**:441

Haswell, Susanna. *See* Rowson, Susanna

Hawthorne, Nathaniel

as Dunbar influence **3**:415

as Malamud influence **7**:916

as O'Connor influence **8**:1136, 1143

as Wright influence **12**:1700

Hawthorne parallels **10**:1413, 1414

H.D. *See* Doolittle, Hilda

Heaney, Seamus **4**:563

Hecht, Ben **1**:45

Heller, Joseph **6**:770

Hellman, Lillian **4**:544, 546, **9**:1188, **10**:1399

as Zindel influence **12**:1713, 1717

Hemingway, Ernest **5**:659-82, **7**:894, **9**:1229, **12**:1635, 1700

Across the River and into the Trees **5**:664, 674

Anderson and **1**:41, 45, 53, **5**:661, 669

as Carver influence **2**:259, 260, 261

as Cormier influence **3**:294, 300

as Ellison influence **4**:460, 464

as Gaines influence **5**:584

as McNickel influence **7**:1004, 1005

as Morrison influence **8**:1051, 1057

as Potok influence **9**:1266

"At Sea" **5**:671

awards and honors **5**:659, 664, 665, 676

background and life **5**:660-65

"Battler, The" **5**:668, 679

Benét and **2**:155

"Big Two-Hearted River" **5**:663, 668, 679

"Bimini" **5**:670-71

bullfighting aesthetic **5**:663, 664, 668, 669, 678

By-Line: Ernest Hemingway, Selected Articles, and Dispatches of Four Decades **5**:674

"Clean, Well-Lighted Place, A" **5**:663, 681

Complete Short Stories, The **5**:674

"Cuba" **5**:671

Dangerous Summer, The **5**:664, 671, 674

Dateline, Toronto: The Complete "Toronto Star" Dispatches, 1920-1924 **5**:674

Death in the Afternoon **5**:663, 668, 674

Ernest Hemingway: Selected Letters, 1917-1961 **5**:674

expatriate experience **5**:659

Farewell to Arms, A **5**:663, 665, 668, 672-74, 675

"Fathers and Sons" **5**:680

Faulkner and **4**:479, 484

Fifth Column and the First Forty-nine Stories, The **5**:664, 665, 674, 678-79

Fifth Column, The **5**:663, 674, 678

"Fifty Grand" **5**:679

film adaptations **5**:673

Fitzgerald and **4**:521, 522, 524, **5**:669

For Whom the Bell Tolls **5**:663, 664, 665, 668, 671, 673, 674, 675-76

"Gambler, the Nun, and the Radio, The" **5**:663, 681

Garden of Eden, The **5**:664, 665, 671, 674, 680

"God Rest You Merry, Gentlemen" **5**:680

"grace under pressure" emphasis **5**:659, 668, 671, 680
Green Hills of Africa **5**:663, 671, 674
Hersey compared with **5**:685
highlights in life **5**:665
"Hills Like White Elephants" **5**:663, 668, 679
iceberg principle in work of **5**:668, 679
"In Another Country" **5**:679
"Indian Camp" **5**:668, 679
influence of **2**:259, 260, 261, **3**:294, 300, **5**:584, **7**:1004, 1005, **8**:1051, 1057, **9**:1266
influences on **5**:669, **8**:1085
In Our Time **5**:663, 665, 674, 679
Islands in the Stream **5**:664, 670-71, 674
"Killers, The" **5**:663, 679
"Light of the World, The" **5**:680
London (Jack) as influence on **7**:878
major works **5**:674-78
Men Without Women **5**:663, 674, 679
"Mother of a Queen, The" **5**:680
Moveable Feast, A **5**:663, 664, 665, 670, 674
Nick Adams Stories, The **5**:670, 674, 680
Norris as influence on **8**:1085
"Now I Lay Me" **5**:679
O'Brien compared with **8**:1125, 1126
Old Man and the Sea, The **5**:659, 664, 665, 674
on Cummings **3**:325
parody of Anderson **1**:45
posthumously published books **5**:670-71
"Sea Change, The" **5**:680
"Short Happy Life of Francis Macomber, The" **5**:663, 668, 678-79
simplicity of style **5**:659, 668
"Snows of Kilimanjaro, The" **5**:663, 678, 679
Snows of Kilimanjaro and Other Stories, The **5**:674
"Soldier's Home" **5**:679
Stein and **5**:699, **10**:1429, 1430, 1431, 1432
Steinbeck and **11**:1453
suicide of **5**:664, 665

Sun Also Rises, The **5**:663, 665, 668, 669, 672, 674, 676-78
"Ten Indians" **5**:679
themes and issues **5**:659, 666, 668, 671, 672-73, 675, 676-77, 680
Three Stories and Ten Poems **5**:674, 678
Today Is Friday **5**:674
To Have and Have Not **4**:479, **5**:663, 674
Torrents of Spring, The **1**:45, **5**:663, 674
True at First Light **5**:664, 665, 670, 671, 674
"Undefeated, The" **5**:679
"Up in Michigan" **5**:678
"Very Short Story, A" **5**:668, 679
"Way You'll Never Be, A" **5**:680
Winner Take Nothing **5**:663, 674, 680-81
Henry, O. **1**:48
Heraclitus **4**:449-50
Hersey, John **5**:683-98
Algiers Motel Incident, The **5**:687, 690
allegory use **5**:691
"AMGOT at Work" **5**:688
Antonietta **5**:690
Aspects of the Presidency: Truman and Ford in Office **5**:690
as war correspondent **5**:684, 685, 686, 687, 688
awards and honors **5**:685, 686, 687, 692
background and life **5**:684-88
Bell for Adano, A **5**:685, 687, 688, 689, 690, 691-92, 695, 696
Blues **5**:690
Call, The **5**:690
Child Buyer, The **5**:686, 688, 689, 690, 696-97
Conspiracy, The **5**:690
Fling and Other Stories **5**:690
Here to Stay: Studies in Human Tenacity **5**:687, 690
highlights in life **5**:687
Hiroshima **5**:683, 686, 687, 689, 690, 692-94, 696
Hiroshima: A New Edition with a Final Chapter Written Forty Years after the Explosion **5**:688, 690
influences on **5**:688
"Intelligence, Choice, and Consent" **5**:688

Into the Valley: A Skirmish of the Marines **5**:685, 688, 690, 697
Key West Tales **5**:690
Letter to the Alumni **5**:690
Life Sketches **5**:690
literary legacy **5**:690
major works **5**:691-96
Marmot Drive, The **5**:686, 690, 691
Men on Bataan **5**:685, 687, 690, 697
My Petition for More Space **5**:689, 690
nonfiction novel and **5**:686, 690, 692, 696
President, The **5**:690
Ralph Ellison: A Collection of Critical Essays (ed.) **5**:690
"Sense of Community, A" **5**:687
Single Pebble, A **5**:686, 687, 689, 690, 692, 698
stylistic clarity **5**:683, 685, 689
themes and issues **5**:683, 689-90, 691, 692, 694-95, 697
Too Far to Walk **5**:690
Under the Eye of the Storm **5**:690
Wall, The **5**:686, 687, 688, 689, 690, 694-96
Walnut Door, The **5**:690
War Lover, The **5**:686, 688, 690
White Lotus **5**:689, 690
Writer's Craft, The (ed.) **5**:690
Hershon, Bob **9**:1205
Hill, Arthur **9**:1172
Hillyer, Robert **3**:313
Hinton, S. E. **5**:699-718
awards and honors **5**:703, 716
background and life **6**:700-703
Big David, Little David **5**:701, 703, 706
character growth portrayal **5**:707-9
film adaptations **5**:701-3
highlights in life **6**:703
influences on **5**:705-6
major works **6**:711-16
Outsiders, The **5**:699, 700, 702, 703, 705, 706, 711-12
plot development **5**:699, 707, 708, 711
Puppy Sister, The **5**:701, 703, 706
Rumble Fish (novel) **5**:699, 700, 701, 702, 703, 706, 716
Rumble Fish (screenplay with Coppola) **5**:700, 702, 703
Taming the Star Runner **5**:701, 703, 705, 706, 710, 713-16

"Teen-Agers Are for Real" **5**:700
Tex **5**:700, 701, 703, 706, 710, 712-13
That Was Then, This Is Now **5**:699, 701, 702, 703, 706, 716-18
  themes and issues **5**:704-5, 706, 707-9, 710, 711, 712, 713, 716
  violence in works **5**:704, 708, 711, 713
Hobart, George V. **4**:502, 503, *504*, 507, 513
Holm, John Cecil **8**:1025
Holmes, Oliver Wendell **3**:312
Homer **2**:204, **6**:742, **8**:1097, 1137, **9**:1248, **11**:1515, 1516
Horace **10**:1413
Howe, Irving **4**:473
Howells, William Dean
  as Anderson influence **1**:45, 49
  as Dunbar influence **3**:399, 403, 405, 407
  Norris and **8**:1085, 1090, 1092
Hubbard, Elbert **10**:1324, 1332-33
Hughes, Langston **1**:59, **5**:644, 653, **6**:725-44, *750, 752*
  Arna Bontemps-Langston Hughes Letters **6**:737
  as Brooks influence **2**:196, 199, 202
  as Ellison influence **4**:461, 464
  Ask Your Mama: Or, Twelve Moods for Jazz **6**:737
  awards and honors **6**:730
  background and life **6**:726-30
  Best of Simple, The **6**:733, *734*, 737, 743
  Best Short Stories by Negro Writers, The: An Anthology from 1899 to the Present (ed.) **6**:737
  Big Sea, The: An Autobiography **6**:737, 738
  Black Magic: A Pictorial History of the Negro in American Entertainment **6**:737
  Black Misery **6**:737
  Black Nativity **6**:737
  blues and **6**:41-42, 731-32, 738, 739-40
  Bontemps and **2**:181, *183*, 185, 186, 187, 193, 196, 199, 202
  Book of Negro Folklore, The (ed. with Bontemps) **2**:187, **6**:737
  Book of Negro Humor, The (ed.) **6**:737

"Christ in Alabama" **6**:744
Collected Poems of Langston Hughes, The **6**:737
confessional poetry **6**:732
critical commentary on **6**:730, 739, 740, 742
Cuba Libre (transl.) **6**:737
Dear Lovely Death **6**:737
Don't You Want to Be Free **6**:737
Dream Keeper and Other Poems, The **6**:737
Dunbar and **3**:397
Famous American Negroes **6**:737
Famous Negro Heroes of America **6**:737
Famous Negro Music Makers **6**:737
Fields of Wonder **6**:737
Fight for Freedom: The Story of the NAACP **6**:737
Fine Clothes to the Jew **6**:728, 730, 737, 739-40
First Book of Africa, The **6**:737
First Book of Jazz, The **6**:737
First Book of Negroes, The **6**:737
First Book of Rhythms, The **6**:737
First Book of the West Indies, The **6**:737
Five Plays (Smalley ed.) **6**:737
folk tradition and **6**:734, 738
Freedom's Plow (play) **6**:737
"Genius Child" **6**:732
Gypsy Ballads (Garcia Lorca; transl.) **6**:737
highlights in life **6**:730
influence of **2**:196, 199, 202, **4**:461, 464
influences on **6**:725, 731, 738, 740, 742, 743
"I, Too, Sing America" (with Bontemps) **2**:185, **6**:728, 742
I Wonder as I Wander: An Autobiographical Journey **6**:728, 737
Jerico-Jim Crow (play) **6**:737
Jim Crow's Last Stand **6**:737
"Justice" **6**:744
Lament for Dark Peoples **6**:737
Langston Hughes Reader, The **6**:737
Laughing to Keep from Crying **6**:737
"Listen Here Blues" **6**:740
Little Ham **6**:737
major works **6**:740-42
Masters of the Dew (Roumain; transl. with Cook) **6**:737

Montage of a Dream Deferred **6**:730, 737, 740-41
"Mother to Son" **6**:727, 732, 741, 742
Mulatto **6**:737
Mule Bone: A Comedy of Negro Life in Three Acts (with Hurston; play) **6**:755
"Negro Artist and the Racial Mountain, The" **6**:729
Negro Mother, The **6**:737
"Negro Speaks of Rivers, The" **6**:727, 730, 731, 742
New Negro Poets: U.S.A. (ed.) **6**:737
New Song, A **6**:737
Not Without Laughter **6**:729, 737
One Way Ticket **6**:737
"On the Road" **6**:743
optimism of **6**:732
Panther and the Lash, The: Or, Poems of Our Times **6**:737
Pictorial History of the Negro in America, A (with Meltzer) **6**:729, 737
Poetry of the Negro, 1746-1949, The (ed. with Bontemps) **2**:187, **6**:737
Popo and Fijina: Children of Haiti (with Bontemps) **2**:186, 187, 188, **6**:737
Prodigal Son, The (play) **6**:737
race consciousness **6**:725, 727, 731, 732, 734, 736, 743, 744
Sandburg as influence **6**:738
"Scottsboro" **6**:744
Scottsboro Limited: Four Poems and a Play in Verse **6**:737, 744
Selected Poems of Gabriela Mistral (transl.) **6**:737
Selected Poems of Langston Hughes **6**:730, 737
Shakespeare in Harlem **6**:737
Simple columns **6**:729, 730, 733-36, *733*, 734-36, 737, 743
Simple Speaks His Mind **6**:737
Simple Stakes a Claim **6**:737
Simple's Uncle Sam **6**:737
Simple Takes a Wife **6**:737
Simply Heavenly (opera libretto) **6**:737
Something in Common and Other Stories **6**:737
"Song of the Soul of Central, A" **6**:727
Street Scene (with Weill and Rice; musical) **6**:737

Sweet Flypaper of Life, The **6:**737
Tambourines to Glory (play) **6:**730, 737
"Theme for English B" **6:**727, 732, 741
themes and issues **6:**725, 731, 732, 734, 740, 741-42
"Town of Scottsboro, The" **6:**744
Troubled Island (opera libretto) **6:**737
vernacular use **6:**738, 740, 743
Ways of White Folks, The **6:**737
"Weary Blues, The" **6:**728, 731
Weary Blues, The **6:**728, 730, 737, 739, 741-42
"When Sue Wears Red" **6:**727, 742
Whitman as influence on **6:**725, 731, 738, 742
Hughes, Ted (Plath husband) **9:**1215-16, 1218, 1220, 1221, 1222, 1224
Hume, David **10:**1413
Hurst, Fannie **6:**747
Hurston, Zora Neale **6:745-62**
African American culture and **6:**745, 750, 751, 752, 755, 757, 758, 761
as anthropologist **6:**745, 747-48, 750, 751, 752, 753, 755
as Bambara influence **6:**751
as Ellison influence **6:**751
as Morrison influence **6:**751
awards and honors **6:**747, 748, 749, 761
background and life **6:**746-49
Barracoon **6:**752
Complete Stories, The **6:**755
Dust Tracks on a Road: An Autobiography **6:**748, 755, 760-61
folklore collection **6:**745, 747, 748, 751, 753, 755, 756
Folklore, Memoirs, and Other Writings by Zora Neale Hurston **6:**755
gender issues and **6:**751, 756, 757, 758
Go Gator and Muddy the Water: Writings by Zora Neale Hurston from the Federal Writers' Project **6:**755
highlights in life **6:**749
"Hoodoo in America" **6:**755
"How It Feels to Be Colored Me" **6:**750

I Love Myself When I Am Laughing…and Then Again When I Am Looking Mean and Impressive: A Zora Neale Hurston Reader (Walker ed.) **6:**755, **11:**1564, 1566, 1575
influence of **6:**751
influences on **6:**747, 752
"John Redding Goes to Sea" **6:**747, 749
Jonah's Gourd Vine **6:**748, 749, 752, 755, 756, 760, 761
linguistic ritual and **6:**748, 750, 752, 753, 758, 761
literary legacy **6:**751-52
major works **6:**753-59
Moses, Man of the Mountain **6:**751, 755, 761
Mule Bone: A Comedy of Negro Life in Three Acts (play with Hughes) **6:**755
Mules and Men **6:**748, 750, 751, 752, 753, 755-56
"My Most Humiliating Jim Crow Experience" **6:**750
"Part One: Folktales" **6:**753
"Part Two: Hoodoo" **6:**753, 755
"'Pet' Negro System, The" **6:**750
Sanctified Church, The **6:**755
Seraph on the Suwanee **6:**748, 755
Spunk: The Selected Short Stories of Zora Neale Hurston **6:**755
Tell My Horse: Voodoo and Life in Haiti and Jamaica **6:**750, 752, 755
Their Eyes Were Watching God **6:**745, 748, 749, 750-51, 752, 755, 756-59
themes and issues **6:**745, 750-51, 753, 755, 756, 758
vernacular use **6:**750, 751, 758
Walker rediscovery of **6:**745, 749, 751, 756, **11:**1564, 1566, 1569, 1575
"What White Publishers Won't Print" **6:**750
Wright and **12:**1706
Huxley, Thomas Henry **3:**380

Ibsen, Henrik
as Foote influence **4:**548
as Miller influence **8:**1020, 1021, 1028
as O'Neill influence **9:**1165, 1167, 1173
as Rich influence **9:**1278

Miller adaptation of **8:**1015, 1018, 1019, 1021, 1025, 1028
Wilder and **12:**1632, 1647
Irving, John **6:763-82**
abortion issue and **6:**768, 770, 773, 774, 775, 776
aphorisms of **6:**777
as social critic **6:**763
awards and honors **6:**763, 765, 767, 768, 773, 774
background and life **6:**764-68
bear motif **6:**765, 769, 772, 773, 776, 777, 779, 781
bizarre events and characters **6:**763, 771, 778, 780, 781
Cider House Rules, The (novel)6.764 **6:**768, 771, 773, 774-76, 781, 782
Cider House Rules, The (screenplay) **6:**767, 768, 773, 774, 775
comedic elements **6:**776, 778
critical commentary on **6:**768, 774, 781
Dickensian novel and **6:**764, 770, 772, 775, 778
dwarf motif **6:**780, 781
family issues and **6:**766, 773, 776, 778, 781
feminist issues and **6:**767, 773, 778, 779, 782
film adaptations **6:**766, 768, 771, 773
highlights in life **6:**768
"Homage" **6:**782
Hotel New Hampshire, The **6:**766, 768, 773, 776-78
Imaginary Girlfriend, An **6:**768, 773, 781
influences on **6:**764, 770, 771, 772, 775, 778, 780, 782
"Interior Space" **6:**781
irony of **6:**770, 771, 776
major works **6:**774-80
My Movie Business: A Memoir **6:**773
158-Pound Marriage, The **6:**765, 773, 780
"Pension Grillparzer" **6:**781
plot emphasis and intricacies **6:**770
Prayer for Owen Meany, A **6:**768, 773, 780-81
prep school motif **6:**773
Setting Free the Bears **6:**765, 767, 773, 781

Son of the Circus, A **6**:768, 773, 781
themes and issues **6**:763, 771, 772-73, 774, 775, 776-77, 778, 779, 780
Three by Irving **6**:768, 773
Trying to Save Piggy Sneed **6**:768, 781-82
Water-Method Man, The **6**:765, 773, 782
"Weary Kingdom" **6**:781-82
Widow for One Year, A **6**:773
"Winter Branch, A" **6**:765
World According to Garp, The **6**:763, 764, 765, 767, 768, 771, 773, 776, 778-80, 781
World War II and **6**:764, 771, 773, 775, 777
wrestling motif **6**:764, 773, 777, 778, 781, 782
Irving, Washington **3**:343

James, Henry **8**:1085, **12**:1637
as Capote influence **2**:241
as Wharton influence **12**:1614, 1615, 1616, 1620, 1626, 1628
Moore and **8**:1039, 1040, 1047
James, William **4**:565, **10**:1419
Jarrell, Randall **4**:563, **9**:1278
Jeffers, Robinson **6**:783-802, **10**:1345
Alpine Christ and Other Poems, The **6**:790
"Answer, The" **6**:789
"At the Birth of an Age" **6**:788
background and life **6**:784-87
Be Angry at the Sun and Other Poems **6**:786, 790
"Bed by the Window, The" **6**:787, 794
Beginning and the End, The **6**:790
"Boats in a Fog" **6**:799-800
Brides of the South Wind **6**:790
Californians **6**:785, 787, 790
Cawdor and Other Poems **6**:786, 790
Collected Poetry of Robinson Jeffers, The **6**:787, 790
Collected Poetry of Robinson Jeffers, Volume I, 1920-1928, The **6**:787, 790
Collected Poetry of Robinson Jeffers, Volume II, 1928-1938, The **6**:787, 790
Collected Poetry of Robinson Jeffers, Volume III, 1939-1962, The **6**:787, 790

Collected Poetry of Robinson Jeffers, Volume IV, Poetry 1903-1920, Prose, and Unpublished Writings, The **6**:787, 790
Cretan Woman, The **6**:790, 796
critical commentary on **6**:786, 788, 798
"Dear Judas" **6**:788
Dear Judas and Other Poems **6**:790
"Deer Lay Down Their Bones, The" **6**:796
Descent to the Dead: Poems Written in Ireland and Great Britain **6**:786, 787, 790
"Divinely Superfluous Beauty" **6**:789
Double Axe and Other Poems, The **6**:786, 787, 790
"Fire on the Hills" **6**:789
Flagons and Apples **6**:784, 787, 790
"Give Your Heart to the Hawks" **6**:789-90
Give Your Heart to the Hawks and Other Poems **6**:786, 790
"Granite and Cypress" **6**:788
highlights in life **6**:787
"Hungerfield" **6**:795-96
Hungerfield and Other Poems **6**:787, 790, 795-96
importance of nature to **6**:789
influences on **6**:788, 796, 799, 801
legends use **6**:788, 789
long narrative poems **6**:783, 786, 788, 789, 795, 796, 798
"Love the Wild Swan" **6**:800
major works **6**:795-99
Medea translation **6**:787, 788, 790, 800-801
"Night" **6**:801-2
"On Building with Stone" **6**:793
philosophical ideas **6**:783, 788, 789, 791, 797, 802
Poems Known and Unknown **6**:790
poetic style and forms **6**:788-89
"Roan Stallion" **6**:789, 796-98
Roan Stallion, Tamar, and Other Poems **6**:786, 790, 796
Rock and Hawk: A Selection of Shorter Poems by Robinson Jeffers **6**:790
Selected Letters of Robinson Jeffers, 1897-1962, The (ed. Ridgeway) **6**:790

Selected Poems **6**:790
Selected Poetry of Robinson Jeffers, The **6**:790
sensational plots **6**:788
Solstice and Other Poems **6**:790
stonemasonry interest **6**:791, 792, 793
Such Counsels You Gave to Me and Other Poems **6**:790
"Tamar" **6**:798-99
Tamar, and Other Poems **6**:783, 786, 787, 788, 790
themes and issues **6**:783, 788, 789, 790, 795, 796, 798
Themes in My Poems **6**:790
Thurso's Landing and Other Poems **6**:786, 790
"Tor House" **6**:793
Tor House (home) **6**:785-86, 787, 791-94
"To the House" **6**:793
"To the Rock That Will Be a Cornerstone of the House" **6**:793
"To the Stone-Cutters" **6**:793
What Odd Expedients and Other Poems **6**:790
Women at Point Sur, The **6**:786, 787, 790
Jewett, Sarah Orne **2**:271, 274
Johnson, Charles Spurgeon **2**:181, 185
Johnson, James Weldon
as Angelou influence **1**:65
as Brooks influence **2**:196, 199, 202
Autobiography of an Ex-Colored Man **1**:65
Bontemps and **2**:181, 185, 187
Johnson, Marguerite Annie. *See* Angelou, Maya
Jones, Edith Newbold. *See* Wharton, Edith
Jones, Gayl **8**:1053
Jones, James **11**:1491
Jones, James Arthur. *See* Baldwin, James
Jordan, June **9**:1280
Joyce, James **5**:598, **7**:894, 971, **9**:1229, **10**:1433
as Anderson influence **1**:45, 49
as Cummings influence **3**:314, 318
as Potok influence **9**:1266
as Wright influence **12**:1700
Wilder and **12**:1632, 1646, 1647
Jung, Carl **3**:343

Kael, Pauline 4:550
Kafka, Franz 6:772, 10:1411
Kant, Immanuel 10:1408
Kaufman, George S. 4:502, 503, 513
Keats, John 4:525, 12:1676
Kennedy, Richard 3:313, 320, 326
Kerouac, Jack 12:1683
Key, Francis Scott 4:516
King, Stephen 11:1510
Kingsley, Charles 7:898
Kingston, Maxine Hong 1:31, 11:1505, 1512
Kinsella, Thomas 10:1371
Kipling, Rudyard
   as Benét influence 2:150
   as London influence 7:877, 881
Knowles, John 6:803-18
   as coming-of-age novelist 6:807, 816
   awards and honors 6:804, 806, 808
   Backcasts: Memories and Recollections of Seventy Years as a Sportsman, Fishing, Hunting, and Other Stories 6:807, 812
   background and life 6:804-8
   critical commentary on 6:812, 814
   "Descent into Proslito" 6:805
   Double Vision: American Thoughts Abroad 6:805, 812
   highlights in life 6:808
   Indian Summer 6:803, 805, 809, 810, 812, 817
   influences on 6:810
   literacy legacy 6:812
   major works 6:813-17
   Morning in Antibes 6:806-7, 810, 812
   Paragon, The 6:803, 810, 812, 817-18
   Peace Breaks Out 6:803, 808, 809, 810, 812, 813-15
   Phineas: Six Stories 6:806, 812
   Private Life of Axie Reed, The 6:806, 812
   Separate Peace, A 6:803, 804, 806, 808, 809, 810, 812, 814, 815-17
   Separate Peace, A: Moods and Settings (Hinkle ed.) 6:806
   Spreading Fires 6:806-7, 812, 818
   Stolen Past, A 6:812
   themes and issues 6:809, 811, 812, 813-14, 815, 816, 817, 818

Vein of Riches, A 6:812
   Wilder as influence 6:810
Konchalovsky, Andrei 12:1722
Kostelanetz, Richard 3:319
Kumin, Maxine 9:1216
   Sexton collaboration 10:1359, 1360, 1361, 1365, 1369, 1371
Kuntsnmakher fun Lublin, Der. *See* Singer, Isaac Bashevis

La Farge, Oliver 7:997, 1002
La Fontaine, Jean de 8:1035, 1036, 1037, 1046
Laforgue, Jules 4:438
Laidlaw, Alice Ann. *See* Munro, Alice
Lardner, Ring 11:1531
Larsen, Nella 11:1569
Lasher, Lawrence M. 7:918
Lathem, Edward Connery 4:561, 567
Laurence, Margaret 6:819-32
   awards and honors 6:819, 821, 822, 823
   background and life 6:820-23
   Bird in the House, A 6:820, 821, 823, 826, 827, 830-31
   Christmas Birthday Story, The 6:827
   Diviners, The 6:822, 823, 825-27, 829
   Fire-Dwellers, The 6:821, 823, 827, 831
   Heart of a Stranger 6:822, 823, 826, 827, 831
   highlights in life 6:823
   influences on 6:826, 832
   Jason's Quest 6:821, 823, 827
   Jest of God, A 6:821, 823, 827, 828, 829, 831
   Long Drums and Cannons: Nigerian Dramatists and Novelists, 1952-1966 6:823, 824, 827
   major works 6:825-30
   Manawaka books 6:819, 821, 822, 823, 824, 827, 830, 831
   "Memorybank Movies" 6:826, 827
   narrative voices 6:824, 830-31
   Olden Days Coat, The 6:827
   "Pillars of the Nation" 6:823
   "Place to Stand On, A" 6:826
   Prophet's Camel Bell, The 6:823, 827
   Selected Letters of Margaret

   Laurence and Adele Wiseman 6:827
   Six Darn Cows 6:827
   "Snapshots" 6:826, 827
   Stone Angel, The 6:821, 823, 827, 831
   "Tales" 6:826, 827
   themes and issues 6:824, 825-26, 829, 830, 831, 832
   This Side Jordan 6:821, 823, 827, 829-30
   Tomorrow-Tamer, The 6:821, 823, 827, 830, 831-32
   Tree for Poverty, A: Somali Poetry and Prose (transl.) 6:821, 823, 827, 832
Lawrence, D. H. 8:1111
   as Anderson influence 1:49
   as T. Williams influence 12:1658
   Malamud and 7:924
Lawrence, Frieda 12:1658
Leacock, Stephen 3:344
Lee, Harper 6:833-42
   awards and honors 6:836
   background and life 6:834-36
   Capote and 2:234, 237
   "Christmas to Me" 6:836, 841
   film adapation 4:539, 542, 543, 550, 6:839, 870
   Foote and 4:539, 542, 543, 550, 551
   highlights in life 6:836
   "High Romance and Adventure" 6:841, 842
   influences on 6:838
   justice issues 6:833, 837, 839, 840, 841
   "Love in Other Words" 6:836, 841, 842
   major work 6:839-41
   racial issues 6:833, 837, 840, 841
   symbolism use 6:833, 841
   themes and issues 6:833, 837-38, 839, 840, 841, 842
   To Kill a Mockingbird 6:833, 834, 835, 836, 837, 838, 839-41, 842
   "When Children Discover America" 6:841, 842
Lessing, Doris 3:371
Levertov, Denise 12:1678
Levy, Newman A. 4:502, 507, 514
Lewis, Oscar 8:1090, 1095
Lewis, Sinclair 6:843-62, 9:1178, 10:1326
   Anderson and 1:45

Ann Vickers **6**:848, 850, 861
Arrowsmith **6**:845, 848, 850, 857-58
awards and honors **6**:843, 846, 847, 848, 851, 858
Babbitt **6**:843, 845, 848, 850, 854-57
background and life **6**:844-48
Bethel Merriday **6**:850
Cass Timberlane: A Novel of Husbands and Wives **6**:848, 850
critical commentary on **6**:850-51
Dodsworth **6**:845-46, 848, 850, 851, 860-61
Dreiser and **3**:378, 383
Elmer Gantry **6**:845, 848, 850, 859-60
film adaptations **6**:855
Free Air **6**:850
From Main Street to Stockholm: Letters of Sinclair Lewis, 1919-1930 (Smith ed.) **6**:850
Gideon Planish **6**:850
God-Seeker, The **6**:848, 850
Hersey and **5**:684, 687
highlights in life **6**:848
If I Were Boss: The Early Business Stories of Sinclair Lewis **6**:850
I'm a Stranger Here Myself and Other Stories **6**:850
influences on **6**:847, 852
Innocents, The: A Story for Lovers **6**:850
It Can't Happen Here (novel) **6**:848, 850, 861-62
It Can't Happen Here (play) **6**:847, 850, 862
Jayhawker: A Play in Three Acts (with Lewis) **6**:850
Job, The: An American Novel **6**:848, 850
Kingsblood Royal **6**:848, 850
literary legacy **6**:850-51
Main Street: The Story of Carol Kennicott **6**:843, 844, 845, 846, 848, 849, 850, 853-54, 861
major works **6**:853-58
Man from Main Street, The: Selected Essays and Other Writings **6**:850
Mantrap **6**:848, 850
Man Who Knew Coolidge, The: Being the Soul of Lowell Schmaltz, Constructive and

Nordic Citizen **6**:848, 850
Our Mr. Wrenn: The Romantic Adventures of a Gentle Man **6**:845, 850
Prodigal Parents, The **6**:850
Selected Short Stories of Sinclair Lewis **6**:848, 850
slang use **6**:850, 855
social satire **6**:843, 845, 850, 852, 853, 854, 856, 857
theatrical work **6**:847, 848, 850
themes and issues **6**:849, 850, 853, 854, 855, 856, 857
Trail of the Hawk, The: A Comedy of the Seriousness of Life **6**:850
Wilder and **12**:1620
women's issues and **6**:861
Work of Art **6**:850
World So Wide **6**:848, 850
Wright and **12**:1694, 1698, 1700
Lewis, Wyndham **5**:670
Liebling, A. J. **11**:1531
Lindsay, Vachel **2**:156, **7**:954
Lish, Gordon **2**:260
Livingston, Douglas **10**:1371
Locke, Alain **2**:185, **6**:754
Loeb, Jacques **3**:380
London, Jack **7**:869-90
Abysmal Brute, The **7**:879
Acorn-Planter, The (play) **7**:879
Adventure **7**:879
as influence on Hemingway **7**:878
as influence on Sinclair **7**:878
Assassination Bureau, Ltd., The (with Fish) **7**:879
as socialist **7**:874, 876, 877, 880, 882, 883, 885-86, 888-89
background and life **7**:870-75
"Batard" **7**:884
Before Adam **7**:876, 879
Burning Daylight **7**:879
Call of the Wild, The **7**:869, 873, 874, 876, 877, 879, 884-85, 886, 887
Children of the Frost **7**:879
critical commentary on **7**:878, 883, 885, 886, 889, 890
Cruise of the Dazzler, The **7**:879, 880
Cruise of the Snark, The **7**:879
Daughter of the Snows, A **7**:874, 879, 880
Dutch Courage and Other Stories **7**:879
effect of environment on **7**:876, 886, 889, 890

Faith of Men and Other Stories, The **7**:879
film adaptations **7**:875
Game, The **7**:879
God of His Fathers and Other Stories, The **7**:879
Hearts of Three **7**:879
highlights in life **7**:874
House of Pride and Other Tales of Hawaii, The **7**:879
Human Drift, The **7**:879
individualism theory **7**:885-86
influences on **7**:876, 877, 881, 887, 889, 890
Iron Heel, The **7**:876, 879, 883, 888-89
Jerry of the Islands **7**:879
John Barleycorn **7**:877, 879
Kempton-Wace Letters, The (with Strunsky) **7**:879
Letters from Jack London (ed Hendricks and Shepard) **7**:879
literary legacy **7**:877-78
Little Lady of the Big House, The **7**:879
Lost Face **7**:879
Love of Life and Other Stories **7**:879
major works **7**:884-87
Martin Eden **7**:877, 879, 883, 885-86
Michael, Brother of Jerry **7**:879
Moon-Face and Other Stories **7**:879
Mutiny of the Elsinore, The **7**:879
Night-Born, The **7**:879
"Odyssey of the North, An" **7**:873
On the Makaloa Mat **7**:879
People of the Abyss, The **7**:873, 877, 879, 880, 882-83
Red One, The **7**:879
Revolution and Other Essays **7**:879
Road, The **7**:876, 879, 883
Scarlet Plague, The **7**:879
Scorn of Women (play) **7**:879
Sea-Wolf, The **7**:869, 873, 877, 879, 886, 889-90
short-story form mastery **7**:878
Smoke Bellew Tales **7**:879
Son of the Sun, A **7**:879
Son of the Wolf, The **7**:874, 879
South Sea Tales **7**:879
Star Rover, The **7**:879
"Story of a Typhoon off the Coast of Japan" **7**:873, 876

Strength of the Strong, The **7**:879
Tales of the Fish Patrol **7**:879
Theft (play) **7**:879
themes and issues **7**:869, 876,
    884, 885, 886
"To Build a Fire" **7**:877, 889, 890
"To the Man on the Trail" **7**:873
Turtles of Tasman, The **7**:879
Valley of the Moon, The **7**:879
War of the Classes, The **7**:879, 883
*When God Laughs and Other
    Stories* **7**:879
White Fang **7**:869, 877, 879,
    886-88
"White Silence, The" **7**:877
Longfellow, Henry Wadsworth
    2:156, **10**:1338, **12**:1613
    as Cummings influence **3**:312,
        313
    Frost and **4**:559, 566
Lorde, Audre **9**:1277, 1280, 1286
Lourie, Dick **9**:1205
Lowell, Amy **10**:1326, 1340
Lowell, Robert **6**:732, **8**:1137,
    12:1678
    Frost and **4**:559
    Plath and **9**:1216, 1218, 1222
    Sexton and **10**:1359, 1360

Machado de Assis, Joachim Maria
    1:65
Mackenzie, Compton **4**:525
MacLeish, Archibald **7**:891-908
    Actfive and Other Poems **7**:896,
        901
    Air Raid: A Verse Play for Radio
        7:901
    American Cause, The **7**:901
    "American Letter" **7**:902
    American Opinion and the War
        7:901
    America Was Promises **7**:901
    "Ars Poetica" **7**:902
    as Benét influence **2**:154
    as Librarian of Congress **7**:894,
        895, 896
    as public servant **7**:891, 894,
        895, 896, 898
    awards and honors **7**:891, 892,
        895
    background and life **7**:892-96
    Background of War **7**:901
    Brave New World **7**:901
    "Broken Promise" **7**:898
    censorship and **7**:896
    Champion of a Cause: Essays and

Addresses on Librarianship
    7:901
Collected Poems, 1917-1952
    7:895, 896, 901
Collected Poems, 1917-1982
    7:895, 900-903, 906
*Collected Poems of Archibald
    MacLeish, The* **7**:901
Conquistador **7**:891, 894, 895,
    900, 901
Continuing Journey, A **7**:901
critical commentary on **7**:905
*Dialogues of Archibald MacLeish
    and Mark Van Doren, The* (with
    Van Doren) **7**:901
Einstein **7**:901
Eleanor Roosevelt Story, The **7**:901
"End of the World, The" **7**:898,
    900-901, 905
*Fall of the City, The: A Verse Play
    for Radio* **7**:901, 905-6
forms and techniques **7**:899
"For the Anniversary of My
    Mother's Death" **7**:901
*Freedom Is the Right to Choose: An
    Inquiry into the Battle for the
    American Future* **7**:901
Frescoes for Mr. Rockefeller's City
    7:901
Great American Frustration, The
    7:901
Hamlet of A. MacLeish, The **7**:901
Happy Marriage, The **7**:901
Herakles: A Play in Verse **7**:901
highlights in life **7**:895
Housing America **7**:901
*Human Season, The: Selected
    Poems, 1926-1972* **7**:901
influence of **2**:154
influences on **7**:894, 897, 898
Irresponsibles, The: A Declaration
    7:901
issues and themes **7**:897, 899
J.B.: A Play in Verse **7**:895, 896,
    901, 903-5, 906
Jews in America **7**:901
Land of the Free **7**:901
"Landscape as a Nude" **7**:902
*Letters of Archibald /aMacLeish:
    1970-1982* (ed Winnick)
    7:901
love poetry **7**:897, 898, 902
major works **7**:900-905
"Memorial Rain" **7**:901
*New and Collected Poems, 1917-
    1976* **7**:895, 901

New Found Land: Fourteen Poems
    7:901
New Poems, 1951-1952 **7**:901
Nobodaddy: A Play **7**:901, 906
On the Beaches of the Moon **7**:901
Panic: A Play in Verse **7**:901, 906
Poems, 1924-1933 **7**:891, 895,
    901
Poetry and Experience **7**:895, 896,
    901, 902
*Poetry and Opinion: The "Pisan
    Cantos" of Ezra Pound* **7**:901
Pot of Earth, The (play) **7**:901
Pot of Earth, The (poetry) **7**:901
Public Speech **7**:901
*Riders on the Earth: Essays and
    Reminiscences* **7**:901
Scratch **7**:901
Six Plays **7**:901
Songs for a Summer's Day **7**:901
Songs for Eve **7**:901, 906
Streets in the Moon **7**:894, 901
themes and issues **7**:897, 899,
    900-902, 903-5
*This Music Crept by Me Upon the
    Waters* (play) **7**:901, 906-7
Time to Act, A: Selected Addresses
    7:901
*Time to Speak, A: The Selected
    Prose of Archibald MacLeish*
    7:901
Tower of Ivory **7**:895, 901
Trojan Horse, The: A Play **7**:901
"What Any Lover Learns" **7**:902
*Wild Old Wicked Man and Other
    Poems, The* **7**:901
"You, Andrew Marvell" **7**:898,
    901-2
Madhubuti, Haki R. **2**:198, 203
Mailer, Norman 3, 362, **2**:245
Malamud, Bernard **7**:909-26
    allegory use **7**:923, 924
    "Angel Levine" **7**:924
    Assistant, The **7**:909, 912, 913,
        916, 917, 918, 919-20, 922,
        923
    awards and honors **7**:909, 912,
        913, 914, 918, 921
    background and life **7**:910-14
    Complete Stories, The **7**:918, 924
    *Conversations with Bernard
        Malamud* (Lasher ed.) **7**:918
    critical commentary on **7**:915,
        916, 918, 919, 921, 923, 924
    Dubin's Lives **7**:916, 917, 918, 924
    fantasy use **7**:909, 915, 918, 924

film adaptations **7**:914
Fixer, The **7**:912, 913, 914, 916, 917, 918, 920-22
God's Grace **7**:918, 924
highlights in life **7**:913
Idiots First **7**:918, 924
influences on **7**:916
Jewish themes **7**:909, 915, 917, 920, 922
"Light Sleeper, The" **7**:911
Magic Barrel, The **7**:912, 913, 918, 924
major works **7**:919-23
Natural, The **7**:912, 913, 915, 917, 918, 920, 922-23
New Life, A **7**:913, 916, 918, 924-25
People and Uncollected Short Stories, The **7**:918
Pictures of Fidelman: An Exhibition **7**:918, 924
Rembrandt's Hat **7**:918, 924
Stories of Bernard Malamud, The **7**:918
symbolism of **7**:922
Talking Horse: Bernard Malamud on Life and Work (Cheuse and Delbanco eds.) **7**:918
Tenants, The **7**:918, 925
themes and issues **7**:909, 915, 917, 919, 920, 921, 922, 923, 924, 925
"Thomas Hardy's Reputation as a Poet in American Periodicals" **7**:911
writing habits **7**:911
Malone, Michael **5**:707, 708
Malory, Sir Thomas, as Steinbeck influence **11**:1446, 1447, 1452, 1454, 1459, 1463, 1465
Malraux, André **4**:461, **11**:1495
Mamet, David **7**:**927-44**
American Buffalo (play) **7**:927, 929, 931, 935, 936-39
American Buffalo (screenplay) **7**:932, 935
American Dream in work of **7**:933
anti-Semitism and **7**:929, 933
awards and honors **7**:927, 929, 931, 936, 938, 939, 942
background and life **7**:928-31
Bar Mitzvah **7**:935
business practice portrayals **7**:927, 929, 932, 936, 938, 939, 940, 941, 942

Cabin, The: Reminiscence and Diversions **7**:930, 935
Camel **7**:928, 931, 935
Cherry Orchard, The (adaptation of Chekhov play) **7**:935
Chinaman, The **7**:935
con artist portrayals **7**:929, 930, 932, 941, 942
critical commentary on **7**:929, 933, 940, 941
Cross Patch (radio play) **7**:935
Cryptogram, The **7**:933, 935, 942-43
dialogue use **7**:927, 928, 932, 942
Dintenfass (radio play) **7**:935
Disappearance of the Jews, The **7**:935
Donald Sultan: Playing Cards (with Jay) **7**:935
Donny March **7**:935
Duck and the Goat, The **7**:935
Duck Variations **7**:929, 935
Edge, The (screenplay) **7**:932, 935
Edmond **7**:929, 935
film adaptations **7**:928-31
Five Television Plays **7**:935
Frog Prince, The **7**:935, 944
Glengarry Glen Ross (play) **7**:927, 928, 929, 931, 933, 935, 939-40
Glengarry Glen Ross (screenplay) **7**:930, 932, 935, *940*
Goldberg Street: Short Plays and Monologues **7**:935
Goldberg Street (radio play) **7**:935
Henrietta **7**:935
Hero Pony, The **7**:935
highlights in life **7**:928-31
Hoffa (screenplay) **7**:932, 935
Homicide (screenplay) **7**:929, 930, 932, 934, 935
House of Games (screenplay) **7**:929, 930, 931, 932, 934, 935, 941
influence of **7**:934
influences on **7**:928, 930, 937
Jafsie and John Henry: Essays on Hollywood, Bad Boys, and Six Hours of Perfect Poker **7**:935
Lakeboat **7**:935
Lansky (teleplay) **7**:932, 934, 935
Life in the Theater, A (play) **7**:935
Life in the Theater, A (teleplay) **7**:932, 934, 935

Life with No Joy in It, and Other Plays and Pieces, A **7**:935
Lip Service (teleplay) **7**:934, 935
literary legacy **7**:934
major works **7**:936-42
Make-Believe Town: Essays and Remembrances **7**:930, 935
No One Will Be Immune, and Other Plays and Pieces **7**:935
Old Neighborhood, The: Three Plays **7**:935
Old Religion, The **7**:935
Oleanna (play) **7**:929, 933, *934*, 935, 943
Oleanna (screenplay) **7**:929, 930, 931, 932, 934, 935
On Directing Film **7**:930, 935
Owl, The **7**:935
Passover **7**:935
Poet and the Rent, The **7**:944
Postman Always Rings Twice, The (screenplay) **7**:929, 931, 932, 935
Prairie de Chien (radio play) **7**:935
profanity in works **7**:927, 929, 932, 940
rapid-action plots **7**:932
Reunion **7**:935
Revenge of the Space Pandas, The **7**:935, 944
Ronin (screenplay) **7**:932, 935
Sexual Perversity in Chicago **7**:929, 931, *933*, 935
Some Freaks **7**:930, 935
Spanish Prisoner, The (play) **7**:935, 941
Spanish Prisoner, The (screenplay) **7**:930, 932, 934, 935, 940-42
Speed-the-Plow **7**:929, 935
State and Main (screenplay) **7**:932, 934, 935
themes and issues **7**:932, 933, 934, 936, 937, 938, 939, 940-41, 943
Things Change (screenplay) **7**:929, 932, 934, 935
Three Children's Plays **7**:935, 943-44
Three Jewish Plays **7**:935
Three Sisters (Chekhov; adaptation by Mamet) **7**:935
Three Uses of the Knife: On the Nature and Purpose of Drama **7**:935
True and False: Heresy and Common Sense for the Actor **7**:935

Uncle Vanya (Chekhov; adaptation by Mamet) **7**:935
Untouchables, The (screenplay) **7**:929, 932, 935
Vanya on 42nd Street (screenplay) **7**:929, 932, 935
Verdict, The (screenplay) **7**:929, 931, 932, 935
Village, The **7**:935
Wag the Dog (screenplay with Henkin) **7**:932, 935
Warm and Cold (with Sultan) **7**:935
Water Engine, The (play) **7**:935
Water Engine, The (teleplay) **7**:930, 932, 934, 935
We're No Angels (screenplay) **7**:932, 935
Whore's Profession, A: Notes and Essays **7**:930, 935
Wilson **7**:935
Winslow Boy, The (play) **7**:935
Winslow Boy, The (screenplay) **7**:930, 932, 934, 935
Woods, The **7**:929, 935
Writing in Restaurants **7**:930, 935
Mann, Thomas **10**:1399, **11**:1495
Mannoni, O. **6**:832
Martin, Robert A. **8**:1025
Marvell, Andrew **7**:898, 901-2
Marx, Karl
   as Dreiser influence **3**:380
   as London influence **7**:877, 881
   as Piercy influence **9**:1202
Masefield, John **1**:45
Masters, Edgar Lee **7:945-60**, **10**:1326
   Across Spoon River **7**:945, 946, 947, 948, 949, 950, 951, 952, 954, 959
   Along the Illinois **7**:954
   Althea (play) **7**:954
   "Anne Rutledge" **7**:957-58
   anti-industrialism of **7**:959, 960
   appearance vs. reality concerns **7**:953, 956
   as Brooks influence **2**:196
   background and life **7**:946-50
   Blood of the Prophets, The **7**:954
   Book of Verses, A **7**:950, 954
   Bread of Idleness, The (play) **7**:954
   Children of the Market Place **7**:950, 954
   Confederacy sympathies **7**:949, 951
   critical commentary on **7**:955

Domesday Book **7**:950, 954
Dramatic Duologues (play) **7**:954
Eileen (play) **7**:954
Fate of the Jury, The: An Epilogue to Domesday Book **7**:954
Gettysburg, Manila, Acoma (play) **7**:954
Godbey (play) **7**:954
Golden Fleece of California, The **7**:954
Great Valley, The **7**:954
"Hannah Armstrong" **7**:957
Harmony of Deeper Music, The: Posthumous Poems **7**:954
highlights in life **7**:950
"Hill, The" **7**:953, 956
Illinois Poem **7**:954
influence of **2**:196
influences on **7**:952
Invisible Landscapes **7**:954
Jack Kelso (play) **7**:954
Kit O'Brien **7**:954
law practice **7**:947-48, 950, 951, 959
Leaves of the Tree, The (play) **7**:954
Lee: A Dramatic Poem (play) **7**:954
Levy Mayer and the New Industrial Era **7**:954
Lichee Nuts **7**:954
Lincoln: The Man **7**:945, 949, 950, 951, 952, 954
Locket, The (play) **7**:954
major works **7**:955-58
Mark Twain: A Portrait **7**:950, 952, 954
Mirage **7**:954
Mitch Miller **7**:950, 954
More People **7**:954
New Spoon River, The **7**:945, 949, 950, 951, 954, 955-56, 959
New World, The **7**:954
Nuptial Flight, The **7**:954
Open Sea, The **7**:954
Poems of People **7**:954
racial bias **7**:952, 955-56
Richmond (play) **7**:954
Sangamon, The **7**:949, 950, 954
Selected Poems **7**:954
Serpent in the Wilderness, The **7**:954
Skeeters Kirby **7**:954
Songs and Satires **7**:954
Songs and Sonnets **7**:954
Songs and Sonnets, Second Series **7**:954

"Spooniad, The" **7**:956
Spoon River Anthology **1**:49, **7**:945, 949, 950, 951, 953, 954, 955, 956-59
Starved Rock **7**:954
Tale of Chicago, The **7**:954
themes and issues **7**:952-53, 955, 956, 957, 958
Tide of Time, The **7**:954, 959-60
Toward the Gulf **7**:954
Trifler, The (play) **7**:954
Vachel Lindsay: A Poet in America **7**:954
Walt Whitman **7**:949, 950, 954, 960
Mather, Cotton **9**:1231, **12**:1690
Matthiessen, Peter **11**:1491
Maugham, W. Somerset **2**:241
Maynard, Joyce **10**:1304, 1306, 1313
McAleer, John J. **3**:381
McCarthy, Cormac **7:961-74**
   All the Pretty Horses (novel) **7**:961, 964, 965, 968, 969-70
   All the Pretty Horses (screenplay) **7**:965, 970
   Appalachian settings **7**:961, 966
   awards and honors **7**:963-64, 965, 969
   background and life **7**:962-65
   Blood Meridian: Or, The Evening Redness in the West **7**:961, 964, 965, 968, 969, 970-71
   Border Trilogy, The **7**:961, 964, 968, 970
   Child of God **7**:963, 965, 970, 973
   Cities of the Plain **7**:964, 965, 970
   critical commentary on **7**:961, 963, 964, 968, 970, 971, 972
   Crossing, The **7**:964, 965, 967, 970
   dark characters and humor **7**:966, 971
   Gardner's Son, The (screenplay) **7**:970
   Gardner's Son, The (teleplay) **7**:963, 965, 970
   highlights in life **7**:962-65
   influences on **7**:968
   major works **7**:969-71
   Orchard Keeper, The **7**:962, 963, 965, 970, 973
   Outer Dark **7**:963, 965, 970, 973-74
   Stonemason, The (play) **7**:964, 965, 970

Suttree **7**:963, 965, 967, 968, 970, 971-73
themes and issues **7**:966, 967-68, 969, 970, 971-72, 973
McCullers, Carson **7:975-92**, **9**:1232
African American characters **7**:980, 987, 988, 989, 990
allegory use **7**:986, 989
as Capote influence **2**:241
as Munro influence **8**:1077
awards and honors **7**:977, 978, 979
background and life **7**:977-79
Ballad of the Sad Café, The **7**:977, 979, 981, 982, 984-86, 989
Ballad of the Sad Café, The: The Novels and Stories of Carson McCullers **7**:978, 983
Ballad of the Sad Café and Collected Short Stories, The **7**:983
character studies **7**:980, 987, 991
Clock Without Hands **7**:978, 979, 983, 985, 990-91
Collected Stories of Carson McCullers **7**:983
critical commentary on **7**:977, 978, 988, 989, 991
female adolescent portrayals **7**:980-81, 988
film adapatations **7**:983
"Flowering Dream, The: Notes on Writing" **7**:981
grotesque characters **7**:981-82, 985, 986, 987
Heart Is a Lonely Hunter, The **7**:975, 977, 979, 980, 981, 982, 983, 985, 986-88, 989
highlights in life **7**:979
Illumination and Night Glare: The Unfinished Autobiography of Carson McCullers **7**:983
individual isolation portrayals **7**:975, 980, 981, 982, 985, 986, 987, 988, 989
influence of **2**:241, **8**:1077
influences on **7**:976, 985
major works **7**:984-89
Member of the Wedding, The: A Play **7**:978, 979, 983, *989*
Member of the Wedding, The (musical) **7**:978
Member of the Wedding, The (novel) **7**:977, 978, 979, 980, 981, 982, 983, 985, 988-90
Mortgaged Heart, The **7**:983

Mute, The **7**:977
pessimism of **7**:980
Reflections in a Golden Eye **7**:977, 978, 979, 981, 982, 983, 985, 991
Square Root of Wonderful, The (play) **7**:978, 979, 983
Sweet as a Pickle, Clean as a Pig **7**:979, 983
themes and issues **7**:975, 980, 981, 982, 984, 985, 986, 987, 988, 989
violence in works **7**:982, 987
"Wunderkind" **7**:977, 979
McHaney, Pearl Amelia **12**:1596
McNickle, D'Arcy **7:993-1006**
as Native American novelist **7**:993, 995, 996, 998, 999, 1000, 1004
background and youth **7**:994-97
critical commentary on **7**:1004
cultural ethnocentrism **7**:999-1000
"Flight of Feather Boy, The" **7**:1005
good vs. evil conflict **7**:1001
"Hard Riding" **7**:1005
"Hawk is Hungry, The" **7**:1005
Hawk Is Hungry and Other Stories, The **7**:997, 1002, 1005
highlights in life **7**:997
"Hungry Generations, The" **7**:997, 1005
Indian Man: A Biography of Oliver La Farge **7**:997, 1002
Indians and Other Americans: Two Ways of Life Meet (with Fey) **7**:997, 1002
influences on **7**:1004
"In the Alien Corn" **7**:1005
literary legacy **7**:1000
major works **7**:1001-5
"Man's Work" **7**:1005
Native American Tribalism: Indian Survivals and Renewals **7**:997, 1002, 1005-6
Runner in the Sun: A Story of Indian Maize **7**:995, 997, 998, 999, 1001, 1002
"Six Beautiful in Paris" **7**:1005
"Snowfall" **7**:1005
Surrounded, The **7**:995, 997, 998, 999, 1000, 1002-3, 1005
symbolism use **7**:1005
themes and issues **7**:995, 998-1000, 1001, 1002, 1003-4, 1005, 1006

They Came Here First: The Epic of the American Indian **7**:1002, 1006
"Train Time" **7**:1005
Wind from an Enemy Sky **7**:995, 997, 998, 999, 1000, 1002, 1003-5, 1006
Mead, Margaret **1**:105, 110
Melville, Herman **4**:467, **7**:971, **11**:1453
Gardner and **5**:598, 600, 601
Mencken, H. L. **10**:1341, **12**:1700
as Dreiser influence **3**:380
on Cather **2**:272
Meredith, William **4**:563
Meriwether, James B. **4**:486
Merlo, Frank **12**:1653, 1654, 1655
Michaels, Leonard **11**:1514
Miller, Arthur **8:1013-32**
After the Fall **8**:1016, 1019, 1020, 1025, 1028
allegory use **8**:1023
All My Sons **8**:1015, 1016, 1017, 1018, 1019, 1021-22, 1025, 1028
American Clock, The **8**:1019, 1025
Archbishop's Ceiling, The **8**:1019, 1025
Arthur Miller and Company (Bigsby ed.) **8**:1025
as International PEN Club president **8**:1013, 1016, 1018
awards and honors **8**:1013, 1014, 1015, 1017, 1018
background and life **8**:1014, 1017
Broken Glass **8**:1025
Chinese Encounters **8**:1025
Clara **8**:1025
Collected Plays **8**:1025
Conversations with Arthur Miller (Roudané ed.) **8**:1025
Creation of the World and Other Business, The **8**:1018, 1019, 1025
critical commentary on **8**:1019, 1028
Crucible, The **8**:1015, 1017, 1018, 1019, 1022-24, 1025
Danger: Memory! **8**:1019, 1025
Death of a Salesman **8**:1013, 1015, 1017, 1018, 1019, 1025-28
Elegy for a Lady **8**:1025
Enemy of the People, An (adaptation of Ibsen play) **8**:1015, 1018, 1019, 1025

Everybody Wins **8**:1025

Fame **8**:1025

father-son relationship portrayals **8**:1017, 1019, 1021, 1022, 1027, 1029, 1031

Focus **8**:1014, 1017, 1018, 1025

"Four Freedoms, The" (radio play) **8**:1017, 1018, 1025

Grandpa and the Statue (radio play) **8**:1025

Guardsman, The (radio adaptation of Molnar play) **8**:1025

"Half-Bridge, The" **8**:1017

highlights in life **8**:1018

Homely Girl, A Life, and Other Stories **8**:1025

Hook, The (screenplay) **8**:1015

I Can't Remember Anything **8**:1025

I Don't Need You Anymore **8**:1025

Incident at Vichy **8**:1016, 1018, 1019, 1025

influences on **8**:1014, 1020, 1021, 1028, 1031

"In Memorium" **8**:1019

In Russia **8**:1018, 1025

Last Yankee, The **8**:1025

liberal causes and **8**:1015

loyalty investigations of **8**:1014, 1015-16, 1018, 1023, 1024

major works **8**:1021-28

Man Who Had All the Luck, The **8**:1014, 1017, 1018, 1025

Memory of Two Mondays, A **8**:1025

Misfits, The (novel) **8**:1019, 1025

Misfits, The (screenplay) 8, **8**:1019, *1020*, 1025

"Misfits, The" (short story) **8**:1016, 1018, 1019

Price, The **8**:1016, 1019, 1025, 1029, 1031

Pussycat and the Expert Plumber Who Was an Honest Man, The; William Ireland's Confession (radio play) **8**:1025

Ride down Mt. Morgan, The **8**:1025

"Salesman" in Beijing **8**:1025

Situation Normal **8**:1025

Some Kind of Love Story **8**:1025

Spain **8**:1025

Story of Gus, The (radio play) **8**:1025

That They May Win **8**:1017, 1025

Theater Essays of Arthur Miller, The (Martin ed.) **8**:1025

themes and issues **8**:1013, 1014, 1015, 1016, 1017, 1019, 1021, 1022-23, 1024, 1025-26, 1028, 1031

"They Too Arise" **8**:1014, 1018

Three Men on a Horse (radio adaptation of Abbott and Holm play) **8**:1025

Timebends: A Life **8**:1013, 1018, 1025

Up from Paradise **8**:1025

View from the Bridge, A **8**:1025, *1030*, 1031

Millgate, Michael **4**:486

Milton, John **5**:598, **11**:1446, 1493
as Bontemps influence **2**:182
as Potok influence **9**:1266

Mistral, Gabriela **6**:737

Mitchell, Margaret **8**:1077, **11**:1455

Mitgang, Herbert **10**:1338

Molnar, Ferenc **8**:1025

Monroe, Harriet **8**:1045, **10**:1325, 1338

Moore, Harry T. **3**:320, 322

Moore, Marianne **8**:**1033-48**
Absentee, The (dramatization of Edgeworth) **8**:1036, 1037, 1043

animals and vegetables as subjects **8**:1040, 1041, 1043, *1047*

as baseball fan **8**:1038, 1039, 1041, 1045, 1046

as modernist poet **8**:1033, 1035, 1040, **11**:1475

as Plath influence **9**:1222

awards and honors **8**:1035, 1036, 1037

background and life **8**:1034-37

Collected Poems **8**:1036, 1037, 1043

Complete Poems of Marianne Moore, The **8**:1036, 1037, 1041-43

Complete Prose of Marianne Moore, The **8**:1036, 1043, 1044-46

compressed simplicity of writing **8**:1033, 1034, 1038, 1042, 1045

"Granite and Steel" **8**:1046

"Henry James as a Characteristic American" **8**:1040

highlights in life **8**:1037

influence of **9**:1222

influences on **8**:1040

"Knife, The" **8**:1046

Like a Bulwark **8**:1036, 1043

literary legacy **8**:1039

major works **8**:1041-46

Marianne Moore Reader, A **8**:1036, 1037, 1043

"Marriage" **8**:1042-43

"Mouse Metamorphosed into a Maid, The" **8**:1046-47

Nevertheless **8**:1043

Observations **8**:1035, 1037, 1043

"Octopus, An" **8**:1043

O to Be a Dragon **8**:1036, 1043

Pangolin and Other Verse, The **8**:1035, 1043

Poems **8**:1043

poetry definitions **8**:1041

Predilections **8**:1036, 1043

Selected Fables of La Fontaine (transl.) **8**:1036, 1037, 1043, 1046

Selected Poems **8**:1035, 1037, 1043

signature tricorn hat **8**:*1038*

Stevens and **11**:1475, 1487

Tell Me, Tell Me **8**:1036, 1043

"Tell Me, Tell Me" **8**:1047-48

themes and issues **8**:1038-39, 1041-42, 1044-46

"To a Snail" **8**:1048

What Are Years **8**:1035, 1037, 1043

wide-ranging interests **8**:1033, 1039, 1040, 1041, 1044, 1046

Morrison, Toni **8**:**1049-70**
African American folklore use **8**:1050, 1057, 1058, 1066, 1070

as book editor **8**:1053, 1054

as influence on Alvarez **1**:31

awards and honors **8**:1049, 1050, 1052, 1053, 1054

background and life **8**:1050-54

Baldwin eulogy by **1**:107

Beloved **8**:1049, 1052, 1054, 1056, 1057, 1058, 1059-60, 1062, 1063-65, 1068

Big Box, The (with Potter) **8**:1064

Birth of a Nation'hood: Gaze, Script, and Spectacle in the O. J. Simpson Case **8**:1064

Bluest Eye, The **8**:1051, 1052, 1053, 1057, 1058, 1064, 1065

complex characterizations **8**:1056

critical commentary on **8**:1052

Dreaming Emmett **8:**1052, 1054, 1064

highlights in life **8:**1052

Hurston as influence on **6:**751

influences on **8:**1050, 1051, 1055-56, 1057, 1058, 1066, 1068, 1070

James Baldwin: Collected Essays (ed.) **1:**110

Jazz **8:**1052, 1054, 1064, 1068

major works **8:**1063-68

Paradise **8:**1054, 1058, 1064, 1068-69

Playing in the Dark: Whiteness and the Literary Imagination **8:**1052, 1056, 1064

Race-ing Justice, En-gendering Power: Essays on Anita Hill, Clarence Thomas, and the Construction of Social Reality (ed.) **8:**1064

Song of Solomon **8:**1051, 1052, 1053, 1057, 1058, 1064, 1066-68

Sula **8:**1052, 1053, 1057, 1058, 1064, 1069-70

supernatural elements in work **8:**1057, 1058, 1063, 1066, 1067

Tar Baby **8:**1052, 1053, 1057, 1058, 1064, 1070

themes and issues **8:**1050, 1055, 1056, 1057, 1058, 1063, 1065, 1066, 1068, 1069, 1070

unreliable narrator use **8:**1068

Morse, Samuel French **11:**1475

Munro, Alice **8:1071-84**

awards and honors **8:**1071, 1074, 1075, 1080, 1082

background and life **8:**1072-75

"Boys and Girls" **8:**1082-83

Canadian voice of **8:**1071

"Carried Away" **8:**1078

Dance of the Happy Shades **8:**1071, 1074, 1075, 1080

female characters **8:**1071, 1076, 1077-78, 1079, 1080, 1081, 1083

"Friend of My Youth" **8:**1077

Friend of My Youth: Stories **8:**1080

genteel facade depictions **8:**1076, 1078, 1084

gothic elements **8:**1073, 1077, 1078, 1084

highlights in life **8:**1075

influences on **8:**1073, 1077

layering technique **8:**1078

"Lichen" **8:**1078

Lives of Girls and Women **8:**1073, 1074, 1075, 1076, 1077, 1079-80, 1082

Love of a Good Woman, The **8:**1075, 1078, 1080

major works **8:**1079-82

"Meneseteung" **8:**1077

"Moons of Jupiter, The" **8:**1074

Moons of Jupiter, The: Stories **8:**1078, 1080

mother-daughter relationship portrayals **8:**1081, 1083

"Office, The" **8:**1074

"Open Secrets" **8:**1078

Open Secrets: Stories **8:**1073, 1074, 1078, 1080

"Ottawa Valley, The" **8:**1073

"Peace of Utrecht, The" **8:**1073, 1075, 1077, 1083-84

Progress of Love, The **8:**1074, 1075, 1078, 1080

"Red Dress—1946" **8:**1077

"Save the Reaper" **8:**1078

Selected Stories **8:**1080

"Something I've Been Meaning to Tell You" **8:**1084

Something I've Been Meaning to Tell You: Thirteen Stories **8:**1074, 1078, 1080

Tan and **11:**1512

themes and issues **8:**1076, 1078, 1079, 1081

Who Do You Think You Are? **8:**1072, 1073, 1074, 1075, 1080-82

"Wilderness Story, A" **8:**1077

"Wild Swans" **8:**1076

Napolin, Leah **10:**1405, 1411

Nathan, George Jean **4:**536

Nègres, Les (Genet) **5:**657

Nestroy, Johann **12:**1632, 1647, 1649

Nietzsche, Friedrich

as Dreiser influence **3:**380

as London influence **7:**877, 889, 890

as O'Neill influence **9:**1157, 1167

Norris, Frank **8:1085-1102, 9:**1157

as Faulkner influence **8:**1085

as Hemingway influence **8:**1085

as naturalistic novelist **8:**1085, 1096, 1098

as Steinbeck influence **8:**1085

as Wright influence **12:**1700

background and life **8:**1086-90

Blix **8:**1089, 1095

Complete Edition of Frank Norris, The **8:**1095

Complete Edition of Frank Norris, The, Vol. 10 **8:**1090

Complete Works **8:**1095

critical commentary on **8:**1102

Deal in Wheat and Other Stories of the New and Old West, A **8:**1095

effective subplots **8:**1096

evil viewed by **8:**1092, 1093

film adapatations **8:**1090

Frank Norris of "The Wave" (Lewis ed.) **8:**1090, 1095

Gettysburg trilogy **8:**1091

Golden Gate Edition of Frank Norris, The **8:**1095

health problems **8:**1088, 1089, 1090

highlights in life **8:**1089

influence of **4:**525, 536, **8:**1085

influences on **8:**1085, 1086, 1087, 1088, 1090, 1092, 1093, 1101

Joyous Miracle, The **8:**1095

Letters of Frank Norris, The (Walker ed.) **8:**1095

Literary Criticism of Frank Norris, The (Pizer ed.) **8:**1095

major works **8:**1094-1100

Man's Woman, A **8:**1089, 1093, 1095, 1101-2

masculine superiority portrayal **8:**1101, 1102

McTeague **8:**1085, 1089, 1093, 1094-97, 1100, 1101, 1102

Moran of the Lady Letty **8:**1089, 1090, *1092*, 1093, 1095, 1101

Novelist in the Making, A: A Collection of Student Themes and the Novels of "Blix" and "Vandover and the Brute" (Hart ed.) **8:**1095

Octopus, The **8:**1085, *1088*, 1089, 1090, 1091, 1093, 1095, 1097-98

Pit, The: A Story of Chicago **8:**1085, 1089, 1090, 1091, 1095, 1098-1100

Responsibilities of the Novelist, The **8:**1095

Surrender of Santiago, The **8:**1095

symbolism use **8**:1095, 1096
themes and issues **8**:1085, 1091-
   93, 1094, 1097-99, 1100,
   1101
Third Circle, The **8**:1095
Two Poems and "Kim" Reviewed
   8:1095
Vandover and the Brute **8**:1090,
   1093, 1095, 1100-1101
Wheat trilogy **8**:1090, 1091,
   1098
"Wolf, The" **8**:1090, 1091
Yvernelle: A Tale of Feudal France
   8:1088, 1089, 1093, 1095,
   1100

Oates, Joyce Carol **8:1103-18**,
   10:1399
All the Good People I've Left Behind
   8:1111
American Appetites **8**:1109, 1110,
   1111
American Gothic Tales (edit) **8**:1111
Angel Fire **8**:1111
Angel of Light **8**:1111
Anonymous Sins **8**:1111
Assassins, The: A Book of Hours
   8:1111
Assignation, The **8**:1111
awards and honors **8**:1103,
   1104, 1105, 1106, 1107
background and life **8**:1104-7
Bad Girls (play) **8**:1109, 1116-17
"Bad Girls" (short story) **8**:1116
Because It Is Bitter, and Because It
   Is My Heart **8**:1109, 1111
Bellefleur **8**:1106, 1111
Best American Essays, The (ed.)
   8:1111
Best American Short Stories of
   1979, The (ed. with Ravenel)
   8:1111
Black Water (novel) **8**:1106,
   1107, 1110, 1111, 1116,
   1117-18
Black Water (opera libretto)
   8:1106, 1107, 1118
Blonde **8**:1106, 1111
Bloodsmoor Romance, A **8**:1106,
   1111
Broke Heart Blues **8**:1111
By the North Gate **8**:1111
Childwold **8**:1111
Collector of Hearts, The **8**:1111
Come Meet Muffin **8**:1111
Contraries: Essays **8**:1111

critical commentary on **8**:1105,
   1106
Crossing the Border **8**:1111
Cybele **8**:1111
Do with Me What You Will **8**:1111
Edge of Impossibility, The: Tragic
   Forms in Literature **8**:1111
Expensive People **8**:1111
Fabulous Beasts, The **8**:1111
film adaptations **8**:1106
First Love **8**:1109, 1111
First Person Singular: Writers on
   Their Craft (ed.) **8**:1111
Foxfire: Confessions of a Girl Gang
   8:1106, 1109, 1111, 1116
Garden of Earthly Delights, A **8**:1111
George Bellows: American Artist
   8:1109, 1111
Goddess and Other Women, The
   8:1111
good vs. evil concerns **8**:1108,
   1109, 1110, 1112, 1113,
   1117
Haunted: Tales of the Grotesque
   8:1111
Heat and Other Stories **8**:1111
highlights in life **8**:1107
Hostile Sun, The: The Poetry of D.
   H. Lawrence **8**:1111
Hungry Ghosts, The **8**:1111
I Lock My Door upon Myself
   8:1111
In Darkest America: Two Plays
   8:1111
influences on **8**:1110
Invisible Woman: New and Selected
   Poems, 1970-1982 **8**:1111
I Stand Before You Naked (play)
   8:1111
Lamb of Abyssalia, The **8**:1111
Last Days **8**:1111
Lives of the Twins (under pseud.
   of Smith) **8**:1111
locale importance **8**:1109-10
Love and Its Derangements **8**:1111
Luxury of Sin, The **8**:1111
major works **8**:1112-16
Man Crazy **8**:1109, 1111
Marriages and Infidelities **8**:1111
Marya: A Life **8**:1109, 1111
Miracle Play **8**:1111
My Heart Laid Bare **8**:1109,
   1110, 1111
Mysteries of Winterthurn **8**:1105,
   1106, 1109, 1110, 1111,
   1112-13

Nemesis (under pseud. of Smith)
   8:1111
New Heaven, New Earth: The
   Visionary Experience in
   Literature **8**:1111
New Plays **8**:1106, 1111, 1116,
   1118
Night-Side **8**:1111
Night Walks: A Bedside Companion
   (ed.) **8**:1111
On Boxing **8**:1111
Oxford Book of American
   Short Stories, The (ed.) **8**:1111
Perfectionist and Other Plays, The
   8:1106, 1111
Perfectionist, The (play) **8**:1107
Poisoned Kiss, The **8**:1111
postmodern elements **8**:1106,
   1113
Profane Art, The: Essays and
   Reviews **8**:1111
prolificity of **8**:1103
psychological realism **8**:1105,
   1108
Raven's Wing **8**:1111
Rise of Life on Earth, The **8**:1109,
   1111
Scenes from American Life:
   Contemporary Short Fiction
   (ed.) **8**:1111
Seduction, The **8**:1111
Sentimental Education, A **8**:1111
Snake Eues (under pseud. of
   Smith) **8**:1111
Solstice **8**:1111
Son of the Morning **8**:1111
Soul/Mate (under pseud. of
   Smith) **8**:1111
Starr Bright Will Be with You
   (under pseud. of Smith)
   8:1111
Sunday Dinner (play) **8**:1107,
   1111
Tenderness **8**:1111
them **8**:1103, 1105, 1107, 1109,
   1111, 1113-15
themes and issues **8**:1103, 1109,
   1112, 1113, 1114, 1115,
   1117
Three Plays **8**:1106, 1111
Time Traveler, The **8**:1111
Triumph of the Spider Monkey, The
   8:1111
Twelve PLays **8**:1106, 1111
Unholy Loves **8**:1111
Upon the Sweeping Flood **8**:1111

We Were the Mulvaneys **8**:1109, 1111

What I Lived For **8**:1103, 1106, 1107, 1109, 1111, 1115-16

Wheel of Love, The **8**:1111

Where Are You Going, Where Have You Been? **8**:1111

Where Is Here? **8**:1111

Will You Always Love Me? **8**:1111

With Shuddering Fall **8**:1104, 1107, 1111

(Woman) Writer: Occasions and Opportunities **8**:1111

Women in Love **8**:1107, 1111

Women Whose Lives Are Food, Men Whose Lives Are Money **8**:1111

Wonderland **8**:1111

You Can't Catch Me (pseud Smith) **8**:1111

You Must Remember This **8**:1109, 1111

Zombie **8**:1111

Obey, André **12**:1631, 1647

O'Brien, Tim **8:1119-34**
  "Ambush" **8**:1132
  awards and honors **8**:1119, 1122, 1123
  background and life **8**:1120-23
  courage as major focus **8**:1122, 1124, 1128, 1129, 1131, 1132-33
  critical commentary on **8**:1119, 1122, 1126, 1129, 1133
  "Evidence" **8**:1130
  "Field Trip" **8**:1132
  Going After Cacciato **8**:1119, 1122, 1123, 1124, 1125, 1127, 1128-29, 1132
  highlights in life **8**:1123
  "How to Tell a True War Story" **8**:1132
  "Hypothesis" **8**:1131
  If I Die in a Combat Zone, Box Me Up and Ship Me Home **8**:1119, 1122, 1123, 1124, 1125, 1127, 1132-33
  In the Lake of the Woods **8**:1119, 1122, 1123, 1124, 1125, 1126, 1127, 1129-31, 1133
  "Lives of the Dead, The" **8**:1132
  major works **8**:1128-32
  Northern Lights **8**:1122, 1123, 1127
  Nuclear Age, The **8**:1122, 1123, 1126, 1127, 1133
  "Observation Post, The" **8**:1129
  "On the Rainy River" **8**:1132

  themes and issues **8**:1121, 1124-25, 1128, 1129, 1131, 1132
  Things They Carried, The **8**:1119, 1122, 1123, 1124, 1125, 1127, 1131-32
  "Things They Carried, The" **8**:1132
  Tomcat in Love **8**:1119, 1123, 1126, 1127, 1133-34
  "Vietnam in Me, The" **8**:1123, 1127

O'Casey, Sean **5**:647

O'Connor, Flannery **8:1135-50**
  "Artificial Nigger, The" **8**:1148
  as Munro influence **8**:1077
  as Potok parallel **9**:1266
  awards and honors **8**:1135, 1138, 1139
  background and life **8**:1136-39
  "Circle of Fire, A" **8**:1135
  Collected Works **8**:1143
  Complete Stories, The **8**:1135, 1139, 1143
  Correspondence of Flannery O'Connor and Brainard Cheneys, The **8**:1143
  critical commentary on **8**:1138, 1143, 1147
  Everything That Rises Must Converge **8**:1138, 1139, 1143
  "Everything That Rises Must Converge" **8**:1135, 1139, 1142, 1148-49
  Flannery O'Connor's Library: Resources of Being **8**:1139
  Foote and **4**:544, 548
  "Geranium, The" **8**:1137, 1139
  Good Man Is Hard to Find, A **8**:1138, 1139, 1143
  "Greenleaf" **8**:1135, 1139, 1142, 1150
  Habit of Being, The: Letters (ed Fitzgerald) **8**:1137, 1143
  highlights in life **8**:1139
  importance as short-story writer **8**:1135
  influences on **8**:1136, 1142, 1143
  "Life You Save May Be Your Own, The" **8**:1135
  love of peacocks **8**:1138, 1139, *1149*
  major works **8**:1144-47
  Mystery and Manners **8**:1143
  Presence of Grace, The **8**:1143
  racial issues and **8**:1141, 1148, 1149

  religious elements **8**:1135, 1140, 1141, 1142, 1143, 1144, 1145, 1146, 1149, 1150
  "Revelation" **8**:1135, 1139, 1143
  southern regionalism **7**:975, **8**:1136, 1142, 1143, *1144*, 1148, **11**:1495, 1512
  themes and issues **8**:1139-40, 1140-43, 1144, 1146, 1147
  violence in works **8**:1136, 1141, 1142, 1144, 1147
  Violent Bear It Away, The **8**:1135, 1138, 1139, 1141, 1143, 1144-46
  Wise Blood **8**:1135, 1137, 1138, 1139, 1141, 1143, 1144, 1145, 1146-48

Odets, Clifford **8**:1020
  Gibson and **5**:613, 614, 615, 619, 620

O'Hara, John **4**:515, 516, 524

Okotp'tek (poet) **11**:1569

O'Neill, Eugene **9:1157-80**, **12**:1635
  Ah, Wilderness! **9**:1166, 1168
  All God's Chillun Got Wings **9**:1164, 1168
  Anna Christie **9**:1159, 1168, 1169-70
  "As Ever, Gene": The Letters of Eugene O'Neill to George Jean Nathan **9**:1168
  as Foote influence **4**:548
  as McCullers influence **7**:976, 985
  as Miller influence **8**:1020
  as realist-naturalist **9**:1157
  awards and honors **9**:1161, 1162, 1163
  background and life **9**:1158-63
  Beyond the Horizon **9**:1161, 1164, 1168
  Bound East for Cardiff **9**:1160, 1163, 1168, 1169
  Calms of Capricorn, The (with Gallup) **9**:1168
  Chris Christophersen **9**:1168
  Complete Plays, The **9**:1168
  Complete Works **9**:1168
  critical commentary on **9**:1171
  Desire Under the Elms **9**:1164, 1168, 1170
  Emperor Jones, The **9**:1164-65, 1168, 1169
  expressionism and **9**:1157, 1164, 1165

film adaptations **9**:1161
Great God Brown, The **9**:1164,
    1168
Hairy Ape, The **9**:1165, 1168
"Haunted, The" **9**:1168, 1179
highlights in life **9**:1163
"Homecoming" **9**:1168, 1179
Hughie **9**:1164, 1168, 1172,
    1177-78
"Hunted, The" **9**:1168, *1170*,
    1179
Iceman Cometh, The **9**:1159,
    1163, 1164, 1166, 1168,
    1171, 1173-75, 1177, 1179
influence of **7**:976, 985, **8**:1020
influences on **9**:1157, 1164,
    1165, 1167
Later Plays **9**:1168
Lazarus Laughed **9**:1165, 1168
Long Day's Journey into Night
    9:1161, 1163, 1166, 1168,
    1172, 1175-77, 1178, 1179
*"Love and Admiration and
    Respect": The O'Neill-Commins
    Correspondence* **9**:1168
major works **9**:1173-77
Marco Millions **9**:1168, 1171-72,
    1178
Moon for the Misbegotten, A
    9:1168, 1172, 1178-79
More Stately Mansions **9**:1162,
    1167, 1168, 1172
Mourning Becomes Electra **9**:1168,
    1170-71, 1179
Nine Plays **9**:1168
Plays **9**:1168
Poems, 1912-1944 (Gallup ed.)
    9:1168
Recklessness **9**:1167
Selected Letters of Eugene O'Neill
    (Bogard and Bryer eds.)
    9:1168
Strange Interlude **9**:1165-66,
    1168, 1171
*Tale of Possessors Self-Dispossessed,
    A* **9**:1162, 1166
*"Theatre We Worked For, The:" The
    Letters of Eugene O'Neill to
    Kenneth MacGowan* **9**:1168
theatrical experimentalism
    9:1164-65, 1169-71
theatrical productions **9**:1169-72
themes and issues **9**:1164, 1168,
    1173, 1174-75
Thirst and Other One-Act Plays
    9:1168

Touch of the Poet, A **9**:1162, 1166,
    1168, 1172
*Unknown O'Neill, The:
    Unpublished or Unfamiliar
    Writings of Eugene O'Neill*
    (Bogard ed.) **9**:1168
Ortiz Cofer, Judith **9:1181-94**
Among the Ancestors **9**:1191
"Arturo's Flight" **9**:1188, 1190
awards and honors **9**:1181,
    1183, 1185, 1193, 1194
background and life **9**:1182-84
"Bad Influence" **9**:1186, 1189
"Beauty Lessons" **9**:1190
"Corazon's Café" **9**:1192
critical commentary on **9**:1183,
    1193, 1194
"Dear Joaquin" **9**:1191-92
genre mixtures **9**:1183, 1184,
    1192
highlights in life **9**:1185
"Home to El Building" **9**:1190
"Hour with Abuelo, An" **9**:1190
influences on **9**:1188
*Island Like You, An: Stories of the
    Barrio* **9**:1185, 1186, 1187,
    1188, 1189-91
"Job for Valentin, A" **9**:1187,
    1190
Latin Deli, The: Prose and Poetry
    9:1183-84, 1185, 1188,
    1191-92
Latin Women Pray **9**:1191
Letters from a Caribbean Island
    9:1191
Line of the Sun, The **9**:1181,
    1183, 1185, 1186, 1191,
    1193
major works **9**:1189-92
"Matoa's Mirror" **9**:1190
"More Room" **9**:1194
"My Grandfather's Hat" **9**:1191
"Nada" **9**:1185
Native Dancer, The **9**:1191
"Olga" **9**:1191
"Paterson Public Library, The"
    9:1188
Peregrina **9**:1191
Puerto Rican experience and
    9:1181, 1183, 1184, 1186,
    1188, 1189, 1191, 1192,
    1193, 1194
Reaching for the Mainland **9**:1185,
    1191
*Reaching for the Mainland and
    Selected New Poems* **9**:1191

*Silent Dancing: A Partial
    Remembrance of a Puerto Rican
    Childhood* **9**:1183, 1185,
    1191, 1193-94
teenage protagonists **9**:1186-87,
    1188, 1189, 1190, 1194
Terms of Survival **9**:1183, 1185,
    1191
themes and issues **9**:1186, 1188,
    1189-90, 1191-92
"To Grandfather, Now
    Forgetting" **9**:1191
"When Latin Women Pray"
    9:1183
"Witch's Husband, The" **9**:1191
*Year of Our Revolution, The: New
    and Selected Stories and Poems*
    9:1184, 1185, 1191, 1194
Osborne, John **7**:937
Ouida **7**:877

Page, Thomas Nelson **3**:415
Parker, Dorothy **4**:502
Parsons, Elsie Clews **7**:1001
Penn, Arthur **4**:546
Piercy, Marge **9:1195-1212**
Art of Blessing the Day, The
    9:1199, 1200, 1202, 1205
"Art of Blessing the Day, The"
    9:1203
autobiographical elements
    9:1203
Available Light **9**:1205, 1209
awards and honors **9**:1197,
    1199, 1200, 1203, 1210
"Baboons in the Perennial Bed"
    9:1209
background and life **9**:1196-
    1200
"Barbie Doll" **9**:1206
"Beauty I Would Suffer For"
    9:1206
Body of Glass. See He, She, and It
Braided Lives **9**:1203, 1205
Breaking Camp **9**:1198, 1199,
    1205
*Circles on the Water: Selected
    Poems of Marge Piercy* **9**:1204-
    7
City of Light **9**:1205
"Crabs" **9**:1206-7
critical commentary on **9**:1201
Dance the Eagle to Sleep **9**:1198,
    1199, 1205
"Daughter of the African
    Evolution" **9**:1209

"Doing It Differently" **9**:1206
Early Grrrl **9**:1205
*Early Ripening: American Women's
    Poetry Now* (ed.) **9**:1205
*Earth Shines Secretly, The: A Book
    of Days* **9**:1205
Eight Chambers of the Heart, The
    9:1205
feminist issues **9**:1195, 1198,
    1201, 1203, 1206, 1209,
    1210
Fly Away Home **9**:1205
Four-Telling (with Hershon,
    Jarrett, and Lourie) **9**:1205
Going Down Fast **9**:1198, 1199,
    1203, 1205
Gone to Soldiers **9**:1202, 1203,
    1205, 1209-10
Grand Coolie Damn, The **9**:1205
Hard Loving **9**:1205
"Hard Time" **9**:1209
He, She, and It **9**:1202, 1205,
    1210
High Cost of Living, The **9**:1205
highlights in life **9**:1196-1200
influences on **9**:1202
Jewish themes **9**:1195, 1196,
    1199, 1200, 1202, 1209,
    1210
*Last White Class, The: A Play
    About Neighborhood Terror*
    (with Wood) **9**:1205
"Learning Experience" **9**:1204-5
literary legacy **9**:1203
Living in the Open **9**:1205
Longings of Women, The **9**:1205
"Loving the Crone" **9**:1209
major works **9**:1204-9
male/female relationship portray-
    als **9**:1206-7, 1211
Mars and Her Children **9**:1205
Moon Is Always Female, The **9**:1205
"Morning love song" **9**:1209
My Mother's Body **9**:1202, 1205
"Open to the Sky" **9**:1209
*Parti-Colored Blocks for a Quilt:
    Poets on Poetry* **9**:1205
"Peaceable Kingdom, The"
    9:*1204*, 1205
"Right to Life" **9**:1206
Small Changes **9**:1205, 1210-11
"Something to Look Forward To"
    9:1209
Stone, Paper, Knife **9**:1205
Storm Tide (with Wood) **9**:1205
Summer People **9**:1205

themes and issues **9**:1195, 1196,
    1198, 1199, 1200, 1201, 1202,
    1203, 1206, 1208, 1209, 1210
Three Women **9**:1205
"Thrifty Lover, The" **9**:1206
To Be of Use **9**:1205
"To Be of Use" **9**:1201
"To the Pay Toilet" **9**:1203
Twelve-Spoked Wheel Flashing, The
    9:1205
"Unclench Yourself" **9**:1206
"Unlearning to Not Speak"
    9:1206
utopian and dystopian elements
    9:1207, 1209, 1210
Vida **9**:1198, 1205
What Are Big Girls Made Of?
    9:1205
"What's That Smell in the
    Kitchen?" **9**:1206
"woman in the ordinary, The"
    9:1206
Woman on the Edge of Time
    9:1195, 1199, 1203, 1205,
    1207-9
"Work of Artifice, A" **9**:1206,
    1207
Written in Bone **9**:1205
"Wrong Monday" **9**:1209
Pierson, Frank **3**:358, 363
Pinter, Harold **7**:937, **12**:1654
Pizer, Donald **3**:381
Plath, Sylvia **6**:732, **9**:**1213-28**
    allegory use **9**:1221
    "Applicant, The" **9**:1221
    Ariel **9**:1217, 1221-22, 1224,
        1225
    autobiographical elements
        9:1213, 1217, 1219, 1222-23,
        1224, 1227
    awards and honors **9**:1215, 1218
    background and life **9**:1214-17
    Bed Book, The **9**:1224
    "Beekeeper's Daughter, The" **9**:1225
    Bell Jar, The (under pseud. of
        Lucas) **9**:1213, 1217, 1219,
        1222-24, 1227
    "Birthday Present, A" **9**:1221
    "Blackberrying" **9**:1222
    Collected Poems, The (Hughes ed.)
        9:1218, 1224
    Colossus and Other Poems, The
        9:1213, 1217-18, 1224-25
    "Comparison, A" **9**:1227
    critical commentary on **9**:1217,
        1218, 1219, 1227

Crossing the Water **9**:1224, 1225
Crystal Gazer **9**:1224
"Eye-Mote, The" **9**:1225
"Fever 103 Degrees" **9**:1221
Fiesta Melons **9**:1224
"Getting There" **9**:1221
"Hermit at Outermost House,
    The" **9**:1225
highlights in life **9**:1218
imagery use **9**:1221, 1222, 1225,
    1226
influences on **9**:1222
*Johnny Panic and the Bible of
    Dreams* **9**:1219, 1224, 1227
Journals of Sylvia Plath, The
    9:1224
"Lady Lazarus" **9**:1221
*Letters Home: Correspondence,
    1950-1963* (ed.. Plath) **9**:1224,
    1227
"Lorelei" **9**:1225
Lyonesse: Poems **9**:1224
major works **9**:1221-25
"Moon and the Yew Tree, The"
    9:1227
"Morning Song" **9**:1221
"Munich Mannequins" **9**:1221
posthumous reponse to **9**:1217
prose of **9**:1219, 1220
Pursuit **9**:1224
"Sculptor, The" **9**:1225
Selected Poems **9**:1224
Sexton and **9**:1216, **10**:1359,
    1360, 1364
"Shadow, The" **9**:1227
suicide and **9**:1213, 1216, 1217,
    1218, 1219, 1221, **10**:1359,
    1364
themes and issues **9**:1213, 1214,
    1221, 1223, 1224-25, 1227
Three Women **9**:1224, 1227
Uncollected Poems **9**:1224
Winter Trees **9**:1224, 1227
Plimpton, George **11**:1491
Poe, Edgar Allan **10**:1413
    as Angelou influence **1**:65
    as Atwood influence **1**:82
    as O'Connor influence **8**:1136
    as W. C. Williams influence
        12:1682-83
    as Wright influence **12**:1700
    Gardner and **5**:600, 601, 608
Pope, Alexander **2**:204, **10**:1340
Porter, Katherine Anne **7**:975,
    9:**1229-44**
    as Welty mentor **12**:1591, 1593

autobiographical elements
9:1231, 1235, 1242
awards and honors 9:1231,
1232, 1233
background and life 9:1230-33
Christmas Story, A 9:1236
*Collected Essays and Occasional
Writings, The* 9:1236
*Collected Stories of Katherine Anne
Porter, The* 9:1232, 1233, 1236
critical commentary on 9:1241
Days Before, The 9:1236
Defense of Circe, A 9:1236
"Flowering Judas" 9:1236, 1241-
42
Flowering Judas and Other Stories
9:1231, 1233, 1234, 1236
Foote and 4:547
"Grave, The" 9:1242-43
Hacienda 9:1236
highlights in life 9:1233
"Holiday" 9:1233
illnesses of 9:1230, 1232, 1233,
1235, 1239
influences on 9:1235
"Jilting of Granny Weatherall,
The" 9:1236, *1242*, 1243
journalism experience 9:1230,
1233, 1234
language precision 9:1236
*Leaning Tower and Other Stories,
The* 9:1231, 1233, 1236
Letters of Katherine Anne Porter
9:1236
literary style 9:1236
major works 9:1237-41
"María Concepción" 9:1230,
1233, 1243
Mexico to Germany voyage of
9:1231, 1233
Miranda stories 9:1235-36,
1242-43
My Chinese Marriage (M. T. F.;
ghostwritten by Porter) 9:1236
Never-Ending Wrong, The 9:1234,
1236
Noon Wine 9:1236, 1237-38
Old Mortality 9:1236
Old Order, The 9:1233, 1236
"Old Order, The" 9:1235
*Outline of Mexican Popular Arts
and Crafts* 9:1236
Pale Horse, Pale Rider 9:1233,
1236, 1238-39
*Pale Horse, Pale Rider: Three Short
Novels* 9:1230, 1236, 1237

*Selected Letters of Katherine Anne
Porter, The* 9:1236
Ship of Fools 9:1229, 1231, 1232,
1233, 1234, 1236, 1239-41
themes and issues 9:1234, 1235,
1237, 1238-39, 1241, 1243
*Uncollected Early Prose of Katherine
Anne Porter* 9:1234, 1236
What Price Marriage? (under
pseud. of Sears) 9:1236
Portis, Charles 9:**1245-58**
background and life 9:1246-49
"Combinations of Jacksons" 9:1249
comedic elements 9:1251-52,
1255, 1258
critical commentary on 9:1247,
1248, 1251
Dog of the South, The 9:1249,
1250, 1251-52, 1253-55
Gringos 9:1249, 1250, 1251,
1254, 1256-57
grotesque characters 9:1251
highlights in life 9:1249
"I Don't Talk Service No More"
9:1249, 1257
influences on 9:1247
journalism experience 9:1245,
1246, 1247, 1249
major works 9:1253-56
Masters of Atlantis 9:1249, 1250,
1254, 1257-58
"new journalism" and 9:1247
"Nights Can Turn Cool in
Viborra" 9:1249
Norwood 9:1247, 1248, 1249,
1250, 1254, 1258
quest portrayals 9:1247-48,
1249, 1250, 1251, 1253,
1254, 1255
themes and issues 9:1250, 1253-
54, 1255, 1256
True Grit 9:1248-49, 1250-51,
1254, 1255-56
Potok, Chaim 9:**1259-76**
as chaplain 9:1260, 1262, 1263,
1275
Asher Lev novels 9:1259, 1265,
1266, 1267, 1274
awards and honors 9:1259, 1260
background and life 9:1260-63
Book of Lights, The 9:1269
Chosen, The 9:1259, 1262, 1263,
1264, *1265*, 1266, *1267*,
1268-70
critical commentary on 9:1262,
1264

Davita's Harp 9:1262, 1263,
1267, 1269
*Ethical Living for a Modern World:
Jewish Insights* 9:1262, 1263,
1269
father-son relationship portrayals
9:1259, 1264-65, 1268, 1270,
1273, 1274
feminist issues 9:1262, 1267,
1270
*Gates of November, The: Chronicles
of the Slepak Family* 9:1263,
1265, 1269, 1273-74
Gift of Asher Lev, The 9:1259,
1269, 1272, 1274
highlights in life 9:1263
I Am the Clay 9:1261, 1267,
1269
influences on 9:1260, 1266
"Inside Modern Paganism" 9:1274
In the Beginning 9:1262, 1266,
1267, 1269
Jewish themes 9:1259, 1260,
1261-62, 1263, 1264, 1265,
1266, 1267, 1268, 1272,
1275
major works 9:1268-73
My First 79 Years (with Stern)
9:1269
My Name Is Asher Lev 9:1259,
1260, 1266, 1269, 1270-72,
1274
Promise, The 9:1259, 1263,
1264-65, 1269, 1272-73
"Rationalism and Skepticism of
Solomon Maimon, The"
9:1261
"Secularism for a Broken World"
9:1275
Sky of Now, The 9:1269
themes and issues 9:1262, 1264-
65, 1267, 1268, 1270, 1272
"Through Ancient Paganism"
9:1274
"Through Classical Paganism"
9:1274
"Through Islam and Christianity"
9:1274
Tobiasse: Artist in Exile 9:1269
Tree of Here, The 9:1269
*Wanderings: Chaim Potok's History
of the Jews* 9:1259, 1263,
1269, 1274-75
Zebra and Other Stories 9:1269
Potter, Beatrix 8:1047
Potter, Giselle 8:1064

Pound, Ezra **8:**1018, **10:**1326
  as Brooks influence **2:**196
  as MacLeish influence **7:**897, 901
  as W. C. Williams influence
    12:1675, 1676, 1677, 1679,
    1684, 1686, 1687, 1690, 1691
  Cummings and **3:**318
  Eliot and **4:**439, 441, 443, 444,
    450, 555, 558, 560, 562, 567
  Frost and **4:**560, 562, 567
  Hemingway and **5:**661, 670
  Moore and **8:**1034, 1035, 1038,
    1040, 1045
  Stein and **10:**1429, 1430, 1432
  Stevens and **11:**1475
Price, Reynolds **11:**1543, 1549
Primeau, Ronald **7:**952
Proust, Marcel **2:**241
Pustau, Erna von **2:**218
Pynchon, Thomas **5:**601, **9:**1251

Rabelais, François **3:**336, 339, 343
Rampersad, Arnold **6:**728, 729,
    731, 736, 739, **12:**1698
Raspberry, William **6:**734
Remarque, Erich Maria **10:**1399
Revelle, Alma **12:**1647
Rice, Elmer **6:**737
Rich, Adrienne **9:**1216, **1277-94**
  Adrienne Rich's Poetry and Prose:
    Poems, Prose, and Criticism
    9:1284
  "After Dark" **9:**1278
  as feminist poet **9:**1277, 1279,
    1280, 1281, 1282, 1283,
    1285, 1286, 1288, 1289,
    1293
  as lesbian **9:**1280, 1281, 1285,
    1289, 1291, 1292
  Atlas of the Difficult World, An:
    Poems, 1988-1991 **9:**1280,
    1284, 1291-92
  "Aunt Jennifer's Tigers" **9:**1282
  awards and honors **9:**1277,
    1279, 1280, 1281, 1291
  background and life **9:**1278-81
  Blood, Bread, and Poetry: Selected
    Prose, 1979-1984 **9:**1284
  Change of World, A **9:**1277, 1279,
    1281, 1284
  Collected Early Poems, 1950-1970
    9:1284
  Dark Fields of the Republic: Poems,
    1991-1995 **9:**1284
  Diamond Cutters and Other Poems,
    The **9:**1284

"Diving into the Wreck" **9:**1286,
  1288
Diving into the Wreck **9:**1277,
  1280, 1281, 1284, 1286,
  1287, 1288-89, 1293
Dream of a Common Language,
  The **9:**1277, 1280, 1284,
  1289, *1290*, 1291, 1293
Fact of a Doorframe, The: Poems
  Selected and New, 1950-1984
  9:1284
"Floating Poem, The" **9:**1291
"Harpers Ferry" **9:**1293
highlights in life **9:**1281
influences on **9:**1278, 1279,
  1285, 1293
Jewish heritage **9:**1285, 1292,
  1293
language and style **9:**1283
Leaflets **9:**1284
major works **9:**1286-91
Midnight Salvage: Poems, 1995-
  1998 **9:**1284
"Mirror in Which Two Are Seen
  as One, The" **9:**1286
Necessities of Life **9:**1284
"Not Somewhere Else, but Here"
  9:1289, 1291
Of Woman Born: Motherhood as
  Experience and Institution
  9:1279, 1284
On Lies, Secrets, and Silence:
  Selected Prose, 1966-1978
  9:1284
"Paula Becker to Clara Westhoff"
  9:1291
"Phantasia for Elvira Shatayev"
  9:1289, 1291
"Phenomenology of Anger, The"
  9:1286
Poems: Selected and New, 1950-
  1974 **9:**1284
"Power" **9:**1289
Selected Poems **9:**1284
"Sibling Mysteries" **9:**1291
Snapshots of a Daughter-in-Law
  9:1284
Sources **9:**1284
"Sources" **9:**1278, 1285
themes and issues **9:**1283-84,
  1286, 1289, 1291
Time's Power: Poems, 1985-1988
  9:1284, 1292-93
"Transcendental Etude" **9:**1291
"Twenty-one Love Poems"
  9:1289, 1291

Twenty-one Love Poems **9:**1280,
  1284
What Is Found There: Notebooks on
  Poetry and Politics **9:**1277,
  1284, 1293-94
Wild Patience Has Taken Me This
  Far, A **9:**1284
Will to Change, The **9:**1284
"Woman Dead in Her Forties, A"
  9:1291
Your Native Land, Your Life
  9:1284, 1285
Ricks, Christopher **11:**1514
Roberts, Meade **12:**1664
Robinson, Edwin Arlington **10:**1345
Rodríguez Feo, José **11:**1484
Roethke, Theodore **4:**563
Roiphe, Anne 12, 1717
Rölvaag, O. E. **7:**1005
Roth, Philip **11:**1495
Roudané, Matthew C. **8:**1025
Roumain, Jacques **6:**737
Rowson, Susanna **3:**312
Rukeyser, Muriel **9:**1284, **11:**1563
Ruskin, John **10:**1332

Saalbach, Robert P. **3:**381
Sade, Marquis de **7:**970
Salinger, J. D. **10:1301-22**
  background and life **10:**1302-34
  Catcher in the Rye, The **10:**1302,
    1303, 1305, 1306, 1308,
    1309, 1310, 1314-15, 1317
  character's realism **10:**1307-8
  "Down at the Dinghy" **10:***1320*,
    1321
  "For Esmé—with Love and
    Squalor" **10:**1303
  "Franny" **10:**1315-16
  Franny and Zooey **10:**1304, 1306,
    1315-17
  Glass family stories **10:**1303,
    1304, 1305, 1308, 1315-18,
    1319, 1321
  "Hapworth 16, 1924" **10:**1304,
    1306
  highlights in life **10:**1306
  "I'm Crazy" **10:**1303
  influences on **10:**1309, 1317
  "Just Before the War with the
    Eskimos" **10:**1319, 1321
  major works **10:**1314-18
  Nine Stories **10:**1303, 1306,
    1310, 1317, 1319, 1321
  "Perfect Day for Bananafish, A"
    10:1303, 1306, 1317, 1319

"Personal Notes of an
Infantryman" **10**:1303
privacy concerns **10**:1301, 1304,
1306, 1309, 1310-13, 1315
"Raise High the Roof Beam,
Carpenters" **10**:1317, 1318
*Raise High the Roof Beam,
Carpenters, and Seymour: An
Introduction* **10**:1304, 1306,
1317-18
"Seymour: An Introduction"
10:1317-18, 1319, 1321
"Slight Rebellion Off Madison"
10:1303, 1306
"Teddy" **10**:1309, 1321
themes and issues **10**:1307,
1308, 1314, 1315, 1316
"This Sandwich Has No
Mayonnaise" **10**:1303
"Uncle Wiggly in Connecticut"
10:1303
"Young Folks, The" **10**:1302, 1306
"Zooey" **10**:1315, 1316
Sandburg, Carl **4**:513, **7**:959,
10:1323-42
Abe Lincoln Grows Up **10**:1338
Abraham Lincoln: The Prairie Years
10:1326, 1328, 1329, 1336-
37, 1338, 1340, 1341, 1350
*Abraham Lincoln: The Prairie Years
and the War Years* **10**:1336,
1338, 1340, 1341
Abraham Lincoln: The War Years
10:1326, 1327, 1328, 1336-
37, 1338, 1340, 1341
"Address Before a Joint Session of
Congress, February 12, 1959"
10:1338
Always the Young Strangers
10:1338, 1340-41
American Songbag, The (ed.)
10:1335, 1338, 1341
"American Vagabond, An"
10:1332
Anderson and **1**:45
as Brooks influence **2**:196
as Hughes influence **6**:738
as Illinois Poet Laureate **2**:195,
198
awards and honors **2**:195, 198,
10:1325, 1326, 1327, 1328
background and life **10**:1324-28
Benét and **2**:151, 156
Breathing Tokens (ed.) **10**:1338
"Chicago" **10**:1325, 1338-39
"Chicago Poems" **10**:1328

Chicago Poems **10**:1326, 1328,
1338, 1340
*Chicago Poems: Poems of the
Midwest* **10**:1338
Chicago Race Riots, The **10**:1338,
1341-42
children's stories **10**:1326
Complete Poems **10**:1327, 1328,
1337-40
Cornhuskers **10**:1326, 1338
critical commentary on **10**:1325,
1337, 1339, 1340, 1342
"Dream Girl" **10**:1325
Early Moon **10**:1338
Ever the Winds of Chance (Sandburg
and Hendrick eds.) **10**:1338
"Fog" **10**:1340
folk song collection **10**:1326,
1333, 1334, 1335, 1341
free verse **10**:1330, 1331, 1339
"Gone" **10**:1339
"Good Morning, America"
10:1330, 1338
"Grass" **10**:1339
"Hangman at Home, The"
10:1339
Harvest Poems, 1910-1960
10:1338
highlights in life **10**:1328
Home Front Memo **10**:1338
Honey and Salt **10**:1338
influences on **10**:1331, 1332,
1338, 1339
In Restless Ecstasy **10**:1325
journalism experience **10**:1324,
1325, 1326, 1328, 1329,
1330, 1334, 1340, 1341-42
Letters of Carl Sandburg, The
(Mitgang ed.) **10**:1338
Lincoln and Whitman Miscellany, A
10:1338
*Lincoln Collector: The Story of
Oliver R. Barrett's Great Private
Collection* **10**:1338
"Mag" **10**:1339
major works **10**:1336-40
"Many Hats" **10**:1339
Mary Lincoln: Wife and Widow
(with Angle) **10**:1338
New American Songbag, The (ed.)
10:1335, 1338
"On a Railroad Right of Way"
10:1339
People, Yes, The **10**:1338
performances by **10**:1325, 1326,
1328, 1332-35

*Photographs of Abraham Lincoln,
The* **10**:1338
poetic form and diction **10**:1329-
30, 1340
Potato Face **10**:1338
"Prairie" **10**:1330, 1339
Prairie-Town Boy **10**:1338
Remembrance Rock **10**:1326,
1330, 1338, 1341, 1342
Rootabaga Pigeons **10**:1326, 1338
Rootabaga Stories **10**:1326, 1328,
1338
Sandburg Range, The **10**:1338
Schaefer and **10**:1344, 1350
Selected Poems of Carl Sandburg
10:1338
Slabs of the Sunburnt West
10:1338
"Sleepyheads" **10**:1339
Smoke and Steel **10**:1326, 1338
"Soiled Dove" **10**:*1330*, 1339
"Southern Pacific" **10**:1339
Steichen the Photographer **10**:1338
*Storm over the Land: A Profile of
the Civil War* **10**:1338
themes and issues **10**:1329,
1336, 1337-38
"To a Contemporary
Bunkshooter" **10**:1339
*Wedding Procession of the Rag Doll
and the Broom Handle and Who
Was in It, The* **10**:1338
Santayana, George **4**:438, 441,
11:1468
Sapin, Louis **12**:1703
Saroyan, William **3**:294, 300,
11:1527
Sartre, Jean-Paul **5**:603, **12**:1647
as Wright influence **12**:1695,
1700
Saul, Oscar **12**:1664
Sayles, John **11**:1521
Schaap, Dick **9**:1247
Schaefer, Jack Warner **10:1343-56**
Adolphe Francis Alphonse Bandelier
10:1352
American Bestiary, An **10**:346,
1352
as environmentalist **10**:1346,
1348
awards and honors **10**:1344,
1347
background and life **10**:1344-47
Big Range, The **10**:1352
Canyon, The **10**:1348-49, 1352,
1355

Collected Stories of Jack Schaefer, The **10**:1352
Company of Cowards **10**:1349, 1352, 1355
Conversations with a Pocket Gopher and Other Outspoken Neighbors **10**:1346, 1352
critical commentary on **10**:1350, 1352, 1354, 1356
film adapations **10**:1349
First Blood **10**:1352
good vs. evil portrayal **10**:1350
Great Endurance Horse Race, The: Six Hundred Miles on a Single Mount, 1908, from Evanston, Wyoming to Denver **10**:1352
Heroes Without Glory: Some Good Men of the Old West **10**:1352
highlights in life **10**:1347
influences on **10**:1350
journalism experience **10**:1345, 1347
Kean Land and Other Stories, The **10**:1349, 1352
literary legacy **10**:1349-50
major works **10**:1351-54
Mavericks **10**:1346, 1348, 1349, 1352, 1355-56
Monte Walsh **10**:1349, 1351-52
New Mexico **10**:1352
Old Ramon **10**:1347, 1349, 1352, 1356
Old West as main subject **10**:1343, 1348, 1350, 1352, 1353, 1355, 1356
Out West: An Anthology of Stories **10**:1352
Pioneers, The **10**:1352
Rider from Nowhere **10**:1345
Shane **10**:1343, 1345, 1347, 1348, 1349-50, 1351, 1352, 1353-54, 1355, 1356
Stubby Pringle's Christmas **10**:1352
themes and issues **10**:1348, 1349, 1350, 1351, 1353, 1355
Schopenhauer, Arthur **3**:380
Schorer, Mark **3**:355
Schwartz, Delmore **1**:129
Scott, Masha **2**:218
Scott, Sir Walter
  as Anderson influence **1**:49
  as Bontemps influence **2**:182, 185
  as Cummings influence **3**:313
  as Norris influence **8**:1086, 1092

Sedges, John (Buck pseudonym) **2**:212, 214, 218, 227
Seidel, Henry **2**:154
Selected Poems (Frost; Cox and Latham eds.) **4**:567, 570
Sexton, Anne **6**:732, **10**:1357-76
  "Addict, The" **10**:1376
  "All My Pretty Ones" **10**:1369, 1371
  All My Pretty Ones **10**:1359, 1361, 1369, *1370*, 1371-72
  Anne Sexton: A Self-Portrait in Letters **10**:1371
  as confessional poet **10**:1357, 1359-60, 1362, 1369, 1372, 1373
  awards and honors **10**:1360, 1361, 1362
  Awful Rowing Toward God, The **10**:1362, 1365, 1367, 1371, 1372-73, 1375
  background and life **10**:1358-61
  "Bestiary U.S.A." **10**:1367
  Book of Folly, The **10**:1371
  Cinderella version **10**:1376
  Complete Poems, The **10**:1361, 1365, 1368, 1371
  critical commentary on **10**:1359, 1366, 1371-72, 1373
  death focus **10**:1367, 1368, 1371
  Death Notebooks, The **10**:1361, 1371, 1375
  Eggs of Things (with Kumin) **10**:1371
  folktale and mythic elements **10**:1357, 1362-63, 1364, 1369, 1375, 1376
  "For Eleanor Boylan Talking with God" **10**:1369
  45 Mercy Street (play) **10**:1360, 1361, 1371
  45 Mercy Street (poetry) **10**:1365, 1371
  free verse **10**:1369, 1372, 1375, 1376
  "Her Kind" **10**:1374
  highlights in life **10**:1361
  "Housewife, The" **10**:1369
  "In Excelsis" **10**:1368
  influences on **10**:1369
  Joey and the Birthday Present (with Kumin) **10**:1371
  literary legacy **10**:1364
  "Live" **10**:1376
  Live or Die **10**:1361, 1371, 1375-76

Love Poems **10**:1371
major works **10**:1369-75
"May 30" **10**:1368
More Eggs of Things (with Kumin) **10**:1371
No Evil Star: Selected Essays, Interviews, and Prose **10**:1371
performance material **10**:1360, 1364
Plath and **9**:1216, **10**:1359, 1360, 1364
Poems (with Kinsella and Livingston) **10**:1371
posthumous publications **10**:1365, 1367
rat imagery **10**:1372
"Rats Live on No Evil Star" **10**:1372
"Red Roses" **10**:1365
religion and **10**:1362, 1365, 1369, 1372-73, 1375
"Rowing" **10**:1372
"Rowing Endeth, The" **10**:1372-73
"Scorpio, Bad Spider, Die" **10**:1367-68
Selected Poems **10**:1371
Selected Poems of Anne Sexton **10**:1371
Snow White version **10**:1376
"Some Foreign Letters" **10**:1374
suicide and **10**:1357, 1359, 1360, 1361, 1362, 1363-64, 1365, 1373, 1376
themes and issues **10**:1362, 1369, 1372, 1373-74, 1375-76
To Bedlam and Part Way Back **10**:1359, 1361, 1371, 1373-75
Transformations **10**:1361, 1363, 1371, 1376
"Truth the Dead Know, The" **10**:1369, 1371
"Unknown Girl in the Maternity Ward" **10**:1374, 1375
violent undertones **10**:1376
"Wanting to Die" **10**:1363-64, 1376
"With Mercy for the Greedy" **10**:1362
Wizard of Tears, The (with Kumin) **10**:1371
"Woman with Girdle" **10**:1369, 1371
women's issues and **10**:1363, 1364, 1365, 1371, 1372, 1374, 1376

Words for Dr. Y: Uncollected Poems with Three Stories **10**:1365, 1367-68, 1371

Shakespeare, William **5**:598, **9**:1190, 1256, **10**:1336, 1371
  and Faulkner **4**:492
  as Angelou influence **1**:65
  as Bontemps influence **2**:182, 185
  as Davies influence **3**:335, 340, 343, 349, 350
  as Didion influence **3**:366
  as Eliot influence **4**:444
  as MacLeish influence **7**:898, 905, 907
  Gibson and **5**:613, 615, 616
  scene from *Tempest* **3**:335

Shaw, George Bernard **4**:535, 540, **12**:1700

Shaw, Irwin **6**:807, **11**:1491

Shelley, Percy Bysshe **7**:952

Sherwood, Robert **4**:502

Simon, John **4**:554

Sinclair, Upton **10**:1377-96
  Affectionately Eve **10**:1392
  American Outpost: A Book of Reminiscences **10**:1381, 1392
  Another Pamela: Or, Virtue Still Rewarded **10**:1392
  as Dreiser influence **3**:380
  as muckraker **10**:1377, 1383
  as Socialist **10**:1381, 1383, 1384, 1386, 1387, 1395
  Autobiography of Upton Sinclair, The **10**:1392
  awards and honors **10**:1377, 1381, 1382, 1396
  Between Two Worlds **10**:1392, 1396
  Bill Porter **10**:1392
  Book of Life, Mind, and Body, The **10**:1392
  Boston **10**:1380-81, 1382, 1384, 1385, 1390-91, 1392
  Brass Check, The: A Study in American Journalism **10**:1380, 1384, 1392, 1395
  California gubernatorial bid **10**:1377, 1381, 1382, 1386-87, *1388*, 1389
  Captain of Industry, A **10**:1379, 1392
  Co-op **10**:1392
  critical commentary on **10**:1385, 1391, 1395
  Cup of Fury, The **10**:1392

Dead Hand series **10**:1379-80, 1382, 1395
Depression Island **10**:1387, 1392
Dragon Harvest **10**:1392, 1396
Dragon's Teeth **10**:1377, 1382, 1392, 1396
education system critique **10**:1384
EPIC campaign **10**:132, 1381, 1386-89
EPIC Plan for California, The **10**:1392
Expect No Peace! **10**:1392
Fasting Cure, The **10**:1392
Flivver King, The **10**:1392
Giant's Strength, A **10**:1392
Gnomobile, The: A Gnice Gnew Gnarrative with Gnonsense, but Gnothing Gnaughty **10**:1392
Goose Step, The: A Study of American Education **10**:1380, 1384, 1392, 1395
Goslings, The: A Study of the American Schools **10**:1380, 1384, 1392, 1395
Hell: A Verse Drama and Photo-Play **10**:1392
I, Candidate for Governor and How I Got Licked **10**:1389, 1392
I, Governor of California and How I Ended Poverty: A True Story of the Future **10**:1387, 1392
Industrial Republic, The **10**:1379, 1392
influence of **3**:380
influences on **7**:878, **10**:1385
It Happened to Didymus **10**:1392
Jimmie Higgins **10**:1392
Journal of Arthur Stirling, The **10**:1392
Jungle, The **10**:1377, 1379, 1382, 1383, 1384, 1385, 1391-94, 1395, **12**:1698
King Coal **10**:1392
Lanny Budd series **10**:1377, 1381, 1382, 1384-85, 1395-96
Letters to Judd **10**:1392
Lewis and **6**:845, 848
"Lie Factory Starts, The" **10**:1387
Little Steel **10**:1392
London (Jack) as influence on **7**:878
Love's Pilgrimage **10**:1379, 1392
major works **10**:1390-95
Mammonart **10**:1380, 1392, 1395

Manassas **10**:1383, 1384, 1392
Marie Antoinette **10**:1392
Mental Radio **10**:1392
Metropolis, The **10**:1379, 1383-84, 1392
Millennium, The **10**:1392
Moneychangers, The **10**:1379, 1383-84, 1392
Money Writes! **10**:1380, 1392, 1395
Mountain City **10**:1392
My Lifetime in Letters **10**:1392
No Pasaran! **10**:1392
Norris and **8**:1085
Oil! A Novel **10**:1380, 1382, 1383, 1384, 1385, 1392, 1394-95
100% **10**:1392
One Clear Call **10**:1392, 1396
O Shepherd, Speak! **10**:1392, 1396
Our Bourgeois Literature **10**:1392
Our Lady **10**:1392
Overman, The **10**:1392
Personal Jesus, A **10**:1392
Plays of Protest **10**:1392
Pot-Boiler, The (play) **10**:1392
Prairie Pirates, The **10**:1378
Presidential Agent **10**:1392, 1396
Presidential Mission **10**:1392, 1396
Prince Hagen **10**:1392
Profits of Religion, The **10**:1380, 1384, 1392, 1395
propagandist tendancy **10**:1393
realism **10**:1384
Return of Lanny Budd, The **10**:1392, 1396
Roman Holiday **10**:1392
Samuel the Seeker **10**:1379, 1384, 1392
Singing Jailbirds **10**:1392
Springtime and Harvest **10**:1378, 1392
Sylvia **10**:1392
Sylvia's Marriage **10**:1392
Terror in Russia: Two Views **10**:1392
Theirs Be the Guilt. See Manassas
themes and issues **10**:1383, 1384, 1390, 1391, 1394
They Call Me Carpenter **10**:1392
Upton Sinclair Presents William Fox **10**:1392
Wally for Queen! **10**:1392
Way Out, The: What Lies Ahead for America? **10**:1387, 1392

Wet Parade, The **10**:1381, 1392
What Didymus Did **10**:1392
What God Means to Me **10**:1392
Wide Is the Gate **10**:1392, 1396
World's End **10**:1392, 1396
World to Win, A **10**:1392, 1396
Wright and **12**:1698
Singer, Isaac Bashevis **7**:916,
　　10:1397-1416
　allegory use **10**:1402
　Alone in the Wild Forest **10**:1411
　"Author's Note" **10**:1413
　awards and honors **10**:1397,
　　1400, 1403
　background and life **10**:1398-1403
　Certificate, The **10**:1400, 1407-9,
　　1411
　Collected Stories, The **10**:1411,
　　1413-14
　*Crown of Feathers and Other
　　Stories, A* **10**:1403, 1411
　*Day of Pleasure, A: Stories of a Boy
　　Growing up in Warsaw*
　　10:1398, 1399, 1403, 1411
　*Death of Methuselah and Other
　　Stories, The* **10**:1411
　Elijah the Slave **10**:1411
　Enemies: A Love Story **10**:1402,
　　1405, 1406, 1411
　Estate, The. See *Manor, The*
　Family Moskat, The **10**:1399,
　　1400, 1402, 1403, 1404,
　　1409-12
　Fearsome Inn, The **10**:1411
　film adaptations **10**:1401, 1406
　*Fools of Chelm and Their History,
　　The* **10**:1411
　*Friend of Kafka and Other Stories,
　　A* **10**:1411
　"Gentleman from Cracow, The"
　　10:1402, 1414
　"Gimpel the Fool" **10**:1400, 1403
　Gimpel the Fool and Other Stories
　　10:1403, 1411
　Golem, The **10**:1411
　Hasidic background **10**:1398,
　　1404, 1408, 1409, 1411,
　　1415, 1416
　highlights in life **10**:1403
　Image and Other Stories, The
　　10:1411
　influences on **10**:1398-99, 1407,
　　1408, 1411
　In My Father's Court **10**:1398,
　　1404, 1411, 1414-16
　"In Old Age" **10**:1399

*Joseph and Koza: Or, The Sacrifice
　to the Vistula* **10**:1411
King of the Fields, The **10**:1411
*Little Boy in Search of God, A:
　Mysticism in a Personal Light*
　10:1411
Lost in America **10**:1411
Magician of Lublin, The **10**:1405,
　1411
major works **10**:1407-13
Manor, The **10**:1403, 1411
*Mazel and Shlimazel; Or, The Milk
　of a Lioness* **10**:1411
Meshugah **10**:1411, 1413
Mirror, The (play) **10**:1411
*Naftali the Storyteller and His
　Horse, Sus, and Other Stories*
　10:1411
Old Love **10**:1411
on purpose of art **10**:1413-14
Penitent, The **10**:1411
philosophical speculations
　10:1413
Power of Light, The: Eight Stories
　10:1411
Purim Gift, The **10**:1416
*Reaches of Heaven: A Story of the
　Baal Shem Tov* **10**:1411
Satan in Goray **10**:1398, 1403,
　1411
Scum **10**:1411
Séance and Other Stories, The
　10:1411
"Secret, The" **10**:1415-16
sex-obsessed characters **10**:1402,
　1404, 1409, 1410-11, 1413,
　1414
Shadows on the Hudson **10**:1399,
　1402, 1404, 1411
Shlemiel the First (play) **10**:1411
Short Friday and Other Stories
　10:1411
Shosha **10**:1399, 1411, 1412-13
Slave, The **10**:1411
Spinoza of Market Street, The
　10:1411
Spinoza's importance to **10**:1398,
　1407, 1408, 1411
Stories for Children **10**:1411
Tale of Three Wishes, A **10**:1411
Teibele and Her Demon **10**:1411
themes and issues **10**:1398,
　1402, 1404, 1407, 1409,
　1410-11, 1412, 1413, 1414
Topsy-Turvy Emperor of China, The
　10:1411

*When Shlemiel Went to Warsaw
　and Other Stories* **10**:1411
Why Noah Chose the Dove
　10:1411
Wicked City, The **10**:1411
"Yearning Heifer, The" **10**:1414
"Yentl, the Yeshiva Boy" **10**:1405,
　1406
Yentl, the Yeshiva Boy (play)
　10:1401, 1405-6, 1411
Yiddish language and **10**:1397,
　1399, 1400, 1403
Young Man in Search of Love, A
　10:1400, 1411
Zionism and **10**:1398, 1407
Zlateh the Goat and Other Stories
　10:1411
Sitwell, Edith **8**:1045
Smalley, Walter **6**:737
Snodgrass, W. D. **10**:1360, 1375
Solzhenitsyn, Alexandr **8**:1016
Sophocles **9**:1167
Spencer, Herbert **7**:876, 877
　as Dreiser influence **3**:380, 389
Spinoza, Baruch, as Singer influence
　10:1398, 1407, 1408, 1409,
　1411
Stark, Inez Cunningham **2**:197,
　199, 202, 208
Steele, Wilbur Daniel **10**:1350
Stegner, Wallace **2**:257, 258
Stein, Gertrude **10**:1417-38, **12**:1700
　abstraction in writing **10**:1422
　as Anderson influence **1**:45, 49
　as McNickle influence **7**:1004
　*Autobiography of Alice B. Toklas,
　　The* **10**:1417, 1421, 1422,
　　1424, 1425, 1431-32, 1436-
　　37
　awards and honors **10**:1421
　background and life **10**:1418-22
　*Bee Time Vine and Other Pieces,
　　1913-1927* **10**:1424
　*Before the Flowers of Friendship
　　Faded, Friendship Faded*
　　10:1424
　Blood on the Dining-Room Floor
　　10:1424
　Brewsie and Willie **10**:1422, 1424,
　　1436, 1437
　Composition as Explanation
　　10:1424
　critical commentary on **10**:1424,
　　1431, 1435, 1436
　cubist movement and **10**:1420,
　　1429, 1434, 1435

dialogue/narrative blurring by 10:1424

Everybody's Autobiography 10:1424, 1436-37

Fernhurst, Q.E.D., and Other Early Writings 10:1424

"Food" 10:1434, 1436

Four Saints in Three Acts (opera libretto) 10:1424, 1425

"Gentle Lena, The" 10:1437, 1438

Geographical History of America, The 10:1424

Geography and Plays 10:1424

"Good Anna, The" 10:1437-38

Hemingway and 5:661, 669, 670, 677

highlights in life 10:1422

How to Write 10:1424

How Writing Is Written 10:1424

Ida: A Novel 10:1424, 1437

In a Garden: An Opera in One Act 10:1424

individualism and 10:1436

influence of 1:45, 49, 7:1004

influences on 10:1423, 1426, 1429

In Savoy: Or, Yes Is for a Very Young Man (A Play of the Resistance in France) 10:1424

Last Operas and Plays 10:1424

Lectures in America 10:1424

Long Gay Book, A 10:1424

Lucretia Borgia 10:1424

Lucy Church Amiably 10:1424

major works 10:1431-36

Making of Americans, The 10:1422, 1423, 1424, 1425, 1429, 1432-34

Matisse, Picasso, and Gertrude Stein, with Two Shorter Stories 10:1424

"Melanctha" 10:1437, 1438

modernism and 10:1417, 1421, 1425, 1426, 1427

Mother of Us All, The (opera libretto) 10:1424

Mrs. Reynolds 10:1437

Mrs. Reynolds and Five Earlier Novelettes, 1931-42 10:1424, 1437

Narration: Four Lectures 10:1424

Novel of Thank You, A 10:1424

"Objects" 10:1434, 1436

opera librettos 10:1424, 1425

Operas and Plays 10:1424

Paris, France 10:1424

Picasso 10:1424

Picasso's importance to 10:1419, 1422, 1423, 1424, 1426, 1434, 1435

Portraits and Prayers 10:1424

punctuation use 10:1423, 1425

Q.E.D. 10:1424, 1425

Reflections on the Atomic Bomb 10:1424

repetition technique 10:1423, 1433

"Rooms" 10:1434, 1436

salon of 10:1419, 1423, 1427, 1429-30

Selected Operas and Plays 10:1424

Stanzas in Meditation and Other Poems, 1929-1933 10:1424

stream of consciousness technique 10:1424, 1433-34

Tender Buttons: Objects, Food, Rooms 1:49, 10:1420, 1422, 1424, 1425, 1434-36

themes and issues 10:1431-32, 1432, 1434

Things as They Are 10:1424, 1425

Three Lives 10:1424, 1425, 1437-38

Toklas relationship 10:1417, 1419, 1420-21, 1422, 1424, 1425, 1426, *1427*, 1429, 1430, 1431-32, 1434, 1436, 1437

Two (Hitherto Unpublished) Poems 10:1424

Wars I Have Seen 10:1422, 1424, 1437

What Are Masterpieces 10:1424

Wilder and 12:1635, 1644

word portraits 10:1420, 1422, 1423, 1425, 1433

World Is Round, The 10:1424

writing techniques 10:1423-24, 1433-34

Steinbeck, John 5:690, **11:1445-66**

Acts of King Arthur and His Noble Knights (Chase ed.) 11:1454

Affaire Lettuceberg, L' 11:1456

America and Americans 11:1454

American Dream reevaluation 11:1450, 1453, 1460, 1461

as war correspondent 11:1451

awards and honors 11:1445, 1447, 1448, 1449, 1451, 1464

background and life 11:1446-49

Bombs Away! 11:1448, 1454

Burning Bright (novel) 11:1454

Burning Bright (play) 11:1454

Cannery Row 11:1448, 1450, 1452, 1454, 1465

critical commentary on 11:1453, 1459, 1460, 1464, 1465

critique of middle-class values 11:1460

Cup of Gold 11:1447, 1451, 1454

East of Eden 11:1448, 1452, 1454, 1466

Faulkner and 4:484

film adaptations 11:1449, 1453, 1455-58

Forgotten Village, The (nonfiction) 11:1454

Forgotten Village, The (screenplay) 11:1453, 1454

"Gift, The" 11:1464-65

Grapes of Wrath, The 11:1445, 1448, 1450, 1451, 1452, 1453, 1454, 1455-56, *1457*, 1458, 1462-64, 12:1698

"Great Mountains, The" 11:1465

highlights in life 11:1451

In Dubious Battle 11:1448, 1450, 1454

influences on 8:1085, 11:1446, 1452, 1463

interchapters use 11:1460, 1464, 1465

Journal of a Novel: The "East of Eden" Letters 11:1454

Letters to Alicia 11:1454

Lifeboat (screenplay) 11:1449, 1453, 1454

"Lifeboat" (short story) 11:1453

literary legacy 11:1453-54

Long Valley, The 11:1448, 1454

major works 11:1459-64

Malory's importance to 11:1446, 1447, 1452, 1454, 1459, 1463, 1465

Medal for Benny, A (screenplay) 11:1449, 1454

migrant worker concerns 11:1456

Moon Is Down, The (novel) 11:1448, 1454

Moon Is Down, The (play) 11:1454

Of Mice and Men (novel) 11:1450, 1452, 1453, 1454, 1456, 1460-62

Of Mice and Men (play) 11:1454

Once There Was a War 11:1454

Pastures of Heaven, The 11:1447, 1454

Pearl, The (novel) **11**:1448, 1454, 1462, 1465-66
Pearl, The (screenplay) **11**:1449, 1453, 1454
"Promise, The" **11**:1465
realism-romance mixture **11**:1452
Red Pony, The (novel) **11**:1447, 1452, 1453, 1454, 1462, 1464-65
Red Pony, The (screenplay) **11**:1449, 1453, 1454
Ricketts friendship **11**:1447, 1448, 1451, 1452, 1454, 1465
Russian Journal, A (with Capa) **11**:1448, 1454
Saint Katy the Virgin **11**:1454
Sea of Cortez (with Ricketts) **11**:1447, 1454
Short Reign of Pippen IV, The **11**:1454
Steinbeck: A Life in Letters (ed. with Wallsten) **11**:1454
Sweet Thursday **11**:1454
sympathy for common people **11**:1450, 1452, *1453*
Their Blood Is Strong **11**:1448, 1454, 1455-56
themes and issues **11**:1450, 1452-53, 1459, 1460-61, 1461-62, 1464
To a God Unknown **11**:1447, 1454
Tortilla Flat **11**:1447, 1450, 1453, 1454, 1459-60, 1462
Travels with Charley: In Search of America **11**:1448, 1454
Viva Zapata! (screenplay) **11**:1453, 1454
Wayward Bus, The **11**:1448, 1454
Winter of Our Discontent, The **11**:1454
Wright and **12**:1698
Stevens, Wallace **11:1467-88**
"Anecdote of the Jar" **11**:1480, 1481
as Rich influence **9**:1279
"Auroras of Autumn, The" **11**:1485
Auroras of Autumn, The **11**:1470, 1471, 1475, 1485-86
"Autumn Refrain" **11**:1482
awards and honors **11**:1470, 1471
background and life **11**:1468-71

"Book of Verse, A" **11**:1469, 1471
Bowl, Cat, and Broomstick **11**:1475
"Burghers of Petty Death" **11**:1487
Carlos Among the Candles (play) **11**:1475
"Carnet de Voyage" **11**:1469, 1471
Collected Poems of Wallace Stevens, The **11**:1470, 1471, 1475, 1486, 1487
complexity of later work **11**:1473, 1474, *1479*, 1481, 1487
critical commentary on **11**:1481-82, 1483, 1485
Description Without Place **11**:1475
"Emperor of Ice-Cream, The" **11**:1480, 1481
essays and plays **11**:1472, 1487
"Esthétique du Mal" **11**:1487
Esthétique du Mal **11**:1471, 1475
experimental artists and **11**:1469, 1484, *1486*
"Fading of the Sun, A" **11**:1482
Florida imagery **11**:1470, 1473, 1480, 1482, 1484
Harmonium **11**:1467, 1470, 1471, 1473, 1475, 1480-82, 1486
highlights in life **11**:1471
"High-Toned Old Christian Woman, A" **11**:1481
"Idea of Order at Key West, The" **11**:1482, 1483
Ideas of Order **11**:1470, 1471, 1473-74, 1475, 1482-83
imagination/reality duality portrayal **11**:1467, 1473, 1480, 1481, 1482, 1483, 1485, 1487
influence of **9**:1279
influences on **11**:1470, 1473, 1474, 1484
Letters of Wallace Stevens **11**:1471, 1475
literary legacy **11**:1474-75
"Little June Book, The" **11**:1469, 1471
major works **11**:1480-83
Man with the Blue Guitar and Other Poems, The **11**:1470, 1471, 1474, 1475
meditations on God **11**:1470, 1472-73, 1474, 1476, 1485

modernism and **11**:1475
Moore and **8**:1038, 1039, 1045
Necessary Angel, The: Essays on Reality and the Imagination **11**:1471, 1475, 1486-87
"Notes Toward a Supreme Fiction" **11**:1487-88
Notes Toward a Supreme Fiction **11**:1475
Opus Posthumous (Morse ed.) **11**:1471, 1475, 1487
Owl's Clover **11**:1475
Parts of a World **11**:1470, 1471, 1475
power of poetry belief **11**:1467, 1472, 1474, 1475, 1482, 1483
"Presence of an External Master of Knowledge" **11**:1476
"Rock, The" **11**:1474, 1486
Roman Catholic conversion of **11**:1470, 1471, 1476-78
"Sad Strains of a Gay Waltz" **11**:1482, *1483*
Selected Poems **11**:1475
"Somnambulisma" **11**:1487
Souvenirs and Prophecies: The Young Wallace Stevens (ed. Stevens) **11**:1475
"Sunday Morning" **11**:*1472,* 1473, 1480, 1481, 1482
symbolism **11**:1473
themes and issues **11**:1473, 1480-81, 1482
Three Academic Pieces **11**:1475
Three Travelers Watch a Sunrise (play) **11**:1475
Transport to Summer **11**:1470, 1471, 1475, 1487
"Waving Adieu, Adieu, Adieu" **11**:1482
wordplay **11**:1467, 1468, 1483
Stevenson, Robert Louis **2**:182, 185, **10**:1378
Stowe, Harriet Beecher **12**:1706
as Anderson influence **1**:49
as Baldwin influence **1**:105
as Dunbar influence **3**:404
Strindberg, August
as Foote influence **4**:548
as O'Neill influence **9**:1164, 1165, 1167
as Wilder influence **12**:1637
Styron, William **11:1489-1504**
as southerner **11**:1489, 1490, 1492, 1494, 1495

awards and honors **11**:1489, 1491, 1492, 1496, 1504
background and life **11**:1490-93
"Benjamin Reid: Aftermath" **11**:1504
Bontemps themes anticipating **2**:188
"Chicago: 1968" **11**:1504
Confessions of Nat Turner, The **11**:1489, 1492, 1494, 1496, 1497-1500, 1504
critical commentary on **11**:1492, 1493, 1494-95
"Darkness Visible" **11**:1496
Darkness Visible: A Memoir of Madness **11**:1489, 1493, 1500
"Death-in-Life of Benjamin Reid, The" **11**:1504
depressive bouts **11**:1489, 1493, 1496
essays and journalism **11**:1503
highlights in life **11**:1496
influences on **11**:1492, 1495
In the Clap Shack **11**:1500
inticately drawn characters **11**:1495
Lie Down in Darkness **11**:1491, 1492, 1494, 1495, 1500, 1502-3
Long March, The **11**:1491, 1495, 1500
major works **11**:1497-1502
racism and **11**:1489, 1493, 1495, 1500
reality/myth relationship and **11**:1494, 1495
"Service, The" **11**:1504
Set This House on Fire **11**:1491-92, 1494, 1495, 1496, 1500
Sophie's Choice **11**:1489, 1493, 1494-95, 1496, 1500-1502
themes and issues **11**:1489, 1492, 1494-95, 1497-98, 1500
"This Quiet Dust" **11**:1504
This Quiet Dust **11**:1500, 1503-4
Tidewater Morning, A: Three Tales from Youth **11**:1493, 1500
violence portrayal **11**:1495, 1499
Swedenborg, Emanuel **4**:556
Swinburne, Algernon Charles **4**:525, **7**:897, **10**:1338
Synge, John Millington **4**:542, **9**:1167

Tan, Amy **11**:**1505-18**
background and life **11**:1506-9

Bildungsroman and **11**:1516
children's books **11**:1508, 1509, 1510, 1514, 1517
Chinese American issues and **11**:1510, 1511
Chinese Siamese Cat, The **11**:1508, 1509, 1514, 1517
Chinese "talk-story" elements **11**:1510, 1512
complex narrative patterns **11**:1510
critical commentary on **11**:1505, 1508, 1517
"Endgame" **11**:1507, 1508
essays **11**:1508, 1510
feng shui and **11**:1508, 1514, 1515, 1517
highlights in life **11**:1507
Hundred Secret Senses, The **11**:1508, 1509, 1511, *1512*, 1514, 1517
influences on **11**:1507, 1512, 1514
Joy Luck Club, The (novel) **11**:1505, 1507, 1508, 1509, 1511, 1512, 1513-15, 1517, 1518
Joy Luck Club, The (screenplay; with Bass) **11**:*1506*, 1508, 1509, 1510, *1513*
Kitchen God's Wife, The **11**:1508, 1509, 1511-12, 1514, 1515-16
"Language of Discretion, The" **11**:1514
major works **11**:1513-16
Moon Lady, The **11**:1508, 1509, 1514, 1517-18
"Moon Lady, The" **11**:1517-18
"Red Candle, The" **11**:1514
"Rules of the Game" **11**:1507
themes and issues **11**:1510-12, 1513-14, 1515-16, 1517, 1518
"What the Library Means to Me" **11**:1507
Tarantino, Quentin **7**:934
Tarkington, Booth **4**:525
Tennyson, Alfred Lord **4**:569, **10**:1338
Terence **12**:1650
Terkel, Studs **11**:**1519-40**
Amazing Grace **11**:1521
American Dreams: Lost and Found **11**:1522, 1523, 1524, 1528, 1532, *1533*, 1534
as radio broadcaster **11**:1520, 1521, 1523, 1524, 1525, 1527

awards and honors **11**:1521, 1522, 1523, 1524-25, 1538
background and life **11**:1520-23
Chicago **11**:1522, 1523
Coming of Age: The Story of Our Century by Those Who've Lived It **11**:1522, 1523, 1537-38
critical commentary on **11**:1522, 1525, 1536, 1538
Division Street: America **11**:1521, 1522, 1523, 1524, 1531, 1538, 1539
Giants of Jazz **11**:1521, 1522, 1523, 1524, 1539
"Good War, The": An Oral History of World War II **11**:1522, 1523, 1524, 1528, 1532, 1538, 1539
Great Divide, The: Second Thoughts on the American Dream **11**:1522, 1523, 1526, 1532, 1534
Hard Times: An Oral History of the Great Depression in America **11**:1522, 1523, 1524, 1525, 1528, 1532, 1534-36, 1538
highlights in life **11**:1523
influences on **11**:1531
journalism experience **11**:1520
major works **11**:532-37
methodology **11**:1525-26, 1528, 1534, 1536
"Miss U.S.A." **11**:1532
My American Century **11**:1522, 1538
"Overture" **11**:1528
"Personal Memoir (and parenthetical comment), A" **11**:1534
"Prologue: Morning, Noon, and Night" **11**:1528
Race: How Blacks and Whites Think and Feel About the American Obsession **11**:1522, 1523, 1526, 1534, 1539
Spectator, The: Talk About Movies and Plays with Those Who Make Them **11**:1522, 1523, 1527-28, 1530
Talking to Myself: A Memoir of My Times **11**:1522, 1523, 1528
themes and issues **11**:1524-25, 1527, 1532, 1534, 1536
Working: People Talk About What They Do All Day and How They Feel About What They Do **11**:1522, 1523, 1524, 1527, 1536-37

Thackeray, William Makepeace **2**:150, **10**:1378
Thomas, Dylan **12**:1700
Thompson, Lawrance **4**:563, 567
Thoreau, Henry David **3**:312, **6**:852
Tjader, Marguerite **3**:381
Tolstoy, Leo **6**:764, **10**:1399, 1406
Toomer, Jean **2**:181, **11**:1569
Trilling, Lionel **4**:559, 561
Turgenev, Ivan **5**:588, 593, **6**:764
Twain, Mark **10**:1352, **11**:1494
    as Anderson influence **1**:42, 49
    as Ellison influence **4**:470
    as Malamud influence **7**:916
    Foote and **4**:540
    Masters study of **7**:950
    Portis compared with **9**:1248
    Wright and **12**:1702, 1717
Tyler, Anne **11**:1541-60
    Accidental Tourist, The **11**:1541, 1545, 1546, 1548, 1550, 1551, 1552, *1553*
    awards and honors **11**:1541, 1543, 1544, 1545, 1546, 1555
    background and life **11**:1542-46
    Breathing Lessons **11**:1541, 1545, 1546, 1551, 1554-55
    "Bridge, The" **11**:1543
    Celestial Navigation **11**:1544, 1549, 1551, 1557-58
    characterizations **11**:1541, 1548, 1549
    Clock Winder, The **11**:1544, 1548, 1550, 1551
    critical commentary on **11**:1544, 1545, 1547, 1549, 1551, 1555, 1557
    Dinner at the Homesick Restaurant **11**:1541, 1545, 1546, 1551, 1555-57
    Earthly Possessions **11**:1548, 1549, 1551, 1558
    family relations focus **11**:1541, 1547-48, 1549, 1550, 1551, 1552, 1554, 1555, 1556-57, 1558, 1560
    film adaptations **11**:1545
    highlights in life **11**:1546
    If Morning Ever Comes **11**:1543, 1546, 1551
    "I Never Saw Morning" **11**:1543
    influences on **11**:1549
    Ladder of Years **11**:1545, 1548, 1551
    "Laura" **11**:1543

    "Lights on the River, The" **11**:1543
    literary legacy **11**:1551
    major works **11**:1552-57
    Morgan's Passing **11**:1545, 1548, 1551
    "Pantaleo" **11**:1545
    Patchwork Planet, A **11**:1545, 1546, 1551, 1558-59
    Saint Maybe **11**:1545, 1551
    "Saints in Caesar's Household, The" **11**:1543
    Searching for Caleb **11**:1544, 1551, 1559-60
    Slipping-Down Life, A **11**:1544, 1551
    themes and issues **11**:1543, 1547-48, 1549, 1552, 1554, 1555
    Tin Can Tree, The **11**:1543, 1546, 1551
    tragicomic vision **11**:1550-51, 1552
    Tumble Tower (Modarressi illus.) **11**:1545, 1546, 1551
    "Winter Birds, Winter Apples" **11**:1543
Tynan, Kenneth **11**:1530

Untermeyer, Louis **4**:558, 565
Updike, John **8**:1143, **11**:1544

Van Doren, Mark **7**:901
Van Vechten, Carl **2**:193, **10**:1429
Vergil. *See* Virgil
Verlaine, Paul **4**:525
Verne, Jules
    as Anderson influence **1**:49
    as Cummings influence **3**:313
Vidal, Gore **6**:810, **12**:1664
Virgil **2**:204, **8**:1097
Vonnegut, Kurt **6**:765, 770

Walker, Alice **11**:1561-82
    Alice Walker Banned **11**:1575
    "Am I Blue?" **11**:1580
    Anything We Love Can Be Saved: A Writer's Activism **11**:1565, 1566, 1567, 1575
    as environmentalist **11**:1567, 1577
    as Hurston popularizer **11**:1564, 1566, 1569, 1575
    awards and honors **11**:1561, 1565, 1566
    background and life **11**:1562-66
    By the Light of My Father's Smile **11**:1575

    campaign against female genital mutilation **11**:1566, 1567, 1581, 1582
    "Child Who Favored Daughter, The" **11**:1579
    Color Purple, The **11**:1561, 1564-65, 1566, 1568, 1570-76, 1581
    Complete Stories, The **11**:1565, 1575
    critical commentary on **11**:1564, 1572-73, 1575
    essays and articles **11**:1561, 1567, 1579
    "Everyday Use" **11**:1579
    "Father" **11**:1580
    film adaptation **11**:1570-73
    Finding the Green Stone **11**:1575
    Good Night, Willie Lee, I'll See You in the Morning: Poems **11**:1575, 1576-77
    Her Blue Body Everything We Know: Earthling Poems, 1965-1990 **11**:1565, 1575, 1576-77
    highlights in life **11**:1566
    Horses Make a Landscape Look More Beautiful **11**:1575, 1576, 1577
    Hurston and **6**:745, 749, 751, 756
    I Love Myself When I Am Laughing…and Then Again When I Am Looking Mean and Impressive: A Zora Neale Hurston Reader (ed.) **6**:755, **11**:1564, 1566, 1575
    influences on **11**:1569
    In Love and Trouble: Stories of Black Women **11**:1564, 1575, 1577-79
    In Search of Our Mothers' Gardens: Womanist Prose **11**:1575
    Langston Hughes: American Poet **11**:1564, 1575
    Living by the Word: Selected Writings, 1973-1987 **11**:1575, 1579-80
    major works **11**:1574-79
    Meridian **11**:1564, 1568, 1575, 1581
    Once: Poems **11**:1563, 1566, 1575, 1576
    Possessing the Secret of Joy **11**:1565, 1566, 1575, 1581-82
    racism and **11**:1561, 1567, 1574, 1578, 1579

"Really, Doesn't Crime Pay?"
11:1579
"Revenge of Hannah Kemhuff,
The" 11:1579
*Revolutionary Petunias and Other
Poems* 11:1564, 1575, 1576
Rich and 9:1277, 1286
"Roselily" 11:1579
*Same River Twice, The: Honoring
the Difficult* 11:1572, 1575
"Strong Horse Tea" 11:1579
Temple of My Familiar, The
11:1575
themes and issues 11:1561,
1566, 1567-68, 1573, 1574,
1576, 1577-79, 1581
Third Life of Grange Copeland, The
11:1564, 1566, 1575
To Hell with Dying (children's
book) 11:1575
"To Hell with Dying" (short
story) 11:1579
*Warrior Marks: Female Genital
Mutilation and the Sexual
Blinding of Women* (nonfiction)
11:1565, 1575
Warrior Marks (screenplay)
11:1566, 1575
*Way Forward Is with a Broken
Heart, The* 11:1569, 1575
"We Have a Beautiful Mother:
Previously Uncollected
Poems" 11:1576
womanist works 11:1561, 1567,
1572, 1575
*You Can't Keep a Good Woman
Down: Short Stories* 11:1575
Walker, Margaret 5:630, 635, 642
Wallsten, Robert 11:1454
Ward, Artemus 6:734
Warren, Robert Penn 12:1591, 1608
Warshawsky, Isaac. *See* Singer, Isaac
Bashevis
Washington, Booker T.
as Dunbar influence 3:404, 405,
409, 411, 413
Bontemps and 2:188
statue of 6:750
Wegener, Frederick 12:1622
Weininger, Otto 10:1399, 1408
Wells, H. G. 4:525, 6:847, 852
Wells, Ida B., Dunbar and 3:399
Welty, Eudora 7:975, 11:1495,
1512, **12:1589-1610**
as Capote influence 2:241
as Foote influence 4:548

as Munro influence 8:1077
as photographer 12:1590, 1591,
1596, 1598, 1606
as Tyler influence 11:1549
autobiography 12:1597-1600
awards and honors 12:1589,
1591, 1592, 1593, 1597, 1608
background and life 12:1590-93
"Blind Weaver" (photograph) 12:*1606*
*Bride of the Innisfallen and Other
Stories, The* 12:1596
characterizations 12:1589, 1591,
1602
*Collected Stories of Eudora Welty,
The* 12:1596
critical commentary on 12:1597,
1598
*Curtain of Green and Other Stories,
A* 12:1591, 1593, 1596
"Death of a Traveling Salesman"
12:1591, 1593, 1607
Delta Wedding 12:1592, 1593,
1596
Eudora Welty: Photographs
12:1596
Eudora Welty, Other Places
12:1596
*Eye of the Story, The: Selected Essays
and Reviews* 12:1589, 1596
family relations portrayals
12:1589, 1595, 1603, 1604
fascination with paradoxes
12:1598, 1603
Golden Apples, The 12:1596,
1601-2, 1606
highlights in life 12:1593
In Black and White 12:1596
influence of 2:241, 4:458,
8:1077, 11:1549
influences on 12:1606
"June Recital" 12:1601, 1602
"Livvie" 12:1592
Losing Battles 12:1592, 1593,
1596, 1598, 1602-4, 1606
major works 12:1601-7
*Miracles of Perception: The Art of
Willa Cather* (with Knopf and
Menuhin) 12:1596
"Moon Lake" 12:1601
Music from Spain (nonfiction)
12:1596
"Music from Spain" (short story)
12:1601
*One Time, One Place: Mississippi in
the Depression, a Snapshot
Album* 12:1596

One Writer's Beginnings 12:1590,
1592, 1593, 1596, 1597-
1600, 1602
Optimist's Daughter, The 12:1592,
1593, 1596, 1598, 1604,
1605, 1606, 1607
oral storytelling tradition
12:1594-95, 1597, 1598,
1600, 1606
Pageant of Birds, A 12:1596
"Petrified Man" 12:1591, 1608,
1609
"Piece of News, A" 12:1591
Place in Fiction 12:1596
Ponder Heart, The 12:1592, 1593,
1596
Porter as mentor 12:1591, 1593
*Reading and Writing of Short
Stories, The* 12:1596
Robber Bridegroom, The 12:1592,
1593, 1594, 1596
Selected Stories of Eudora Welty
12:1596
Shoe Bird, The 12:1596
Short Stories 12:1596
"Shower of Gold" 12:1601
"Sir Rabbit" 12:1601
southern settings 12:1589, 1595
themes and issues 12:1595-96,
1597, 1598, 1601, 1602,
1604, 1606, 1607
Three Papers on Fiction 12:1596
"Wanderers, The" 12:1601
"Whole World Knows, The"
12:1601
"Why I Live at the P.O." 12:1608
"Wide Net, The" 12:1592
Wide Net and Other Stories, The
12:1596
"Worn Path, A" 12:1592, 1608
*Writer's Eye, A: Collected Book
Reviews* (ed McHaney)
12:1596
Wemyss, Jean Margaret. *See*
Laurence, Margaret
Wharton, Edith **12:1611-28**
Age of Innocence, The 12:1611,
1615, 1616, 1618, 1619,
1620, 1621-23
Artemis to Actaeon 12:1622
awards and honors 12:1611,
1615, 1616
background and life 12:1612-16
Backward Glance, A 12:1615,
1622
Buccaneers, The 12:1615, 1622

Certain People **12**:1622
Children, The **12**:1620, 1622
Collected Short Stories of Edith Wharton, The **12**:1622
critical commentary on **12**:1611, 1620, 1621
Crucial Instances **12**:1614, 1622
Cruise of the Vanadis, The **12**:1622
Custom of the Country, The **12**:1622
Decoration of Houses, The (with Codman) **12**:1614, 1615, 1622
Descent of Man, The **12**:1622
Ethan Frome **12**:1618, 1619, 1622, 1623-24, 1628
Fast and Loose **12**:1613, 1615, 1622
Fighting France from Dunkerque to Belfort **12**:1622
film adaptation **12**:1617, 1619, 1620
French Ways and Their Meanings **12**:1622
Fruit of the Tree, The **12**:1622
Ghosts **12**:1622
Glimpses of the Moon, The **12**:1620, 1622
Gods Arrive, The **12**:1622
Greater Inclination, The **12**:1614, 1615, 1622
Here and Beyond **12**:1622
Hermit and the Wild Woman, The **12**:1622
highlights in life **12**:1615
House of Mirth, The **12**:1611, 1614, 1615, 1616, 1617, 1618, 1619, 1622-23, 1625-26
Hudson River Bracketed **12**:1622
Human Nature **12**:1622
influences on **12**:1614, 1615, 1616, 1620, 1626, 1628
In Morocco **12**:1622
Italian Backgrounds **12**:1622
Italian Villas and Their Gardens **12**:1622
James friendship **12**:1614, 1615, 1616, 1620, 1626, 1628
Letters of Edith Wharton, The **12**:1622
literary legacy **12**:1619-20
Madame de Treymes **12**:1618, 1622
major works **12**:1621-26
Marne, The **12**:1622
Mother's Recompense, The **12**:1622

Motor-Flight Through France, A **12**:1622
"Mrs. Manstey's View" **12**:1614, 1615
narrative technique **12**:1624
New York high society portrayals **12**:1611, 1614, 1615, 1617, 1619, 1621, 1622, 1625, 1626
nonfiction **12**:1619
Old New York **12**:1622
position in New York society **12**:1612, 1613
Reef, The **12**:1618, 1622, 1626-28
Sanctuary **12**:1622
social class representations **12**:1618, 1625, 1626
Son at the Front, A **12**:1622
stage adaptations **12**:1619
Summer **12**:1622, 1628
Tales of Men and Ghosts **12**:1622
themes and issues **12**:1611, 1618-19, 1621, 1622-23, 1625
Touchstone, The **12**:1614, 1622
Twelve Poems **12**:1622
Twilight Sleep **12**:1620, 1622
Uncollected Critical Writings, The (ed Wegener) **12**:1622
Valley of Decision, The **12**:1614, 1615, 1622
Verses **12**:1613, 1615, 1622
World Over, The **12**:1622
Writing of Fiction, The **12**:1622
Xingu and Other Stories **12**:1622
White, William Allen **4**:502, 503
Whitman, Walt **4**:564, **10**:1340, **12**:1676, 1682, 1683, 1684, 1689, 1691
as Anderson influence **1**:45, 49, 56
as Bontemps influence **2**:185
as Hughes influence **6**:725, 731, 738, 742
as Piercy influence **9**:1202
as Rich influence **9**:1293
as Sandburg influence **10**:1331, 1332, 1338, 1339
chalk sketch of **6**:*731*
Cummings and **3**:317, 318
Masters study of **7**:949, 950, 960
Whittier, John Greenleaf **3**:313
Wiesel, Elie **11**:1495
Wilbur, Richard **4**:563, **7**:896
Wilde, Oscar **4**:535
Wilder, Thornton **12**:1629-50
Alcestiad, The. See Life in the Sun, A

American Characteristics and Other Essays **12**:1647
Angel That Troubled the Waters and Other Plays, The **12**:1637, 1647
as Benét influence **2**:154
as Knowles influence **6**:810
as theatrical innovator **12**:1629, 1635, 1637, 1638, 1649
awards and honors **12**:1629, 1631, 1632, 1633, 1634, 1636
background and life **12**:1630-34
Bridge of San Luis Rey, The **12**:1629, 1631, 1634, 1636, 1637, 1643-44, 1647
Cabala, The **12**:1631, 1634, 1635, 1636, 1647
Childhood **12**:1647
critical commentary on **12**:1629, 1631, 1635, 1646-47
Doll's House, A (Ibsen; adaptation by Wilder) **12**:1632, 1647
Drunken Sisters, The **12**:1647
Eighth Day, The **12**:1633, 1634, 1647, 1648-49
essays of **12**:1647
film adaptations **12**:1631
Happy Journey to Trenton and Camden, The **12**:1647
Heaven's My Destination **12**:1631, 1647
highlights in life **12**:1634
Ides of March, The **12**:1647
Infancy **12**:1647
influence of **2**:154, **6**:810
influences on **12**:1629, 1635, 1637, 1638, 1644
Intent of the Artist, The **12**:1647
Journals of Thornton Wilder, 1939-1961, The **12**:1647
Life in the Sun, A **12**:1632, 1634, 1647
Long Christmas Dinner, The (opera libretto) **12**:1632, 1634, 1647
Long Christmas Dinner, The (play) **12**:1638
Long Christmas Dinner and Other Plays in One Act, The **12**:1631, 1647
Love and How to Cure It **12**:1647
Lucrece (Obey; adaptation by Wilder) **12**:1631, 1647
major works **12**:1631-47
Matchmaker, The (Nestroy; adaptation by Wilder) **12**:1629, 1632, 1634, 1638, 1647, 1649

Merchant of Yonkers, The. See Matchmaker, The
minimalist staging **12**:1638
modernism's importance to **12**:1629, 1635, 1637, 1638, 1644
optimism of **12**:1629, 1633, 1636, 1637
Our Town (play) **12**:1629, 1632, 1634, *1636*, 1637, 1638, 1639, 1641, *1642*, 1644-45, 1646, 1647, 1648, 1649, 1650
Our Town (screenplay with Craven and Chantlee) **12**:1631, 1647
"Perhaps an Accident" **12**:1644
"Perhaps an Intention" **12**:1644
philosophical speculation **12**:1649
plagiarism charge against **12**:1632, 1646-47
Plays for Bleecker Street **12**:1634, 1647
Pullman Car Hiawatha **12**:1647
Queens of France **12**:1647
Shadow of a Doubt (with Benson and Revelle) **12**:1632, 1634, 1639, *1640*, 1641, 1647, 1650
Skin of Our Teeth, The **12**:1629, 1632, 1634, 1637, 1639, 1641, 1646-47, 1649, 1650
Someone from Assisi **12**:1647
Such Things Only Happen in Books **12**:1647
themes and issues **12**:1629, 1635, 1636, 1637, 1643, 1644, 1645, 1646, 1649-50
Theophilus North **12**:1633, 1634, 1647
Trumpet Shall Sound, The **12**:1630, 1631, 1634, 1647
Victors, The (Sartre; transl. Wilder) **12**:1647
Woman of Andros, The **12**:1631, 1636, 1647, 1649-50
Williams, Tennessee **4**:542, **12:1651-74**
American Blues: Five Short Plays **12**:1664
Androgyne, Mon Amour **12**:1664
"Angel in the Alcove, The" **12**:1655
as Foote influence **4**:548
as Mamet influence **7**:937
as Zindel influence **12**:1717, 1720
awards and honors **12**:1651, 1652-53, 1654

Baby Doll (screenplay) **12**:1663, 1664
background and life **12**:1652-55
Battle of Angels **12**:1653, 1654, 1664
Camino Real **12**:1653, 1664
Candles to the Sun **12**:1652
Cat on a Hot Tin Roof **12**:1653, 1654, 1657, 1664, 1669-70
Clothes for a Summer Hotel **12**:1655, 1664
Collected Stories **12**:1664
Confessional **12**:1664
critical commentary on **12**:1655, 1659, 1670
"Desire and the Black Masseur" **12**:1655
Dragon Country **12**:1664
Eccentricities of a Nightingale, The **12**:1664
Eight Mortal Ladies Possessed: A Book of Stories **12**:1664
Enemy, The: Time **12**:1664
essays **12**:1162, 1660
female characters **12**:1656, 1658, 1668
film adaptations **12**:1663, *1667*
Fugitive Kind, The (screenplay with Roberts) **12**:1663, 1664
"Gentleman Caller, The." See *Glass Menagerie, The*
Glass Menagerie, The (play) **12**:1651, 1653, 1654, 1656, 1658, 1659, *1661*, 1662, 1663-64, *1665*, 1666
Glass Menagerie, The (screenplay with Berneis) **12**:1653, 1663, 1664
Hard Candy: A Book of Stories **12**:1664
highlights in life **12**:1655
House Not Meant to Stand, A **12**:1664
influence of **7**:937, **12**:1717, 1720
influences on **12**:1658
In the Bar of a Tokyo Hotel **12**:1655, 1664
In the Winter of Cities **12**:1664
I Rise in Flame, Cried the Phoenix **12**:1658, 1664
Kingdom of Earth. See Seven Descents of Myrtle, The
Knightly Quest, The: A Novella and Four Short Stories **12**:1664
Lady of Larkspur Lotion, The **12**:1664

Long Stay Cut Short, The: Or, The Unsatisfactory Supper **12**:1664
Lovely Sunday for Creve Coeur, A **12**:1664
major works **12**:1663-70
McCullers and **7**:975, 978, 979, 991
Memoirs **12**:1654, 1655, 1659-60, 1664
Milk Train Doesn't Stop Here Anymore, The **12**:1655, 1664
Moise and the World of Reason **12**:1655, 1664
"Mutilated, The" **12**:1657
Night of the Iguana, The (play) **12**:1653, 1654, 1657, 1659, 1664, 1673
"Night of the Iguana, The" (short story) **12**:1655
"One Arm" **12**:1655
One Arm and Other Stories **12**:1664
Orpheus Descending **12**:1664
Out Cry **12**:1655, 1664
Period of Adjustment **12**:1664
"Poem for Paul" **12**:1657
"Portrait of a Girl in Glass" **12**:1655
"Production Notes to *The Glass Menagerie*" **12**:1662
Red Devil Battery Sign, The **12**:1655, 1664
Roman Spring of Mrs. Stone, The **12**:1653, 1664
Rose Tattoo, The (play) **12**:1653, 1654, 1664, 1672
Rose Tattoo, The (screenplay with Kanter) **12**:1653, 1663, 1664
Seven Descents of Myrtle, The **12**:1655, 1664
Slapstick Tragedy: The Mutilated and the Gnädiges Fraulein **12**:1664
Small Craft Warnings **12**:1654, 1655, 1659, 1664
Steps Must Be Gentle **12**:1658, 1664
Stopped Rocking and Other Screenplays **12**:1664
Streetcar Named Desire, A (play) **12**:1651, 1653, 1654, 1655, 1656, 1657, 1664, 1666, *1667*, 1668-69
Streetcar Named Desire, A (screenplay with Saul) **12**:1653, 1655, 1663, 1664
Suddenly Last Summer **12**:1653, 1664

Suddenly Last Summer (screenplay with Vidal) **12**:1663, 1664
Summer and Smoke **12**:1653, 1656, 1664, 1671-72
Sweet Bird of Youth **12**:1653, 1664, 1672-73
symbolism use **12**:1651, 1656, 1662, 1668, *1671*, 1672, 1673
"Tennessee Williams Presents His POV" **12**:1662
Terkel interview of **11**:1528
Theatre of Tennessee Willliams, The **12**:1664
themes and issues **12**:1656-57, 1660, 1663-64, 1666, 1668, 1669, 1670, 1672
"Three Players of a Summer Game" **12**:1655
Twenty-seven Wagons Full of Cotton and Other Plays **12**:1664
Two-Character Play, The **12**:1664
"Vengeance of Nitocris, The" **12**:1652, 1654
Vieux Carré **12**:1664
Where I Live: Selected Essays **12**:1660, 1662, 1664
You Touched Me (with Windham) **12**:1658, 1664
Williams, William Carlos **10**:1340, **12**:1675-92
Adam and Eve and the City **12**:1686
Al Que Quiere! **12**:1681, 1686
Alvarez and **1**:31
as Imagist poet **12**:1675, 1677, 1682, 1684
as modernist **12**:1680, 1682
"Asphodel, That Greeny Flower" **12**:1679
Autobiography of William Carlos Williams, The **12**:1686
awards and honors **12**:1678, 1679
background and life **12**:1676-79
"Ballad of Faith" **12**:1682
"Bird Song" **12**:1682
Broken Span, The **12**:1686
Build-up, The **12**:1686, 1692
Clouds, The **12**:1686
Collected Earlier Poems **12**:1686
Collected Later Poems **12**:1686
Collected Poems, 1921-1931 **12**:1686
Collected Poems of William Carlos Williams, The: Volume 1, 1909-1939 **12**:1686

Collected Poems of William Carlos Williams, The: Volume 2, 1939-1962 **12**:1686
Complete Collected Poems of William Carlos Williams, 1906-1938, The **12**:1686
critical commentary on **12**:1679, 1683, 1684, 1685, 1687, 1689, 1691
Cummings and **3**:318
"Descent, The" **12**:1683
Desert Music and Other Poems, The **12**:1686
Doctor Stories, The **12**:1686
Dream of Love, A **12**:1678, 1679, 1686
Early Martyr and Other Poems, An **12**:1686
Embodiment of Knowledge, The **12**:1686
essays **12**:1677, 1686, 1690
Farmers' Daughters, The: The Collected Stories of William Carlos Williams **12**:1686
Great American Novel, The **12**:1686
highlights in life **12**:1679
influence on later poets **12**:1675, 1678, 1680, 1682, 1683
influences on **12**:1675, 1676, 1677, 1679, 1681, 1682-83, 1684, 1686, 1687, 1689, 1690, 1691
In the American Grain **12**:1685, 1686, 1690-91
In the Money **12**:1686, 1692
I Wanted to Write a Poem **12**:1686
Journey to Love **12**:1679, 1686
Knife of the Times and Other Stories, The **12**:1686
Kora in Hell: Improvisations **12**:1686
Life Along the Passaic River **12**:1686
major works **12**:1679-90
Make Light of It: Collected Stories **12**:1678, 1686
Many Loves and Other Plays **12**:1686
medical practice of **12**:1675, 1677, 1678, 1680
Moore and **8**:1034, 1035, 1038, 1039, **18**:1040
Novelette and Other Prose, A **12**:1686
"Ol' Bunk's Band" **12**:1682

Paterson **3**:318, **12**:1684, 1685-90
Pictures from Brueghel and Other Poems **12**:1679, 1686
Poems **12**:1677, 1686
poetic innovations **12**:1683
Pound/Williams: Selected Letters of Ezra Pound and William Carlos Williams (Witmeyer ed.) **12**:1686
Recognizable Image, A **12**:1686
"Red Wheelbarrow, The" **12**:1681
"Rumba! Rumba!" **12**:1682
Selected Letters of William Carlos Williams, The **12**:1686
Selected Poems **12**:1686
"Some Simple Measures in the American Idiom" **12**:1683
"Song (Beauty Is a Shell)" **12**:1682
"Song (Pluck the Florets)" **12**:1682
"Song (Russia! Russia!)" **12**:1682
"Sort of a Song, A" **12**:1682
Sour Grapes **12**:1686
Spring and All **12**:1686, 1691
Stein and **10**:1429, 1430
symbolism use **12**:1680-81
Tempers, The **12**:1677, 1679, 1686
themes and issues **12**:1677, 1685-87, 1691
"Use of Force, The" **12**:1678
Voyage to Pagany, A **12**:1686
Wedge, The **12**:1686
White Mule **12**:1686, 1691-92
William Carlos Williams and James Laughlin: Selected Letters **12**:1686
William Carlos Williams, John Sanford: A Corrspondence **12**:1686
Wills, Garry **11**:1528
Wilson, August **11**:1527
Wilson, Edmund **7**:978
Fitzgerald and **4**:517, 524, 531, 532, 537
on Cather **2**:272
Windham, Donald **12**:1658, 1664
Witmeyer, Hugh **12**:1686
Wofford, Chloe Anthony. *See* Morrison, Toni
Wolfe, Thomas (novelist) **3**:294, 300, **11**:1495
Wolfe, Tom (journalist), Portis mentored by **9**:1247, 1252
Wolff, Cynthia Griffin **12**:1624

(Woman) Writer: Occasions and
    Opportunities (Oates) **8**:1111
Woolf, Virginia **8**:1045, **9**:1188,
    10:1434
    as Morrison influence **8**:1051,
        1057, 1058
Woollcott, Alexander **4**:*502*
Wordsworth, William **4**:569
Wright, Richard **5**:644, **6**:752,
    12:1693-1710
    American Hunger **12**:1701, 1703
    as Brooks influence **2**:197
    as Ellison influence **4**:461, 462,
        463, 464, 473
    awards and honors **12**:1695,
        1697, 1705-6
    background and life **12**:1694-97
    Baldwin and **1**:105
    "Big Boy Leaves Home" **12**:1698,
        1706, 1707
    Black Boy **12**:1693, 1694, 1695,
        1697, 1698, 1700, 1701-4,
        1706
    *Black Boy (American Hunger): A
        Record of Childhood and Youth*
        12:1701
    *Black Power: A Record of Reactions
        in a Land of Pathos* **12**:1697,
        1703
    "Bright and Morning Star"
        12:1706, 1707
    *Color Curtain, The: A Report on the
        Bandung Conference* **12**:1697,
        1703
    critical commentary on **12**:1695,
        1697, 1698, 1699, 1703,
        1704, 1706, 1707, 1708
    Daddy Goodness (play with Sapin)
        12:1703
    "Decision" **12**:1709
    "Descent" **12**:1709
    "Down by the Riverside"
        12:1699, 1706-7
    "Dread" **12**:1709
    "Dream" **12**:1709
    Dunbar and **3**:410
    Eight Men **12**:1697, 1703, 1707-8
    "Ethics of Living Jim Crow, The"
        12:1706, 1707
    "Fate" **12**:1704
    "Fear" **12**:1704
    "Fire and Cloud" **12**:1699, 1707
    "Flight" **12**:1704
    highlights in life **12**:1697
    "Horror and the Glory, The"
        12:1701, 1703

"I Have Seen Black Hands"
    12:1695
    imagery **12**:1699
    influence of **2**:197, **4**:461, 462,
        463, 464, 473
    influences on **12**:1696, 1700,
        1709
    Lawd Today **12**:1700, 1703
    literary legacy **12**:1699
    "Long Black Song" **12**:1707
    Long Dream, The **12**:1697, 1703
    major works **12**:1701-7
    "Man Who Lived Underground,
        The" **12**:1699, 1707, 1708
    "Man Who Was Almost a Man,
        The" **12**:1698, 1707
    McCullers and **7**:977, 985, 987,
        988
    Morrison and **8**:1053, 1055
    *Native Son; The Biography of a
        Young American* (play with
        Green) **12**:1695, 1703, 1705
    Native Son (novel) **1**:67, 105,
        3:410, **8**:1053, **12**:1693,
        1695, 1697, 1698, 1703,
        1704-5, 1707, 1708, 1709
    Native Son (screenplay) **12**:1696,
        1697, 1703, 1705
    Outsider, The **12**:1696, 1697,
        1703, 1708-9
    Pagan Spain **12**:1697, 1703
    Rite of Passage **12**:1703
    Savage Holiday **12**:1697, 1703
    "Southern Nights" **12**:1701,
        1702
    themes and issues **12**:1698,
        1701-2, 1703, 1704, 1705-6,
        1709
    Twelve Million Black Voices
        12:1695, 1699, 1703
    Uncle Tom's Children **12**:1693,
        1695, 1697, 1698, 1699,
        1703, 1704, 1705-7
    White Man, Listen! **12**:1697,
        1700, 1703

Yeats, William Butler **4**:567, **8**:1045,
    9:1167, **12**:1601
    as Didion influence **3**:366
    as Eliot influence **4**:440
Yen, James **2**:218
Young, Philip **5**:670, 680

Zimmerman, Robert Allen. *See*
    Dylan, Bob
Zindel, Paul **12**:1711-26

Alice in Wonderland (teleplay)
    12:1717, *1718*, 1722
*Amazing and Death-Defying Diary
    of Eugene Dingman, The*
    12:1722
Amulets Against the Dragon Forces
    12:1722
And Miss Reardon Drinks a Little
    12:1714, 1722
Attack of the Killer Fishsticks
    12:1715, 1722
awards and honors **12**:1711,
    1713, 1714, 1720, 1721, 1724
Babes in Toyland (teleplay)
    12:1717, 1722
background and life **12**:1712-14
Begonia for Miss Applebaum, A
    12:1722
City Safari **12**:1715, 1722
Confessions of a Teenage Baboon
    12:1722
*Connecticut Yankee in King Arthur's
    Court, A* (teleplay) **12**:1717,
    1722
critical commentary on **12**:1714,
    1715, 1717
David and Della **12**:1715, 1722
Destiny with Half Moon Street, A
    12:1722
Dimensions of Peacocks **12**:1713,
    1722
Doom Stone, The **12**:1722
Dream of Swallows, A **12**:1722
*Effect of Gamma Rays on Man-in-
    the-Moon Marigolds, The*
    12:1711, 1713, 1714, 1715,
    1719-21, 1722
Euthanasia and the Endless Hearts
    12:1722
*Every Seventeen Minutes the Crowd
    Goes Crazy!* **12**:1722
Fifth Grade Safari **12**:1722
Fright Party **12**:1715, 1722
Girl Who Wanted a Boy, The
    12:1722
*Harry and Hortense at Hormone
    High* **12**:1722, 1724-25
highlights in life **12**:1721
I Love My Mother **12**:1722
I Never Loved Your Mind **12**:1722
influences on **12**:1713, 1717,
    1720
Ladies at the Alamo **12**:1722
*Let Me Hear You Whisper and The
    Ladies Should Be in Bed: Two
    Plays* **12**:1717, 1722

Let Me Hear You Whisper (teleplay) **12**:1717, 1722
literary legacy **12**:1717-18
Loch **12**:1715, 1722
major works **12**:1719-24
Mame (screenplay) **12**:1717, 1722
Maria's Lovers (screenplay with Brach and Konchalovsky) **12**:1717, 1722
My Darling, My Hamburger **12**:1714, 1722, 1725
100% Laugh Riot, The **12**:1715, 1722
Pardon Me, You're Stepping on My Eyeball! **12**:1715, 1722

Pigman, The **12**:1711, 1714, 1721-24, 1725
Pigman and Me, The **12**:1722, 1725-26
Pigman's Legacy, The **12**:1722
Raptor **12**:1715, 1722
Rats **12**:1715, 1722
Reef of Death **12**:1722
Runaway Train (screenplay) **12**:1722
Secret Affairs of Mildred Wild, The **12**:1722
Star for the Latecomer, A (with Zindel) **12**:1722
themes and issues **12**:1715, 1717, 1719, 1721

To Take a Dare (with Dragonwagon) **12**:1722
Undertaker's Gone Bananas, The **12**:1722
Up the Sandbox (screenplay) **12**:1717, 1722
When a Darkness Falls **12**:1722
Zola, Emile, as Norris influence **8**:1085, 1088, 1092
Zolotow, Charlotte **12**:1713
Zweig, Stefan **10**:1399

Index of Literary Works

Abe Lincoln Grows Up (Sandburg) **10**:1338

Abraham Lincoln: The Prairie Years (Sandburg) **10**:1326, 1328, 1329, 1336-37, 1338, 1340, 1341, 1350

Abraham Lincoln: The Prairie Years and the War Years (Sandburg) **10**:1336, 1338, 1340, 1341

Abraham Lincoln: The War Years (Sandburg) **10**:1326, 1327, 1328, 1336-37, 1338, 1340, 1341

Abraham Lincoln (Benét; screenplay) **2**:153, 155

Absalom, Absalom! (Faulkner) **4**:478, 481, 482, 483, 486, 495-97

Absentee, The (Edgeworth) **8**:1036, 1037

Absentee, The (Moore dramatization of Edgeworth) **8**:1036, 1037, 1043

Abysmal Brute, The (London) **7**:879

"Acceptance" (Frost) **4**:571

Accidental Tourist, The (Tyler) **11**:1541, 1545, 1546, 1548, 1550, 1551, 1552, *1553*

Acorn-Planter, The (London) **7**:879

"Acquainted with the Night" (Frost) **4**:571

Across Spoon River (Masters) **7**:945, 946, 947, 948, 949, 950, 951, 952, 954, 959

Across the River and into the Trees (Hemingway) **5**:664, 674

Actfive and Other Poems (MacLeish) **7**:896, 901

Acts of King Arthur and His Noble Knights (Steinbeck; Chase ed.) **11**:1454

Actual, The (Bellow) **1**:132, 133, 138

Adam and Eve and the City (W. C. Williams) **12**:1686

"Addict, The" (Sexton) **10**:1376

"Address Before a Joint Session of Congress, February 12, 1959" (Sandburg) **10**:1338

Adolphe Francis Alphonse Bandelier (Schaefer) **10**:1352

Adrienne Rich's Poetry and Prose: Poems, Prose, and Criticism (Rich; Gelpi and Gelpi eds.) **9**:1284

"Adventure" (Anderson) **1**:52

Adventure (London) **7**:879

Adventures in Value (Cummings; photos by Morehouse) **3**:319

Adventures of Augie March, The (Bellow) **1**:125, 126, 132

Aeneid (Virgil) **2**:204, **8**:1097

Affaire Lettuceberg, L' (Steinbeck) **11**:1456

Affectionately Eve (Sinclair) **10**:1392

"African Fragment" (Brooks) **2**:208

African Queen, The (Agee; screenplay) **1**:11, 13, 14, 17

African Queen, The (Forester) **1**:16, 17

"After Apple-Picking" (Frost) **4**:569

"After Dark" (Rich) **9**:1278

After Henry (Didion) **3**:359, 360, 361, 363, 372

Afternoon of an Author: A Selection of Uncollected Stories and Essays (Fitzgerald) **4**:532

After the Fall (Miller) **8**:1016, 1019, 1020, 1025, 1028

After the First Death (Cormier) **3**:296, 299, 301, 307

"Against Cinderella" (Alvarez) **1**:38

Agee on Film: Five Film Scripts (Agee; screenplays) **1**:17

Agee on Film: Reviews and Comments (Agee) **1**:17

Age of Innocence, The (Wharton) **12**:1611, 1615, 1616, 1618, 1619, 1620, 1621-23

Ah, Wilderness! (O'Neill) **9**:1166, 1168

Air Raid: A Verse Play for Radio (MacLeish) **7**:901

Alcestiad, The (Wilder). *See Life in the Sun, A*

Alexander's Bridge (Cather) **2**:274, 278

Algiers Motel Incident, The (Hersey) **5**:687, 690

Alias Grace (Atwood) **1**:84, 89, 90, 91

Alice in Wonderland (Carroll) **12**:1717, *1718*

Alice in Wonderland (Zindel; teleplay) **12**:1717, *1718*, 1722

Alice Walker Banned (Walker) **11**:1575

"All Along the Watchtower" (Dylan) **3**:429-30

All God's Children Need Traveling Shoes (Angelou) **1**:60, 68, 73-74

All God's Chillun Got Wings (O'Neill) **9**:1164, 1168

"All I Gotta Do" (Giovanni) **5**:639

"All in green went my love riding" (Cummings) **3**:329

Alliterative "Morte d'Arthure," "The Owl and the Nightingale," and Five Other Middle English Poems, The (Gardner ed.) **5**:602

All Men Are Brothers (Shih Nai-an; Buck transl.) **2**:212, 213, 218

"All My Pretty Ones" (Sexton) **10**:1369, 1371

All My Pretty Ones (Sexton) **10**:1359, 1361, 1369, *1370*, 1371-72

All My Sons (Miller) **8**:1015, 1016, 1017, 1018, 1019, 1021-22, 1025, 1028

All That Money Can Buy (Benét; screenplay) **2**:153, 155

All the Good People I've Left Behind (Oates) **8**:1111

All the Pretty Horses (McCarthy; novel) **7**:961, 964, 965, 968, 969-70

All the Pretty Horses (McCarthy; screenplay) **7**:965, 970

All the Sad Young Men (Fitzgerald) **4**:532

All Under Heaven (Buck) **2**:218

"Almos' a Man" (Wright). *See* "Man Who Was Almost a Man, The"
Alone in the Wild Forest (Singer) **10**:1411
Aloneness (Brooks) **2**:203
Along the Illinois (Masters) **7**:954
Alpine Christ and Other Poems, The (Jeffers) **6**:790
Al Que Quiere! (W. C. Williams) **12**:1681, 1686
Althea (Masters) **7**:954
Always the Young Strangers (Sandburg) **10**:1338, 1340-41
Amazing and Death-Defying Diary of Eugene Dingman, The (Zindel) **12**:1722
Amazing Grace (Terkel) **11**:1521
"Ambush" (O'Brien) **8**:1132
Amen Corner, The (Baldwin) **1**:104, 105, 110, 111-13
America and Americans (Steinbeck) **11**:1454
America (Benét) **2**:152, 155
America Is Worth Saving (Dreiser) **3**:381
American Appetites (Oates) **8**:1109, 1110, 1111
American Argument: With Eslanda Goode Robeson (Buck) **2**:218
American Beauty (Ferber) **4**:504, 507
American Bestiary, An (Schaefer) **10**:1346, 1352
American Blues: Five Short Plays (T. Williams) **12**:1664
American Buffalo (Mamet; play) **7**:927, 929, 931, 935, 936-39
American Buffalo (Mamet; screen-play) **7**:932, 935
American Cause, The (MacLeish) **7**:901
American Characteristics and Other Essays (Wilder) **12**:1647
American Clock, The (Miller) **8**:1019, 1025
American Diaries, 1902-1926 (Dreiser) **3**:381
American Dreams: Lost and Found (Terkel) **11**:1522, 1523, 1524, 1528, 1532, *1533*, 1534
American Gothic Tales (Oates ed.) **8**:1111
American Hunger (Wright) **12**:1701, 1703
"American Letter" (MacLeish) **7**:902
American Negro Poetry (Bontemps ed.) **2**:187

American Opinion and the War (MacLeish) **7**:901
American Outpost: A Book of Reminiscences (Sinclair) **10**:1381, 1392
American Primitive (Gibson). *See John and Abigail*
American Songbag, The (Sandburg ed.) **10**:1335, 1338, 1341
American Stuff (WPA anthology) **12**:1706
American Tragedy, An (Dreiser) **3**:378, 380, 381, 384, 385-86
American Unity and Asia (Buck) **2**:218
"American Vagabond, An" (Sandburg) **10**:1332
America Was Promises (MacLeish) **7**:901
"AMGOT at Work" (Hersey) **5**:688
"Am I Blue?" (Walker) **11**:1580
Among the Ancestors (Ortiz Cofer) **9**:1191
& (Cummings) **3**:315, 316, 319, 330
Amulets Against the Dragon Forces (Zindel) **12**:1722
And Miss Reardon Drinks a Little (Zindel) **12**:1714, 1722
Andria (Terence) **12**:1650
Androgyne, Mon Amour (T. Williams) **12**:1664
"And So On" (Cormier) **3**:294
And Still I Rise (Angelou) **1**:67, 68
"Anecdote of the Jar" (Stevens) **11**:1480, 1481
Angel Fire (Oates) **8**:1111
"Angel in the Alcove, The" (T. Williams) **12**:1655
"Angel Levine" (Malamud) **7**:924
Angel of Light (Oates) **8**:1111
Angel That Troubled the Waters and Other Plays, The (Wilder) **12**:1637, 1647
Anglican Book of Common Prayer **3**:347
Angry Wife, The (Buck under Sedges pseud.) **2**:218
Animals in the Country, The (Atwood) **1**:90
Animal U. (Davies) **3**:344
Anna Christie (O'Neill) **9**:1159, 1168, 1169-70
Anna Karenina (Tolstoy) **10**:1406
Anna's Pet (Atwood and Barkhouse) **1**:90

"Anne Rutledge" (Masters) **7**:957-58
Anne Sexton: A Self-Portrait in Letters (Sexton) **10**:1371
"Anniad, The" (Brooks) **2**:204, 207
Annie Allen (Brooks) **2**:195, 197, 199, 203, 204-5, 207
Ann Vickers (Lewis) **6**:848, 850, 861
Anonymous Sins (Oates) **8**:1111
Another Country (Baldwin) **1**:104, 105, 110, 120, **11**:1492
"Another of Mike's Girls" (Cormier) **3**:308
Another Pamela: Or, Virtue Still Rewarded (Sinclair) **10**:1392
Another Side of Bob Dylan (Dylan; record album) **3**:425
"Answer, The" (Jeffers) **6**:789
Answered Prayers: The Unfinished Novel (Capote) **2**:237, 238, 241, 242, 245
"Ante-Bellum Sermon, An" (Dunbar) **3**:403, 407, 408
Anthropos: The Future of Art (Cummings) **3**:319
Antonietta (Hersey) **5**:690
"anyone lived in a pretty how town" (Cummings) **3**:326, 327
Anyplace but Here (Bontemps and Conroy) **2**:184, 187
Anything We Love Can Be Saved: A Writer's Activism (Walker) **11**:1565, 1566, 1567, 1575
Appalachian Elders: A Warm Hearth Sampler (Giovanni and Dennison eds.) **5**:635
"Applicant, The" (Plath) **9**:1221
Apprentice Fiction of F. Scott Fitzgerald, The (Fitzgerald) **4**:532
April Twilights (Cather) **2**:278
Arabian Nights **1**:29, **11**:1446
Ara Vos Prec (Eliot) **4**:450
Archbishop's Ceiling, The (Miller) **8**:1019, 1025
"Are You a Doctor?" (Carver) **2**:257
Are You There God? It's Me, Margaret (Blume) **2**:165, 166, 167, 168, 170, 171-73, 180
Ariel (Plath) **9**:1217, 1221-22, 1224, 1225
Arna Bontemps-Langston Hughes Letters, 1925-1967 (Nichols ed.) **2**:187, **6**:737
Arrowsmith (Lewis) **6**:845, 848, 850, 857-58
"Ars Poetica" (MacLeish) **7**:902
Artemis to Actaeon (Wharton) **12**:1622

Arthur Miller and Company (Miller; Bigsby ed.) **8**:1025

"Artificial Nigger, The" (O'Connor) **8**:1148

Art of Blessing the Day, The (Piercy) **9**:1199, 1200, 1202, 1205

"Art of Blessing the Day, The" (Piercy) **9**:1203

Art of Fiction, The: Notes on Craft for Young Writers (Gardner) **5**:602

"Art of Fiction, The" (Ellison) **4**:473

Art of Living and Other Stories, The (Gardner) **5**:598, 599, 602

"Arturo's Flight" (Ortiz Cofer) **9**:1188, 1190

"As Ever, Gene": The Letters of Eugene O'Neill to George Jean Nathan (Roberts and Roberts eds.) **9**:1168

As Ever, Scott Fitzgerald (Fitzgerald) **4**:532

Asher Lev novels (Potok) **9**:1259, 1265, 1266, 1267, 1274

Ash Wednesday (Eliot) **4**:440, 450, 455-56

As I Lay Dying (Faulkner) **4**:478, 481, 486, 490-92, **11**:1494

Ask Your Mama: Or, Twelve Moods for Jazz (Hughes) **6**:737

Aspects of the Presidency: Truman and Ford in Office (Hersey) **5**:690

"Asphodel, That Greeny Flower" (W. C. Williams) **12**:1679

Aspirant, The (Dreiser) **3**:381

Assassination Bureau, Ltd., The (London and Fish) **7**:879

Assassins, The: A Book of Hours (Oates) **8**:1111

Assignation, The (Oates) **8**:1111

Assistant, The (Malamud) **7**:909, 912, 913, 916, 917, 918, 919-20, 922, 923

At Budokan (Dylan; record album) **3**:425

At Home in the World (Maynard) **10**:1304, 1313

Atlas of the Difficult World, An: Poems, 1988-1991 (Rich) **9**:1280, 1284, 1291-92

At My Heart's Core (Davies) **3**:344

At Night the Salmon Move (Carver) **2**:257, 258, 261

"At Sea" (Hemingway) **5**:671

"At Shaft 11" (Dunbar) **3**:413, 415

Attack of the Killer Fishsticks (Zindel) **12**:1715, 1722

"At the Birth of an Age" (Jeffers) **6**:788

At the Gates of the Righteous (Davies) **3**:344

"At Your Age" (Fitzgerald) **4**:518

"Aunt Helen" (Eliot) **4**:451, 453

Auntie Mame (Dennis) **12**:1717

"Aunt Jennifer's Tigers" (Rich) **9**:1282

Aurora (Brooks) **2**:203

Auroras of Autumn, The (Stevens) **11**:1470, 1471, 1475, 1485-86

"Auroras of Autumn, The" (Stevens) **11**:1485

"Author's Note" (Singer) **10**:1413

Autobiography of Alice B. Toklas, The (Stein) **10**:1417, 1421, 1422, 1424, 1425, 1431-32, 1436, 1437

Autobiography of an Ex-Colored Man, The (Johnson) **1**:65, **2**:187

Autobiography of Benjamin Franklin, The **12**:1702

Autobiography of Miss Jane Pittman, The (Gaines) **5**:585, 586, 588, 589, 590-91

Autobiography of Miss Jane Pittman, The (television film) **5**:584, 585, 586, 589

Autobiography of Upton Sinclair, The (Sinclair) **10**:1392

Autobiography of William Carlos Williams, The (W. C. Williams) **12**:1686

"Autumn Refrain" (Stevens) **11**:1482

Available Light (Piercy) **9**:1205, 1209

Awake and Sing (Odets) **8**:1020

"Awakening, An" (Anderson) **1**:53

Awful Rowing Toward God, The (Sexton) **10**:1362, 1365, 1367, 1371, 1372-73, 1375

"Ax-Helve, The" (Frost) **4**:563

Babbitt (Lewis) **6**:843, 845, 848, 850, 854-57, **9**:1178

Babes in Toyland (Herbert; operetta) **12**:1722

Babes in Toyland (Zindel; teleplay) **12**:1717, 1722

"Baboons in the Perennial Bed" (Piercy) **9**:1209

Baby Doll (T. Williams; screenplay) **12**:1663, 1664

Babylon Revisited and Other Stories (Fitzgerald) **4**:532

Baby, the Rain Must Fall (Foote; screenplay) **4**:541, 544, 547

Backcasts: Memories and Recollections of Seventy Years as a Sportsman, Fishing, Hunting, and Other Stories (Knowles) **6**:807, 812

Background of War (MacLeish) **7**:901

Backward Glance (Wharton) **12**:1615, 1622

Bad Girls (Oates; play) **8**:1109, 1116-17

"Bad Girls" (Oates; short story) **8**:1116

"Bad Influence" (Ortiz Cofer) **9**:1186, 1189

"Bad Time for Fathers, A" (Cormier) **3**:308

"Ballad of Faith" (W. C. Williams) **12**:1682

Ballad of the Duke's Mercy, The (Benét) **2**:155

Ballad of the Sad Café, The (McCullers; novella) **7**:977, 979, 981, 982, 984-86, 989

Ballad of the Sad Café, The (Albee adaptation as play) **7**:978, 982

Ballad of the Sad Café, The: The Novels and Stories of Carson McCullers (McCullers) **7**:978, 983

Ballad of the Sad Café and Collected Short Stories, The (McCullers) **7**:983

"Ballad of William Sycamore, 1790-1871, The" (Benét) **2**:151, 160

Ballads and Poems, 1915-1930 (Benét) **2**:155

"Banjo Song, A" (Dunbar) **3**:399, 407

"Barbie Doll" (Piercy) **9**:1206

Bar Mitzvah (Mamet) **7**:935

Barn Burning (Foote; teleplay) **4**:479, 547

Barracoon (Hurston) **6**:752

Basement Tapes, The (Dylan; record album) **3**:419, 425

Basil and Josephine Stories, The (Fitzgerald) **4**:532

Basil Duke Lee stories (Fitzgerald) **4**:517

"Batard" (London) **7**:884

"Bath, The" (Carver) **2**:262-63

Battle of Angels (T. Williams) 12.1653, 12.1654, 12.1664., *See also Orpheus Descending*

"Battle Royal" (Ellison) **4**:469

"Battler, The" (Hemingway) **5**:668, 679

Bean Eaters, The (Brooks) **2**:197-98, 203, 206-7

"Bean Eaters, The" (Brooks) **2**:206

Be Angry at the Sun and Other Poems (Jeffers) **6**:786, 790

"Bear, The" (Faulkner) **4**:479, 481, 496, 497

Beat the Devil (Capote and Huston; screenplay) **2**:235, 238, 242

Beautiful and Damned, The (Fitzgerald) **4**:518, 522, 525, 532, 536

"Beauty I Would Suffer For" (Piercy) **9**:1206

"Beauty Lessons" (Ortiz Cofer) **9**:1190

Because It Is Bitter, and Because It Is My Heart (Oates) **8**:1109, 1111

Becket: Ou, l'Honneur de Dieu (*Becket: Or, The Honor of God*) (Anouilh) **4**:443

Beckonings (Brooks) **2**:203

Bed Book, The (Plath) **9**:1224

"Bed by the Window, The" (Jeffers) **6**:787, 794

"Beekeeper's Daughter, The" (Plath) **9**:1225

Bee Time Vine and Other Pieces, 1913-1927 (Stein) **10**:1424

Before Adam (London) **7**:876, 879

Before the Flood (Dylan; record album) **3**:425

Before the Flowers of Friendship Faded, Friendship Faded (Stein) **10**:1424

Beggar Maid, The: Stories of Flo and Rose (Munro). *See Who Do You Think You Are?* (Munro)

Beginning and the End, The (Jeffers) **6**:790

Beginning of Wisdom, The (Benét) **2**:151, 152, 155

Begonia for Miss Applebaum, A (Zindel) **12**:1722

"Being and Nothingness (to quote a philosopher)" (Giovanni) **5**:639

Bellarosa Connection, The (Bellow) **1**:132, 138-40

Bellefleur (Oates) **8**:1106, 1111

Bell for Adano, A (Hersey) **5**:685, 687, 688, 689, 690, 691-92, 695, 696

Bell Jar, The (Plath) **9**:1213, 1217, 1219, 1222-24, 1227

Bellow Plays, The. See Under the Weather

Beloved (Morrison) **8**:1049, 1052, 1054, 1056, 1057, 1058, 1059-60, 1062, 1063-65, 1068

"Benjamin Reid: Aftermath" (Styron) **11**:1504

Beowulf (epic) **5**:604

Best American Essays, The (Oates ed.) **8**:1111

Best American Short Stories, The (1967 edition) **2**:257, 258

Best American Short Stories of 1979, The (Oates and Ravenel eds.) **8**:1111

"Bestiary U.S.A." (Sexton) **10**:1367

Best of Simple, The (Hughes) **6**:733, 734, 737, 743

Best Short Stories by Negro Writers, The: An Anthology from 1899 to the Present (Hughes ed.) **6**:737

Best Short Stories (Dreiser; Farrell ed.) **3**:381

Best Stories of Paul Laurence Dunbar, The (Brawley ed.) **3**:406, 413, 415

Best Stories of Theodore Dreiser, The (Fast ed.) **3**:381, 384

Bethel Merriday (Lewis) **6**:850

Between Two Worlds (Sinclair) **10**:1392, 1396

Beyond Desire (Anderson) **1**:46, 48

Beyond Spoon River: The Legacy of Edgar Lee Masters (Primeau) **7**:952

Beyond the Chocolate War (Cormier) **3**:300, 301, 304

Beyond the Horizon (O'Neill) **9**:1161, 1164, 1168

Big Box, The (Morrison, Morrison, and Potter) **8**:1064

"Big Boy Leaves Home" (Wright) **12**:1698, 1706, 1707

Big David, Little David (Hinton) **5**:701, 703, 706

Big Range, The (Schaefer) **10**:1352

Big Sea, The: An Autobiography (Hughes) **6**:737, 738

Big Sleep, The (Chandler) **4**:479

Big Sleep, The (Faulkner; screenplay) **4**:479, 486

"Big Two-Hearted River" (Hemingway) **5**:663, 668, 679

Big Wave, The (Buck) **2**:214, 218

Big Woods (Faulkner) **4**:486, 497

"Bilingual Sestina" (Alvarez) **1**:38

Bill Porter (Sinclair) **10**:1392

"Bimini" (Hemingway) **5**:670-71

Biograph (Dylan; record album) **3**:425

"Birches" (Frost) **4**:570, 571

Bird in the House, A (Laurence) **6**:820, 821, 823, 826, 827, 830-31

"Bird Song" (W. C. Williams) **12**:1682

"Birthday Present, A" (Plath) **9**:1221

Birth of a Nation'hood: Gaze, Script, and Spectacle in the O. J. Simpson Case (Morrison) **8**:1064

Birth of Tragedy, The (Nietzsche) **9**:1167

Bits of Paradise (Fitzgerald) **4**:532

Black Beauty (Soul) **1**:124

"Blackberrying" (Plath) **9**:1222

Black Book, The: Three Hundred Years of African American Life (anthology) **8**:1053, 1060

Black Boy (Wright) **12**:1693, 1694, 1695, 1697, 1698, 1700, 1701-4, 1706

Black Boy (American Hunger): A Record of Childhood and Youth (Wright) **12**:1701

"Black Boys and Native Sons" (Howe) **4**:473

Black Feeling, Black Talk/Black Judgement (Giovanni) **5**:630, 635, 636, 638

Black Feeling, Black Talk (Giovanni) **5**:630, 631, 635, 636

Black Judgement (Giovanni) **5**:630, 631, 635, 636

Black Love (Brooks) **2**:203

Black Magic: A Pictorial History of the Negro in American Entertainment (Hughes and Meltzer) **6**:737

Black Misery (Hughes; Arouni illus.) **6**:737

Black Nativity (Hughes) **6**:737

Black Power: A Record of Reactions in a Land of Pathos (Wright) **12**:1697, 1703

Blacks (Brooks) **2**:203

Blacks, The (Genet) **1**:59, 60

Black Steel: Joe Frazier and Muhammad Ali (Brooks) **2**:203

Black Thunder (Bontemps) **2**:183, 184, 187, 188, 189-90, 191, 192

Black Water (Oates; novel) **8**:1106, 1107, 1110, 1111, 1116, 1117-18

Black Water (Oates; opera libretto) **8**:1106, 1107, 1118

Blancs, Les: The Collected Last Plays of Lorraine Hansberry (Hansberry; Nemiroff ed.) **5**:649, 654, 657

Blind Assassin, The (Atwood) **1**:85, 90

Blix (Norris) **8**:1089, 1095

Blonde (Oates) **8**:1106, 1111

Blonde on Blonde (Dylan; record album) **3**:419, 421, 425

Blood, Bread, and Poetry: Selected Prose, 1979-1985 (Rich) **9**:1284

Bloodline (Gaines) **5**:585, 586, 589

Blood Meridian: Or, The Evening Redness in the West (McCarthy) **7**:961, 964, 965, 968, 969, 970-71

"Blood of Martyrs, The" (Benét) **2**:154-55

Blood of the Prophets, The (Masters) **7**:954

Blood on the Dining-Room Floor (Stein) **10**:1424

Blood on the Tracks (Dylan; record album) **3**:420, 425

Bloodsmoor Romance, A (Oates) **8**:1106, 1111

"Blowin' in the Wind" (Dylan; song) **3**:419, 425-26, 428

Blubber (Blume) **2**:166, 167, 170, 172, 173-74

Bluebeard's Egg (Atwood) **1**:90

"Blueberries" (Frost) **4**:563

Blues: For All the Changes: New Poems (Giovanni) **5**:635

Blues for Mister Charlie (Baldwin) **1**:104, 105, 110, 113-14

Bluest Eye, The (Morrison) **8**:1051, 1052, 1053, 1057, 1058, 1064, 1065

"Boats in a Fog" (Jeffers) **6**:799-800

Bob Dylan (Dylan; record album) **3**:419, 421, 425

Bodily Harm (Atwood) **1**:90

Body and the Wheel, The: A Play Made from the Gospels (Gibson) **5**:614, 615, 619

Body of Glass (Piercy). *See He, She, and It*

Bombs Away! (Steinbeck) **11**:1448, 1454

Book About Myself, A (Dreiser) **3**:381

"Bookmaking" (Alvarez) **1**:38

Book of Americans, A (Benét and Benét) **2**:151, 154, 155

Book of Common Prayer **5**:679

Book of Common Prayer, A (Didion) **3**:357, 358, 361, 363, 372

Book of Folly, The (Sexton) **10**:1371

Book of Knowledge, The (encyclopedia) **7**:910, 914

Book of Life, Mind, and Body, The (Sinclair) **10**:1392

Book of Lights, The (Potok) **9**:1269

Book of Negro Folklore, The (Bontemps and Hughes eds.) **2**:187, **6**:737

Book of Negro Humor, The (Hughes ed.) **6**:737

"Book of the Grotesque, The" (Anderson) **1**:52

"Book of Verse, A" (Stevens) **11**:1469, 1471

Book of Verses, A (Masters) **7**:950, 954

Bootleg Series, Vol. 1-3, The: Rare and Unreleased, 1961-1991 (Dylan; record album) **3**:425

"Boots of Spanish Leather" (Dylan; song) **3**:422

Border Trilogy, The (McCarthy) **7**:961, 964, 968, 970

Boston Evening Transcript, The (Eliot) **4**:451

Boston (Sinclair) **10**:1380-81, 1382, 1384, 1385, 1390-91, 1392

Bound East for Cardiff (O'Neill) **9**:1160, 1163, 1168, 1169

Bound for Glory (Guthrie) **3**:418

Bowl, Cat, and Broomstick (Stevens) **11**:1475

"Boys and Girls" (Munro) **8**:1082-83

Boy's Will, A (Frost) **4**:558, 560, 566-68, 570

"Boy's Will, A" (Longfellow) **4**:566

Braided Lives (Piercy) **9**:1203, 1205

Brass Check, The: A Study in American Journalism (Sinclair) **10**:1380, 1384, 1392, 1395

Brave and Startling Truth, A (Angelou) **1**:68

Brave New World (MacLeish) **7**:901

Bravo! (Ferber and Kaufman) **4**:507

"Bread" (Atwood) **1**:98, 99

Bread of Idleness, The (Masters) **7**:954

Breakfast at Tiffany's: A Short Novel and Three Stories (Capote) **2**:235, 242, *244*, 245

Breaking Camp (Piercy) **9**:1198, 1199, 1205

Breathing Lessons (Tyler) **11**:1541, 1545, 1546, 1551, 1554-55

Breathing Tokens (Sandburg) **10**:1338

Brewsie and Willie (Stein) **10**:1422, 1424, 1436, 1437

Bride Comes to Yellow Sky, The (Agee; screenplay) **1**:17

Bride of the Innisfallen and Other Stories, The (Welty) **12**:1596

Brideshead Revisited (Waugh) **9**:1260, 1266

Brides of the South Wind (Jeffers) **6**:790

"Bridge, The" (Tyler) **11**:1543

Bridge for Passing, A (Buck) **2**:218

Bridge of San Luis Rey, The (Wilder) **12**:1629, 1631, 1634, 1636, 1637, 1643-44, 1647

Bridges: A Journal for Jewish Feminists and Our Friends **9**:1281

"Bright and Morning Star" (Wright) **12**:1706, 1707

Bright Procession (Buck under Sedges pseud.) **2**:218

Bringing It All Back Home (Dylan; record album) **3**:419, 421, 425

Broke Heart Blues (Oates) **8**:1111

Broken Glass (Miller) **8**:1025

"Broken Promise" (MacLeish) **7**:898

Broken Span, The (W. C. Williams) **12**:1686

Bronzeville Boys and Girls (Brooks) **2**:197, 203

"Bronzeville Mother Loiters in Mississippi, A. Meanwhile, a Mississippi Mother Burns Bacon" (Brooks) **2**:206-7

Brothers Karamazov, The (Dostoyevski) **8**:1014, 1020

Buccaneers, The (Wharton) **12**:1615, 1622

"Buffalo Bill's" (Cummings) **3**:319, 329-30

Build-up, The (W. C. Williams) **12**:1686, 1692

Bulwark, The (Dreiser) **3**:381, 384

Bumblebee Flies Anyway, The (Cormier) **3**:296, 298, 301

Bumblebees and Their Ways (O. Plath) **9**:1214, 1222

"Burghers of Petty Death" (Stevens) **11**:1487

"Burial of the Dead, The" (Eliot) **4**:454

Burning Bright (Steinbeck; novel) **11**:1454

Burning Bright (Steinbeck; play)
11:1454

Burning City (Benét) 2:152, 155

Burning Daylight (London) 7:879

"Burnt Norton" (Eliot) 4:449-50

Buttered Side Down (Ferber) 4:507

Butterfingers Angel, Mary and Joseph, Herod the Nut, and the Slaughter of Twelve Hit Carols in a Pear Tree, The (Gibson) 5:614, 619, 621, 626

By-Line: Ernest Hemingway, Selected Articles, and Dispatches of Four Decades (Hemingway) 5:674

By the Light of My Father's Smile (Walker) 11:1575

By the North Gate (Oates) 8:1111

Cabala, The (Wilder) 12:1631, 1634, *1635*, 1636, 1647

Cabaret for Freedom (Angelou and Cambridge) 1:59, 60, 68

Cabin, The: Reminiscence and Diversions (Mamet) 7:930, 935

Californians (Jeffers) 6:785, 787, 790

Call, The (Hersey) 5:690

Call of the Wild, The (London) 7:869, 873, 874, 876, 877, 879, 884-85, 886, 887

Calms of Capricorn, The (O'Neill and Gallup) 9:1168

"Cambridge ladies who live in furnished souls, the" (Cummings) 3:329

Camel (Mamet) 7:928, 931, 935

Camino Real (T. Williams) 12:1653, 1664

Candle-Lightin' Time (Dunbar) 3:406

Candles to the Sun (T. Williams) 12:1652

Cannery Row (Steinbeck) 11:1448, 1450, 1452, 1454, 1465

Canterbury Tales, The (Chaucer) 11:1514

Cantos (Pound) 3:318

Canyon, The (Schaefer) 10:1348-49, 1352, 1355

Capote Reader, A (Capote) 2:238, 242

Capsule Course in Black Poetry Writing, A (Brooks) 2:293

Captain of Industry, A (Sinclair) 10:1379, 1392

Carnegie Works at Pittsburgh, The (Dreiser) 3:381

"Carnet de Voyage" (Stevens) 11:1469, 1471

"Carried Away" (Munro) 8:1078

Cass Timberlane: A Novel of Husbands and Wives (Lewis) 6:848, 850

Catcher in the Rye, The (Salinger) 10:1302, 1303, 1305, 1306, 1308, 1309, 1310, 1314-15, 1317

Cathedral (Carver) 2:257, 258, 259, 261, 262

"Cathedral" (Carver) 2:263

Catherine Cormier (Gaines) 5:584, 585, 588-89, 593-94

Cat on a Hot Tin Roof (T. Williams) 12:1653, 1654, 1657, 1664, 1669-70

Cat's Eye (Atwood) 97, 1:81, 82, 90

Cats (musical) 4:440, 441, 443, *447*, 448

Cawdor and Other Poems (Jeffers) 6:786, 790

Celebration (Foote) 4:547

Celestial Navigation (Tyler) 11:1544, 1549, 1551, 1557-58

Certain People (Wharton) 12:1622

Certificate, The (Singer) 10:1400, 1407-9, 1411

Chains: Lesser Novels and Stories (Dreiser) 3:381

Champion of a Cause: Essays and Addresses on Librarianship (MacLeish) 7:901

Change of World, A (Rich) 9:1277, 1279, 1281, 1284

Chariot in the Sky: A Story of the Jubilee Singers (Bontemps) 2:187

Charlotte Temple (Rowson) 3:312

Chase, The (Foote; novel) 4:542, 543, 544, 546, 547

Chase, The (Foote; play) 4:542, 547

Cheerful—By Request (Ferber) 4:507

Cheers for Miss Bishop (Benét; screenplay) 2:153, 155

Cherry Orchard, The (Chekhov; Mamet adaptation) 7:935

"Chicago: 1968" (Styron) 11:1504

Chicago Poems: Poems of the Midwest (Sandburg) 10:1326, 1328, 1338, 1340

"Chicago Poems" (Sandburg) 10:1328

Chicago Race Riots, The (Sandburg) 10:1338, 1341-42

"Chicago" (Sandburg) 10:1325, 1338-39

Chicago (Terkel) 11:1522, 1523

Child Buyer, The (Hersey) 5:686, 688, 689, 690, 696-97

Childhood (Wilder) 12:1647

Child Is Born, A: A Modern Drama of the Nativity (Benét) 2:155

Child of God (McCarthy) 7:963, 965, 970, 973

Children, The (Wharton) 12:1620, 1622

Children Coming Home (Brooks) 2:203

Children for Adoption (Buck) 2:218

Children of the Frost (London) 7:879

Children of the Market Place (Masters) 7:950, 954

Child's Bestiary, A (Gardner) 5:602

"Child Who Favored Daughter, The" (Walker) 11:1579

Child Who Never Grew, The (Buck) 2:218

Childwold (Oates) 8:1111

"China and the West" (Buck) 2:211, 212

China as I See It (Buck) 2:218

China Flight (Buck) 2:218

China in Black and White (Buck) 2:218

Chinaman, The (Mamet) 7:935

China Past and Present (Buck) 2:218

China Sky (Buck) 2:218

Chinese Encounters (Miller; photos by Morath) 8:1025

Chinese Novel, The (Buck) 2:218

Chinese Siamese Cat, The (Tan; Shields illus.) 11:1508, 1509, 1514, 1517

"Chinese Woman Speaks, A" (Buck) 2:212, 215

Chocolate War, The (Cormier) 3:295-96, 297, 298, 299, 300, 301, 302-4, 305, 307

"Choice, The" (Dunbar) 3:407

Chosen, The (Potok) 9:1259, 1262, 1263, 1264, *1265*, 1266, *1267*, 1268-70

Chris Christophersen (O'Neill) 9:1168

"Christ in Alabama" (Hughes) 6:744

Christmas Birthday Story, The (Laurence) 6:827

Christmas Memory, A (Capote) 2:242

Christmas Story, A (Porter) 9:1236

"Christmas to Me" (Lee) 6:836, 841

Chronicles (Froissart) 8:1087, 1092

Cider House Rules, The (Irving;

novel) **6:**764, 768, 771, 773, 774-76, 781, 782

Cider House Rules, The (Irving; screenplay) **6:**767, 768, 773, 774, 775

Cimarron (Ferber) **4:**506-8

CIOPW (Cummings) **3:**319

Circle Game, The (Atwood) **1:**85, 90

"Circle of Fire, A" (O'Connor) **8:**1135

Circles on the Water: Selected Poems of Marge Piercy **9:**1204-7

Cities of the Plain (McCarthy) **7:**964, 965, 970

City of Light (Piercy) **9:**1205

City Safari (Zindel) **12:**1715, 1722

Clara (Miller) **8:**1025

"Clean, Well-Lighted Place, A" (Hemingway) **5:**663, 681

Clearings in the Thicket (collection) **6:**842

Cliff Faraday stories (Sinclair under Fitch pseud.) **10:**1378

Clock Winder, The (Tyler) **11:**1544, 1548, 1550, 1551

Clock Without Hands (McCullers) **7:**978, 979, 983, 985, 990-91

Clorindy: Or, The Origin of the Cakewalk (Dunbar) **3:**401, 406

Closing of the American Mind, The (Bloom) **1:**129

Clothes for a Summer Hotel (T. Williams) **12:**1655, 1664

Clouds, The (W. C. Williams) **12:**1686

Cobweb, The (Gibson; screenplay) **5:**613, 615, 619

Cobweb, The (Gibson under Mass pseud.) **5:**613, 615, 616, 619

Cocktail Party, The (Eliot) **4:**440, 446, 448, 450

"Code, The" (Frost) **4:**563

Collected Earlier Poems (W. C. Williams) **12:**1686

Collected Early Poems, 1950-1970 (Rich) **9:**1284

Collected Essays and Occasional Writings, The (Porter) **9:**1236

Collected Later Poems (W. C. Williams) **12:**1686

Collected Plays (Miller) **8:**1025

Collected Poems, 1909-1935 (Eliot) **4:**450

Collected Poems, 1909-1962 (Eliot) **4:**450

Collected Poems, 1917-1952

(MacLeish) **7:**895, 896, 901

Collected Poems, 1917-1982 (MacLeish) **7:**895, 900-903, 906

Collected Poems, 1921-1931 (W. C. Williams) **12:**1686

Collected Poems (Cummings) **3:**315, 316, 319

Collected Poems (Frost) **4:**561, 567, 570

Collected Poems (Moore) **8:**1036, 1037, 1043

Collected Poems of Archibald MacLeish, The **7:**901

Collected Poems of James Agee, The **1:**17

Collected Poems of Langston Hughes, The **6:**737

Collected Poems of Wallace Stevens, The **11:**1470, 1471, 1475, 1486, 1487

Collected Poems of William Carlos Williams, The: Volume 1, 1909-1939 **12:**1686

Collected Poems of William Carlos Williams, The: Volume 2, 1939-1962 **12:**1686

Collected Poems (Plath; Hughes ed.) **9:**1218, 1224

Collected Poetry of Paul Laurence Dunbar, The (Dunbar; ed. Braxton) **3:**406, 407

Collected Poetry of Robinson Jeffers, Volume I, 1920-1928, The **6:**787, 790

Collected Poetry of Robinson Jeffers, Volume II, 1928-1938, The **6:**787, 790

Collected Poetry of Robinson Jeffers, Volume III, 1939-1962, The **6:**787, 790

Collected Poetry of Robinson Jeffers, Volume IV, Poetry 1903-1920, Prose, and Unpublished Writings, The **6:**787, 790

Collected Short Prose of James Agee, The **1:**17

Collected Short Stories of Edith Wharton, The **12:**1622

Collected Short Stories of William Faulkner **4:**486

Collected Stories (Faulkner) **7:**924

Collected Stories, The (Singer) **10:**1411, 1413-14

Collected Stories of Carson McCullers **7:**983

Collected Stories of Eudora Welty, The **12:**1596

Collected Stories of Jack Schaefer, The **10:**1352

Collected Stories of Katherine Anne Porter, The **9:**1232, 1233, 1236

Collected Stories (T. Williams) **12:**1664

Collected Works (O'Connor) **8:**1143

Collector of Hearts, The (Oates) **8:**1111

Color Curtain, The: A Report on the Bandung Conference (Wright) **12:**1697, 1703

"Colored Soldiers, The" (Dunbar) **3:**407

Color of a Great City, The (Dreiser) **3:**381

Color Purple, The (Walker) **11:**1561, 1564-65, 1566, 1568, 1570-76, 1581

Colossus and Other Poems, The (Plath) **9:**1213, 1217-18, 1224-25

"Combinations of Jacksons" (Portis) **9:**1249

Come and Get It (Ferber) **4:**504, 505, 507, 508

"Comeback" (Gaines) **5:**584, 585

Come Meet Muffin (Oates) **8:**1111

Come, My Beloved (Buck) **2:**218

Coming of Age: The Story of Our Century by Those Who've Lived It (Terkel) **11:**1522, 1523, 1537-38

Command the Morning (Buck) **2:**218

Company of Cowards (Schaefer) **10:**1349, 1352, 1355

"Comparison, A" (Plath) **9:**1227

Complete Collected Poems of Maya Angelou, The (Angelou) **1:**68, 78

Complete Collected Poems of William Carlos Williams, 1906-1938, The **12:**1686

Complete Edition of Frank Norris, The **8:**1095

Complete Edition of Frank Norris, The, Vol. 10 **8:**1090

Complete Plays, The (O'Neill) **9:**1168

Complete Poems, 1913-1962 (Cummings) **3:**319

Complete Poems and Plays, The (1962) (Eliot) **4:**450

Complete Poems and Plays, The (1969) (Eliot) **4:**450

Complete Poems (Frost) **4:**567, 570

Complete Poems of Marianne Moore, The **8:**1036, 1037, 1041-43

Complete Poems of Paul Laurence Dunbar, The **3**:402, 406, 407-9

Complete Poems (Sandburg) **10**:1327, 1328, 1337-40

Complete Prose of Marianne Moore, The **8**:1036, 1043, 1044-46

Complete Short Stories, The (Hemingway) **5**:674

Complete Stories, The (Hurston) **6**:755

Complete Stories, The (Malamud) **7**:918, 924

Complete Stories, The (O'Connor) **8**:1135, 1139, 1143

Complete Stories, The (Walker) **11**:1565, 1575

Complete Works (Norris) **8**:1095

Complete Works of the Gawain-Poet, The (Gardner ed.) **5**:597, 602

Complete Works (O'Neill) **9**:1168

Composition as Explanation (Stein) **10**:1424

"Concord Hymn, The" (Emerson) **3**:313

Confessional (T. Williams) **12**:1664

Confessions of a Teenage Baboon (Zindel) **12**:1722

Confessions of Nat Turner, The (Styron) **2**:188, **11**:1489, 1492, 1494, 1496, 1497-1500, 1504

Confidential Clerk, The (Eliot) **4**:448, 450

Congressional Record **11**:1458

Connecticut Yankee in King Arthur's Court, A (Twain) **12**:1717

Connecticut Yankee in King Arthur's Court, A (Zindel; teleplay) **12**:1717, 1722

Conspiracy, The (Hersey) **5**:690

Construction of Christian Poetry in Old English, The (Gardner) **5**:602

Construction of the Wakefield Cycle, The (Gardner) **5**:602

Continuing Journey, A (MacLeish) **7**:901

Contraries: Essays (Oates) **8**:1111

Conversations with a Pocket Gopher and Other Outspoken Neighbors (Schaefer) **10**:1346, 1352

Conversations with Arthur Miller (Roudané ed.) **8**:1025

Conversations with Bernard Malamud (Lasher ed.) **7**:918

Conversations with James Baldwin (Standley and Pratt eds.) **1**:110

Convicts (Foote; screenplay) **4**:547

Co-op (Sinclair) **10**:1392

"Corazon's Café" (Ortiz Cofer) **9**:1192

Cornhuskers (Sandburg) **10**:1326, 1338

Cornish trilogy (Davies) **3**:337, 338

"Corn Song, The" (Whittier) **3**:313

"Corn Stalk Fiddle, The" (Dunbar) **3**:408

Correspondence of Flannery O'Connor and Brainard Cheneys, The **8**:1143

Cotton Candy on a Rainy Day (Giovanni) **5**:631, 635, 638-39, 641

"Cotton Candy on a Rainy Day" (Giovanni) **5**:638-39

"Council of State, A" (Dunbar) **3**:412

Count of Monte-Cristo, The (Dumas) **9**:1158

Courtship (Foote; novel) **4**:547, 553

Courtship (Foote; play) **4**:547, 553

Courtship (Foote; screenplay) **4**:547

"Cousin Nancy" (Eliot) **4**:451

Cousins (Foote) **4**:547

"Crabs" (Piercy) **9**:1206-7

"Crack-Up, The" (Fitzgerald) **4**:519

Crack-Up, The (Fitzgerald; Wilson ed.) **4**:524, 532

Creation of the World and Other Business, The (Miller) **8**:1018, 1019, 1025

"Cretan Woman, The" (Jeffers) **6**:790, 796

Crime and Punishment (Dostoyevsky) **12**:1705

Crossing the Border (Oates) **8**:1111

Crossing, The (McCarthy) **7**:964, 965, 967, 970

Crossing the Water (Plath) **9**:1224, 1225

Cross Patch (Mamet; radio play) **7**:935

Crown of Feathers and Other Stories, A (Singer) **10**:1403, 1411

Crucial Instances (Wharton) **12**:1614, 1622

Crucible, The (Miller) **8**:1015, 1017, 1018, 1019, 1022-24, 1025

Cruise of the Dazzler, The (London) **7**:879, 880

Cruise of the Snark, *The* (London) **7**:879

Cruise of the Vanadis, The (Wharton) **12**:1622

Cry of Players, A (Gibson) **5**:613, 615, 616, 617, 619, 621

Cryptogram, The (Mamet) **7**:933, 935, 942-43

Crystal Gazer (Plath) **9**:1224

"Crystal Stair, The". See *Raisin in the Sun, A*

"Cuba" (Hemingway) **5**:671

Cuba Libre (Guillén; Hughes and Carruthers transl.) **6**:737

Cultivation of Christmas Trees, The (Eliot) **4**:450

Cunning Man, The (Davies) **3**:337, 344

Cup of Fury, The (Sinclair) **10**:1392

Cup of Gold (Steinbeck) **11**:1447, 1451, 1454

Curtain of Green and Other Stories, A (Welty) **12**:1591, 1593, 1596

Custom of the Country, The (Wharton) **12**:1622

Cybele (Oates) **8**:1111

Daddy Goodness (Wright and Sapin) **12**:1703

Dance of the Happy Shades (Munro) **8**:1071, 1074, 1075, 1080

Dance the Eagle to Sleep (Piercy) **9**:1198, 1199, 1205

Dancing Girls (Atwood) **1**:90

Danger: Memory! (Miller) **8**:1019, 1025

Dangerous Summer, The (Hemingway) **5**:664, 671, 674

Dangling Man (Bellow) **1**:124, 126, 132

Dark Fields of the Republic: Poems, 1991-1995 (Rich) **9**:1284

Dark Laughter (Anderson) **1**:45, 46, 48

Darkness Visible: A Memoir of Madness (Styron) **11**:1489, 1493, 1500

"Darkness Visible" (Styron) **11**:1496

Dateline, Toronto: The Complete "Toronto Star" Dispatches, 1920-1924 (Hemingway) **5**:674

"Daughter of the African Evolution" (Piercy) **9**:1209

Daughter of the Snows, A (London) **7**:874, 879, 880

David and Della (Zindel) **12**:1715, 1722

David Copperfield (Dickens) **6**:772, **10**:1315

Davita's Harp (Potok) **9**:1262, 1263, 1267, 1269

Dawn (Dreiser) **3**:381

Dawn O'Hara: The Girl Who Laughed (Ferber) **4**:501, 503, 507

Day of Pleasure, A: Stories of a Boy Growing up in Warsaw (Singer) **10**:1398, 1399, 1403, 1411

Days Before, The (Porter) **9**:1236

"Day's Work, A" (Capote) **2**:252

Dead Hand series (Sinclair) **10**:1379-80, 1382, 1395

Deal in Wheat and Other Stories of the New and Old West, A (Norris) **8**:1095

Dean's December, The (Bellow) **1**:127, 132, 140

Dearest of Friends, The (Foote) **4**:547

"Dear Joaquin" (Ortiz Cofer) **9**:1191-92

Dear Judas and Other Poems (Jeffers) **6**:790

"Dear Judas" (Jeffers) **6**:788

Dear Lovely Death (Hughes) **6**:737

Dear Scott/Dear Max: The Fitzgerald-Perkins Correspondence **4**:532

Death and the Maiden (Gardner) **5**:602

"Death by Water" (Eliot) **4**:454

Death Comes for the Archbishop (Cather) **2**:269, 272, 274, 276-77, 278, 279-81

Death ("Hungerfield") **6**:795, 796

"Death-in-Life of Benjamin Reid, The" (Styron) **11**:1504

Death in the Afternoon (Hemingway) **5**:663, 668, 674

Death in the Castle (Buck) **2**:218

"Death in the Desert, A" (Cather) **2**:275

Death in the Family, A (Agee) **1**:11, 13, 14, 15, 17, 18-20

"Death in the Woods" (Anderson) **1**:54

Death in the Woods and Other Stories (Anderson) **1**:44, 48, 54

Death Notebooks, The (Sexton) **10**:1361, 1371, 1375

Death of a Salesman (Miller) **8**:1013, 1015, 1017, 1018, 1019, 1025-28

"Death of a Traveling Salesman" (Welty) **12**:1591, 1593, 1607

Death of Methuselah and Other Stories, The (Singer) **10**:1411

Death of Papa, The (Foote) **4**:547, 553, 554

"Death of the Hired Man, The" (Frost) **4**:563, 569

"Death Song, A" (Dunbar) **3**:401

"Decision" (Wright) **12**:1709

Decoration of Houses, The (Wharton and Codman) **12**:1614, 1615, 1622

Deenie (Blume) **2**:167, 169, 170, 172, 176-78

"Deer Lay Down Their Bones, The" (Jeffers) **6**:796

Deer Park, The (Mailer) **3**:362

Defense of Circe, A (Porter) **9**:1236

"Delia" (Dylan; song) **3**:423

Delta Wedding (Welty) **12**:1592, 1593, 1596

Democracy (Didion) **3**:360, 361, 362-63, 372

Depression Island (Sinclair) **10**:1387, 1392

Deptford trilogy (Davies) **3**:335, 337, 338, 340, 343, 345, 347, 350

"Descent, The" (W. C. Williams) **12**:1683

"Descent into Proslito" (Knowles) **6**:805

Descent of Man, The (Wharton) **12**:1622

Descent to the Dead: Poems Written in Ireland and Great Britain (Jeffers) **6**:786, 787, 790

"Descent" (Wright) **12**:1709

Description Without Place (Stevens) **11**:1475

Desert Music and Other Poems, The (W. C. Williams) **12**:1686

"Desert Places" (Frost) **4**:571

"Design" (Frost) **4**:571

"Desire and the Black Masseur" (T. Williams) **12**:1655

Desire (Dylan; record album) **3**:425

Desire Under the Elms (O'Neill) **9**:1164, 1168, 1170

"Despair" (Wright) **12**:1709

Destiny with Half Moon Street, A (Zindel) **12**:1722

Devil and Daniel Webster, The (Benét; play) **2**:155

"Devil and Daniel Webster, The" (Benét; story) **2**:151, 152, 157

Devil and Daniel Webster, The (opera) **2**:153

Devil Finds Work, The (Baldwin) **1**:106, 110

Dialogue, A: James Baldwin and Nikki Giovanni (Baldwin and Giovanni) **1**:106, 110, **5**:631, 635, 642

Dialogues of Archibald MacLeish and Mark Van Doren, The (MacLeish and Van Doren) **7**:901

"Diamond as Big as the Ritz, The" (Fitzgerald) **4**:522

Diamond Cutters and Other Poems, The (Rich) **9**:1284

Diary of Samuel Marchbanks, The (Davies) **3**:335, 344

Dimensions of Peacocks (Zindel) **12**:1713, 1722

Dinner at Eight (Ferber and Kaufman; play) **4**:507

Dinner at the Homesick Restaurant (Tyler) **11**:1541, 1545, 1546, 1551, 1555-57

Dinny and the Witches: A Frolic on Grave Matters (Gibson) **5**:619

Dintenfass (Mamet; radio play) **7**:935

Disappearance of the Jews, The (Mamet) **7**:935

Displaced Person, The (Foote; teleplay) **4**:544, 547

Displaced Person, The (O'Connor) **4**:544

Dividing the Estate (Foote) **4**:547

Divine Comedy, The (Dante) **3**:330, **11**:1484

"Divinely Superfluous Beauty" (Jeffers) **6**:789

Diviners, The (Laurence) **6**:822, 823, 825-27, 829

Diving into the Wreck (Rich) **9**:1277, 1280, 1281, 1284, 1286, *1287*, 1288-89, 1293

"Diving into the Wreck" (Rich) **9**:1286, 1288

Division Street: America (Terkel) **11**:1521, 1522, 1523, 1524, 1531, 1538, 1539

"Doc Mellhorn and the Pearly Gates" (Benét) **2**:151

Doctor Martino and Other Stories (Faulkner) **4**:486

Doctor Stories, The (W. C. Williams) **12**:1686

Dodsworth (Lewis) **6**:845-46, 848, 850, 851, 860-61

Dog of the South, The (Portis) **9**:1249, 1250, 1251-52, 1253-55

Dogs Bark, The: Public People and Private Places (Capote) **2**:242, 251

"Doing It Differently" (Piercy) **9**:1206

Doll's House, A (Ibsen) **9**:1278, **12**:1632, 1647

Doll's House, A (Ibsen; Wilder adaptation) **12**:1632, 1647

Dom Casmurro (Machado de Assis) **1**:65

Domesday Book (Masters) **7**:950, 954

Donald Sultan: Playing Cards (Mamet and Jay) **7**:935

"Don't Think Twice, It's All Right" (Dylan; song lyric) **3**:429

Don't You Want to Be Free (Hughes) **6**:737

Doom Stone, The (Zindel) **12**:1722

Double Axe and Other Poems, The (Jeffers) **6**:786, 787, 790

Double Persephone (Atwood) **1**:83, 85, 90

Double Vision: American Thoughts Abroad (Knowles) **6**:805, 812

Do with Me What You Will (Oates) **8**:1111

"Down at the Cross: Letter from a Region in My Mind" (Baldwin) **1**:120-21

"Down at the Dinghy" (Salinger) **10**:*1320*, 1321

"Down by the Riverside" (Wright) **12**:1699, 1706-7

Down in the Groove (Dylan; record album) **3**:425

Dragon Country (T. Williams) **12**:1664

Dragon, Dragon and Other Tales (Gardner) **5**:602

Dragon Harvest (Sinclair) **10**:1392, 1396

Dragon Seed (Buck) **2**:218

Dragon's Teeth (Sinclair) **10**:1377, 1382, 1392, 1396

Dramatic Duologues (Masters) **7**:954

"Dread" (Wright) **12**:1709

Dream Catcher, The (M. Salinger) **10**:1313

"Dream Girl" (Sandburg) **10**:1325

Dreaming Emmett (Morrison) **8**:1052, 1054, 1064

Dream Keeper and Other Poems, The (Hughes) **6**:737

Dream of a Common Language, The (Rich) **9**:1277, 1280, 1284, 1289, *1290*, 1291, 1293

Dream of Love, A (W. C. Williams) **12**:*1678*, 1679, 1686

Dream of Swallows, A (Zindel) **12**:1722

Dream Play, A (Strindberg) **12**:1637

Dreams in the Mirror: A Biography of E. E. Cummings (Kennedy) **3**:320

"Dream" (Wright) **12**:1709

Dreiser Looks at Russia (Dreiser) **3**:378, 381, 384, *394*

Drinking Gourd, The (Hansberry; teleplay; Nemiroff ed.) **5**:648, 654, 657

Drugstore: Sunday Noon (Foote; teleplay) **4**:547

Drums at Dusk (Bontemps) **2**:183, 186, 187, 188, 191-93

Drunken Sisters, The (Wilder) **12**:1647

"Dry Salvages, The" (Eliot) **4**:438, 451

Dubin's Lives (Malamud) **7**:916, 917, 918, 924

Duck and the Goat, The (Mamet) **7**:935

Duck Variations (Mamet) **7**:929, 935

Dust Tracks on a Road: An Autobiography (Hurston) **6**:748, 755, 760-61

Dutch Courage and Other Stories (London) **7**:879

Dylan and the Dead (Dylan; record album) **3**:425

Early Grrrl (Piercy) **9**:1205

Early Martyr and Other Poems, An (W. C. Williams) **12**:1686

Early Moon (Sandburg) **10**:1338

Early Ripening: American Women's Poetry Now (Piercy ed.) **9**:1205

Earthly Possessions (Tyler) **11**:1548, 1549, 1551, 1558

Earth Shines Secretly, The: A Book of Days (Piercy; artwork by Blaine) **9**:1205

East and West and the Novel (Buck) **2**:218

East and West (Buck) **2**:218

"East Coker" (Eliot) **4**:450-51

East of Eden (Steinbeck) **11**:1448, 1452, 1454, 1466

East Wind: West Wind (Buck) **2**:213, 218

Eccentricities of a Nightingale, The (T. Williams) **12**:1664

Ecclesiastes, Book of **5**:677

Edge, The (Mamet; screenplay) **7**:932, 935

Edge of Impossibility, The: Tragic Forms in Literature (Oates) **8**:1111

Edible Woman, The (Atwood) **1**:81, 85, 90

Edmond (Mamet) **7**:929, 935

E. E. Cummings: A Selection of Poems (Cummings) **3**:319

E. E. Cummings: The Growth of a Writer (Friedman) **3**:320, 322

Effect of Gamma Rays on Man-in-the-Moon Marigolds, The (Zindel) **12**:1711, 1713, 1714, 1715, 1719-21, 1722

"Egg, The" (Anderson) **1**:41, 46, 54-55

Eggs of Things (Sexton and Kumin) **10**:1371

Ego-Tripping and Other Poems for Young Readers (Giovanni) **5**:635

"Ego-Tripping" (Giovanni) **5**:639

Eight Chambers of the Heart, The (Piercy) **9**:1205

"Eighteen-Year-Old Looks Back on Life, An" (Maynard) **10**:1313

Eight Harvard Poets (collection) **3**:313, 316

Eighth Day, The (Wilder) **12**:1633, 1634, 1647, 1648-49

Eight Men (Wright) **12**:1697, 1703, 1707-8

Eight Mortal Ladies Possessed: A Book of Stories (T. Williams) **12**:1664

Eight Plus One (Cormier) **3**:297, 300, 301, 308

Eileen (Masters) **7**:954

Eimi (Cummings) **3**:315, 316, 319, 330-31

Einstein (MacLeish) **7**:901

Elder Statesman, The (Eliot) **4**:441, 445, 448, 450

Eleanor Roosevelt Story, The (MacLeish) **7**:901

Elegy for a Lady (Miller) **8**:1025

Elephant and Other Stories (Carver) **5**:261

Elijah the Slave (Singer) **10**:1411

Elmer Gantry (Lewis;) **6**:845, 848, 850, 859-60

Embodiment of Knowledge, The (W. C. Williams) **12**:1686

Emma McChesney and Co. (Ferber) **4**:507, 513

Emma McChesney series (Ferber) **4**:501, 503, 513

Emperor Jones, The (O'Neill) **9**:1164-65, 1168, 1169

"Emperor of Ice-Cream, The" (Stevens) **11**:1480, 1481

Empire Burlesque (Dylan; record album) 3:425

"Endgame" (Tan) 11:1507, 1508

"End of the World, The" (MacLeish) 7:898, 900-901, 905

"End to Dreams, An" (Benét) 2:151, 152

Enemies: A Love Story (Singer) 10:1402, 1405, 1406, 1411

Enemy, The: Time (T. Williams) 12:1664

Enemy of the People, An (Ibsen; Miller adaptation) 8:1015, 1018, 1019, 1025

Enormous Room, The (Cummings) 3:314, 316, 319, 320, 324-25, 329, 330

Enthusiasms of Robertson Davies, The (Davies) 3:344

EPIC Plan for California, The (Sinclair) 10:1392

Epitaph: A Poem (Dreiser) 3:381

Ernest Hemingway: Selected Letters, 1917-1961 5:674

Eros at Breakfast (Davies) 3:344

"Errand" (Carver) 2:264-65

Essays, Speeches, and Public Letters (Faulkner; Meriwether ed.) 4:486

Estate, The (Singer). *See Manor, The* (Singer)

Esthétique du Mal (Stevens) 11:1471, 1475

"Esthétique du Mal" (Stevens) 11:1487

Etcetera: The Unpublished Poems of E. E. Cummings (Cummings) 3:319

"Ethan Frome: `This Vision of His Story'" (Wolff) 12:1624

Ethan Frome (Wharton) 12:1618, 1619, 1622, 1623-24, 1628

Ethical Living for a Modern World: Jewish Insights (Potok) 9:1262, 1263, 1269

"Ethics of Living Jim Crow, The" (Wright) 12:1706, 1707

Ethics (Spinoza) 10:1407, 1408, 1409

Étranger, L' (Camus) 11:1492

Eudora: A Writer's Life (Waldron) 12:1597

Eudora Welty: Photographs (Welty) 12:1596

Eudora Welty, Other Places (Welty) 12:1596

Euthanasia and the Endless Hearts (Zindel) 12:1722

Even the Stars Look Lonesome (Angelou) 1:68

"Eventide" (Brooks) 2:197

Ever the Winds of Chance (Sandburg; Sandburg and Hendrick eds.) 10:1338

Everybody's Autobiography (Stein) 10:1424, 1436-37

"Everybody's Protest Novel" (Baldwin) 1:105

Everybody Wins (Miller) 8:1025

"Everyday Use" (Walker) 11:1579

Every Seventeen Minutes the Crowd Goes Crazy! (Zindel) 12:1722

Everything That Rises Must Converge (O'Connor) 8:1138, 1139, 1143

"Everything That Rises Must Converge" (O'Connor) 8:1135, 1139, 1142, 1148-49

"Evidence" (O'Brien) 8:1130

Evidence of Things Not Seen, The (Baldwin) 1:106, 110

"Evil Eye, The" (Fitzgerald; musical lyrics) 4:517

Exile, The (Buck) 2:215, 218

Expect No Peace! (Sinclair) 10:1392

Expeditions (Atwood) 1:90

Expensive People (Oates) 8:1111

"Eye-Mote, The" (Plath) 9:1225

Eye of the Story, The: Selected Essays and Reviews (Welty) 12:1589, 1596

Fable, A (Faulkner) 4:486

Fables choisies, mises en vers (La Fontaine) 8:1035, *1036*, 1037, 1046

Fabulous Beasts, The (Oates) 8:1111

"Face, A" (Moore) 8:1042

Fact of a Doorframe, The: Poems Selected and New, 1950-1984 (Rich) 9:1284

Fade (Cormier) 3:300, 301, 304-5

"Fading of the Sun, A" (Stevens) 11:1482

Faith of Men and Other Stories, The (London) 7:879

Fall of the City, The: A Verse Play for Radio (MacLeish) 7:901, 905-6

Fame (Miller) 8:1025

Familye Mushkat, Di (Singer). *See Family Moskat, The*

Family Moskat, The (Singer) 10:1399, 1400, 1402, 1403, 1404, 1409-12

Family Reunion, The (Eliot) 4:445-46, 450

Famous American Negroes (Hughes) 6:737

Famous Negro Athletes (Bontemps) 2:187

Famous Negro Heroes of America (Hughes) 6:737

Famous Negro Music Makers (Hughes) 6:737

Fanatics, The (Dunbar) 3:401, 402, 406

Fanny Herself (Ferber) 4:502, 507

Far and Near, Stories of Japan, China, and America (Buck) 2:218

Farewell: A Memoir of a Texas Childhood (Foote) 4:543, 544, 547

Farewell to Arms, A (Hemingway) 5:663, 665, 668, 672-74, 675

"Farewell to Florida" (Stevens) 11:1482-83

"Farmer in the Dell, The" (nursery rhyme) 3:306

Farmers' Daughters, The: The Collected Stories of William Carlos Williams 12:1686

Farm Servants and Other People (Frost). *See North of Boston*

Fast and Loose (Wharton) 12:1613, 1615, 1622

Fasting Cure, The (Sinclair) 10:1392

Fast Sooner Hound, The (Bontemps and Conroy) 2:187

Fate of the Jury, The: An Epilogue to Domesday Book (Masters) 7:954

"Fate" (Wright) 12:1704

Father of the Blues (Handy and Bontemps) 2:187

"Fathers and Sons" (Hemingway) 5:680

Fathers and Sons (Turgenev) 5:588, 593

"Father" (Walker) 11:1580

Faulkner at West Point (Fant and Ashley ed.) 4:486

Faulkner-Cowley File, The: Letters and Memories, 1944-1962 (Cowley ed.) 4:486

Faulkner Reader, The (Faulkner) 4:486

Faulkner's MGM Screenplays (Kawin ed.) 4:486

Fearsome Inn, The (Singer) 10:1411

"Fear" (Wright) 12:1704

Fernhurst, Q.E.D., and Other Early Writings (Stein) 10:1424, 1425

"Fever 103 Degrees" (Plath) 9:1221

"Fie! Fie! Fi-Fi!" (Fitzgerald; musical book and lyrics) **4**:517

Fields of Wonder (Hughes) **6**:737

"Field Trip" (O'Brien) **8**:1132

Fiesta Melons (Plath) **9**:1224

Fifth Business (Davies) **3**:337, 338, 344, 345-47, 350

Fifth Column and the First Forty-nine Stories, The (Hemingway) **5**:663, 664, 665, 674, 678-79

Fifth Grade Safari (Zindel) **12**:1722

"Fifty Grand" (Hemingway) **5**:679

Fifty Poems (Cummings) **3**:319

Fight for Freedom: The Story of the NAACP (Hughes) **6**:737

Fighting Angel: Portrait of a Soul (Buck) **2**:215, 218

Fighting France from Dunkerque to Belfort (Wharton) **12**:1622

"Figlia che Piange, La" (Eliot) **4**:451

Financier, The (Dreiser) **3**:378, 380, 381, 384, 392, 395

Finding the Green Stone (Walker) **11**:1575

Fine Clothes to the Jew (Hughes) **6**:728, 730, 737, 739-40

Fine Furniture (Dreiser) **3**:381

Finnegans Wake (Joyce) **12**:1632, 1646

"Fire and Cloud" (Wright) **12**:1699, 1707

"Fire and Ice" (Frost) **4**:571

Fire-Dwellers, The (Laurence) **6**:821, 823, 827, 831

Fire Next Time, The (Baldwin) **1**:104, 105, 110, 120-21, **5**:642

"Fire on the Hills" (Jeffers) **6**:789

Fires: Essays, Poems, Stories (Carver) **2**:261

"Fires" (Carver) **2**:261

"Fire Sermon, The" (Eliot) **4**:454

"First Wife, The" (Buck) **2**:215

First Blood (Schaefer) **10**:1352

First Book of Africa, The (Hughes) **6**:737

First Book of Jazz, The (Hughes) **6**:737

First Book of Negroes, The (Hughes) **6**:737

First Book of Rhythms, The (Hughes) **6**:737

First Book of the West Indies, The (Hughes) **6**:737

First Love (Oates) **8**:1109, 1111

First Person Singular: Writers on Their Craft (Oates ed.) **8**:1111

First Principles (Spencer) **3**:380

First Wife and Other Stories, The (Buck) **2**:218

"F is for foetus" (Cummings) **3**:327

Five Men and Pompey (Benét) **2**:150, 152, 155

Five Plays (Hughes; Smalley ed.) **6**:737

Five Television Plays (Mamet) **7**:935

Fixer, The (Malamud) **7**:912, 913, 914, 916, 917, 918, 920-22

Flagons and Apples (Jeffers) **6**:784, 787, 790

Flags in the Dust (Faulkner; Day ed.) **4**:478, 483, 484, 486, 489

Flannery O'Connor's Library: Resources of Being (O'Connor) **8**:1139

Flappers and Philosophers (Fitzgerald) **4**:532

Flight (Foote; teleplay) **4**:542, 547

"Flight of Feather Boy, The" (McNickle) **7**:1005

"Flight" (Wright) **12**:1704

Fling and Other Stories (Hersey) **5**:690

Flivver King, The (Sinclair) **10**:1392

"floatfloafloff" (Cummings) **3**:327

"Floating Poem, The" (Rich) **9**:1291

"Flowering Dream, The: Notes on Writing" (McCullers) **7**:981

Flowering Judas and Other Stories (Porter) **9**:1231, 1233, 1234, 1236

"Flowering Judas" (Porter) **9**:1236, 1241-42

Fly Away Home (Piercy) **9**:1205

Flying Home and Other Stories (Ellison) **4**:465, 466, 472-73

"Flying Home" (Ellison) **4**:462, 466, 472, 473

Focus (Miller) **8**:1014, 1017, 1018, 1025

"Fog" (Sandburg) **10**:1340

Folklore, Memoirs, and Other Writings by Zora Neale Hurston **6**:755

Folks from Dixie (Dunbar) **3**:401, 402, 406, 413

"Food" (Stein) **10**:1434, 1436

Fools of Chelm and Their History, The (Singer) **10**:1411

"For Eleanor Boylan Talking with God" (Sexton) **10**:1369

"For Esmé—with Love and Squalor" (Salinger) **10**:1303

Forever... (Blume) **2**:166, 168, 172, 174-76

Forgotten Village, The (Steinbeck; nonfiction) **11**:1454

Forgotten Village, The (Steinbeck; screenplay) **11**:1453, 1454

Forms of Fiction, The (Gardner and Dunlap eds.) **5**:602

"For Once, Then, Something" (Frost) **4**:571

"For the Anniversary of My Mother's Death" (MacLeish) **7**:901

Fortune, My Foe (Davies) **3**:338, 344

45 Mercy Street (Sexton; play) **10**:1360, 1361, 1371

45 Mercy Street (Sexton; poetry) **10**:1365, 1371

For Whom the Bell Tolls (Hemingway) **5**:663, 664, 665, 668, 671, 673, 674, 675-76

For Your Eye Alone: Robertson Davies' Letters, 1976-1995 (Grant ed.) **3**:344

Foster, John **12**:1717

Four Early Stories by James Agee (Agee) **1**:17

"Four Freedoms, The" (Miller; radio play) **8**:1017, 1018, 1025

Four Quartets (Eliot) **4**:437, 438, 440, 441, 449-51, 456

Four Saints in Three Acts (Stein; opera libretto) **10**:1424, 1425

Fourteen Stories (Buck) **2**:218

Four-Telling (Piercy, Hershon, Jarrett, and Lourie) **9**:1205

Foxfire: Confessions of a Girl Gang (Oates) **8**:1106, 1109, 1111, 1116

Frankenstein (Gardner; libretto) **5**:602

Frank Norris of "The Wave" (Norris; Lewis ed.) **8**:1090, 1095

Franny and Zooey (Salinger) **10**:1304, 1306, 1315-17

"Franny" (Salinger) **10**:1315-16

Freckle Juice (Blume) **2**:166, 172

Freddy's Book (Gardner) **5**:598, 599, 602

Frederick Douglass: Slave, Fighter, Freeman (Bontemps) **2**:187, 188, 193

"Frederick Douglass" (Dunbar) **3**:407

Free Air (Lewis) **6**:850

Free and Easy (Bontemps and Cullen) **2**:184, 187, 188

Free and Other Stories (Dreiser) **3**:381

Free at Last: The Life of Frederick Douglass (Bontemps) **2**:187, 188, 193

Freedom Is the Right to Choose: An Inquiry into the Battle for the American Future (MacLeish) **7**:901

"Freedom's Hard-Bought Thing" (Benét) **2**:152

Freedom's Plow (Hughes) **6**:737

Freewheelin' Bob Dylan, The (Dylan; record album) **3**:421, 425

Frenchtown Summer (Cormier) **3**:301

French Ways and Their Meanings (Wharton) **12**:1622

Frescoes for Mr. Rockefeller's City (MacLeish) **7**:901

Friend of Kafka and Other Stories, A (Singer) **10**:1411

Friend of My Youth: Stories (Munro) **8**:1080

"Friend of My Youth" (Munro) **8**:1077

Friend to Friend: A Candid Exchange Between Pearl S. Buck and Carlos P. Romulo (Buck and Romulo) **2**:218

Fright Party (Zindel) **12**:1715, 1722

Frog Prince, The (Mamet) **7**:935, 944

From Main Street to Stockholm: Letters of Sinclair Lewis, 1919-1930 (Smith ed.) **6**:850

From Uncertain to Blue (Foote and Carter) **4**:547

Frost: Collected Poems, Prose, and Plays **4**:571

Fruit of the Tree, The (Wharton) **12**:1622

F. Scott Fitzgerald on Authorship (Fitzgerald) **4**:532

F. Scott Fitzgerald's Ledger (Fitzgerald) **4**:532

Fudge-a-Mania (Blume) **2**:167, 172

"Fudge" series (Blume) **2**:166, 167, 170

Fugitive Kind, The (T. Williams and Roberts; screenplay) **12**:1663, 1664

Furious Seasons and Other Stories (Carver) **2**:261

Further Range, A (Frost) **4**:561, 567, 571

Gallery of Women, A (Dreiser) **3**:381

"Gambler, the Nun, and the Radio, The" (Hemingway) **5**:663, 681

Gambling Heart, The (Foote; teleplay) **4**:547

Game, The (London) **7**:879

"Game of Chess, A" (Eliot) **4**:454

Garden of Cyrus, The (Browne) **9**:1251

Garden of Earthly Delights, A (Oates) **8**:1111

Garden of Eden, The (Hemingway) **5**:664, 665, 671, 674, 680

Gardner's Son, The (McCarthy; screenplay) **7**:970

Gardner's Son, The (McCarthy; teleplay) **7**:963, 965, 970

"Gates of Eden" (Dylan; song) **3**:422

Gates of November, The: Chronicles of the Slepak Family (Potok) **9**:1263, 1265, 1269, 1273-74

Gathering of Old Men, A (Gaines) **5**:585, 586, 588, 589, 591-92

Gather Together in My Name (Angelou) **1**:60, 68, 76, 78-80

Gemini: An Extended Autobiographical Statement on My First Twenty-five Years of Being a Black Poet (Giovanni) **5**:631, 635, 642

Genie in the Jar, The (Giovanni) **5**:635

"Genius," The (Dreiser) **3**:381, 384, 395

"Genius Child" (Hughes) **6**:732

"Gentle Lena, The" (Stein) **10**:1437, 1438

"Gentleman Caller, The" (T. Williams). See *Glass Menagerie, The*

"Gentleman from Cracow, The" (Singer) **10**:1402, 1414

Geographical History of America, The (Stein) **10**:1424

Geography and Plays (Stein) **10**:1424

George Bellows: American Artist (Oates) **8**:1109, 1111

"Geranium, The" (O'Connor) **8**:1137, 1139

"Gerontion" (Eliot) **4**:454

"Getting There" (Plath) **9**:1221

Gettysburg trilogy (Norris) **8**:1091

Ghost Sonata, The (Strindberg) **12**:1637

Ghosts (Wharton) **12**:1622

Giant (Ferber) **4**:503, 507, 512-13

Giants of Jazz (Terkel) **11**:1521, 1522, 1523, 1524, 1539

Giant's Strength, A (Sinclair) **10**:1392

Gideon Planish (Lewis) **6**:850

"Gift, The" (Steinbeck) **11**:1464-65

Gift of Asher Lev, The (Potok) **9**:1259, 1269, 1272, 1274

"Gift Outright, The" (Frost) **4**:555, 559, 561, 571

Gifts They Bring, The: Our Debt to the Mentally Retarded (Buck) **2**:218

Gigolo (Ferber) **4**:507

Gilgamesh (Gardner and Maier transl.) **5**:602

Gimpel the Fool and Other Stories (Singer) **10**:1403, 1411

"Gimpel the Fool" (Singer) **10**:1400, 1403

Giovanni's Room (Baldwin) **1**:105, 110

Girl in the Coffin, The (Dreiser) **3**:381

Girls, The (Ferber) **4**:507, 513

Girl Who Wanted a Boy, The (Zindel) **12**:1722

"Give Your Heart to the Hawks" (Jeffers) **6**:789-90

Give Your Heart to the Hawks and Other Poems (Jeffers) **6**:786, 790

"Gladys Poems, The" (Alvarez) **1**:38

Glass family stories (Salinger) **10**:1303, 1304, 1308, 1315-18, 1319, 1321

Glass Menagerie, The (T. Williams; play) **12**:1651, 1653, 1654, 1656, 1658, 1659, *1661*, 1662, 1663-64, *1665*, 1666, 1720

Glass Menagerie, The (T. Williams and Berneis; screenplay) **12**:1653, 1663, 1664

Glengarry Glen Ross (Mamet; play) **7**:927, 928, 929, 931, 933, 935, 939-40

Glengarry Glen Ross (Mamet; screenplay) **7**:930, 932, 935, *940*

Glimpses of the Moon, The (Wharton) **12**:1620, 1622

Gnomobile, The: A Gnice Gnew Gnarrative with Gnonsense, but Gnothing Gnaughty (Sinclair) **10**:1392

Godbey (Masters) **7**:954

Goddess Abides, The (Buck) **2**:218

Goddess and Other Women, The (Oates) **8**:1111

"Godliness: A Tale in Four Parts" (Anderson) **1**:52

God of His Fathers and Other Stories, The (London) **7**:879

Go Down, Moses (Faulkner) **4**:479, 481, 486, *496*, 497

"God Rest You Merry, Gentlemen" (Hemingway) **5**:680

Gods Arrive, The (Wharton) **12**:1622

God-Seeker, The (Lewis) **6**:848, 850

God Sends Sunday (Bontemps) **2**:182, 183, 184, 187, 188, 193

God's Grace (Malamud) **7**:918, 924

God's Men (Buck) **2**:215, 218

God's Pictures (Foote) **4**:547

Go Gator and Muddy the Water: Writings by Zora Neale Hurston from the Federal Writers' Project **6**:755

Going After Cacciato (O'Brien) **8**:1119, 1122, 1123, 1124, 1125, 1127, 1128-29, 1132

Going Down Fast (Piercy) **9**:1198, 1199, 1203, 1205

Going to Meet the Man (Baldwin) **1**:110

Going to the Territory (Ellison) **4**:463, 464, 466, 473

Golda (Gibson) **5**:614, 615, 617, 619, 621, 624-26

Goldberg Street: Short Plays and Monologues (Mamet) **7**:935

Golden Apples, The (Welty) **12**:1596, 1601-2, 1606

Golden Boy (Gibson; musical with Strouse and Adams) **5**:614, 619

Golden Boy, The (Odets) **5**:614, 619, 620

Golden Fleece of California, The (Masters) **7**:954

Golden Gate Edition of Frank Norris, The **8**:1095

Golden Slippers: An Anthology of Negro Poetry for Young Readers (Bontemps ed.) **2**:187

Golem, The (Singer) **10**:1411

"Golgotha Is a Mountain" (Bontemps) **2**:184, 188, 193

"Gone" (Sandburg) **10**:1339

Gone to Soldiers (Piercy) **9**:1202, 1203, 1205, 1209-10

Gone with the Wind (Foote) **4**:547

Gone with the Wind (Mitchell) **8**:1077, **11**:1455

"Good Anna, The" (Stein) **10**:1437-38

Good Bones (Atwood) **1**:90

"Goodbye to All That" (Didion) **3**:355, 364, 369

Goodbye to Richmond (Foote) **4**:547

"Good Country People" (O'Connor) **8**:1143

Good Deed and Other Stories, The (Buck) **2**:218

Good Earth, The (Buck) **2**:211, 212, 213, 215, 218, 223-24, 227

"Good Hours" (Frost) **4**:569

Goodly Creatures (Gibson) **5**:614, 619

"Good Man Is Hard to Find, A" (O'Connor) **8**:1142, 1149-50

Good Man Is Hard to Find, A (O'Connor) **8**:1138, 1139, 1143

"Good Morning, America" (Sandburg) **10**:1330, 1338

Good Night, Willie Lee, I'll See You in the Morning: Poems (Walker) **11**:1575, 1576-77

"*Good War, The*": An Oral History of World War II (Terkel) **11**:1522, 1523, 1524, 1528, 1532, 1538, 1539

Goose Step, The: A Study of American Education (Sinclair) **10**:1380, 1384, 1392, 1395

Goslings, The: A Study of the American Schools (Sinclair) **10**:1380, 1384, 1392, 1395

Go Tell It on the Mountain (Baldwin) **1**:105, 110, 115-16, **5**:642

Go Tell It on the Mountain (television adaptation) **1**:106

"Gotta Serve Somebody" (Dylan; song) **3**:423

Gottschalk and the Grande Tarantelle (Brooks) **2**:203

Grand Coolie Damn, The (Piercy) **9**:1205

Grand Fathers: Reminiscences, Poems, Recipes, and Photos of the Keepers of our Traditions (Giovanni ed.) **5**:635

Grand Mothers: Poems, Reminiscences, and Short Stories About the Keepers of our Traditions (Giovanni ed.) **5**:635

Grandpa and the Statue (Miller; radio play) **8**:1025

"Granite and Cypress" (Jeffers) **6**:788

"Granite and Steel" (Moore) **8**:1046

Grapes of Wrath, The (Steinbeck) **11**:1445, 1448, 1450, 1451, 1452, 1453, 1454, 1455-56, 1457, 1458, 1462-64, **12**:1698

Grass Harp, The (Capote) **2**:240, 242, 245, 246-48, 246

Grass Harp, The: A Play (Capote) **2**:235, 238, 242

"Grass" (Sandburg) **10**:1339

"Grave, The" (Porter) **9**:1242-43

Great American Frustration, The (MacLeish) **7**:901

Great Divide, The: Second Thoughts on the American Dream (Terkel) **11**:1522, 1523, 1526, 1532, 1534

Great Endurance Horse Race, The: Six Hundred Miles on a Single Mount, 1908, from Evanston, Wyoming to Denver (Schaefer) **10**:1352

Greater Inclination, The (Wharton) **12**:1614, 1615, 1622

Greatest, The: My Own Story (Ali) **8**:1053

Great Expectations (Dickens) **6**:764, 772

Great Gatsby, The (Fitzgerald) **4**:515, 518, 520, 521, 522, 523-24, 525, 526, 528-29, 530-33, 536, **5**:30-33, **11**:1494

Great God Brown, The (O'Neill) **9**:1164, 1168

"Great Mountains, The" (Steinbeck) **11**:1465

"Great Pax Whitie, The" (Giovanni) **5**:636

Great Slave Narratives (Bontemps ed.) **2**:187

Great Son (Ferber) **4**:505, 507

Great Valley, The (Masters) **7**:954

Green Bough, A (Faulkner) **4**:486

Green Hills of Africa (Hemingway) **5**:663, 671, 674

"Greenleaf" (O'Connor) **8**:1135, 1139, 1142, 1150

Green Magic (Agee; screenplay) **1**:17

Grendel (Gardner) **2**:256, **5**:598, 599, 602, 603-4

Grimm's Fairy Tales **10**:1369

Gringos (Portis) **9**:1249, 1250, 1251, 1254, 1256-57

"Gringuita, La" (Alvarez) **1**:39

Guardsman, The (Molnar; Miller radio adaptation) **8**:1025

Gudgekin the Thistle Girl and Other Tales (Gardner) **5**:602

Gypsy Ballads (García Lorca; Hughes transl.) **6**:737

Habitation of Dragons, The (Foote; play) **4**:547

Habitation of Dragons, The (Foote; teleplay) **4**:547

Habit of Being, The: Letters

(O'Connor; Fitzgerald ed.) **8**:1137, 1143

Hacienda (Porter) **9**:1236

Hairy Ape, The (O'Neill) **9**:1165, 1168

"Half-Bridge, The" (Miller) **8**:1017

Half Portions (Ferber) **4**:507

Hamlet, The (Faulkner) **4**:478, 483, 486

"Hamlet" (Eliot) **4**:442

Hamlet of A. MacLeish, The (MacLeish) **7**:901

Hamlet (Shakespeare) **7**:905, **9**:1256

"Handcarved Coffins: A Nonfiction Account of an American Crime" (Capote) **2**:238, 252

Handmaid's Tale, The (Atwood) **1**:81, 84, 85, 90, 91-95

Hand of the Potter, The: A Tragedy in Four Acts (Dreiser) **3**:381

"Hands" (Anderson) **1**:52

Handy Dandy (Gibson) **5**:619

"Hannah Armstrong" (Masters) **7**:957

Happy Alchemy: On the Pleasures of Music and the Theatre (Davies; Surridge and Davies eds.) **3**:344

"Happy Endings" (Atwood) **1**:99

Happy Journey to Trenton and Camden, The (Wilder) **12**:1647

Happy Marriage, The (MacLeish) **7**:901

"Hapworth 16, 1924" (Salinger) **10**:1304, 1306

Hard Candy: A Book of Stories (T. Williams) **12**:1664

Hard Loving (Piercy) **9**:1205

Hard Rain (Dylan; record album) **3**:425

"Hard Rain's A-Gonna Fall, A" (Dylan; song lyrics) **3**:422

"Hard Riding" (McNickle) **7**:1005

"Hard Time" (Piercy) **9**:1209

Hard Times: An Oral History of the Great Depression in America (Terkel) **11**:1522, 1523, 1524, 1525, 1528, 1532, 1534-36, 1538

Hardy Boys book series **12**:1714

"Harlem" (Hughes) **5**:653, **6**:740-41

Harlem Book of the Dead, The (Van Der Zee) **8**:1068

"Harlem Ghetto, The" (Baldwin) **1**:105

Harlem Renaissance Remembered, The (Bontemps ed.) **2**:187

"Harlem Then and Now" (Baldwin) **1**:105

Harmonium (Stevens) **11**:1467, 1470, 1471, 1473, 1475, 1480-82, 1486

Harmony of Deeper Music, The: Posthumous Poems (Masters) **7**:954

"Harpers Ferry" (Rich) **9**:1293

Harry and Hortense at Hormone High (Zindel) **12**:1722, 1724-25

"Harvest (for Rosa Parks)" (Giovanni) **5**:641-42

Harvest Poems, 1910-1960 (Sandburg) **10**:1338

Haunted: Tales of the Grotesque (Oates) **8**:1111

"Haunted, The" (O'Neill) **9**:1168, 1179

"Hawk is Hungry, The" (McNickle) **7**:1005

Hawk Is Hungry and Other Stories, The (McNickle) **7**:997, 1002, 1005

"Head and Shoulders" (Fitzgerald) **4**:518

Headless Horseman, The (Benét) **2**:155

Heart Is a Lonely Hunter, The (McCullers) **7**:975, 977, 979, 980, 981, 982, 983, 985, 986-88, 989

Heart of a Stranger (Laurence) **6**:822, 823, 826, 827, 831

Heart of a Woman, The (Angelou) **1**:68, 80

Heart of Happy Hollow, The (Dunbar) **3**:402, 406, 415

Hearts Come Home and Other Stories (Buck) **2**:218

"Heart's Needle" (Snodgrass) **10**:1375

Hearts of Three (London) **7**:879

Heat and Other Stories (Oates) **8**:1111

Heavens and Earth (Benét) **2**:151, 155

Heaven's My Destination (Wilder) **12**:1631, 1647

Hedda Gabler (Ibsen) **9**:1165

Helen: A Court Ship (Faulkner) **4**:486

Hell: A Verse Drama and Photo-Play (Sinclair) **10**:1392

Hello, Dolly! (musical based on Wilder play) **12**:1632, 1634

Hello Towns! (Anderson column) **1**:45, 48

Henderson the Rain King (Bellow) **1**:129, 130, 132, *132*, 140

Henrietta (Mamet) **7**:935

"Henry James as a Characteristic American" (Moore) **8**:1040

Herakles: A Play in Verse (MacLeish) **7**:901

Her Blue Body Everything We Know: Earthling Poems, 1965-1990 (Walker) **11**:1565, 1575, 1576-77

Here and Beyond (Wharton) **12**:1622

Here's to You, Rachel Robinson (Blume) **2**:167, 172

Here to Stay: Studies in Human Tenacity (Hersey) **5**:687, 690

"Her Kind" (Sexton) **10**:1374

Hermit and the Wild Woman, The (Wharton) **12**:1622

"Hermit at Outermost House, The" (Plath) **9**:1225

Heroes Without Glory: Some Good Men of the Old West (Schaefer) **10**:1352

"Heroines" (Alvarez) **1**:38

Hero Pony, The (Mamet) **7**:935

Herzog (Bellow) **1**:125, 132, 133, 134-36

He, She, and It (Piercy) **9**:1202, 1205, 1210

Hey, Rub-a-Dub-Dub! (Dreiser) **3**:381

Hidden Flower, The (Buck) **2**:214, 215, 218

High Cost of Living, The (Piercy) **9**:1205

"High Romance and Adventure" (Lee) **6**:841, 842

High Spirits (Davies) **3**:344

"High-Toned Old Christian Woman, A" (Stevens) **11**:1481

Highway 61 Revisited (Dylan; record album) **3**:419, 421, 425

"Hill, The" (Masters) **7**:953, 956

"Hills Like White Elephants" (Hemingway) **5**:663, 668, 679

Him (Cummings) **3**:315, 316, 319

Him with His Foot in His Mouth and Other Stories (Bellow) **1**:132

Hiroshima: A New Edition with a Final Chapter Written Forty Years after the Explosion (Hersey) **5**:688, 690

Hiroshima (Hersey) **5**:683, 686, 687, 688, 689, 690, 692-94, 696

History of Alabama, and Incidentally of Georgia and Mississippi, from the Earliest Period (Pickett) **6**:842

Hoffa (Mamet; screenplay) **7:**932, 935

Hold Fast to Dreams: Poems Old and New (Bontemps ed.) **2:**187

"Holiday" (Porter) **9:**1233

"Hollow Men, The" (Eliot) **4:**441, 456-57

"Homage" (Irving) **6:**782

"Home Burial" (Frost) **4:**563, 569

Homecoming: New and Collected Poems (Alvarez) **1:**28, 29, 32, 37-38

Homecoming: Poems (Alvarez) **1:**28, 29, 32, 37

Homecoming (Foote) **4:**547

"Homecoming" (O'Neill) **9:**1168, 1179

Home Front Memo (Sandburg) **10:**1338

Homely Girl, A Life, and Other Stories (Miller) **8:**1025

"Homely Heroine, The" (Ferber) **4:**501, 503

"Home to El Building" (Ortiz Cofer) **9:**1190

Home Town (Anderson) **1:**45, 48

Homicide (Mamet; screenplay) **7:**929, 930, 932, 934, 935

Honey and Salt (Sandburg) **10:**1338

"Hoodoo in America" (Hurston) **6:**755

Hook, The (Miller; screenplay) **8:**1015

Hoosier Holiday, A (Dreiser) **3:**381

"Hope" (Bontemps) **2:**184

Hope Deferred (Davies) **3:**344

"Horror and the Glory, The" (Wright) **12:**1701, 1703

Horses and Men: Tales Long and Short (Anderson) **1:**45, 46, 48

Horses Make a Landscape Look More Beautiful (Walker) **11:**1575, 1576, 1577

Hostile Sun, The: The Poetry of D. H. Lawrence (Oates) **8:**1111

Hotel New Hampshire, The (Irving) **6:**766, 768, 773, 776-78

"Hour with Abuelo, An" (Ortiz Cofer) **9:**1190

House Divided, A (Buck) **2:**218

"Housekeeper, The" (Frost) **4:**563

House Not Meant to Stand, A (T. Williams) **12:**1664

House of Earth (Buck) **2:**218

House of Flowers (Capote and Arlen) **2:**235, 238, 242

House of Games (Mamet; screenplay) **7:**929, 930, 931, 932, 934, 935, 941

House of Mirth, The (Wharton) **12:**1611, 1614, 1615, 1616, 1617, 1618, 1619, 1622-23, 1625-26

House of Pride and Other Tales of Hawaii, The (London) **7:**879

"Housewife, The" (Sexton) **10:**1369

Housing America (MacLeish) **7:**901

"How It Feels to Be Colored Me" (Hurston) **6:**750

How it Happens: Talk About the German People, 1914-33, with Ema von Pustau (Buck and Pustau) **2:**218

Howl (Ginsberg) **12:**1678

How the García Girls Lost Their Accents (Alvarez) **1:**28, 29, 32, 33-34

"How to Tell a True War Story" (O'Brien) **8:**1132

How to Write (Stein) **10:**1424

How Writing Is Written (Stein) **10:**1424

Hoyf, Der (Singer). See *Manor, The*

Huckleberry Finn (Twain) **4:**540, **10:**1352

Hudson River Bracketed (Wharton) **12:**1620, 1622

Hughie (O'Neill) **9:**1164, 1168, 1172, 1177-78

Human Drift, The (London) **7:**879

Human Nature (Wharton) **12:**1622

Human Season, The: Selected Poems, 1926-1972 (MacLeish) **7:**901

Humboldt's Gift (Bellow) **1:**125, 127, 129, *130,* 132, 133, 136-37, 140

"Hummingbird" (Carver) **2:***260*

"Hundred Collars, A" (Frost) **4:**563

Hundred Secret Senses, The (Tan) **11:**1508, 1509, 1511, *1512,* 1514, 1517

Hungerfield and Other Poems (Jeffers) **6:**787, 790, 795-96

"Hungerfield" (Jeffers) **6:**795-96

Hunger (Hamsun) **10:**1399

"Hungry Generations, The" (McNickle) **7:**997, 1005

Hungry Ghosts, The (Oates) **8:**1111

"Hunted, The" (O'Neill) **9:**1168, *1170,* 1179

Hunting Stuart (Davies) **3:**344

Hurry Sundown (Foote and Ryan; screenplay) **4:**544, 546-47

Hydriotaphia, Urne-Buriall (Browne) **11:**1502

"Hyla Brook" (Frost) **4:**571

"Hypothesis" (O'Brien) **8:**1131

i: six nonlectures (Cummings) **3:**319

I Am the Cheese (Cormier) **3:**296, 297, 298, 299, 301, 305-7

I Am the Clay (Potok) **9:**1261, 1267, 1269

I, Candidate for Governor and How I Got Licked (Sinclair) **10:**1389, 1392

I Can't Remember Anything (Miller) **8:**1025

Iceman Cometh, The (O'Neill) **9:**1159, 1163, 1164, 1166, 1168, 1171, 1173-75, 1177, 1179

Ice Palace (Ferber) **4:**505, 507

Ida: A Novel (Stein) **10:**1424, 1437

"Idea of Order at Key West, The" (Stevens) **11:**1482, 1483

Ideas of Order (Stevens) **11:**1470, 1471, 1473-74, 1475, 1482-83

Ides of March, The (Wilder) **12:**1647

Idiots First (Malamud) **7:**918, 924

I Don't Need You Anymore (Miller) **8:**1025

"I Don't Talk Service No More" (Portis) **9:**1249, 1257

"I Dreamed I Saw St. Augustine" (Dylan; song lyric) **3:**423

If Beale Street Could Talk (Baldwin) **1:**106, 110, 121-22

If I Die in a Combat Zone, Box Me Up and Ship Me Home (O'Brien) **8:**1119, 1122, 1123, 1124, 1125, 1127, 1132-33

If I Were Boss: The Early Business Stories of Sinclair Lewis (Lewis) **6:**850

If Morning Ever Comes (Tyler) **11:**1543, 1546, 1551

Iggie's House (Blume) **2:**163, 165, 166, 172

I, Governor of California and How I Ended Poverty: A True Story of the Future (Sinclair) **10:**1387, 1392

"I Have Seen Black Hands" (Wright) **12:**1695

I Have Words to Spend: Reflections of a Small Town Editor (Cormier) **3:**297, 301

"II" (Brooks) **2:**204

I Know Why the Cage Bird Sings (Angelou) **1:**60, 62, 68, 74-76

I Know Why the Cage Bird Sings (television adaptation) **1**:60

I Lay in Zion (Gibson) **5**:613, 615, 619

Iliad (Homer) **2**:204, **8**:1097, 1137

"i like my body when it is with your" (Cummings) **3**:330

Illinois Poem (Masters) **7**:954

Illumination and Night Glare: The Unfinished Autobiography of Carson McCullers **7**:983

I Lock My Door upon Myself (Oates) **8**:1111

I Love My Mother (Zindel) **12**:1722

I Love Myself When I Am Laughing…and Then Again When I Am Looking Mean and Impressive: A Zora Neale Hurston Reader (Walker ed.) **6**:755, **11**:1564, 1566, 1575

"I love those little booths at Benvenuti's" (Brooks) **2**:205

Image and Other Stories, The (Singer) **10**:1411

Imaginary Girlfriend, An (Irving) **6**:768, 773, 781

I'm a Stranger Here Myself and Other Stories (Lewis) **6**:850

"I'm Crazy" (Salinger) **10**:1303

Imperial Woman (Buck) **2**:215, 217, 218, 224-26

In a Coffin in Egypt (Foote) **4**:547

In a Garden: An Opera in One Act (Stein) **10**:1424

"In Another Country" (Hemingway) **5**:679

In Black and White (Welty) **12**:1596

"In China, Too" (Buck) **2**:211, 212

Incident at Vichy (Miller) **8**:1016, 1018, 1019, 1025

In Cold Blood (Capote) **2**:233, 237, 238, 240, 242, 244, 245, *245*, 248-50, *250*, 251, **6**:836

In Darkest America: Two Plays (Oates) **8**:1111

"Index 1916" (Cummings) **3**:313

"Indian Camp" (Hemingway) **5**:668, 679

Indian Man: A Biography of Oliver La Farge (McNickle) **7**:997, 1002

Indians and Other Americans: Two Ways of Life Meet (McNickle and Fey) **7**:997, 1002

Indian Summer (Knowles) **6**:803, 805, 809, 810, 812, 817

Indian Tribes of the United States, The:

Ethnic and Cultural Survival (McNickle). *See Native American Tribalism: Indian Survivals and Renewals*

In Dubious Battle (Steinbeck) **11**:1448, 1450, 1454

Industrial Republic, The (Sinclair) **10**:1379, 1392

I Never Loved Your Mind (Zindel) **12**:1722

"I Never Saw Morning" (Tyler) **11**:1543

"In Excelsis" (Sexton) **10**:1368

Infancy (Wilder) **12**:1647

Inferno (Dante) **3**:330

Infidels (Dylan; record album) **3**:425

"Ingrate, The" (Dunbar) **3**:404, 411, 413

"In Hardwood Groves" (Frost) **4**:567

"in Just-spring when the world is mud-luscious" (Cummings) **3**:317, 329

In Love and Trouble: Stories of Black Women (Walker) **11**:1564, 1575, 1577-79

"In Memorium" (Miller) **8**:1019

In Morocco (Wharton) **12**:1622

In My Beginning (Foote) **4**:547

In My Father's Court (Singer) **10**:1398, 1404, 1411, 1414-16

In My Father's House (Gaines) **5**:585, 586, 588, 589, 594

Innocents, The: A Story for Lovers (Lewis) **6**:850

Innocents, The (Capote; screenplay) **2**:237, 238, 242

"In Old Age" (Singer) **10**:1399

In Old Plantation Days (Dunbar) **3**:401, 402, 406, *414*, 415

In Our Time (first version; Hemingway) **5**:679

In Our Time (second version) (Hemingway) **5**:663, 665, 674, 679

In Restless Ecstasy (Sandburg) **10**:1325

In Russia (Miller; photos by Morath) **8**:1018, 1025

In Savoy: Or, Yes Is for a Very Young Man (A Play of the Resistance in France) (Stein) **10**:1424

In Search of J. D. Salinger (Hamilton) **10**:1304, 1306, 1311, 1313

In Search of Our Mothers' Gardens: Womanist Prose (Walker) **11**:1575

"Inside Modern Paganism" (Potok) **9**:1274

"Intelligence, Choice, and Consent" (Hersey) **5**:688

Intent of the Artist, The (Wilder) **12**:1647

"Interior Space" (Irving) **6**:781

Interlunar (Atwood) **1**:90

"In the Alien Corn" (McNickle) **7**:1005

In the American Grain (W. C. Williams) **12**:1685, 1686, 1690-91

In the Bar of a Tokyo Hotel (T. Williams) **12**:1655, 1664

In the Beginning (Potok) **9**:1262, 1266, 1267, 1269

In the Clap Shack (Styron; play) **11**:1500

In the Clearing (Frost) **4**:567, 570

In the Lake of the Woods (O'Brien) **8**:1119, 1122, 1123, 1124, 1125, 1126, 1127, 1129-31, 1133

In the Mecca (Brooks) **2**:198, 203

In the Middle of the Night (Cormier) **3**:301

In the Money (W. C. Williams) **12**:1686, 1692

In the Name of Salomé (Garcia) **1**:32

"In the Region of Ice" (Oates) **8**:1104

In the Suicide Mountains (Gardner) **5**:602

In the Time of the Butterflies (Alvarez) **1**:28, 29, 30, 32, 34-36

In the Winter of Cities (T. Williams) **12**:1664

"Into Egypt" (Benét) **2**:155

Into the Valley: A Skirmish of the Marines (Hersey) **5**:685, 688, 690, 697

Intruder in the Dust (Faulkner) **4**:479, 484, 486

Inventions of the March Hare: Poems, 1909-1917 (Eliot; Ricks ed.) **4**:441, 450

Invisible Landscapes (Masters) **7**:954

Invisible Man (Ellison) **1**:67, **3**:410, **4**:459, 460, 462, 463, 464, 465, 466, 467, 468-70, 471, 472, 473, **12**:1708

Invisible Woman: New and Selected Poems, 1970-1982 (Oates) **8**:1111

"I Remember Grandpa: A Story" (Capote) **2**:242

I Rise in Flame, Cried the Phoenix (T. Williams) **12**:1658, 1664

Iron Heel, The (London) **7:**876, 879, 883, 888-89

Irresponsibles, The: A Declaration (MacLeish) **7:**901

Is 5 (Cummings) **3:**319, 331-32

Isaac McCaslin ("Bear") **4:**496, 497

I Shall Not be Moved: Poems (Angelou) **1:**68

"i sing of Olaf glad and big" (Cummings) **3:**326

Island Like You, An: Stories of the Barrio (Ortiz Cofer) **9:**1185, 1186, 1187, 1188, 1189-91

Islands in the Stream (Hemingway) **5:**664, 670-71, 674

I Stand Before You Naked (Oates) **8:**1111

"Is There a Case for Foreign Missions?" (Buck) **2:**213

"It Ain't Me Babe" (Dylan; song lyric) **3:**423

Italian Backgrounds (Wharton) **12:**1622

Italian Villas and Their Gardens (Wharton) **12:**1622

It All Ends Up: From the Dim Past to the Uncertain Future (Bellow) **1:**132

It Can't Happen Here (Lewis; novel) **6:**848, 850, 861-62

It Can't Happen Here (Lewis; play) **6:**847, 850, *862*

It Happened to Didymus (Sinclair) **10:**1392

"I, Too, Sing America" (Bontemps and Hughes) **2:**185, **6:**728, 742

"It's Alright Ma, I'm Only Bleeding" (Dylan; song lyric) **3:**423

It's Not the End of the World (Blume) **2:**172, 178

Ivanhoe (Scott) **2:**182

I-wan (*Patriot*) **2:**229

I Wanted to Write a Poem (W. C. Williams) **12:**1686

"I Want to Know Why" (Anderson) **1:**55, *56*

I Wonder as I Wander: An Autobiographical Journey (Hughes) **6:**728, 737

Jack Kelso (Masters) **7:**954

"Jacob and the Indians" (Benét) **2:**160-61

Jafsie and John Henry: Essays on Hollywood, Bad Boys, and Six Hours of Perfect Poker (Mamet) **7:**935

James Baldwin: Collected Essays (Morrison ed.) **1:**106, 110

James Shore's Daughter (Benét) **2:**155

Jane Eyre (Brontë) **6:**775

Jason and Medea (Gardner) **5:**598, 602

Jason's Quest (Laurence) **6:**821, 823, 827

Jayhawker: A Play in Three Acts (Lewis and Lewis) **6:**850

Jazz (Morrison) **8:**1052, 1054, 1064, 1068

J.B.: A Play in Verse (MacLeish) **7:**895, 896, 901, 903-5, 906

Jean Huguenot (Benét) **2:**151, 155

Jennie Gerhardt (Dreiser) **3:**378, 380, 381, 384, 386-89

Jerico-Jim Crow (Hughes) **6:**737

Jerry of the Islands (London) **7:**879

Jest of God, A (Laurence) **6:**821, 823, 827, 828, 829, 831

Jig for the Gipsy, A (Davies) **3:**337, 344

"Jilting of Granny Weatherall, The" (Porter) **9:**1236, *1242*, 1243

Jim Crow's Last Stand (Hughes) **6:**737

Jimmie Higgins (Sinclair) **10:**1392

Jimmy Blevins (*All the Pretty Horses*) **7:**969

Jimmy Dell (*Spanish Prisoner*) **7:**941

Jimmy Louie (*Kitchen God's Wife*) **11:**1516

Jimmy's Blues: Selected Poems (Baldwin) **1:**106, 110

"Jimsella" (Dunbar) **3:**413, 415

Job, The: An American Novel (Lewis) **6:**848, 850

"Job for Valentin, A" (Ortiz Cofer) **9:**1187, 1190

"Joe Poems, The" (Alvarez) **1:**38

Joey and the Birthday Present (Sexton and Kumin) **10:**1371

John and Abigail (Gibson) **5:**617, 619

John Barleycorn (London) **7:**877, 879

John Brown's Body (Benét) **2:**149, 151, 152, 153-54, 155, 158-59

Johnny Jack and His Beginnings (Buck) **2:**218

Johnny Panic and the Bible of Dreams (Plath) **9:**1219, 1224, 1227

"Johnny Pye and the Fool-Killer" (Benét) **2:**151, 155

"John Redding Goes to Sea" (Hurston) **6:**747, 749

John Wesley Harding (Dylan; record album) **3:**419-20, 421, 425

Jonah's Gourd Vine (Hurston) **6:**748, 749, 752, 755, 756, *760*, 761

Joseph and Koza: Or, The Sacrifice to the Vistula (Singer) **10:**1411

Journal of a Novel: The "East of Eden" Letters (Steinbeck) **11:**1454

Journal of Arthur Stirling, The (Sinclair) **10:**1392

Journals of Susanna Moodie, The (Atwood) **1:**84, 89, 90, 95, 97-99

Journals of Sylvia Plath, The (Plath) **9:**1224

Journals of Thornton Wilder, 1939-1961, The (Wilder) **12:**1647

"Journey, The" (Porter). *See Old Order, The*

Journey to Love (W. C. Williams) **12:**1679, 1686

Joy Luck Club, The (Tan; novel) **11:**1505, 1507, 1508, 1509, 1511, 1512, 1513-15, 1517, 1518

Joy Luck Club, The (Tan and Bass; screenplay) **11:***1506*, 1508, 1509, *1510*, *1513*

Joy of Children, The (Buck) **2:**218

Joyous Miracle, The (Norris) **8:**1095

Jubilee (Walker) **5:**642

Jump Bad: A New Chicago Anthology (Brooks ed.) **2:**203

"June Recital" (Welty) **12:**1601, 1602

Juneteenth (Ellison) **4:**462, 463, 465, 466, 467, 470-72

Jungle, The (Sinclair) **3:**380, **10:**1377, 1379, 1382, 1383, 1384, 1385, 1391-94, 1395, **12:**1698

Just Above My Head (Baldwin) **1:**106, 110

Just as Long as We're Together (Blume) **2:**167, 172

"Just Before the War with the Eskimos" (Salinger) **10:**1319, 1321

Just Give Me a Cool Drink of water 'fore I Diiie (Angelou) **1:**60, 68, 78

"Justice" (Hughes) **6:**744

"Just Like a Woman" (Dylan; song lyric) **3:**429

Kaleidoscopes Baroque: A Poem (Atwood) **1:**90

Kean Land and Other Stories, The (Schaefer) **10**:1349, 1352

Kempton-Wace Letters, The (London and Strunsky) **7**:879

Kennedy Women, The: A Personal Appraisal (Buck) **2**:218

Key West Tales (Hersey) **5**:690

Kidnapped (Stevenson) **2**:182

"Killers, The" (Hemingway) **5**:663, 679

Kind of Magic, A (Ferber) **4**:502, 503, 505, 507

Kinfolk (Buck) **2**:215, 218

King Arthur legends **7**:922, 923

King Coal (Sinclair) **10**:1392

"King David" (Benét) **2**:151, 155

Kingdom of Art, The: Willa Cather's First Principles and Critical Statements, 1893-1896 (Cather) **2**:278

Kingdom of Earth (T. Williams). *See Seven Descents of Myrtle, The*

King Lear (Shakespeare) **3**:366

King of the Bingo Game and Flying Home (Ellison) **4**:466

"King of the Bingo Game" (Ellison) **4**:462, 466, 472-73

King of the Fields, The (Singer) **10**:1411

King of the Hummingbirds and Other Tales, The (Gardner) **5**:602

King Phoenix (Davies) **3**:344

Kingsblood Royal (Lewis) **6**:848, 850

"King's Indian, The: A Tale" (Gardner; Fink illus.) **5**:608

King's Indian, The: Stories and Tales (Gardner; Fink illus.) **5**:598, 599, 600-601, 602, 608

Kipling, Rudyard **4**:505

Kit Brandon (Anderson) **1**:45, 46, 48, 55

"kitchenette folks" (Brooks) **2**:207

Kitchen God's Wife, The (Tan) **11**:1508, 1509, 1511-12, 1514, 1515-16

Kit O'Brien (Masters) **7**:954

"Knife, The" (Moore) **8**:1046

Knife of the Times and Other Stories, The (W. C. Williams) **12**:1686

Knightly Quest, The: A Novella and Four Short Stories (T. Williams) **12**:1664

Knight's Gambit (Faulkner) **4**:486

Knocked Out Loaded (Dylan; record album) **3**:425

"Knoxville: Summer of 1915" (Agee) **1**:13, 15

"Knoxville, Tennessee" (Giovanni) **5**:636

Knoxville, Tennessee (Giovanni) **5**:635

Kofi and His Magic (Angelou and Courtney-Clarke) **1**:68

Kora in Hell: Improvisations (W. C. Williams) **12**:1686

Ladder of Years (Tyler) **11**:1545, 1548, 1551

Ladies at the Alamo (Zindel) **12**:1722

"Lady Lazarus" (Plath) **9**:1221

Lady of Larkspur Lotion, The (T. Williams) **12**:1664

Lady Oracle (Atwood) **1**:83, 85, 90, 95-96

Lakeboat (Mamet) **7**:935

Lamb of Abyssalia, The (Oates) **8**:1111

Lament for Dark Peoples (Hughes) **6**:737

Land Is Bright, The (Ferber and Kaufman) **4**:507

Land of the Free (MacLeish) **7**:901

Land of the Pharaohs (Faulkner; screenplay) **4**:486

"Landscape as a Nude" (MacLeish) **7**:902

Langston Hughes: American Poet (Walker) **11**:1564, 1575

Langston Hughes Reader, The (Hughes) **6**:737

"Language of Discretion, The" (Tan) **11**:1514

Lanny Budd series (Sinclair) **10**:1377, 1381, 1382, 1384-85, 1395-96

Lansky (Mamet; teleplay) **7**:932, 934, 935

Lapse of Memory (Cormier) **3**:298

Larry of the Little League (book) **8**:1120

Last Analysis, The (Bellow) **1**:132

Last Circle, The: Stories and Poems (Benét) **2**:155

Last Days (Oates) **8**:1111

Last Operas and Plays (Stein) **10**:1424

Last Thing He Wanted, The (Didion) **3**:358, 361, 363, 372-74

Last Tycoon, The (Fitzgerald) **3**:362, **4**:520, 522, 523, 524, 525, 532, 536, 536-37

Last White Class, The: A Play About Neighborhood Terror (Piercy and Wood) **9**:1205

Last Yankee, The (Miller) **8**:1025

Later Plays (O'Neill) **9**:1168

Latin Deli, The: Prose and Poetry (Ortiz Cofer) **9**:1183-84, 1185, 1188, 1191-92

Latin Women Pray (Ortiz Cofer; play) **9**:1191

Latin Women Pray (Ortiz Cofer; short story collection) **9**:1191

Laughing to Keep from Crying (Hughes) **6**:737

Laura Dennis (Foote) **4**:547

"Laura" (Tyler) **11**:1543

Lawd Today (Wright) **12**:1700, 1703

"Lay, Lady, Lay" (Dylan; song lyric) **3**:423

Lazarus Laughed (O'Neill) **9**:1165, 1168

Leaflets (Rich) **9**:1284

Leaning Tower and Other Stories, The (Porter) **9**:1231, 1233, 1236

"Learning Experience" (Piercy) **9**:1204-5

Leaven of Malice (Davies) **3**:337, 340, 341, 344, 347-48, 351

Leaves of Grass (Whitman) **2**:185, **6**:731, **7**:960, **12**:1684

Leaves of the Tree, The (Masters) **7**:954

Lectures in America (Stein) **10**:1424

Lee: A Dramatic Poem (Masters) **7**:954

"Legend Beautiful, The" (Longfellow) **3**:313

Lesson Before Dying, A (Gaines) **5**:585, 586, 588, 589, 592-93

Let Me Hear You Whisper and The Ladies Should Be in Bed: Two Plays (Zindel) **12**:1717, 1722

Let Me Hear You Whisper (Zindel; teleplay) **12**:1717, 1722

"Letter from Baltimore, A" (Hughes) **6**:734

Letter from Peking (Buck) **2**:218

Letters from a Caribbean Island (Ortiz Cofer) **9**:1191

Letters from Jack London (Hendricks and Shepard ed.) **7**:879

Letters Home: Correspondence, 1950-1963 (Plath; A. Plath ed.) **9**:1224, 1227

Letters of Archibald MacLeish: 1970-1982 (Winnick ed.) **7**:901

Letters of Carl Sandburg, The (Mitgang ed.) **10**:1338

Letters of Edith Wharton, The (Wharton) **12**:1622

Letters of Frank Norris, The (Norris; Walker ed.) **8**:1095

Letters of F. Scott Fitzgerald, The (Fitzgerald) **4**:532

Letters of James Agee to Father Flye (Agee) **1**:17

Letters of Katherine Anne Porter (Porter) **9**:1236

Letters of Robert Frost to Louis Untermeyer (with commentary by Louis Untermeyer) **4**:567

Letters of Sherwood Anderson, The (Anderson) **1**:48

Letters of Theodore Dreiser (Dreiser) **3**:381

Letters of T. S. Eliot, The: Volume 1, 1898-1922 (Eliot ed.) **4**:441, 450

Letters of Wallace Stevens (Stevens ed.) **11**:1471, 1475

Letters to Alicia (Steinbeck) **11**:1454

Letters to Bab: Sherwood Anderson to Marietta D. Finley (Anderson) **1**:48

Letters to His Daughter (Fitzgerald) **4**:532

Letters to Judd (Sinclair) **10**:1392

Letters to Judy: What Your Kids Wish They Could Tell You (Blume) **2**:166, 167, 172

Letters to Louise (Dreiser) **3**:381

Letter to the Alumni (Hersey) **5**:690

Let Us Now Praise Famous Men (Agee and Evans) **1**:11, 13, 14, 15, 17, 19, 20-22

Levy Mayer and the New Industrial Era (Masters) **7**:954

Lichee Nuts (Masters) **7**:954

"Lichen" (Munro) **8**:1078

Lie Down in Darkness (Styron) **11**:1491, 1492, 1494, 1495, 1500, 1502-3

"Lie Factory Starts, The" (Sinclair) **10**:1387

Life Along the Passaic River (W. C. Williams) **12**:1686

Life and Death of Mr. Badman, The (Bunyan) **11**:1497

Life and Times of Chaucer, The (Gardner) **5**:598, 602

Life Before Man (Atwood) **1**:90

Lifeboat (Steinbeck; screenplay) **11**:1449, 1453, 1454

"Lifeboat" (Steinbeck; short story) **11**:1453

Life Doesn't Frighten Me (Angelou and Basquiat) **1**:68

Life in the Sun, A (Wilder) **12**:1632, 1634, 1647

Life in the Theater, A (Mamet; play) **7**:935

Life in the Theater, A (Mamet; teleplay) **7**:932, 934, 935

"Life of Lincoln West, The" (Brooks) **2**:207

Life Sketches (Hersey) **5**:690

Life Studies (R. Lowell) **10**:1360

Life with No Joy in It, and Other Plays and Pieces, A (Mamet) **7**:935

"Life You Save May Be Your Own, The" (O'Connor) **8**:1135

Light in August (Faulkner) **4**:478, 481, 484, 486, 497

"Light of the World, The" (Hemingway) **5**:680

"Light Sleeper, The" (Malamud) **7**:911

"Lights on the River, The" (Tyler) **11**:1543

Like a Bulwark (Moore) **8**:1036, 1043

"Like a Rolling Stone" (Dylan; song lyric) **3**:423, 427

Lily Dale (Foote; play) **4**:547

Lily Dale (Foote; screenplay) **4**:547

Lincoln and Whitman Miscellany, A (Sandburg) **10**:1338

Lincoln Collector: The Story of Oliver R. Barrett's Great Private Collection (Sandburg) **10**:1338

Lincoln: The Man (Masters) **7**:945, 949, 950, 951, 952, 954

Line of the Sun, The (Ortiz Cofer) **9**:1181, 1183, 1185, 1186, 1191, 1193

Lion in the Garden: Interviews with William Faulkner, 1926-1962 (Faulkner; ed. Meriwether and Millgate) **4**:486

Lip Service (Mamet; teleplay) **7**:934, 935

"Listen Here Blues" (Hughes) **6**:740

"Listen to the People" (Benét) **2**:155

"Litany of Dictatorships" (Benét) **2**:154

Literary Criticism of Frank Norris, The (Norris; Pizer ed.) **8**:1095

"Litter of Rose Leaves, The" (Benét) **2**:155

Little Boy in Search of God, A: Mysticism in a Personal Light (Singer) **10**:1411

"Little Gidding" (Eliot) **4**:451

"Little Girl Speakings" (Angelou) **1**:78

Little Ham (Hughes) **6**:737

"Little June Book, The" (Stevens) **11**:1469, 1471

Little Lady of the Big House, The (London) **7**:879

Little Man, Little Man: A Story of Childhood (Baldwin) **1**:106, 110

Little Raw on Monday Morning, A (Cormier) **3**:295, 301

Little Steel (Sinclair) **10**:1392

Little Stream, A (Gaines) **5**:584

"Little Things That Count, The" (Cormier) **3**:294, 297

Live or Die (Sexton) **10**:1361, 1371, 1375-76

"Live" (Sexton) **10**:1376

Lives of Girls and Women (Munro) **8**:1073, 1074, 1075, 1076, 1077, 1079-80, 1082

"Lives of the Dead, The" (O'Brien) **8**:1132

Lives of the Twins (Oates; under Smith pseud.) **8**:1111

Living by the Word: Selected Writings, 1973-1987 (Walker) **11**:1575, 1579-80

Living in the Open (Piercy) **9**:1205

Living Reed, The (Buck) **2**:214, 218

Local Color (Capote) **2**:235, 238, 242

Loch (Zindel) **12**:1715, 1722

Locket, The (Masters) **7**:954

"Loneliness: An American Malady" (McCullers) **7**:986

Lonely, The (Foote) **4**:547

Lonesome Boy (Bontemps) **2**:187

"Lone Striker, A" (Frost) **4**:571

"Long Black Song" (Wright) **12**:1707

Long Christmas Dinner, The (Wilder; opera libretto) **12**:1632, 1634, 1647

Long Christmas Dinner, The (Wilder; play) **12**:1638

Long Christmas Dinner and Other Plays in One Act, The (Wilder) **12**:1631, 1647

Long Day in November, A (Gaines) **5**:587, 589

"Long Day in November, A" (Gaines) **5**:587

Long Day's Journey into Night (O'Neill) **9**:1161, 1162, 1163, 1166, 1168, 1172, 1175-77, 1178, 1179

Long Dream, The (Wright) **12:**1697, 1703

Long Drums and Cannons: Nigerian Dramatists and Novelists, 1952-1966 (Laurence) **6:**823, 824, 827

Long Gay Book, A (Stein) **10:**1424

Longings of Women, The (Piercy) **9:**1205

Long Love, The (Sedges; under Buck pseud.) **2:**218

Long March, The (Styron) **11:**1491, 1495, 1500

Long Stay Cut Short, The: Or, The Unsatisfactory Supper (T. Williams) **12:**1664

Long Valley, The (Steinbeck) **11:**1448, 1454

"Lord Randal" (ballad) **3:**422

"Lorelei" (Plath) **9:**1225

Losing Battles (Welty) **12:**1592, 1593, 1596, 1598, 1602-4, 1606

Lost Face (London) **7:**879

Lost in America (Singer) **10:**1411

Lost Lady, A (Cather) **2:**274, 278

"Love and Admiration and Respect": The O'Neill-Commins Correspondence (O'Neill and Commins; Commins ed.) **9:**1168

Love and How to Cure It (Wilder) **12:**1647

Love and Its Derangements (Oates) **8:**1111

Love and Libel: Or, The Ogre of the Provincial World (Davies) **3:**337, 341, 344, 348

Love and Trouble: Stories of Black Women (Walker) **11:**1564

Love, Honor, and Behave (film) **2:**153

"Love in Other Words" (Lee) **6:**836, 841, 842

Lovely Sunday for Creve Coeur, A (T. Williams) **12:**1664

Love Medicine (Erdrich) **11:**1507, 1512, 1514

Love of a Good Woman, The (Munro) **8:**1075, 1078, 1080

Love of Landry, The (Dunbar) **3:**401, 402, 406

Love of Life and Other Stories (London) **7:**879

Love of the Last Tycoon, The: A Western (Fitzgerald) **4:**520, 522, 524, 525, 532, 536, 537

Love Poems (Giovanni) **5:**635

Love Poems (Sexton) **10:**1371

Lovers and Other Stories, The (Buck) **2:**218

"Love Song of J. Alfred Prufrock, The" (Eliot) **4:**437, 439, 441, 442, 451, 452-53, 457

Love's Pilgrimage (Sinclair) **10:**1379, 1392

"Love the Wild Swan" (Jeffers) **6:**800

"Loving the Crone" (Piercy) **9:**1209

Lower Depths, The (Gorky) **9:**1173

Lucrece (Obey; Wilder adaptation) **12:**1631, 1647

Lucretia Borgia (Stein) **10:**1424

Lucy Church Amiably (Stein) **10:**1424

Lucy Gayheart (Cather) **2:**274, 278

Luxury of Sin, The (Oates) **8:**1111

Lyonesse: Poems (Plath) **9:**1224

Lyre of Orpheus, The (Davies) **3:**337, 344

Lyrical Ballads (Wordsworth) **4:**569

Lyrics, 1962-1985 (Dylan; song lyric texts) **3:**425

Lyrics, 1962-1999 (Dylan; song lyric texts) **3:**425

Lyrics of Love and Laughter (Dunbar) **3:**401, 402, 406

Lyrics of Lowly Life (Dunbar) **3:**399, 406, 407

Lyrics of Sunshine and Shadow (Dunbar) **3:**401, 402, 406

Lyrics of the Hearthside (Dunbar) **3:**401, 402, 406

Macbeth (Shakespeare) **4:**492-93, **10:**1371

Madame Bovary (Flaubert) **2:**241, **8:**1057, **10:**1406

Madame de Treymes (Wharton) **12:**1618, 1622

Maggie: A Girl of the Streets (Crane) **3:**380, **8:**1092

Magic Barrel, The (Malamud) **7:**912, 913, 918, 924

Magician of Lublin, The (Singer) **10:**1405, 1411

"Mag" (Sandburg) **10:**1339

Main Street: The Story of Carol Kennicott (Lewis) **6:**843, *844*, 845, 846, 848, 849, 850, 853-54, 861

Majors and Minors (Dunbar) **3:**399, 402, 403, 406

Make-Believe Town: Essays and Remembrances (Mamet) **7:**930, 935

Make Light of It: Collected Stories (W. C. Williams) **12:**1678, 1686

Making of Americans, The (Stein) **10:**1422, 1423, 1424, 1425, 1429, 1432-34

"Making Our Beds" (Alvarez) **1:**37-38

"Making Up the Past" (Alvarez) **1:**38

Mame (Zindel; screenplay) **12:**1717, 1722

Mammonart (Sinclair) **10:**1380, 1392, 1395

Manassas (Sinclair) **10:**1383, 1384, 1392

Manawaka books (Laurence) **6:**819, 821, 822, 823, 824, 827, 830, 831

Manchild in the Promised Land (Brown) **8:**1051

Man Crazy (Oates) **8:**1109, 1111

Mandala (Buck) **2:**218

Man from Main Street, The: Selected Essays and Other Writings (Lewis) **6:**850

Man of the House, The (Foote; screenplay) **4:**547

Manor, The (Singer) **10:**1403, 1411

Mansion, The (Faulkner) **4:**480, 486

"Man's Story, The" (Anderson) **1:**46

Man's Woman, A (Norris) **8:**1089, 1093, 1095, 1101-2

"Man's Work" (McNickle) **7:**1005

Manticore, The (Davies) **3:**337, 344, 350

Mantrap (Lewis) **6:**848, 850

Man Who Changed China, The: The Story of Sun Yat-Sen (Buck) **2:**218

Man Who Climbed Pecan Trees, The (Foote) **4:**547

Man Who Had All the Luck, The (Miller) **8:**1014, 1017, 1018, 1025

Man Who Knew Coolidge, The: Being the Soul of Lowell Schmaltz, Constructive and Nordic Citizen (Lewis) **6:**848, 850

"Man Who Lived Underground, The" (Wright) **12:**1699, 1707, 1708

Man Who Married a Dumb Wife, The (play) **3:**336

"Man Who Was Almost a Man, The" (Wright) **12:**1698, 1707

Man with the Blue Guitar and Other Poems, The (Stevens) **11:**1470, 1471, 1474, 1475

Man with the Golden Arm, The (Algren) **11:**1531

Many Loves and Other Plays (W. C. Williams) **12**:1686

Many Marriages (Anderson) **1**:45, 46, 48, 55-56

"Many Thousands Gone" (Baldwin) **1**:105

"Maple" (Frost) **4**:563

Marble Faun, The (Faulkner) **4**:477, 486

Marchbanks' Almanack (Davies) **3**:344

Marching Men (Anderson) **1**:45, 48

Marco Millions (O'Neill) **9**:1168, 1171-72, 1178

Margaret Atwood: Conversations (Atwood) **1**:90

María Concepción (Porter) **9**:1230, 1233, 1243

Marianne Moore Reader, A (Moore) **8**:1036, 1037, 1043

Maria's Lovers (Zindel, Brach, and Konchalovsky; screenplay) **12**:1717, 1722

Marie Antoinette (Sinclair) **10**:1392

Marionettes, The: A Play in One Act (Faulkner; Polk ed.) **4**:486

Mark Mallory stories (Sinclair under Garrison pseud.) **10**:1378

Mark Twain: A Portrait (Masters) **7**:952, 954

Marmot Drive, The (Hersey) **5**:686, 690, 691

Marne, The (Wharton) **12**:1622

"Marriage" (Moore) **8**:1042-43

Marriages and Infidelities (Oates) **8**:1111

Mars and Her Children (Piercy) **9**:1205

Martin Eden (London) **7**:877, 879, 883, 885-86

Marya: A Life (Oates) **8**:1109, 1111

Mary Lincoln: Wife and Widow (Sandburg and Angle) **10**:1338

Masque of Mercy, A (Frost) **4**:567, 572

Masque of Reason, A (Frost) **4**:567, 573

Mass for the Dead, A (Gibson) **5**:615, 619, 624

"Master Charge Blues" (Giovanni) **5**:639

Masters of Atlantis (Portis) **9**:1249, 1250, 1254, 1257-58

Masters of the Dew (Roumain; Hughes and Cook transl.) **6**:737

Matisse, Picasso, and Gertrude Stein, with Two Shorter Stories (Stein) **10**:1424

"Matoa's Mirror" (Ortiz Cofer) **9**:1190

Maud Martha (Brooks) **2**:197, 203, 207

Mavericks (Schaefer) **10**:1346, 1348, 1349, 1352, 1355-56

"May 30" (Sexton) **10**:1368

Mayday (Faulkner) **4**:486

"may i feel said he" (Cummings) **3**:326

Mayn Tatn's Bes-din Shtub (Singer). See *In My Father's Court*

Mazel and Shlimazel; Or, The Milk of a Lioness (Singer) **10**:1411

McTeague (Norris) **8**:1085, 1089, 1093, 1094-97, 1100, 1101, 1102

Medal for Benny, A (Steinbeck; screenplay) **11**:1449, 1454

Medea (Euripides; Jeffers transl.) **6**:787, 788, 788, 790, 800-801

"Melanctha" (Stein) **10**:1437, 1438

Member of the Family (Foote; teleplay) **4**:547

Member of the Wedding, The: A Play (McCullers) **7**:978, 979, 983, *989*

Member of the Wedding, The (McCullers; musical) **7**:978

Member of the Wedding, The (McCullers; novel) **7**:977, 978, 979, 980, 981, 982, 983, 985, 988-90

Memoirs (T. Williams) **12**:1654, 1655, 1659, 1660, 1664

"Memorial Rain" (MacLeish) **7**:901

"Memorybank Movies" (Laurence) **6**:826, 827

Memory of Two Mondays, A (Miller) **8**:1025

"Mending Wall" (Frost) **4**:568, 569

"Meneseteung" (Munro) **8**:1077

Men on Bataan (Hersey) **5**:685, 687, 690, 697

Mental Radio (Sinclair) **10**:1392

Men Without Women (Hemingway) **5**:663, 674, 679

Meridian (Walker) **11**:1564, 1568, 1575, 1581

Merry Heart, The: Reflections on Reading, Writing, and the World of Books (Davies) **3**:344

Meshugah (Singer) **10**:1411, 1413

"Mess of Pottage, A" (Dunbar) **3**:412-13

Metropolis, The (Sinclair) **10**:1379, 1383-84, 1392

"Metropolitan Nigthmare" (Benét) **2**:154

Miami (Didion) **3**:357, 360, 363

Michael, Brother of Jerry (London) **7**:879

Mickelsson's Ghosts (Gardner) **5**:598, 599, 601, 602

Mid-American Chants (Anderson) **1**:44, 45, 48, 56

"Midnight Reader, The" (Gardner) **5**:608

Midnight Salvage: Poems, 1995-1998 (Rich) **9**:1284

Milk Train Doesn't Stop Here Anymore, The (T. Williams) **12**:1655, 1664

Millennium, The (Sinclair) **10**:1392

"Mine on Thursdays" (Cormier) **3**:308

Minick (Ferber and Kaufman; play) **4**:502, 507

Miracle Play (Oates) **8**:1111

Miracles of Perception: The Art of Willa Cather (Welty, Knopf, and Menuhin) **12**:1596

Miracle Worker, The (Gibson) **5**:611, 612, 613, 614, 615, 616-17, 618-21, 623, 625

Miracle Worker, The (Gibson; screenplay) **5**:613, 615, 619

Miracle Worker, The (Gibson; teleplay) **5**:611, 613, 615, 619

Mirage (Masters) **7**:954

Miranda stories (Porter) **9**:1235-36, 1242-43

Mirror, The (Singer) **10**:1411

"Mirror in Which Two Are Seen as One, The" (Rich) **9**:1286

"Mirrors (for Billie Jean King)" (Giovanni) **5**:641

Misfits, The (Miller; novel) **8**:1019, 1025

Misfits, The (Miller; screenplay) **8**:1016, 1019, *1020*, 1025

"Misfits, The" (Miller; short story) **8**:1016, 1018, 1019

Mississippi Poems (Faulkner) **4**:486

Miss Julie (Strindberg) **9**:1165

"Miss U.S.A." (Terkel) **11**:1532

"Mister Tambourine Man" (Dylan; song lyric) **3**:423, 428-29

Mitch Miller (Masters) **7**:950, 954

Mixture of Frailties, A (Davies) **3**:337, 340-41, 344, 351

Moby Dick (Melville) **4**:467, **5**:598, 600, 608, **11**:1453
Modern Writer, The (Anderson) **1**:48
Moise and the World of Reason (T. Williams) **12**:1655, 1664
Monday after the Miracle (Gibson) **5**:614, 615, 617, 619
Moneychangers, The (Sinclair) **10**:1379, 1383-84, 1392
Money Writes! (Sinclair) **10**:1380, 1392, 1395
Monkey's Paw, The (Jacobs) **12**:1712
Montage of a Dream Deferred (Hughes) **5**:653, **6**:730, 737, 740-41
Monte Walsh (Schaefer) **10**:1349, 1351-52
Moods: Cadenced and Declaimed (Dreiser) **3**:381
"Moon and the Yew Tree, The" (Plath) **9**:1227
Moon-Face and Other Stories (London) **7**:879
Moon for the Misbegotten, A (O'Neill) **9**:1168, 1172, 1178-79
Moon Is Always Female, The (Piercy) **9**:1205
Moon Is Down, The (Steinbeck; novel) **11**:1448, 1454
Moon Is Down, The (Steinbeck; play) **11**:1454
Moon Lady, The (Tan; Shields illus.) **11**:1508, 1509, 1514, 1517-18
"Moon Lake" (Welty) **12**:1601
"mOOn Over tOwns mOOn" (Cummings) **3**:327
Moons of Jupiter, The: Stories (Munro) **8**:1078, 1080
"Moons of Jupiter, The" (Munro) **8**:1074
Moran of the Lady Letty (Norris) **8**:1089, 1090, *1092*, 1093, 1095, 1101
More Die of Heartbreak (Bellow) **1**:132, 140-41
More Eggs of Things (Sexton and Kumin) **10**:1371
More People (Masters) **7**:954
"More Room" (Ortiz Cofer) **9**:1194
More Stately Mansions (O'Neill) **9**:1162, 1167, 1168, 1172
Morgan's Passing (Tyler) **11**:1545, 1548, 1551
Morning in Antibes (Knowles) **6**:806-7, 810, 812
Morning in the Burned House (Atwood) **1**:90

"Morning love song" (Piercy) **9**:1209
"Morning Song" (Plath) **9**:1221
Morning Watch, The (Agee) **1**:13, 14, 16-17, 17, 23
Morte d'Arthur, Le (Malory) **11**:1446, 1447, 1451, 1459, 1465
Mortgaged Heart, The (McCullers) **7**:983
Mort sans sépulture (Sartre) **12**:1647
Mosby's Memoirs and Other Stories (Bellow) **1**:132
Moses, Man of the Mountain (Hurston) **6**:751, 755, 761
Mosquitoes (Faulkner) **4**:486
"mother, the" (Brooks) **2**:205
Mother, The (Buck) **2**:215, 217, 218
Mother Courage (Brecht) **12**:1658
Mother Knows Best (Ferber) **4**:507
"Mother of a Queen, The" (Hemingway) **5**:680
Mother of Us All, The (Stein; opera libretto) **10**:1424
Mother's Recompense, The (Wharton) **12**:1622
"Mother's Tale, A" (Agee) **1**:17
"Mother to Son" (Hughes) **6**:727, 732, 741, 742
Motor-Flight Through France, A (Wharton) **12**:1622
Mountain City (Sinclair) **10**:1392
Mountain Interval (Frost) **4**:560, 567, 571
"Mountain Whippoorwill, The" (Benét) **2**:151
Mourning Becomes Electra (O'Neill) **9**:1168, 1170-71, 1179
"Mouse Metamorphosed into a Maid, The" (Moore) **8**:1046-47
Moveable Feast, A (Hemingway) **5**:663, 664, 665, 670, 674, **10**:1430
Movement, The: Documentary of a Struggle for Equality (Hansberry) **5**:654, 658
"Mowing" (Frost) **4**:566, 567
"Mr. Cornelius, Office Seeker" (Dunbar) **3**:412
Mr. Kelso's Lion (Bontemps) **2**:187
Mr. Sammler's Planet (Bellow) **1**:132, 140
Mrs. Reynolds and Five Earlier Novelettes, 1931-42 (Stein) **10**:1424, 1437
Mrs. Reynolds (Stein) **10**:1437
MTV Unplugged (Dylan; record album) **3**:425

Mulatto (Hughes) **6**:737
Mule Bone: A Comedy of Negro Life in Three Acts (Hurston and Hughes) **6**:755
Mules and Men (Hurston) **6**:748, 750, 751, 752, 753, 755-56
"Munich Mannequins" (Plath) **9**:1221
Murder in the Cathedral (Eliot) **4**:440, 441, 442, 445, *446*, 449, 450, 457
Murder in the Dark (Atwood) **1**:90, 98, 99
Murther and Walking Spirits (Davies) **3**:334, *334*, 337, 338, 344
Muses Are Heard, The (Capote) **2**:235, 238, 242
Music for Chameleons (Capote) **2**:238, 242, 251-52
Music from Spain (Welty; nonfiction) **12**:1596
"Music From Spain" (Welty; short story) **12**:1601
Mute, The (McCullers) **7**:977
"Mutilated, The" (T. Williams) **12**:1657
Mutiny of the Elsinore, The (London) **7**:879
My American Century (Terkel) **11**:1522, 1538
My Antonia (Cather) **2**:269, 272, 274, 275-76, 278
"My Back Pages" (Dylan; song lyric) **3**:423
"My Butterfly" (Frost) **4**:557, 560
My Chinese Marriage (M. T. F.; ghostwritten by Porter) **9**:1236
My City (Dreiser) **3**:381
My Darling, My Hamburger (Zindel) **12**:1714, 1722, 1725
"My Dungeon Shook: Letter to My Nephew on the One Hundredth Anniversary of the Emancipation" (Baldwin) **1**:120
My First 79 Years (Stern and Potok) **9**:1269
"My First Negro" (Cormier) **3**:308
My Foolish Heart (film) **10**:1303
"my girl's tall with hard long eyes" (Cummings) **3**:330
"My Grandfather's Hat" (Ortiz Cofer) **9**:1191
My Heart Laid Bare (Oates) **8**:1109, 1110, 1111
My House (Giovanni) **5**:631, 635
My Lifetime in Letters (Sinclair) **10**:1392

My Mortal Enemy (Cather) **2**:278

"My Most Humiliating Jim Crow Experience" (Hurston) **6**:750

My Mother's Body (Piercy) **9**:1202, 1205

My Movie Business: A Memoir (Irving) **6**:773

My Name Is Asher Lev (Potok) **9**:1259, 1260, 1266, 1269, 1270-72, 1274

"My November Guest" (Frost) **4**:567

My Painted House, My Friendly Chicken, and Me (Angelou and Courtney-Clarke) **1**:68

My Petition for More Space (Hersey) **5**:689, 690

My Several Worlds: A Personal Record (Buck) **2**:218

Mysteries of Winterthurn (Oates) **8**:1105, 1106, 1109, 1110, 1111, 1112-13

Mystery and Manners (O'Connor) **8**:1143

"Mystery of the Raymond Mortgage, The" (Fitzgerald) **4**:516

"my sweet old etcetera" (Cummings) **3**:331

"Nada" (Ortiz Cofer) **9**:1185

Naftali the Storyteller and His Horse, Sus, and Other Stories (Singer) **10**:1411

Nancy Drew book series **12**:1714

Narration: Four Lectures (Stein) **10**:1424

Narrative of Arthur Gordon Pym, The (Poe) **5**:600

Narrative of the Life of Frederick Douglass, an American Slave, Written by Himself (Douglass) **1**:67, **12**:1702

Narrenschiff, Das (Brant) **9**:1240-41

Nashville Skyline (Dylan; record album) **3**:420, 421, 424, 425

Native American Tribalism: Indian Survivals and Renewals (McNickle) **7**:997, 1002, 1005-6

Native Dancer, The (Ortiz Cofer) **9**:1191

Native Son: The Biography of a Young American (Wright and Green; play) **12**:1695, 1703, *1705*

Native Son (Wright; novel) **1**:67, 105, **3**:410, **8**:1053, **12**:1693, 1695, 1697, 1698, 1703, 1704-5, 1707, 1708, 1709

Native Son (Wright; screenplay) **12**:1696, 1697, 1703, 1705

Natural, The (Malamud) **7**:912, 913, 915, 917, 918, 920, 922-23

Near-Johannesburg Boy, The (Brooks) **2**:203

Near Klamath (Carver) **2**:257, 258, 261

Necessary Angel, The: Essays on Reality and the Imagination (Stevens) **11**:1471, 1475, 1486-87

Necessities of Life (Rich) **9**:1284

"Negro Artist and the Racial Mountain, The" (Hughes) **6**:725

"Negro Love Song, A" (Dunbar) **3**:405-6, 407, 408

Negro Mother, The (Hughes) **6**:737

Negro Poetry and Drama (Brown) **3**:403

"Negro Speaks of Rivers, The" (Hughes) **2**:193, **6**:727, 730, 731, 742

"Negro Writer and His Roots, The" (Hansberry) **5**:658

"Neighbors" (Carver) **2**:265-66

Nemesis (Oates; under Smith pseud.) **8**:1111

Nerves (Benét and Farrar) **2**:155

Neshome Ekspeditsyes (Singer). *See Shosha*

"Never Again Would Birds' Song Be the Same" (Frost) **4**:571

Never-Ending Wrong, The (Porter) **9**:1234, 1236

Nevertheless (Moore) **8**:1043

New American Songbag, The (Sandburg ed.) **10**:1335, 1338

New and Collected Poems, 1917-1976 (MacLeish) **7**:895, 901

New Found Land: Fourteen Poems (MacLeish) **7**:901

New Hampshire: A Poem with Notes and Grace Notes (Frost) **4**:561, 563, 567

New Heaven, New Earth: The Visionary Experience in Literature (Oates) **8**:1111

New Hope (*As I Lay Dying*) **4**:490

New Life, A (Malamud) **7**:913, 916, 918, 924-25

New Mexico (Schaefer) **10**:1352

New Morning (Dylan; record album) **3**:425

New Negro Poets: U.S.A. (Hughes ed.) **6**:737

New Orleans Sketches (Faulkner; Collins ed.) **4**:486

New Path to the Waterfall, A (Carver) **2**:258, 261

New Plays (Oates) **8**:1106, 1111, 1116, 1118

New Poems, 1951-1952 (MacLeish) **7**:901

New Song, A (Hughes) **6**:737

Newspaper Days (Dreiser). *See Book About Myself, A*

New Spoon River, The (Masters) **7**:945, 949, 950, 951, 954, 955-56, 959

New Testament, A (Anderson) **1**:48

New Wind in a Dry Land (Laurence). *See Prophet's Camel Bell, The*

New World, The (Masters) **7**:954

New Year, The (Buck) **2**:218

"next to of course god America i" (Cummings) **3**:331

Nickel Mountain: A Pastoral Novel (Gardner) **5**:597, 598, 601, 602, 608, 609

Nick Adams Stories, The (Hemingway) **5**:670, 674, 680

"Nigger/Can You Kill?" (Giovanni) **5**:630, 636

Nigger Heaven (Van Vechten) **2**:193

Night-Born, The (London) **7**:879

Night Comes Softly: Anthology of Black Female Voices (Giovanni ed.) **5**:630, 635

Nightingale (Foote) **4**:547

"Night" (Jeffers) **6**:801-2

"Nightmare at Noon" (Benét) **2**:154

Night of the Hunter, The (Agee; screenplay) **1**:11, 13, 14, 17

Night of the Hunter, The (Grubb) **1**:17

Night of the Iguana, The (T. Williams) **12**:1653, 1654, 1657, 1659, 1664, 1673

"Night of the Iguana, The" (T. Williams) **12**:1655

Night of the Storm, The (*Roots in a Parched Ground*) (Foote; teleplay) **4**:547

Night of the Storm, The (*Roots in a Parched Land*) (Foote; play) **4**:547, 553

"Nights Can Turn Cool in Viborra" (Portis) **9**:1249

Night Seasons (Foote; 1977 play) **4**:547

Night Seasons (Foote; 1993 play) **4**:547

Night-Side (Oates) **8**:1111

Night Walks: A Bedside Companion (edit Oates) **8**:1111

"Nikki-Rosa" (Giovanni) **5**:636

Nine Plays (O'Neill) **9**:1168

Nine Stories (Salinger) **10**:1303, 1306, 1310, 1317, 1319, 1321

Ninety-five Poems (Cummings) **3**:316, 319

Noa Noa (Agee; screenplay) **1**:17

Nobodaddy: A Play (MacLeish) **7**:901, 906

"Nobody Knows" (Anderson) **1**:52-53

Nobody Knows My Name: More Notes of a Native Son (Baldwin) **1**:105, 110

Nobody's in Town (Ferber) **4**:507

"Nocturne at Bethesda" (Bontemps) **2**:188

No Evil Star: Selected Essays, Interviews, and Prose (Sexton) **10**:1371

No Heroics, Please: Uncollected Writings (Carver) **2**:261

"No More Auction Block for Me" (song lyric) **3**:425

No Name in the Street (Baldwin) **1**:105, 110

No One Will Be Immune, and Other Plays and Pieces (Mamet) **7**:935

Noon Wine (Porter) **9**:1236, 1237-38

No Pasaran! (Sinclair) **10**:1392

Northern Lights (O'Brien) **8**:1122, 1123, 1127

North of Boston (Frost) **4**:558, 560, 562, 563, 567, 568-70

Norwood (Portis) **9**:1247, 1248, 1249, 1250, 1254, 1258

No Swank (Anderson) **1**:45, 48

Notebooks of F. Scott Fitzgerald, The (Fitzgerald) **4**:532

Notes of a Native Son (Baldwin) **1**:110, 122

Notes on How to Turn a Phoenix into Ashes: The Story of the Stage Production, with the Text, of "Golda" (Gibson) **5**:619, 625

Notes on Life (Dreiser; Tjader and McAleer eds.) **3**:381

"Notes Toward a Supreme Fiction" (Stevens) **11**:1487-88

Notes Toward a Supreme Fiction (Stevens) **11**:1475

No Thanks (Cummings) **3**:315, 319

"Nothing Gold Can Stay" (Frost) **4**:571

Nothing Personal (Baldwin and Avedon) **1**:110

"Not Somewhere Else, but Here" (Rich) **9**:1289, 1291

Not Under Forty (Cather) **2**:274, 278

Not Without Laughter (Hughes) **6**:729, 737

Novelette and Other Prose, A (W. C. Williams) **12**:1686

Novelist in the Making, A: A Collection of Student Themes and the Novels of "Blix" and "Vandover and the Brute" (Norris; Hart ed.) **8**:1095

Novel of Thank You, A (Stein) **10**:1424

Novels into Films (Tibbets and Welsh) **10**:1353

Now and at the Hour (Cormier) **3**:295, 297, 301

"Now I Lay Me" (Hemingway) **5**:679

Now Not to Be King (Frost) **4**:567

Now Sheba Sings the Song (Angelou) **1**:68

Nuclear Age, The (O'Brien) **8**:1122, 1123, 1126, 1127, 1133

Nuptial Flight, The (Masters) **7**:954

Oak and Ivy (Dunbar) **3**:398-99, 402, 406

Oberto ("kitchenette folks") **2**:207

"obituary for a living lady" (Brooks) **2**:205

"Objects" (Stein) **10**:1434, 1436

Obscure Destinies (Cather) **2**:274, 278

"Observation Post, The" (O'Brien) **8**:1129

Observations (Capote and Avedon) **2**:242

Observations (Moore) **8**:1035, 1037, 1043

"O Captain, My Captain" (Whitman) **7**:960

October Light (Gardner) **2**:256, **5**:595, 598, 599, 602, 604-6

"Octopus, The" (Norris) **8**:1043

Octopus, The (Norris) **8**:1085, *1088*, 1089, 1090, 1091, 1093, 1095, 1097-98

"Ode to Ethiopia" (Dunbar) **3**:399, 407

"Ode to the Austrian Socialists" (Benét) **2**:154

"Odor of Verbena, An" (Faulkner) **4**:487-89

Odyssey (Homer) **8**:1137, **9**:1248, **11**:*1515*, 1516

"Odyssey of the North, An" (London) **7**:873

"Office, The" (Munro) **8**:1074

Of Love and Dust (Gaines) **5**:585, 586, 589

Of Men and Women (Buck) **2**:212, 218, 230

Of Mice and Men (Foote; screenplay) **4**:547

Of Mice and Men (Steinbeck; novel) **11**:1450, 1452, 1453, 1454, 1456, 1460-62

Of Mice and Men (Steinbeck; play) **11**:1454

Of Woman Born: Motherhood as Experience and Institution (Rich) **9**:1279, 1284

O. Henry Prize Stories (1974 edition) **2**:257

O. Henry Prize Stories (1975 edition) **2**:257

O. Henry Prize Stories of 1939 **12**:1591, 1608

Oh Mercy (Dylan; record album) **3**:425

Oh Pray My Wings Are Gonna Fit Me Well (Angelou) **1**:60, 68

Oil! A Novel (Sinclair) **10**:1380, 1382, *1383*, 1384, 1385, 1392, 1394-95

"Ol' Bunk's Band" (W. C. Williams) **12**:1682

Old Age Ain't for Sissies (Alvarez and Oldham eds.) **1**:28, 29, 32

Old Beauty and Others, The (Cather) **2**:274, 278

Olden Days Coat, The (Laurence) **6**:827

Old Friends, The (Foote) **4**:547

Old Love (Singer) **10**:1411

Old Maid, The (Akins) **12**:1619

Old Man and the Sea, The (Hemingway) **5**:659, 664, 665, 674, **11**:1453

Old Man (Foote; teleplay) **4**:542, 543, 547

"Old Man River" (song) **4**:511

"Old Men, The" (Gardner) **5**:597

Old Mortality (Porter) **9**:1236

Old Neighborhood, The: Three Plays (Mamet) **7**:935

Old New York (Wharton) **12**:1622

Old Order, The (Porter) **9**:1233, 1236

"Old Order, The" (Porter) **9**:1235

Old Possum's Book of Practical Cats (Eliot) **4**:440, 441, 443, *447*, 448, 450

Old Ramon (Schaefer) **10**:1347, 1349, 1352, 1356

Old Religion, The (Mamet) **7**:935

Old South, The: "A Summer Tragedy" and Other Stories of the Thirties (Bontemps) **2**:187, 188

Old Times on the Mississippi (Twain) **12**:1702

Oleanna (Mamet; play) **7**:929, 933, *934*, 935, 943

Oleanna (Mamet; screenplay) **7**:929, 930, 931, 932, 934, 935

"Olga" (Ortiz Cofer) **9**:1191

Oliver Twist (Dickens) **6**:772, 775

"Ol' Tunes, The" (Dunbar) **3**:408

"On a Railroad Right of Way" (Sandburg) **10**:1339

On Becoming a Novelist (Gardner) **5**:602

On Boxing (Oates) **8**:1111

"On Building with Stone" (Jeffers) **6**:793

Once: Poems (Walker) **11**:1563, 1566, 1575, 1576

"Once by the Pacific" (Frost) **4**:571

Once There Was a War (Steinbeck) **11**:1454

Once upon a Christmas (Buck) **2**:218

On Directing Film (Mamet) **7**:930, 935

100% Laugh Riot, The (Zindel) **12**:1715, 1722

100% (Sinclair) **10**:1392

One Arm and Other Stories (T. Williams) **12**:1664

One-Armed Man, The (Foote) **4**:547

"One Arm" (T. Williams) **12**:1655

One Basket (Ferber) **4**:507

One Bright Day and Other Stories for Children (Buck) **2**:218

"One Christmas" (Capote) **2**:242

One Clear Call (Sinclair) **10**:1392, 1396

One Day When I Was Lost: A Scenario Based on "The Autobiography of Malcolm X" (Baldwin) **1**:106, 110

One Half of Robertson Davies (Davies) **3**:344

One Hundred Years of Negro Freedom (Bontemps) **2**:187

One Hundred Years of Solitude (García Márquez) **11**:1517

One in the Middle Is the Green Kangaroo, The (Blume) **2**:165, 166, 172

"One Man's Fortune" (Dunbar) **3**:412, 413

One of Ours (Cather) **2**:273, 274, 278

One Time, One Place: Mississippi in the Depression, a Snapshot Album (Welty) **12**:1596

1 x 1 (Cummings) **3**:319

1/20 Poems (Cummings) **3**:319

One Way Ticket (Hughes) **6**:737

One Writer's Beginnings (Welty) **12**:1590, 1592, 1593, 1596, 1597-1600, 1602

On Lies, Secrets, and Silence: Selected Prose, 1966-1978 (Rich) **9**:1284

Only the Heart (Foote) **4**:542, 547

Only the Heart (Foote; play) **4**:542, 547

Only the Heart (Foote; teleplay) **4**:547

On Moral Fiction (Gardner) **5**:595, 598, 599, 601, 602, 608-9

On the Beaches of the Moon (MacLeish) **7**:901

On the Makaloa Mat (London) **7**:879

On the Origin of Species by Means of Natural Selection (Darwin) **3**:380, **7**:877, **8**:1092

"On the Pulse of Morning" (Angelou) **1**:61, 68, 78

"On the Pulse of Morning" (Angelou; recording) **1**:69

"On the Rainy River" (O'Brien) **8**:1132

"On the Road" (Hughes) **6**:743

On Valentine's Day (Foote; screenplay) **4**:541, 547

Open Sea, The (Masters) **7**:954

Open Secrets: Stories (Munro) **8**:1073, 1074, 1078, 1080

"Open Secrets" (Munro) **8**:1078

"Open to the Sky" (Piercy) **9**:1209

Operas and Plays (Stein) **10**:1424

O Pioneers! (Cather) **2**:269, 272, 274, 275, 278, 279, 281-84

O Pioneers! (television film) **2**:273

Optimist's Daughter, The (Welty) **12**:1592, 1593, 1596, 1598, 1604, *1605*, 1606, 1607

Opus Posthumous (Stevens; Morse ed.) **11**:1471, 1475, 1487

Orange Soufflé (Bellow) **1**:132

Orchard Keeper, The (McCarthy) **7**:962, 963, 965, 970, 973

Oresteia (Aeschylus) **9**:1179

Orphans' Home cycle (Foote) **4**:543, 544, 553-54

Orpheus Descending (T. Williams) **12**:1664

O Shepherd, Speak! (Sinclair) **10**:1392, 1396

Other Bells for Us to Ring (Cormier) **3**:301

Other Gods: An American Legend (Buck) **2**:215, 218

Other Side, The: El Otro Lado (Alvarez) **1**:28, 29, 32, 38

"Other Side, The": *El Otro Lado* (Alvarez) **1**:38

Other Voices, Other Rooms (Capote) **2**:234, 238, 242, 245, 252

Otherwise Known as Sheila the Great (Blume) **2**:166, 172

O to Be a Dragon (Moore) **8**:1036, 1043

"Ottawa Valley, The" (Munro) **8**:1073

Our Bourgeois Literature (Sinclair) **10**:1392

Our Lady (Sinclair) **10**:1392

"Our Martyred Soldiers" (Dunbar) **3**:402

Our Mrs. McChesney (Ferber and Hobart; play) **4**:502, 503, 504, 507, 513

Our Mr. Wrenn: The Romantic Adventures of a Gentle Man (Lewis) **6**:845, 850

Our Town (Wilder) **12**:1629, 1632, 1634, *1636*, 1637, 1638, 1639, 1641, *1642*, 1644-45, 1646, 1647, 1648, 1649, 1650

Our Town (Wilder, Craven, and Chantlee; screenplay; 1940) **12**:1631, 1647

Out Cry (T. Williams) **12**:1655, 1664

Outer Dark (McCarthy) **7**:963, 965, 970, 973-74

Out from Under (Bellow) **1**:132

Outline of Mexican Popular Arts and Crafts (Porter) **9**:1236

Out of My House (Foote) **4**:542, 547

Outsider, The (Wright) **12**:1696, 1697, 1703, 1708-9

Outsiders, The (Hinton) **5**:699, 700, 702, 703, 705, 706, 711-12

Out West: An Anthology of Stories (Schaefer) **10**:1352

"Oven Bird, The" (Frost) **4**:571

Overlaid (Davies) **3**:341, 344

Overman, The (Sinclair) **10**:1392

"Overture" (Terkel) **11**:1528

Owl, The (Mamet) **7**:935

Owl's Clover (Stevens) **11**:1475

Oxford Bood of Canadian Verse in English, The (Atwood ed.) **1**:90

Oxford Book of American Short Stories, The (Oates ed.) **8**:1111

Pagan Spain (Wright) **12**:1697, 1703

Pageant of Birds, A (Welty) **12**:1596

Pale Horse, Pale Rider: Three Short Novels (Porter) **9**:1230, 1236, 1237

Pale Horse, Pale Rider (Porter) **9**:1233, 1236, 1238-39

Palgrave's Golden Treasury **4**:565

Pangolin and Other Verse, The (Moore) **8**:1035, 1043

Panic: A Play in Verse (MacLeish) **7**:901, 906

Panic in Needle Park, The (Didion and Dunne; screenplay) **3**:355, 357, 358, 363

"Pantaleo" (Tyler) **11**:1545

Panther and the Lash, The: Or, Poems of Our Times (Hughes) **6**:737

"Paper Pills" (Anderson) **1**:52

Papers on the Art and Age of Geoffrey Chaucer (Gardner and Joost eds.) **5**:602

Paradise Lost (Milton) **11**:1493

Paradise Lost (Odets) **8**:1020

Paragon, The (Knowles) **6**:803, 810, 812, 817-18

Pardon Me, You're Stepping on My Eyeball! (Zindel) **12**:1715, 1722

Parti-Colored Blocks for a Quilt: Poets on Poetry (Piercy) **9**:1205

Part of a Long Story: Eugene O'Neill as a Young Man in Love (Boulton) **9**:1161

"Part One: Folktales" (Hurston) **6**:753

Parts of a World (Stevens) **11**:1470, 1471, 1475

"Part Two: Hoodoo" (Hurston) **6**:753, 755

Passions and Other Stories (Singer) **10**:1411

Passover (Mamet) **7**:935

Pasteboard Bandit, The (Bontemps) **2**:187

"Pastoral" (Carver) **2**:256

"Pastoral" (Gardner) **2**:256

Pastor's Son (Foote; screenplay) **4**:547

"Pasture, The" (Frost) **4**:569

Pastures of Heaven, The (Steinbeck) **11**:1447, 1454

Patchwork Planet, A (Tyler) **11**:1545, 1546, 1551, 1558-59

"Paterson Public Library, The" (Ortiz Cofer) **9**:1188

Paterson (W. C. Williams) **3**:318, **12**:1684, 1685-90

Pat Garrett and Billy the Kid (Dylan; record album) **3**:425

Pat Hobby Stories, The (Fitzgerald) **4**:520, 522, 532

Patriot, The (Buck) **2**:218, 229

"Paula Becker to Clara Westhoff" (Rich) **9**:1291

Paul Laurence Dunbar: Poet of His People (Brawley) **3**:401

"Paul Robeson" (Brooks) **2**:207

"Paul's Case" (Cather) **2**:271, 275, 285-86

Pavilion of Women (Buck) **2**:215, 217, 218, *229*, 230

"Peaceable Kingdom, The" (Piercy) **9**:*1204*, 1205

Peace Breaks Out (Knowles) **6**:803, 808, 809, 810, 812, 813-15

"Peace of Utrecht, The" (Munro) **8**:1073, 1075, 1077, 1083-84

Pearl, The (Steinbeck; novel) **11**:1448, 1454, 1462, 1465-66

Pearl, The (Steinbeck; screenplay) **11**:1449, 1453, 1454

Pearl S. Buck's America (Buck) **2**:218

Peculiar Treasure, A (Ferber) **4**:507

Penitent, The (Singer) **10**:1411

"Pension Grillparzer" (Irving) **6**:781

Peony (Buck) **2**:218

People and Uncollected Short Stories, The (Malamud) **7**:918

People in the Show (Foote) **4**:547

People of Japan, The (Buck) **2**:218

People of the Abyss, The (London) **7**:873, 877, 879, 880, 882-83

People, Yes, The (Sandburg) **10**:1338

Peregrina (Ortiz Cofer) **9**:1191

"Perfect Day for Bananafish, A" (Salinger) **10**:1303, 1306, 1317, 1319

Perfectionist, The (Oates) **8**:1107

Perfectionist and Other Plays, The (Oates) **8**:1106, 1111

"Perhaps an Accident" (Wilder) **12**:1644

"Perhaps an Intention" (Wilder) **12**:1644

Perhaps Women (Anderson) **1**:45, 48

Period of Adjustment (T. Williams) **12**:1664

Permit Me Voyage (Agee) **1**:12-13, 15, 17

Personal Art, The: Reading to Good Purpose (Davies) **3**:344

Personality Plus (Ferber) **4**:507, 513

Personal Jesus, A (Sinclair) **10**:1392

"Personal Memoir (and parenthetical comment), A" (Terkel) **11**:1534

"Personal Notes of an Infantryman" (Salinger) **10**:1303

Personals (Bontemps) **2**:187

Peter Pan: Or, the Boy Who Wouldn't Grow Up (Barrie) **4**:505

"'Pet' Negro System, The" (Hurston) **6**:750

"Petrified Man" (Welty) **12**:1591, 1608, *1609*

Phaedra (Greek tragedy) **6**:796

Phenomenal Woman: Four Poems Celebrating Women (Angelou) **1**:68

"Philosopher, The" (Anderson) **1**:52

Phineas: Six Stories (Knowles) **6**:806, 812

Photographs of Abraham Lincoln, The (Sandburg) **10**:1338

Picasso (Stein) **10**:1424

"Picky Eater" (Alvarez) **1**:39

Pictorial History of the Negro in America, A (Hughes and Meltzer) **6**:729, 737

Pictures from Brueghel and Other Poems (W. C. Williams) **12**:1679, 1686

Pictures of Fidelman: An Exhibition (Malamud) **7**:918, 924

"Piece of News, A" (Welty) **12**:1591

Pigman, The (Zindel) **12**:1711, 1714, 1721-24, 1725

Pigman and Me, The (Zindel) **12**:1722, 1725-26

Pigman's Legacy, The (Zindel) **12**:1722

Pilgrim's Progress from This World to That Which Is to Come, The (Bunyan) **3**:325, 330

"Pillars of the Nation" (Laurence) **6**:823

"Pinch of Salt, A" (Foote) **4**:541

Pioneers, The (Schaefer) **10**:1352

Pit, The; A Story of Chicago (Norris) **8**:1085, 1089, 1090, 1091, 1095, 1098-1100

"pity this busy monster,manunkind" (Cummings) **3**:326, 327

Place in Fiction (Welty) **12**:1596

Places I Never Meant to Be: Original Stories by Censored Writers (Blume ed.) **2**:167, 172

"Place to Stand On, A" (Laurence) **6**:826

Planet Waves (Dylan; record album) **3**:425

Playing in the Dark: Whiteness and the Literary Imagination (Morrison) **8**:1052, 1056, 1064

Play It as It Lays (Didion) **3**:357, 358, 359, 361, 363, 364-66, 371

Play It as It Lays (Didion and Dunne; screenplay) **3**:355, 357, 358, 360, 363, 364

Plays: Winesburg, Ohio, and Others (Anderson) **1**:48

Plays for Bleecker Street (Wilder) **12**:1634, 1647

Plays of Protest (Sinclair) **10**:1392

Plays of the Natural and Supernatural (Dreiser) **3**:381

Plays (O'Neill) **9**:1168

"Poem for Paul" (T. Williams) **12**:1657

"Poem (for TW)" (Giovanni) **5**:638

Poem of Angela Yvonne Davis (Giovanni) **5**:635

Poems: Maya Angelou (Angelou) **1**:68

Poems, 1909-1925 (Eliot) **4**:450

Poems, 1912-1944 (O'Neill; Gallup ed.) **9**:1168

Poems, 1923-1954 (Cummings) **3**:316, 319, 325-27

Poems, 1924-1933 (MacLeish) **7**:891, 895, 901

Poems 1965-1975 (Atwood) **1**:90

Poems 1976-1989 (Atwood) **1**:90

Poems (Eliot) **4**:450

Poems (Gardner) **5**:602

Poems Known and Unknown (Jeffers) **6**:790

Poems (Moore) **8**:1043

Poems of Cabin and Field (Dunbar) **3**:406

Poems of People (Masters) **7**:954

Poems (Sexton, Kinsella, and Livingston) **10**:1371

Poems: Selected and New, 1950-1974 (Rich) **9**:1284

Poems (W. C. Williams) **12**:1677, 1686

Poems Written in Early Youth (Eliot) **4**:450

"Poet, The" (Dunbar) **3**:403, 405, 407

Poet and the Rent, The (Mamet) **7**:944

Poetic Equation, A: Conversations Between Nikki Giovanni and Margaret Walker (Giovanni and Walker) **5**:635, 642

Poetry: A Magazine of Verse **10**:1325, 1328, 1338, 1339

Poetry and Experience (MacLeish) **7**:895, 896, 901, 902

Poetry and Opinion: The "Pisan Cantos" of Ezra Pound (MacLeish) **7**:901

"Poetry" (Moore) **8**:1041

Poetry of Chaucer, The (Gardner) **5**:598, 602

Poetry of Robert Frost, The (Frost; Lathem ed.) **4**:561, 567, 570-72

Poetry of the Negro, 1746-1949, The (Bontemps and Hughes ed.) **2**:187, **6**:737

Poetry of the Negro, 1746-1970, The (Bontemps ed.) **2**:187

Poisoned Kiss, The (Oates) **8**:1111

Ponder Heart, The (Welty) **12**:1592, 1593, 1596

Ponder Heart, The (Welty; stage adaptation) **12**:1593

Poor White (Anderson) **1**:41, 44, 45, 46, 48, 49-51

Popo and Fifina: Children of Haiti (Bontemps and Hughes) **2**:186, 187, 188, **6**:737

Portable Faulkner, The (Faulkner; Cowley ed.) **4**:479, 482, 485, 486

Portable F. Scott Fitzgerald, The (Fitzgerald) **4**:515, 524, 532

"Portrait of a Girl in Glass" (T. Williams) **12**:1655

"Portrait of a Lady" (Eliot) **4**:441, 451, 453

Portrait of a Marriage (Buck) **2**:214, 218

Portrait of the Artist as a Young Man, A (Joyce) **9**:1266

Portraits and Prayers (Stein) **10**:1424

Possessing the Secret of Joy (Walker) **11**:1565, 1566, 1575, 1581-82

Postman Always Rings Twice, The (Cain; novel) **7**:929, 935

Postman Always Rings Twice, The (Mamet; screenplay) **7**:929, 931, 932, 935

Potato Face (Sandburg) **10**:1338

Pot-Boiler, The (Sinclair) **10**:1392

Pot of Earth, The (MacLeish; play) **7**:901

Pot of Earth, The (MacLeish; poetry) **7**:901

Pound/Williams: Selected Letters of Ezra Pound and William Carlos Williams (Witmeyer ed.) **12**:1686

Power of Light, The: Eight Stories (Singer) **10**:1411

Power Politics (Atwood) **1**:90

"Power" (Rich) **9**:1289

Prairie de Chien (Mamet; radio play) **7**:935

Prairie Pirates, The (Sinclair) **10**:1378

"Prairie" (Sandburg) **10**:1330, 1339

Prairie-Town Boy (Sandburg) **10**:1338

Prayer for Owen Meany, A (Irving) **6**:768, 773, 780-81

Predilections (Moore) **8**:1036, 1043

"Preludes" (Eliot) **4**:453

"Presence of an External Master of Knowledge" (Stevens) **11**:1476

Presence of Grace, The (O'Connor) **8**:1143

President, The (Hersey) **5**:690

Presidential Agent (Sinclair) **10**:1392, 1396

Presidential Mission (Sinclair) **10**:1392, 1396

"Previous Condition" (Baldwin) **1**:105, 122

Price, The (Miller) **8**:1016, 1019, 1025, 1029, 1031

Price of the Ticket, The: Collected Nonfiction, 1948-1985 (Baldwin) **1**:106, 110

Price Was High, The: The Last Uncollected Stories of F. Scott Fitzgerald (Fitzgerald) **4**:532

Primer for Blacks (Brooks) **2**:203

Prince Hagen (Sinclair) **10**:1392

Princess Prunella and the Purple Peanut (Atwood and Kowalski) **1**:90

Prisoner's Song, The (Foote) **4**:547

Private Life of Axie Reed, The (Knowles) **6**:806, 812

Procedures for Underground (Atwood) **1**:90

Prodigal Parents, The (Lewis) **6**:850

Prodigal Son, The (Hughes) **6**:737

"Production Notes to *The Glass Menagerie*" (T. Williams) **12**:1662

Profane Art, The: Essays and Reviews (Oates) **8**:1111

Professor's House, The (Cather) **2**:272, 274, 277, 278

Profits of Religion, The (Sinclair) **10**:1380, 1384, 1392, 1395

Progress of Love, The (Munro) **8**:1074, 1075, 1078, 1080

"Prologue: Morning, Noon, and Night" (Terkel) **11**:1528

Promise, The (Buck) **2**:218

Promise, The (Potok) **9**:1259, 1263, 1264-65, 1269, 1272-73

"Promise, The" (Steinbeck) **11**:1465

Prophet's Camel Bell, The (Laurence) **6**:823, 827

Prospero and Caliban: The Psychology of Colonization (Mannoni) **6**:832

"Provide, Provide" (Frost) **4**:571

Prufrock and Other Observations (Eliot) **4**:441, 450, 451-53

Public Speech (MacLeish) **7**:901

Pullman Car Hiawatha (Wilder) **12**:1647

Puppy Sister, The (Hinton) **5**:701, 703, 706

Purim Gift, The (Singer) **10**:1416

Pursuit (Plath) **9**:1224

Pussycat and the Expert Plumber Who Was an Honest Man, The; William Ireland's Confession (Miller; radio play) **8**:1025

"Putting in the Seed" (Frost) **4**:571

"Put Yourself in My Shoes" (Carver) **2**:257, 261

Puzzled America (Anderson) **1**:45, 48

Pylon (Faulkner) **4**:486

Q.E.D. (Stein) **10**:1424, 1425

Queens of France (Wilder) **12**:1647

Question Time (Davies) **3**:344

Quiet One, The (Agee; documentary narration) **1**:14, 16

Race: How Blacks and Whites Think and Feel About the American Obsession (Terkel) **11**:1522, 1523, 1526, 1534, 1539

Race-ing Justice, En-gendering Power: Essays on Anita Hill, Clarence Thomas, and the Construction of Social Reality (Morrison ed.) **8**:1064

Racism 101 (Giovanni) **5**:635, 642, 644

Raggedy Ann and Andy (Gibson and Raposo) **5**:619

Rainbow, The (Buck) **2**:218

"Rainy Day Women #12 & 35" (Dylan) **3**:423

Raise High the Roof Beam, Carpenters, and Seymour: An Introduction (Salinger) **10**:1304, 1306, 1317-18

"Raise High the Roof Beam, Carpenters" (Salinger) **10**:1317, 1318

Raisin in the Sun, A (Hansberry; play) **5**:645, 648, 649, 650, 651, 652, 653-55, **6**:741

Raisin in the Sun, A (Hansberry; screenplay) **5**:648, 649, 651-52, 654

Raisin in the Sun, A (Hansberry; teleplay) **5**:652

Ralph Ellison: A Collection of Critical Essays (Hersey ed.) **5**:690

"Range-Finding" (Frost) **4**:571

Rape of the Lock, The (Pope) **2**:204

Rap on Race, A (Baldwin with Mead) **1**:105, 110

Raptor (Zindel) **12**:1715, 1722

"Rationalism and Skepticism of Solomon Maimon, The" (Potok) **9**:1261

"Rats Live on No Evil Star" (Sexton) **10**:1372

Rats (Zindel) **12**:1715, 1722

Ravelstein (Bellow) **1**:129, 132

Raven's Wing (Oates) **8**:1111

Re: Creation (Giovanni) **5**:630, 635, 639-41

Reaches of Heaven: A Story of the Baal Shem Tov (Singer) **10**:1411

Reaching for the Mainland and Selected New Poems (Ortiz Cofer) **9**:1191

Reaching for the Mainland (Ortiz Cofer) **9**:1185, 1191

Reading and Writing (Davies) **3**:344

Reading and Writing of Short Stories, The (Welty) **12**:1596

Real Live (Dylan; record album) **3**:425

"Really, Doesn't Crime Pay?" (Walker) **11**:1579

Rebel Angels, The (Davies) **3**:337, 344

Recklessness (O'Neill) **9**:1167

Recognizable Image, A (W. C. Williams) **12**:1686

Record of a Friendship, The (Frost; Bartlett ed.) **4**:567

Red and Blue Club (drawing) **4**:477

Red Badge of Courage, The (Agee; screenplay) **1**:17

Red Badge of Courage, The (Crane) **8**:1124, **12**:1698

"Red Candle, The" (Tan) **11**:1514

Red Devil Battery Sign, The (T. Williams) **12**:1655, 1664

"Red Dress—1946" (Munro) **8**:1077

Red Front, The (Aragon; Cummings transl.) **3**:319

Red One, The (London) **7**:879

Red Pony, The (Steinbeck; novel) **11**:1447, 1452, 1453, 1454, 1462, 1464-65

Red Pony, The (Steinbeck; screenplay) **11**:1449, 1453, 1454

"Red Roses for a Blue Lady" (song) **10**:1365

"Red Roses" (Sexton) **10**:1365

"Red Wheelbarrow, The" (W. C. Williams) **12**:1681

"Redwing Sonnets" (Alvarez) **1**:38

Reef, The (Wharton) **12**:1618, 1622, 1626-28

Reef of Death (Zindel) **12**:1722

Reflections in a Golden Eye (McCullers) **7**:977, 978, 979, 981, 982, 983, 985, 991

Reflections on the Atomic Bomb (Stein) **10**:1424

Reivers, The (Faulkner) **4**:486

"Reluctance" (Frost) **4**:567

Rembrandt's Hat (Malamud) **7**:918, 924

Remembrance of Things Past (Proust) **2**:241

Remembrance Rock (Sandburg) **10**:1326, 1330, 1338, 1341, 1342

Renown at Stratford: A Record of the Shakespeare Festival in Canada, 1953 (Davies and Guthrie) **3**:336, 344

"Report from Part One" (Brooks) **2**:208

Report from Part One: An Autobiography (Brooks) **2**:198, 203, 207-8

Report from Part Two (Brooks) **2**:203

"Representing T. A. Buck" (Ferber) **4**:501

Requiem for a Nun (Faulkner) 4:486

Responsibilities of the Novelist, The (Norris) 8:1095

Resurrection, The (Gardner) 5:597-98, 599, 601, 602, 609

"Return, The" (Bontemps) 2:184, 188

Return (Foote) 4:547

Return of Lanny Budd, The (Sinclair) 10:1392, 1396

Reunion (Mamet) 7:935

"Revelation" (O'Connor) 8:1135, 1139, 1143

"Revenge of Hannah Kemhuff, The" (Walker) 11:1579

Revenge of the Space Pandas, The (Mamet) 7:935, 944

Revolution and Other Essays (London) 7:879

Revolutionary Petunias and Other Poems (Walker) 11:1564, 1575, 1576

"Rhapsody on a Windy Night" (Eliot) 4:451, 453

"Rich Boy, The" (Fitzgerald) 4:521

Richmond (Masters) 7:954

Ride Down Mt. Morgan, The (Miller) 8:1025

Rider from Nowhere (Schaefer) 10:1345

Riders on the Earth: Essays and Reminiscences (MacLeish) 7:901

"Right to Life" (Piercy) 9:1206

Riot (Brooks) 2:203

Rise of Life on Earth, The (Oates) 8:1109, 1111

Rite of Passage (Wright) 12:1703

Road, The (London) 7:876, 879, 883

"Road Not Taken, The" (Frost) 4:565, 571

Roads to Home (Foote; teleplay) 4:547

Roads to Home, The (Foote trilogy: *Nightingale, The Dearest of Friends,* and *Spring Dance*) 4:547

"Roan Stallion" (Jeffers) 6:789, 796-98

Roan Stallion, Tamar, and Other Poems (Jeffers) 6:786, 790, 796

"Roast Beef Medium" (Ferber) 4:501

Roast Beef Medium (Ferber) 4:507, 513

Robber Bride, The (Atwood) 1:81, 90, 99

Robber Bridegroom, The (Welty) 12:1592, 1593, 1594, 1596

Robinson Crusoe (Defoe) 2:182

Rock, The (Eliot) 4:440, 445, 450

"Rock, The" (Stevens) 11:1474, 1486

Rock and Hawk: A Selection of Shorter Poems by Robinson Jeffers 6:790

Rocking Chair (Foote; teleplay) 4:547

Roman Holiday (Sinclair) 10:1392

Roman Spring of Mrs. Stone, The (T. Williams) 12:1653, 1664

"Romantic Egoist, The" (Fitzgerald) 4:518, 525

Ronin (Mamet; screenplay) 7:932, 935

"Rooms" (Stein) 10:1434, 1436

Rootabaga Pigeons (Sandburg) 10:1326, 1338

Rootabaga Stories (Sandburg) 10:1326, 1328, 1338

Roots in a Parched Ground. See Night of the Storm, The

Rose for Emily, A (television film) 4:479

"Roselily" (Walker) 11:1579

Rose Tattoo, The (T. Williams; play) 12:1653, 1654, 1664, 1672

Rose Tattoo, The (T. Williams and Kanter; screenplay) 12:1653, 1663, 1664

Rover Boys stories 4:540

"Rowing Endeth, The" (Sexton) 10:1372-73

"Rowing" (Sexton) 10:1372

Royal Family, The (Ferber and Kaufman; play) 4:503, 504, 507, 513-14

Ruby, The (Gibson) 5:616

"Rules of the Game" (Tan) 11:1507

"Rumba! Rumba!" (W. C. Williams) 12:1682

Rumble Fish (Hinton; novel) 5:699, 700, 701, 702, 703, 706, 716

Rumble Fish (Hinton and Coppola; screenplay) 5:700, 702, 703, 707, 708, 717

Rumpelstiltskin (Gardner; libretto) 5:602

Runaway Train (Zindel; screenplay) 12:1722

Runner in the Sun: A Story of Indian Maize (McNickle) 7:995, 997, 998, 999, 1001, 1002

Run River (Didion) 3:355, 358, 359, 360, 361, 363

Russian Journal, A (Steinbeck and Capa) 11:1448, 1454

Sacred Cows and Other Edibles (Giovanni) 5:635

Sacred Wood, The (Eliot) 4:441, 450

Sad-Faced Boy (Bontemps) 2:186, 187

"Sad Strains of a Gay Waltz" (Stevens) 11:1482, *1483*

"Safety First" (Fitzgerald; musical lyrics) 4:517

Saint Katy the Virgin (Steinbeck) 11:1454

Saint Maybe (Tyler) 11:1545, 1551

"Saints in Caesar's Household, The" (Tyler) 11:1543

"Salesman" in Beijing (Miller) 8:1025

Salinger: A Biography (Alexander) 10:1306

Salterton trilogy (Davies) 3:337, 338, 340-41, 347, 348, 349, 351

Salvador (Didion) 3:357, 363, 372

Same River Twice, The: Honoring the Difficult (Walker) 11:1572, 1575

Sam Patch: The High, Wide, and Handsome Jumper (Bontemps and Conroy) 2:187

Samuel the Seeker (Sinclair) 10:1379, 1384, 1392

Sanctified Church, The (Hurston) 6:755

Sanctuary (Faulkner) 4:478, 486

Sanctuary (Wharton) 12:1622

Sandburg Range, The (Sandburg) 10:1338

Sangamon, The (Masters) 7:949, 950, 954

Santa Claus: A Morality (Cummings) 3:319

Sapphira and the Slave Girl (Cather) 2:274, 278

Saratoga Trunk (Ferber) 4:504, 507

Sartoris (Faulkner) 4:478, 481, 486

Satan in Goray (Singer) 10:1398, 1403, 1411

Satan Never Sleeps (Buck) 2:218

Savage Holiday (Wright) 12:1697, 1703

Saved (Dylan; record album) 3:425

Save Me the Waltz (Z. Fitzgerald) 4:533

"Save the Reaper" (Munro) 8:1078

Scarlet Plague, The (London) 7:879

Scenes from American Life: Contemporary Short Fiction (Oates ed.) 8:1111

Scorn of Women (London) 7:879

"Scorpio, Bad Spider, Die" (Sexton) 10:1367-68

"Scottsboro" (Hughes) 6:744

Scottsboro Limited: Four Poems and a Play in Verse (Hughes) 6:737, 744

Scratch (MacLeish) **7**:901

"Sculptor, The" (Plath) **9**:1225

Scum (Singer) **10**:1411

"Sea Change, The" (Hemingway) **5**:680

Seagull, The (Chekhov) **12**:1658

Séance and Other Stories, The (Singer) **10**:1411

Sea of Cortez (Steinbeck and Ricketts) **11**:1447, 1454

Searching for Caleb (Tyler) **11**:1544, 1551, 1559-60

Season in Heaven, A (Gibson) **5**:619

Sea-Wolf, The (London) **7**:869, 873, 877, 879, 886, 889-90

"Second Coming, The" (Yeats) **3**:366

Second Sex, The (de Beauvoir) **9**:1280

Second Words: Selected Critical Prose (Atwood) **1**:90

"Secret, The" (Singer) **10**:1415-16

Secret Affairs of Mildred Wild, The (Zindel) **12**:1722

Secret Footprints, The (Alvarez) **1**:28, 32

Secrets of the Heart (Buck) **2**:218

"Secularism: Messiah for a Broken World" (Potok) **9**:1275

Seduction, The (Oates) **8**:1111

Seesaw Log, The: A Chronicle of the Stage Production, with the Text, of "Two for the Seesaw" (Gibson) **5**:614, 619

Seize the Day (Bellow) **1**:123, 129, 132, 133, 137-38

Selected Essays of William Carlos Williams **12**:1686

Selected Fables of La Fontaine (Moore transl.) **8**:1036, 1037, 1043, 1046

Selected Journalism, ed. Paul Ashdown (Agee) **1**:17

Selected Letters (Faulkner; Blotner ed.) **4**:486

Selected Letters of E. E. Cummings **3**:319

Selected Letters of Eugene O'Neill (Bogard and Bryer eds.) **9**:1168

Selected Letters of Katherine Anne Porter, The **9**:1236

Selected Letters of Margaret Laurence and Adele Wiseman (Laurence and Wiseman) **6**:827

Selected Letters of Robert Frost (Thompson ed.) **4**:567

Selected Letters of Robinson Jeffers, 1897-1962, The (Ridgeway ed.) **6**:790

Selected Letters of Stephen Vincent Benét **2**:155

Selected Letters of William Carlos Williams, The **12**:1686

Selected Magazine Articles of Theodore Dreiser (Hakutani ed.) **3**:381

Selected Operas and Plays (Stein) **10**:1424

Selected Poems (Atwood) **1**:90

Selected Poems (Brooks) **2**:198, 203

Selected Poems (Dreiser; Saalbach ed.) **3**:381

Selected Poems II (Atwood) **1**:90

Selected Poems (Jeffers) **6**:790

Selected Poems (Masters) **7**:954

Selected Poems (Moore) **8**:1035, 1037, 1043

Selected Poems of Anne Sexton **10**:1371

Selected Poems of Carl Sandburg **10**:1338

Selected Poems of Gabriela Mistral (Hughes transl.) **6**:737

Selected Poems of Langston Hughes **6**:730, 737

Selected Poems of Nikki Giovanni **5**:635

Selected Poems (Plath) **9**:1224

Selected Poems (Rich) **9**:1284

Selected Poems (Sexton) **10**:1371

Selected Poems (Stevens) **11**:1475

Selected Poems (W. C. Williams) **12**:1686

Selected Poetry of Robinson Jeffers, The **6**:790

Selected Short Stories of Sinclair Lewis **6**:848, 850

Selected Stories (Munro) **8**:1080

Selected Stories of Eudora Welty **12**:1596

Selected Works of Stephen Vincent Benét **2**:155

Selected Writings (Capote) **2**:242

Self Portrait (Dylan; record album) **3**:425

"Sense of Community, A" (Hersey) **5**:687

"Sensible Thing, The" (Fitzgerald) **4**:521

Sentimental Education, A (Oates) **8**:1111

Separate Peace, A: Moods and Settings (Knowles; Hinkle ed.) **6**:806

Separate Peace, A (Gilsenan; play) **6**:806

Separate Peace, A (Knowles; novel) **6**:803, 804, 806, 808, 809, 810, 812, 814, 815-17

Seraph on the Suwanee (Hurston) **6**:748, 755

Serpent in the Wilderness, The (Masters) **7**:954

Servant Girl, The (Atwood; screenplay) **1**:90

Servant Girl, The (Atwood; teleplay) **1**:84

"Servant to Servants, A" (Frost) **4**:569

"Service, The" (Styron) **11**:1504

Set This House on Fire (Styron) **11**:1491-92, 1494, 1495, 1496, 1500

Setting Free the Bears (Irving) **6**:765, 767, 773, 781

Seven Descents of Myrtle, The (T. Williams) **12**:1655, 1664

Seven Trees (Alvarez) **1**:28, 29, 32

Seventy-three Poems (Cummings) **3**:319

Sexual Perversity in Chicago (Mamet) **7**:929, 931, *933*, 935

"Seymour: An Introduction" (Salinger) **10**:1317-18, 1319, 1321

"Shadow, The" (Plath) **9**:1227

Shadow and Act (Ellison) **4**:463, 465, 466, 473

Shadow of a Doubt (Wilder, Benson, and Revelle; screenplay; 1943 film) **12**:1632, 1634, 1639, *1640*, 1641, 1647, 1650

Shadows on the Hudson (Singer) **10**:1399, 1402, 1404, 1411

Shadows on the Rock (Cather) **2**:269, 272-73, 274, 277, 278

Shaker, Why Don't You Sing? (Angelou) **1**:68

Shakespeare's Game (Gibson) **5**:619

Shakespeare for Younger Players: A Junior Course (Davies) **3**:335, 338, 344

Shakespeare in Harlem (Hughes) **6**:737

Shakespeare's Boy Actors (Davies) **3**:335, 338, 344

Shane (Schaefer) **10**:1343, 1345, 1347, 1348, 1349-50, 1351, 1352, 1353-54, 1355, 1356

Shape of the River, The (Foote; teleplay) **4**:547

"she being Brand" (Cummings) **3**:331, 332

Sherwood Anderson: Selected Letters **1**:48

Sherwood Anderson's Memoirs **1**:44, 46, 48

Sherwood Anderson's Notebook **1**:44, 48

Shimmy Shimmy Shimmy Like My Sister Kate: Looking at the Harlem Renaissance Through Poems (Giovanni ed.) **5**:635, 644

Ship of Fools (Porter) **9**:1229, 1231, 1232, 1233, 1234, 1236, 1239-41

Shlemiel the First (Singer) **10**:1411

Shoe Bird, The (Welty) **12**:1596

Short Friday and Other Stories (Singer) **10**:1411

"Short Happy Life of Francis Macomber, The" (Hemingway) **5**:663, 668, 678-79

Short Reign of Pippen IV, The (Steinbeck) **11**:1454

Short Stories (Welty) **12**:1596

Short Teller's Story, A (Anderson) **1**:44

Shosha (Singer) **10**:1399, 1411, 1412-13

Shot of Love (Dylan; record album) **3**:425

Show Boat (Ferber) **4**:499, 507, 509-11

Show Boat (musical) **4**:503, 504, 510, 511

"Shower of Gold" (Welty) **12**:1601

"Sibling Mysteries" (Rich) **9**:1291

Signa (Ouida) **7**:877

Sign in Sidney Brustein's Window, The (Hansberry) **5**:649, 650-51, 654, 655-57

Silent Dancing: A Partial Remembrance of a Puerto Rican Childhood (Ortiz Cofer) **9**:1183, 1185, 1191, 1193-94

"Silken Tent, The" (Frost) **4**:571

"Silver Dish, A" (Bellow) **1**:126

"Silver Jemmy" (Benét) **2**:154

Simple columns (Hughes) **6**:729, 730, 733-36, 743

Simple Speaks His Mind (Hughes) **6**:737

Simple Stakes a Claim (Hughes) **6**:737

Simple's Uncle Sam (Hughes) **6**:737

Simple Takes a Wife (Hughes) **6**:737

Simply Heavenly (Hughes; opera libretto) **6**:737

Singin' and Swingin' and Gettin' Merry Like Christmas (Angelou) **1**:60, 68, 76-78

Singing Jailbirds (Sinclair) **10**:1392

Single Pebble, A (Hersey) **5**:686, 687, 689, 690, 692, 698

Sinister Street (Mackenzie) **4**:525

Sister Carrie (Dreiser) **1**:49, **3**:378, 379-80, 381, 384, 386, 389-92, **8**:1090

Situation Normal (Miller) **8**:1025

"Six Beautiful in Paris" (McNickle) **7**:1005

Six Darn Cows (Laurence) **6**:827

"Six of One —" (Fitzgerald) **4**:523

Six Plays (MacLeish) **7**:901

Skeeters Kirby (Masters) **7**:954

Skin of Our Teeth, The (Wilder) **12**:1629, 1632, 1634, 1637, 1639, 1641, 1646-47, 1649, 1650

"Sky Is Gray, The" (Gaines) **5**:586, 587

Sky of Now, The (Potok) **9**:1269

Slabs of the Sunburnt West (Sandburg) **10**:1338

Slappy Hooper: The Wonderful Sign Painter (Bontemps and Conroy) **2**:187

Slapstick Tragedy: The Mutilated and the Gnädiges Fraulein (T. Williams) **12**:1664

Slave, The (Singer) **10**:1411

Slave Ship (Faulkner; screenplay) **4**:486

"Sleepyheads" (Sandburg) **10**:1339

"Slight Rebellion off Madison" (Salinger) **10**:1303, 1306

Slipping-Down Life, A (Tyler;) **11**:1544, 1551

Slouching Towards Bethlehem (Didion) **3**:353, 355, 358, 363, 364, 366, 368-69, 371

Slow Train Coming (Dylan; record album) **3**:420, 421, 425

Small Changes (Piercy) **9**:1205, 1210-11

Small Craft Warnings (T. Williams) **12**:1654, 1655, 1659, 1664

"Small, Good Thing, A" (Carver) **2**:262-63

Smart Women (Blume) **2**:167, 172

Smoke and Steel (Sandburg) **10**:1326, 1338

Smoke Bellew Tales (London) **7**:879

Snake Eyes (Oates; under Smith pseud.) **8**:1111

Snake Poems (Atwood) **1**:90

"Snapshots" (Laurence) **6**:826, 827

Snapshots of a Daughter-in-Law (Rich) **9**:1284

Snopes trilogy (Faulkner) **4**:478, 480

Snowbird (Atwood; screenplay) **1**:90

Snowbird (Atwood; teleplay) **1**:84

"Snowfall" (McNickle) **7**:1005

"Snows of Kilimanjaro, The" (Hemingway) **4**:521, **5**:663, 678, 679

Snows of Kilimanjaro and Other Stories, The (Hemingway) **5**:674

Snow White (Sexton version) **10**:1376

"Soiled Dove" (Sandburg) **10**:*1330*, 1339

"Soldier's Home" (Hemingway) **5**:679

Soldiers' Pay (Faulkner) **4**:478, 481, 486

Solstice and Other Poems (Jeffers) **6**:790

Solstice (Oates) **8**:1111

"Some Foreign Letters" (Sexton) **10**:1374

Some Freaks (Mamet) **7**:930, 935

Some Kind of Love Story (Miller) **8**:1025

Someone from Assisi (Wilder) **12**:1647

"Some Simple Measures in the American Idiom" (W. C. Williams) **12**:1683

Something in Common and Other Stories (Hughes) **6**:737

Something I've Been Meaning to Tell You: Thirteen Stories (Munro) **8**:1074, 1078, 1080

"Something I've Been Meaning to Tell You" (Munro) **8**:1084

Something to Declare (Alvarez) **1**:28, 29, 30, 31, 32, 39

"Something to Look Forward To" (Piercy) **9**:1209

Something to Remember Me By: Three Tales (Bellow) **1**:132

"somewhere i have never traveled gladly beyond" (Cummings) **3**:326

"Somnambulisma" (Stevens) **11**:1487

Son at the Front, A (Wharton) **12**:1622

"Song, A" (Dunbar) **3**:408

"Song (Beauty Is a Shell)" (W. C. Williams) **12**:1682

"Song of Myself" (Whitman) **3**:318

Song of Solomon (Morrison) **8**:1051, 1052, 1053, 1057, 1058, 1064, 1066-68

Song of the Lark, The (Cather) **2**:272, 274, 275, 278

"Song of the Soul of Central, A" (Hughes) **6**:727

"Song of the Wandering Aengus, The" (Yeats) **12**:1601

"Song of the Woods, A" (Benét) **2**:150

"Song (Pluck the Florets)" (W. C. Williams) **12**:1682

"Song (Russia! Russia!)" (W. C. Williams) **12**:1682

Songs and Satires (Masters) **7**:954

Songs and Sonnets (Masters) **7**:954

Songs and Sonnets, Second Series (Masters) **7**:954

Songs for a Summer's Day (MacLeish) **7**:901

Songs for Eve (MacLeish) **7**:901, 906

Songs of Bob Dylan from 1966 Through 1975, The (Dylan; lyric texts) **3**:425

Sonim, de Geshichte fun a Liebe (Singer). *See Enemies: A Love Story*

Sonnet 29 (Shakespeare) **1**:65

"Sonny's Blues" (Baldwin) **1**:117-18

Son of the Circus, A (Irving) **6**:768, 773, 781

Son of the Morning (Oates) **8**:1111

Son of the Sun, A (London) **7**:879

Son of the Wolf, The (London) **7**:874, 879

Sons (Buck) **2**:218

Sophie's Choice (Styron) **11**:1489, 1493, 1494-95, 1496, 1500-1502

"Sophistication" (Anderson) **1**:53

"Sort of a Song, A" (W. C. Williams) **12**:1682

Sotn in Gorey, Der (Singer). *See Satan in Goray*

Soul/Mate (Oates; under Smith pseud.) **8**:1111

Soul on Ice (Cleaver) **1**:104, 107, **3**:371

Sound and the Fury, The (Faulkner) **4**:475, 478, 481, 483, 484, 486, 490, 492-95, **11**:1494

"Sources and Illuminations" (Brooks) **2**:208

"Sources" (Rich) **9**:1278, 1285

Sources (Rich) **9**:1284

Sour Grapes (W. C. Williams) **12**:1686

Southerner, The (Faulkner; screenplay) **4**:486

"Southern Nights" (Wright) **12**:1701, 1702

"Southern Pacific" (Sandburg) **10**:1339

South Sea Tales (London) **7**:879

Souvenirs and Prophecies: The Young Wallace Stevens (Stevens ed.) **11**:1475

Spain (Miller) **8**:1025

Spanish Bayonet (Benét) **2**:151, 155, 161

Spanish Prisoner, The (Mamet; play) **7**:935, 941

Spanish Prisoner, The (Mamet; screenplay) **7**:930, 932, 934, 935, 940-42

Spectator, The: Talk About Movies and Plays with Those Who Make Them (Terkel) **11**:1522, 1523, 1527-28, 1530

Speeches for Dr. Frankenstein (Atwood) **1**:90

Speed-the-Plow (Mamet) **7**:929, 935

Spin a Soft Black Song: Poems for Children (Giovanni) **5**:631, 635

Spinoza of Market Street, The (Singer) **10**:1411

"Spooniad, The" (Masters) **7**:956

Spoon River Anthology (Masters) **1**:49, **7**:945, 949, 950, 951, 953, 954, 955, 956-59

Sport of the Gods, The (Dunbar) **3**:401, 402, 406, 409-10, 416

Spreading Fires (Knowles) **6**:806-7, 812, 818

Spring and All (W. C. Williams) **12**:1686, 1691

Spring Dance (Foote) **4**:547

Springtime and Harvest (Sinclair) **10**:1378, 1392

Spunk: The Selected Short Stories of Zora Neale Hurston **6**:755

Square Root of Wonderful, The (McCullers) **7**:978, 979, 983

Stage Door (Ferber and Kaufman; play) **4**:507

Stalking Moon, The (Foote; screenplay) **4**:547

Stanzas in Meditation and Other Poems, 1929-1933 (Stein) **10**:1424

Star for the Latecomer, A (Zindel and Zindel) **12**:1722

Star Is Born, A (Didion, Dunne, and Pierson; screenplay) **3**:358, 363

Starr Bright Will Be With You (Oates under Smith pseud.) **8**:1111

Starring Sally J. Freedman as Herself (Blume) **2**:170, 172

Star Rover, The (London) **7**:879

Starved Rock (Masters) **7**:954

State and Main (Mamet; screenplay) **7**:932, 934, 935

State of the Language, The (Ricks and Michaels ed.) **11**:1514

"Staying Up Alone" (Alvarez) **1**:38

Steeple Bush (Frost) **4**:567

Steichen the Photographer (Sandburg) **10**:1338

Steinbeck: A Life in Letters (Steinbeck and Wallsten eds.) **11**:1454

Stephen Leacock: Feast of Stephen (Davies) **3**:344

Stephen Vincent Benét: Selected Poetry and Prose (Benét) **2**:155

Stephen Vincent Benét on Writing: A Great Writer's Letters of Advice to a Young Beginner (Benét) **2**:155

Steps Must Be Gentle (T. Williams) **12**:1658, 1664

"Stillness" and "Shadows" (Gardner; Delbanco ed.) **5**:599, 602

St. Louis Woman (Bontemps and Cullen) **2**:184, 187, 188

Stoic, The (Dreiser) **3**:378, 381, 384, 394-95

Stolen Past, A (Knowles) **6**:812

Stone Angel, The (Laurence) **6**:821, 823, 827, 831

Stonemason, The (McCarthy) **7**:964, 965, 970

Stone Mason of Tor House, The (Bennett) **6**:791

Stone, Paper, Knife (Piercy) **9**:1205

Stopped Rocking and Other Screenplays (T. Williams) **12**:1664

"Stopping by Woods on a Snowy Evening" (Frost) **4**:571

Stories for Children (Singer) **10**:1411

Stories for Little Children (Buck) **2**:218

Stories of Bernard Malamud, The (Malamud) **7**:918

Storm Fear (Foote; screenplay) **4**:542, 543, 547

Storm over the Land: A Profile of the Civil War (Sandburg) **10**:1338

Storm Tide (Piercy and Wood) **9**:1205

Story Bible, The (Buck) **2**:218

Story of a Marriage, The (Foote; teleplay) **4**:547

"Story of a Typhoon off the Coast of Japan" (London) **7**:873, 876

Story of George Washington Carver, The (Bontemps) **2**:187, 188

Story of Gus, The (Miller; radio play) **8**:1025

Story of the Negro, The (Bontemps) **2**:184, 187

Story Teller's Story, A (Anderson) **1**:45, 48

Strange Interlude (O'Neill) **9**:1165-66, 1168, 1171

Stranger, The (Camus) **12**:1709

"Stranger in the Village" (Baldwin) **1**:118-20

Strange Things: the Malevolent North in Canadian Literature (Atwood) **1**:90

Streetcar Named Desire, A (T. Williams; play) **12**:1651, 1653, 1654, 1655, 1656, 1657, 1664, 1666, 1667, 1668-69

Streetcar Named Desire, A (T. Williams and Saul; screenplay) **12**:1653, 1655, 1663, 1664

Street in Bronzeville, A (Brooks) **2**:197, 199, 203, 205-6, 207

Street-Legal (Dylan; record album) **3**:425

Street Scene (Hughes, Weill, and Rice; musical) **6**:737

Streets in the Moon (MacLeish) **7**:894, 901

"Strength of Gideon, The" (Dunbar) **3**:411, 413

Strength of Gideon and Other Stories, The (Dunbar) **3**:401, 402, 406, 410-13

Strength of the Strong, The (London) **7**:879

"Strong Horse Tea" (Walker) **11**:1579

Stubby Pringle's Christmas (Schaefer) **10**:1352

"Subverted Flower, The" (Frost) **4**:571

Such Counsels You Gave to Me and Other Poems (Jeffers) **6**:790

Such Things Only Happen in Books (Wilder) **12**:1647

Suddenly Last Summer (T. Williams; play) **12**:1653, 1664

Suddenly Last Summer (T. Williams and Vidal; screenplay) **12**:1663, 1664

Sula (Morrison) **8**:1052, 1053, 1057, 1058, 1064, 1069-70

Summer and Smoke (T. Williams) **12**:1653, 1656, 1664, 1671-72

Summer People (Piercy) **9**:1205

Summer Sisters (Blume) **2**:166, 167, 172, 178-79

"Summer Tragedy, A" (Bontemps) **2**:184, 188, 192, 193-94

Summer (Wharton) **12**:1622, 1628

"Summons to Be Free, A" (Benét) **2**:155

Sun Also Rises, The (Hemingway) **5**:663, 665, 668, 669, 672, 674, 676-78

Sunday Dinner (Oates) **8**:1107, 1111

"Sunday Morning" (Stevens) **11**:*1472, 1473, 1480, 1481, 1482*

"Sundays of Satin Legs Smith, The" (Brooks) **2**:197, 205-6

Sun Is So Quiet, The: Poems (Giovanni) **5**:635

Sunlight Dialogues, The (Gardner) **2**:256, **5**:595, 597, 598, 599, 600, 601, 602, 606-7, 609

"Sunset" (Didion) **3**:355

Surfacing (Atwood) **1**:81, 90

Surrender of Santiago, The (Norris) **8**:1095

Surrounded, The (McNickle) **7**:995, 997, 998, 999, 1000, 1002-3, 1005

Survival: A Thematic Guide to Canadian Literature (Atwood) **1**:85, 90

Suttree (McCarthy) **7**:963, 965, 967, 968, 970, 971-73

Sweeney Agonistes (Eliot) **4**:445, 450

Sweet as a Pickle, Clean as a Pig (McCullers) **7**:979, 983

Sweet Bird of Youth (T. Williams) **12**:1653, 1664, 1672-73

Sweet Flypaper of Life, The (Hughes; photographs by De Carava) **6**:737

Sweet Thursday (Steinbeck) **11**:1454

Sylvia (Sinclair) **10**:1392

Sylvia's Marriage (Sinclair) **10**:1392

Symbolist Movement in Literature, The (Symons) **4**:438

"Sympathy" (Dunbar) **3**:405

Table Talk of Samuel Marchbanks, The (Davies) **3**:335-36, 344

Tailor of Gloucester, The (Potter) **8**:1047

Take Me Where the Good Times Are (Cormier) **3**:295, 301

Tale of Chicago, The (Masters) **7**:954

Tale of Possessors Self-Dispossessed, A (O'Neill) **9**:1162, 1166

Tale of Three Wishes, A (Singer) **10**:1411

Tale of Two Cities, A (Dickens) **1**:102

Tales Before Midnight (Benét) **2**:155

"Tales" (Laurence) **6**:826, 827

Tales of a Fourth-Grade Nothing (Blume) **2**:166, 172

Tales of Men and Ghosts (Wharton) **12**:1622

"Tales of Queen Louisa" (Gardner) **5**:608

Tales of the Fish Patrol (London) **7**:879

Tales of the Jazz Age (Fitzgerald) **4**:532

Talismans for Children (Atwood) **1**:90

Talk About Russia: With Masha Scott (Buck and Scott) **2**:218

Talking Horse: Bernard Malamud on Life and Work (Malamud; Cheuse and Delbanco ed.) **7**:918

Talking Pictures (Foote) **4**:547

Talking to Myself: A Memoir of My Times (Terkel) **11**:1522, 1523, 1528

Tamar, and Other Poems (Jeffers) **6**:783, 786, 787, 788, 790

"Tamar" (Jeffers) **6**:798-99

Tambourines to Glory (Hughes) **6**:730, 737

Taming the Star Runner (Hinton) **5**:701, 703, 705, 706, 710, 713-16

Taps at Reveille: The Stories of F. Scott Fitzgerald (Fitzgerald) **4**:532

Tar: A Midwest Childhood (Anderson) **1**:44, 48

Tarantula (Dylan; writing) **3**:425

Tar Baby (Morrison) **8**:1052, 1053, 1057, 1058, 1064, 1070

Tarzan stories (Burroughs) **10**:1344

"Teddy" (Salinger) **10**:1309, 1321

"Teen-Agers Are for Real" (Hinton) **5**:700

Teibele and Her Demon (Singer) **10**:1411

Telling Stories (Didion) **3**:363

Tell Me How Long the Train's Been Gone (Baldwin) **1**:105, 110

Tell Me, Tell Me (Moore) **8**:1036, 1043

"Tell Me, Tell Me" (Moore) **8**:1047-48

Tell My Horse: Voodoo and Life in Haiti and Jamaica (Hurston) **6**:750, 752, 755

Tell the People: Talks with James Yen About the Mass Education Movement (Buck and Yen) **2**:218

Tempers, The (W. C. Williams) **12**:1677, 1679, 1686

Tempest, The (Shakespeare) **3**:335, 340, 348, 349, **7**:907

Tempest-Tost (Davies) **3**:337, 340, 344, 347, 348, 349-50

Temple of My Familiar, The (Walker) **11**:1575

Temptation Game, The (Gardner; radio play) **5**:602

Tenants, The (Malamud) **7**:918, 925

Tender Buttons: Objects, Food, Rooms (Stein) **1**:49, **10**:1420, 1422, 1424, 1425, 1434-36

Tender Mercies (Foote; screenplay) **4**:539, 541, 543, 544, 546, 547, 549-50

Tenderness (Cormier) **3**:301, 308

Tenderness (Oates) **8**:1111

"Ten Indians" (Hemingway) **5**:679

"Tennessee Williams Presents His POV" (T. Williams) **12**:1662

Terms of Survival (Ortiz Cofer) **9**:1183, 1185, 1191

Terror in Russia: Two Views (Sinclair) **10**:1392

Tess of the D'Urbervilles (Hardy) **3**:380

"Testimony Against Gertrude Stein" (article) **10**:1432

Texas Town (Foote) **4**:542, 547

Tex (Hinton) **5**:700, 701, 703, 706, 710, 712-13

Thanksgiving Visitor, The (Capote) **2**:242

That Awful Mrs. Eaton (Benét and Farrar) **2**:155

"That Same Pain, That Same Pleasure" (Ellison) **4**:473

That They May Win (Miller) **8**:1017, 1025

That Was Then, This Is Now (Hinton) **5**:699, 701, 702, 703, 706, 716-18

Theater Essays of Arthur Miller, The (Martin ed.) **8**:1025

"*Theatre We Worked For, The:*" The Letters of Eugene O'Neill to Kenneth MacGowan (O'Neill; Bryer and Alvarezn eds.) **9**:1168

Theft, A (Bellow) **1**:132

Theft (London) **7**:879

Their Blood Is Strong (Steinbeck) **11**:1448, 1454, 1455-56

Their Eyes Were Watching God (Hurston) **6**:745, 748, 749, 750-51, 752, 755, 756-59

Theirs Be the Guilt (Sinclair). *See Manassas*

"Theme for English B" (Hughes) **6**:727, 732, 741

Themes in My Poems (Jeffers) **6**:790

them (Oates) **8**:1103, 1105, 1107, 1109, 1111, 1113-15

Then Again, Maybe I Won't (Blume) **2**:166, 167, 169, 172, 179-80

Theodore Dreiser: A Selection of Uncollected Prose (Pizer ed.) **3**:381

Theophilus North (Wilder) **12**:1633, 1634, 1647

These Thirteen (Faulkner) **4**:486

They Brought Their Women (Ferber) **4**:507

They Call Me Carpenter (Sinclair) **10**:1392

They Came Here First: The Epic of the American Indian (McNickle) **7**:1002, 1006

They Seek a City (Bontemps and Conroy) **2**:187

"They Too Arise" (Miller) **8**:1014, 1018

Things as They Are (Stein) **10**:1424, 1425

Things Change (Mamet; screenplay) **7**:929, 932, 934, 935

"Things Have Changed" (Dylan; song lyric) **3**:421

Things They Carried, The (O'Brien) **8**:1119, 1122, 1123, 1124, 1125, 1127, 1131-32

"Things They Carried, The" (O'Brien) **8**:1132

Thinking of Home: William Faulkner's Letters to His Mother and Father, 1918-1925 (Faulkner; Watson ed.) **4**:486

Third Circle, The (Norris) **8**:1095

Third Life of Grange Copeland, The (Walker) **11**:1564, 1566, 1575

Thirst and Other One-Act Plays (O'Neill) **9**:1168

"Thirteen O'Clock" (Benét) **2**:155

Thirtieth Anniversary Concert Celebration, The (Dylan; record album) **3**:425

"This Is Not for John Lennon" (Giovanni) **5**:641

This Music Crept by Me Upon the Waters (MacLeish) **7**:901, 906-7

This Property Is Condemned (T. Williams) **12**:1664

This Proud Heart (Buck) **2**:212, 213, 215, 218, 230-31

This Quiet Dust (Styron) **11**:1500, 1503-4

"This Quiet Dust" (Styron) **11**:1504

"This Sandwich Has No Mayonnaise" (Salinger) **10**:1303

This Side Jordan (Laurence) **6**:821, 823, 827, 829-30

This Side of Paradise (Fitzgerald) **4**:517, 518, 522, 523, 524, 525, 532, 534-37

This Water (Carver) **2**:258, 261

"Thomas Hardy's Reputation as a Poet in American Periodicals" (Malamud) **7**:911

Those Who Ride the Night Winds (Giovanni) **5**:635, 641-42

Thoughtbook of Francis Scott Fitzgerald (Fitzgerald) **4**:532

Three Academic Pieces (Stevens) **11**:1475

Three by Irving (Irving) **6**:768, 773

Three by Truman Capote (Capote) **2**:242

Three Children's Plays (Mamet) **7**:935, 943-44

Three Comrades (Fitzgerald; screenplay) **4**:523, 532

Three Daughters of Madame Liang, The (Buck) **2**:218, 231-32

Three Famous Novels (Faulkner) **4**:486

Three Jewish Plays (Mamet) **7**:935

Three Lives (Stein) **10**:1424, 1425, 1437-38

Three Men on a Horse (Abbott and Holm; play) **8**:1025

Three Men on a Horse (Miller radio adaptation) **8**:1025

Three Papers on Fiction (Welty) **12**:1596

"Three Players of a Summer Game" (T. Williams) **12**:1655

Three Plays (Oates) **8**:1106, 1111

Three Sisters (Chekhov; Mamet adaptation) **7**:935

Three Stories and Ten Poems (Hemingway) **5:**674, 678

Three Travelers Watch a Sunrise (Stevens) **11:**1475

Three Uses of the Knife: On the Nature and Purpose of Drama (Mamet) **7:**935

Three Women (Piercy) **9:**1205

Three Women (Plath) **9:**1224, 1227

Thrice the Brinded Cat Hath Mew'd: A Record of the Stratford Shakespearean Festival in Canada, 1955 (Davies and Guthrie) **3:**336, 344

"Thrifty Lover, The" (Piercy) **9:**1206

"Through Ancient Paganism" (Potok) **9:**1274

"Through Classical Paganism" (Potok) **9:**1274

"Through Islam and Christianity" (Potok) **9:**1274

Thurso's Landing and Other Poems (Jeffers) **6:**786, 790

Thus Spake Zarathustra (Nietzsche) **9:**1167

Tide of Time, The (Masters) **7:**954, 959-60

Tidewater Morning, A: Three Tales from Youth (Styron) **11:**1493, 1500

Tiger Eyes (Blume) **2:**166, 167, 172

Tiger Joy (Benét) **2:**155

Tiger Who Wore White Gloves, The: Or, You Are What You Are (Brooks) **2:**203

Timebends: A Life (Miller) **8:**1013, 1018, 1025

Time Is Noon, The (Buck) **2:**218

Time out of Mind (Dylan; record album) **3:**420, 421, 425

Time's Power: Poems, 1985-1988 (Rich) **9:**1284, 1292-93

Times They Are A-Changin', The (Dylan; record album) **3:**419, 421, 425

Time to Act, A: Selected Addresses (MacLeish) **7:**901

Time to Speak, A: The Selected Prose of Archibald MacLeish **7:**901

Time Traveler, The (Oates) **8:**1111

"Timmy" (O'Brien) **8:**1121

Tin Can Tree, The (Tyler) **11:**1543, 1546, 1551

Tin Drum, The (Grass) **6:**780

Titan, The (Dreiser) **3:**378, 381, 392, 394

"To a Contemporary Bunkshooter" (Sandburg) **10:**1339

To a God Unknown (Steinbeck) **11:**1447, 1454

"To a Mouse" (Burns) **11:**1460

"To a Snail" (Moore) **8:**1048

To Bedlam and Part Way Back (Sexton) **10:**1359, 1361, 1371, 1373-75

"To Be of Use" (Piercy) **9:**1201

To Be of Use (Piercy) **9:**1205

To Be Young, Gifted, and Black: Lorraine Hansberry in Her Own Words (Hansberry; Nemiroff ed.) **5:**646, 649, 654, 657, 658

To Be Young, Gifted, and Black: Lorraine Hansberry in Her Own Words (Hansberry; play) **5:**649, 654

Tobiasse: Artist in Exile (Potok) **9:**1269

"To Build a Fire" (London) **7:**877, 889, 890

Today and Forever (Buck) **2:**218

Today Is Friday (Hemingway) **5:**674

Today We Live (Faulkner; screenplay) **4:**479, 486

To Disembark (Brooks) **2:**203

"To Grandfather, Now Forgetting" (Ortiz Cofer) **9:**1191

To Have and Have Not (Faulkner; screenplay) **4:**479, 486

To Have and Have Not (Hemingway) **4:**479, **5:**663, 674

To Hell with Dying (Walker; children's book) **11:**1575

"To Hell with Dying" (Walker; short story) **11:**1579

"To His Coy Mistress" (Marvell) **7:**901-2

To Jerusalem and Back: A Personal Account (Bellow) **1:**130, 132

To Kill a Mockingbird (Foote; screenplay) **4:**539, 542, 543, 546, 547, 550-52

To Kill a Mockingbird (Lee; novel) **2:**234, **4:**539, 542, 543, 550, **6:**833, 834, 835, 836, 837, 838, 839-41, 842

Toklas, Alice B. **10:**1417, 1419, 1420-21, 1422, 1424, 1425, 1426, *1427*, 1429, 1430, 1431-32, 1434, 1436-37

Tom: A Ballet (Cummings) **3:**319

Tom and Viv (Hastings; play) **4:**441

"Tombstone Blues" (Dylan) **3:**423

Tomcat in Love (O'Brien) **8:**1119, 1123, 1126, 1127, 1133-34

Tomorrow (Foote; play) **4:**547

Tomorrow (Foote; screenplay) **4:**547

Tomorrow (Foote; teleplay) **4:**542, 547

Tomorrow-Tamer, The (Laurence) **6:**821, 823, 827, 830, 831-32

Tom Sawyer (Twain) **4:**540

Tom Swift stories, Foote and **4:**540

To My Daughters with Love (Buck) **2:**218

Too Far to Walk (Hersey) **5:**690

Topsy-Turvy Emperor of China, The (Singer) **10:**1411

Torah **10:**1401, 1404, 1406, 1409, 1414

"Tor House" (Jeffers) **6:**793

Torrents of Spring, The (Hemingway) **1:**45, **5:**663, 674

Tortilla Flat (Steinbeck; novel) **11:**1447, 1450, 1453, 1454, 1459-60, 1462

To Take a Dare (Zindel and Dragonwagon) **12:**1722

"To the House" (Jeffers) **6:**793

"To the Man on the Trail" (London) **7:**873

"To the Pay Toilet" (Piercy) **9:**1203

"To the Rock That Will Be a Cornerstone of the House" (Jeffers) **6:**793

"To the Stone-Cutters" (Jeffers) **6:**793

Touch of the Poet, A (O'Neill) **9:**1162, 1166, 1168, 1172

Touch of the Poet, A (television film) **9:**1161

Touchstone, The (Wharton) **12:**1614, 1622

Toward the Gulf (Masters) **7:**954

Tower of Ivory (MacLeish) **7:**895, 901

Town, The (Faulkner) **4:**480, 486

"Town of Scottsboro, The" (Hughes) **6:**744

Townsman, The (Sedges; pseud. of Buck) **2:**212, 214, 215, 218, 226-28

Toys in the Attic (Hellman) **12:**1713

"Tradition and the Individual Talent" (Eliot) **4:**442, 457

"Tragedy at Three Forks, The" (Dunbar) **3:**412

Tragedy of Faust, The (Goethe) **7:**952

Tragic America (Dreiser) **3:**381

Trail of the Hawk, The: A Comedy of the Seriousness of Life (Lewis) **6**:850

"Train Time" (McNickle) **7**:1005

"Transcendental Etude" (Rich) **9**:1291

Transformations (Sexton) **10**:1361, 1363, 1371, 1376

Transport to Summer (Stevens) **11**:1470, 1471, 1475, 1487

Traveler at Forty, A (Dreiser) **3**:378, 381

Travelers, The (Foote; teleplay) **4**:547

Traveling Lady, The (Foote) **4**:542, 544, 547

Travels with Charley: In Search of America (Steinbeck) **11**:1448, 1454

Treasure Island (Stevenson) **2**:182, **10**:1378

Tree for Poverty, A: Somali Poetry and Prose (Laurence transl.) **6**:821, 823, 827, 832

Tree of Here, The (Potok) **9**:1269

Tree of Night and Other Stories, A (Capote) **2**:235, 238, 242

Trees Die at the Top (Ferber) **4**:507

"Trial by Existence, The" (Frost) **4**:567

Trifler, The (Masters) **7**:954

Trilogy: An Experiment in Multimedia (Capote, Perry, and Perry) **2**:242

"trilogy of desire" (Dreiser) **3**:378, 392, 393, 394

Triple Crown: Chicano, Puerto Rican, and Cuban-American Poetry (amthology) **9**:1185, 1191

Trip to Bountiful, The (Foote; play) **4**:542, 547, 554

Trip to Bountiful, The (Foote; screenplay) **4**:541, 543, 546, 547, 554

Trip to Bountiful, The (Foote; teleplay) **4**:542, 547, 554

Triumphal March (Eliot) **4**:450

Triumph of the Egg, The: A Book of Impressions from American Life in Tales and Poems (Anderson) **1**:44, 45, 46, 48, 54, 55

Triumph of the Spider Monkey, The (Oates) **8**:1111

Trojan Horse, The: A Play (MacLeish) **7**:901

Troll Garden, The (Cather) **2**:271, 274, 278, 285

Troubled Island (Hughes; opera libretto) **6**:737

True and False: Heresy and Common Sense for the Actor (Mamet) **7**:935

True at First Light (Hemingway) **5**:664, 665, 670, 671, 674

True Confessions (Didion and Dunne; screenplay) **3**:357, 363

True Grit (Portis) **9**:1248-49, 1250-51, 1254, 1255-56

True Stories (Atwood) **1**:90

Trumpet Shall Sound, The (Wilder) **12**:1630, 1631, 1634, 1647

Trumpets of Summer, The (Atwood and Beckwith) **1**:84

Truth (Giovanni; record album) **5**:632

Truth Is on Its Way (Giovanni; record album) **5**:630, 631, 632

"Truth the Dead Know, The" (Sexton) **10**:1369, 1371

Trying to Save Piggy Sneed (Irving) **6**:768, 781-82

"Tuft of Flowers, A" (Frost) **4**:567, 568

Tulips and Chimneys (Cummings) **3**:314, 316, 319, 320, 327-30

"Tulips and Chimneys" (Cummings) **3**:328

Tumble Tower (Tyler; Modarressi illus.) **11**:1545, 1546, 1551

Tunes for Bears to Dance To (Cormier) **3**:300, 301, 309

"Turtles, The" (Gaines) **5**:584

Turtles of Tasman, The (London) **7**:879

$1200 a Year (Ferber and Levy; play) **4**:502, 507, 514

Twelve Men (Dreiser) **3**:381

Twelve Million Black Voices (Wright) **12**:1695, 1699, 1703

Twelve Plays (Oates) **8**:1106, 1111

Twelve Poems (Wharton) **12**:1622

Twelve-Spoked Wheel Flashing, The (Piercy) **9**:1205

Twenty-five Short Stories (Benét) **2**:155

Twenty-one Love Poems (Rich) **9**:1280, 1284

"Twenty-one Love Poems" (Rich) **9**:1289, 1291

Twenty-seven Stories (Buck) **2**:218

Twenty-seven Wagons Full of Cotton and Other Plays (T. Williams) **12**:1664

Twice Have the Trumpets Sounded: A Record of the Stratford Shakespearean Festival in Canada, 1954 (Davies and Guthrie) **3**:336, 344

Twilight (Frost) **4**:557

Twilight Sleep (Wharton) **12**:1620, 1622

Two-Character Play, The (T. Williams) **12**:1664

Two for the Seesaw (Gibson) **5**:612, 613-14, 615, 616, 619, 621-23, 624

Two Girls with Blue Aprons (painting) **12**:1691

Two-Headed Poems (Atwood) **1**:90

Two (Hitherto Unpublished) Poems (Stein) **10**:1424

Two Poems and "Kim" Reviewed (Norris) **8**:1095

Two Poems (Carver) **2**:261

Two Southern Idylls: Miss Lou and The Girls (Foote) **4**:547

"Two Tramps at Mud Time" (Frost) **4**:571

Ultramarine (Carver) **2**:258, 261

Ulysses (Joyce) **5**:598, **7**:971

Uncalled, The (Dunbar) **3**:401, 402, 406, 415-16

Uncle Eph's Christmas (Dunbar) **3**:401, 406

"Unclench Yourself" (Piercy) **9**:1206

Uncle Remus: His Songs and His Sayings (Harris) **8**:1058

Uncle Tom's Cabin (Stowe) **12**:1706
Baldwin critique of **1**:105

Uncle Tom's Children (Wright) **12**:1693, 1695, 1697, 1698, 1699, 1703, 1704, 1705-7

Uncle Valentine and Other Stories: Willa Cather's Collected Short Fiction, 1915-1929 (Cather) **2**:278

Uncle Vanya (Chekhov; Mamet adaptation) **7**:935

"Uncle Wiggly in Connecticut" (Salinger) **10**:1303

Uncollected Critical Writings, The (Wharton; Wegener ed.) **12**:1622

Uncollected Early Prose of Katherine Anne Porter **9**:1234, 1236

Uncollected Poems (Plath) **9**:1224

Uncollected Stories of William Faulkner (Faulkner; Blotner ed.) **4**:486

"Undefeated, The" (Hemingway) **5**:679

Undertaker's Gone Bananas, The (Zindel) **12**:1722

Under the Biltmore Clock (television film) **4:**519

Under the Eye of the Storm (Hersey) **5:**690

Under the Red Sky (Dylan; record album) **3:**425

Under the Weather (Bellow) **1:**132

Unholy Loves (Oates) **8:**1111

"Unknown Girl in the Maternity Ward" (Sexton) **10:**1374, 1375

Unknown O'Neill, The: Unpublished or Unfamiliar Writings of Eugene O'Neill (Bogard ed.) **9:**1168

"Unlearning to Not Speak" (Piercy) **9:**1206

"Untold Lie, The" (Anderson) **1:**52

Untouchables, The (Mamet; screenplay) **7:**929, 932, 935

Untouchables, The (television series) **7:**929

Unvanquished, The (Faulkner) **4:**486, 487-89

Up Close and Personal (Didion and Dunne; screenplay) **3:**357, 363

Up from Paradise (Miller) **8:**1025

"Up in Michigan" (Hemingway) **5:**678

Upon the Sweeping Flood (Oates) **8:**1111

Up the Sandbox (Zindel; screenplay) **12:**1717, 1722

Up the Tree (Atwood) **1:**90

Upton Sinclair Presents William Fox (Sinclair) **10:**1392

Ursinus College **10:**1302

"Use of Force, The" (W. C. Williams) **12:**1678

Vacation Time: Poems for Children (Giovanni) **5:**635

Vachel Lindsay: A Poet in America (Masters) **7:**954

Valentine's Day (Foote) **4:**547, 554

Valley of Decision, The (Wharton) **12:**1614, 1615, 1622

Valley of the Moon, The (London) **7:**879

Vandover and the Brute (Norris) **8:**1090, 1093, 1095, 1100-1101

Vanya on 42nd Street (Mamet; screenplay) **7:**929, 932, 935

Vegetable, The: Or, From President to Postman (Fitzgerald; play) **4:**532

Vein of Riches, A (Knowles) **6:**812

"Vengeance of Nitocris, The" (T. Williams) **12:**1652, 1654

Verdict, The (Mamet; screenplay) **7:**929, 931, 932, 935

Verdict, The (Reed; novel) **7:**935

Verses (Wharton) **12:**1613, 1615, 1622

"Very Short Story, A" (Hemingway) **5:**668, 679

Very Young Poets (Brooks) **2:**203

Victim, The (Bellow) **1:**132

Victors, The (Sartre; Wilder transl.) **12:**1647

"Vietnam in Me, The" (O'Brien) **8:**1123, 1127

Vieux Carré (T. Williams) **12:**1664

View from the Bridge, A (Miller) **8:**1025, *1030*, 1031

Village, The (Mamet) **7:**935

"Viney's Free Papers" (Dunbar) **3:**411

Viol de Lucrèce, Le (Obey) **12:**1631, 1647

Violent Bear It Away, The (O'Connor) **8:**1135, 1138, 1139, 1141, 1143, 1144-46

Violent Duality (Grace) **1:**85

Vision in Spring (Faulkner; Sensibar ed.) **4:**486

Viva Zapata! (Steinbeck; screenplay) **11:**1453, 1454

Voice from the Attic, A (Davies) **3:**344

Voice of the People, The (Davies) **3:**344

Voices in the House (Sedges; Buck pseud.) **2:**218

Voyage to Pagany, A (W. C. Williams) **12:**1686

Wag the Dog (Mamet and Henkin; screenplay) **7:**932, 935

Waiting for Lefty (Odets) **8:**1020

Wall, The (Brooks) **2:**203

Wall, The (Hersey) **5:**686, 687, 688, 689, 690, 694-96

Wally for Queen! (Sinclair) **10:**1392

Walnut Door, The (Hersey) **5:**690

Walt Whitman (Masters) **7:**949, 954, 960

"Wanderers, The" (Welty) **12:**1601

Wanderings: Chaim Potok's History of the Jews (Potok) **9:**1259, 1263, 1269, 1274-75

"Wanting to Die" (Sexton) **10:**1363-64, 1376

War Lover, The (Hersey) **5:**686, 688, 690

Warm and Cold (Mamet and Sultan) **7:**935

"Warning to Free Nations" (Buck) **2:**214

War of the Classes, The (London) **7:**879, 883

Warrior Marks: Female Genital Mutilation and the Sexual Blinding of Women (Walker; nonfiction) **11:**1565, 1575

Warrior Marks (Walker; screenplay) **11:**1566, 1575

Wars I Have Seen (Stein) **10:**1422, 1424, 1437

Waste Land, The: A Facsimile and Transcript of the Original Drafts Including the Annotations of Ezra Pound (Eliot) **4:**441, 450

Waste Land, The (Eliot) **4:**437, 439, 440, 441, 442, 450, 451, 453-55, **12:**1677, 1684

Watch on the Rhine (play) **11:**1530

Water Babies, The (Kingsley) **7:**898

Water Engine, The (Mamet; play) **7:**935

Water Engine, The (Mamet; teleplay) **7:**930, 932, 934, 935

Water-Method Man, The (Irving) **6:**765, 773, 782

"Waving Adieu, Adieu, Adieu" (Stevens) **11:**1482

Way Forward Is with a Broken Heart, The (Walker) **11:**1569, 1575

Way of the Pilgrim, The (book in Glass stories) **10:**1315, 1316

Way Out, A (Frost) **4:**567

Way Out, The: What Lies Ahead for America? (Sinclair) **10:**1387, 1392

Ways of White Folks, The (Hughes) **6:**737

Wayward Bus, The (Steinbeck) **11:**1448, 1454

"Way You'll Never Be, A" (Hemingway) **5:**680

We All Fall Down (Cormier) **3:**301, 310

"We Are the World" (song) **3:**421

"Weary Blues, The" (Hughes) **6:**728, 731

Weary Blues, The (Hughes) **6:**728, 730, 737, 741-42

"Weary Kingdom" (Irving) **6:**781-82

Web and the Rock, The (Wolfe) **3:**300

Wedding Procession of the Rag Doll and the Broom Handle and Who

Was in It, The (Sandburg) **10**:1338

Wedge, The (W. C. Williams) **12**:1686

"We Have a Beautiful Mother: Previously Uncollected Poems" (Walker) **11**:1576

We Have Tomorrow (Bontemps) **2**:187, 188

Welcome Table, The (Baldwin; uncompleted) **1**:111, 113

Well-Tempered Critic, The (Davies) **3**:344

Wen, A (Bellow) **1**:132

"We Real Cool" (Brooks) **2**:203, 206

We're No Angels (Mamet; screenplay) **7**:932, 935

We Stand United, and Other Radio Scripts (Benét; radio plays) **2**:155

"We Stand United" (Benét) **2**:155

Western Star (Benét) **2**:149, 152, 155

"West-Running Brook" (Frost) **4**:571

West-Running Brook (Frost) **4**:567

Wet Parade, The (Sinclair) **10**:1381, 1392

"We Wear the Mask" (Dunbar) **3**:403, 405, 407

We Were the Mulvaneys (Oates) **8**:1109, 1111

Wharton Dance, The (Foote) **4**:547

What America Means to Me (Buck) **2**:218

"What Any Lover Learns" (MacLeish) **7**:902

What Are Big Girls Made Of? (Piercy) **9**:1205

What Are Masterpieces (Stein) **10**:1424

What Are Years (Moore) **8**:1035, 1037, 1043

What Didymus Did (Sinclair) **10**:1392

What God Means to Me (Sinclair) **10**:1392

What I Lived For (Oates) **8**:1103, 1106, 1107, 1109, 1111, 1115-16

What Is Found There: Notebooks on Poetry and Politics (Rich) **9**:1277, 1284, 1293-94

"What Kind of Husbands Do `Jimmies' Make" (Fitzgerald) **4**:522

What Odd Expedients and Other Poems (Jeffers) **6**:790

What Price Marriage? (Porter under Sears pseud.) **9**:1236

What's Bred in the Bone (Davies) **3**:337, 344

"What's That Smell in the Kitchen?" (Piercy) **9**:1206

"What the Library Means to Me" (Tan) **11**:1507

"What the Thunder Said" (Eliot) **4**:454

What Use Are Flowers?: A Fable in One Act (Hansberry; Nemiroff ed.) **5**:654, 658

What We Talk About When We Talk About Love (Carver) **2**:255, 257, 258, 259, 261, 262

"What We Talk About When We Talk About Love" (Carver) **2**:266-67

"What White Publishers Won't Print" (Hurston) **6**:750

Wheat trilogy (Norris) **8**:1090, 1091, 1098

Wheel of Love, The (Oates) **8**:1111

When a Darkness Falls (Zindel) **12**:1722

"When Children Discover America" (Lee) **6**:841, 842

When God Laughs and Other Stories (London) **7**:879

"When Latin Women Pray" (Ortiz Cofer) **9**:1183

"When Malindy Sings" (Dunbar) **3**:407

When Shlemiel Went to Warsaw and Other Stories (Singer) **10**:1411

"When Sue Wears Red" (Hughes) **6**:727, 742

When We Dead Awaken (Ibsen) **9**:1278

Where Are You Going, Where Have You Been? (Oates) **8**:1111

Where I Live: Selected Essays (T. Williams) **12**:1660, 1662, 1664

Where I'm Calling From (Carver) **2**:258, 259, 261, 262

Where Is Here? (Oates) **8**:1111

Where Water Comes Together with Other Water (Carver) **2**:258, 261

White Album, The (Didion) **3**:354, 358, 362, 363, 369, 371

White Fang (London) **7**:869, 877, 879, 886-88

White Lotus (Hersey) **5**:689, 690

White Mane (Agee; screenplay) **1**:17

White Man, Listen! (Wright) **12**:1697, 1700, 1703

White Mule (W. C. Williams) **12**:1686, 1691-92

"White Silence, The" (London) **7**:877

White Rose of Memphis, The (Falkner) **4**:476

Who Do You Think You Are? (Munro) **8**:1072, 1073, 1074, 1075, 1080-82

"Whole World Knows, The" (Welty) **12**:1601

Whore's Profession, A: Notes and Essays (Mamet) **7**:930, 935

"Why Don't You Dance?" (Carver) **2**:266

"Why I Live at the P.O." (Welty) **12**:1608

Why Noah Chose the Dove (Singer) **10**:1411

Wicked City, The (Singer) **10**:1411

Wide Is the Gate (Sinclair) **10**:1392, 1396

"Wide Net, The" (Welty) **12**:1592

Wide Net and Other Stories, The (Welty) **12**:1596

Widow Claire, The (Foote) **4**:547

Widow for One Year, A (Irving) **6**:773

Wifey (Blume) **2**:166, 167, 172

Wild Duck, The (Ibsen) **9**:1173

"Wilderness Story, A" (Munro) **8**:1077

Wilderness Tips (Atwood) **1**:90

Wild Old Wicked Man and Other Poems, The (MacLeish) **7**:901

Wild Palms, The (Faulkner) **4**:486

Wild Patience Has Taken Me This Far, A (Rich) **9**:1284

"Wild Swans" (Munro) **8**:1076

Willa Cather in Europe (Cather) **2**:278

Willa Cather's Collected Short Fiction, 1892-1912 (Cather) **2**:278

William Carlos Williams and James Laughlin: Selected Letters **12**:1686

William Carlos Williams, John Sanford: A Corrspondence **12**:1686

William Faulkner: Early Prose and Poetry (Collins ed.) **4**:486

William Wilson (Gardner; libretto) **5**:602

William Styron's "Nat Turner": Ten Black Writers Respond (Clarke ed.) **11**:1492

Will to Change, The (Rich) **9**:1284

Will You Always Love Me? (Oates)
8:1111

Will You Please Be Quiet, Please?
(Carver) 2:255, 257, 258, 259,
261

"Will You Please Be Quiet, Please?"
(Carver) 2:257, 258, 267-68

Wilson (Mamet) 7:935

"Wind and Water" (Tan). *See Joy
Luck Club, The*

Wind from an Enemy Sky (McNickle)
7:995, 997, 998, 999, 1000,
1002, 1003-5, 1006

Wind Song (Sandburg) 10:1338

Windy McPherson's Son (Anderson)
1:44, 45, 46, 48

Winesburg, Ohio (Anderson) 1:41,
42, 44, 46, 47, 48, 49, 50, 51-54

Winner Take Nothing (Hemingway)
5:663, 674, 680-81

Winnie (Brooks) 2:203

"Winter Birds, Winter Apples"
(Tyler) 1543

"Winter Branch, A" (Irving) 6:765

Winter Crook (Gibson) 5:615, 619

Winter Insomnia (Carver) 2:261

Winter of Our Discontent, The
(Steinbeck) 11:1454

Winter of Our Discontent, The (television film) 11:1449

Winter Trees (Plath) 9:1224, 1227

Wise Blood (O'Connor) 8:1135,
1137, 1138, 1139, 1141, 1143,
1144, 1145, 1146-48

Wishing Tree, The (Faulkner) 4:486

"Witch's Husband, The" (Ortiz
Cofer) 9:1191

"With Mercy for the Greedy"
(Sexton) 10:1362

With Shuddering Fall (Oates) 8:1104,
1107, 1111

Witness Tree, A (Frost) 4:561, 567

Wizard of Tears, The (Sexton and
Kumin) 10:1371

"Wolf, The" (Norris) 8:1090, 1091

"Woman Dead in Her Forties, A"
(Rich) 9:1291

"Womanhood, The" (Brooks) 2:204

"woman in the ordinary, The"
(Piercy) 9:1206

Woman of Andros, The (Wilder)
12:1631, 1636, 1647, 1649-50

Woman on the Edge of Time (Piercy)
9:1195, 1199, 1203, 1205, 1207-9

*Woman Who Was Changed and Other
Stories, The* (Buck) 2:218

"Woman with Girdle" (Sexton)
10:1369, 1371

*(Woman) Writer: Occasions and
Opportunities* (Oates) 8:1111

Women and the Men, The (Giovanni)
5:631, 635

Women at Point Sur, The (Jeffers)
6:786, 787, 790

Women in Love (Oates) 8:1107, 1111

*Women Whose Lives Are Food, Men
Whose Lives Are Money* (Oates)
8:1111

Wonderland (Oates) 8:1111

"Wood-Pile, The" (Frost) 4:569

Woods, The (Mamet) 7:929, 935

word portraits (Stein) 10:1420,
1422, 1423, 1425, 1433

*Words for Dr. Y: Uncollected Poems
with Three Stories* (Sexton)
10:1365, 1367-68, 1371

Words for Music (Eliot) 4:450

*Working: People Talk About What
They Do All Day and How They
Feel About What They Do* (Terkel)
11:1522, 1523, 1524, 1527,
1536-37

Working: The Musical 11:1536

"Work of Artifice, A" (Piercy)
9:1206, 1207

Work of Art (Lewis) 6:850

World According to Garp, The (Irving)
6:763, 764, 765, 767, 768, 771,
773, 776, 778-80, 781

"World and the Jug, The" (Ellison)
4:473

*World and the Parish, The: Willa
Cather's Articles and Reviews,
1893-1902* 2:278

World Gone Wrong (Dylan; record
album) 3:420, 425

World Is Round, The (Stein) 10:1424

World of Gwendolyn Brooks, The
(Brooks) 2:198, 203

World of Wonders (Davies) 3:337,
344, 347

World Over, The (Wharton) 12:1622

World's End series (Sinclair). *See
Lanny Budd series*

World's End (Sinclair) 10:1392, 1396

World So Wide (Lewis) 6:848, 850

World to Win, A (Sinclair) 10:1392,
1396

"Worn Path, A" (Welty) 12:1592,
1608

*Wouldn't Take Nothing for My Journey
Now* (Angelou) 1:60, 68, 71

"Wounds of Jesus, The" (Hurston)
6:761

Wreckage of Agathon, The (Gardner)
5:598, 601, 602, 609-10

Wrecker, The (Bellow) 1:132

Writer's Craft, The (Hersey ed.)
5:690

Writer's Experience, The (Ellison)
4:466

*Writer's Eye, A: Collected Book
Reviews* (Welty; McHaney ed.)
12:1596

Writing in Restaurants (Mamet)
7:930, 935

Writing of Fiction, The (Wharton)
12:1622

Writings and Drawings (Dylan) 3:425

*Writings from Willa Cather's Campus
Years* (Cather) 2:278

Written in Bone (Piercy) 9:1205

"Wrong Monday" (Piercy) 9:1209

"Wunderkind" (McCullers) 7:977,
979

Wuthering Heights (Brontë) 8:1073,
1077

W[ViVa]: Seventy New Poems
(Cummings) 3:319

Xaipe (Cummings) 3:319

Xingu and Other Stories (Wharton)
12:1622

XLI Poems (Cummings) 3:315, 316,
319

"Yearning Heifer, The" (Singer)
10:1414

*Year of Our Revolution, The: New and
Selected Stories and Poems* (Ortiz
Cofer) 9:1184, 1185, 1191, 1194

"Yentl, the Yeshiva Boy" (Singer;
story) 10:1405, 1406

Yentl, the Yeshiva Boy (Singer and
Napolin; play) 10:1401, 1405-6,
1411

!Yo! (Alvarez) 1:28, 29, 30, 32, 34,
36-37

Yoknapatawpha saga (Faulkner)
4:475, 478, 479, 481, 482-83,
489, 495, 497, 548

"You, Andrew Marvell" (MacLeish)
7:898, 901-2

You Are Happy (Atwood) 1:90

You Can't Catch Me (Oates; under
Smith pseud.) 8:1111

*You Can't Keep a Good Woman Down:
Short Stories* (Walker) 11:1575

You Can't Pet a Possom (Bontemps) **2**:186, 187

You Must Remember This (Oates) **8**:1109, 1111

Young Adventure: A Book of Poems (Benét) **2**:150, 155

Young Booker: Booker T. Washington's Early Days (Bontemps) **2**:187, 188

"Young Folks, The" (Salinger) **10**:1302, 1306

Young Lady of Property, A (Foote) **4**:547

Young Man from Atlanta, The (Foote) **4**:539, 543, 544, 547, 552-53

Young Man in Search of Love, A (Singer) **10**:1400, 1411

Young People's Pride (Benét) **2**:151, 155

Young Poets' Primer (Brooks) **2**:203

Young Revolutionist, The (Buck) **2**:218

Your Native Land, Your Life (Rich) **9**:1284, 1285

Youth and the Bright Medusa (Cather) **2**:274, 278

"You Touched Me" (Lawrence) **12**:1658

You Touched Me (T. Williams and Windham; play) **12**:1658, 1664

Yvernelle: A Tale of Feudal France (Norris) **8**:1088, 1089, 1093, 1095, 1100

Zebra and Other Stories (Potok) **9**:1269

Zlateh the Goat and Other Stories (Singer) **10**:1411

Zombie (Oates) **8**:1111

"Zooey" (Salinger) **10**:1315, 1316

Index of Visual Arts

Achelous and Hercules (painting), 7:959

Acrobats, or Masks and Ruins (painting), 3:342

Adrift in Soho (painting), 9:1217

Africa (painting), 11:1581

After Tea (painting), 11:1472

Alice B. Toklas (painting), 10:1431

Amazons, The (painting), 11:1580

America (painting), 11:1524

American Rudder (painting), 7:937

American Village (painting), 6:846

angel image (painting), 5:614

Anxiety (painting), 4:442

Apple Harvest, The (painting), 6:805

Arnold Comes of Age (painting), 1:52

Arts of the South (painting), 8:1146

As Seen on TV (watercolor), 9:1210

Automobile Industry (painting), 11:1537

Ball, The (painting), 12:1621

Ballo della Vita, Il (painting), 11:1483

Banjo Lesson, The (painting), 2:182

Baptism (painting), 11:1503

Bare Bones #34/Constellation (painting), 9:1192

Barque sur la Marne, En (painting), 3:385

Bartholeme de Las Casas (painting), 12:1643

Baseball at Night (painting), 7:923

Beach Scene with Female Bather Holding an Umbrella: Morning (watercolor), 10:1319

Belle (painting), 8:1141

Betrayal (painting), 5:715

Between the Wars #3 (painting), 5:624

Bikini (image), 5:693

Birches (woodcut), 4:570

Birem, Iguana of the Rocks (painting), 12:1673

Birthday Dress, The (painting), 7:981

Blank Signature, The (painting), 3:328

"Blind Weaver" (photograph), 12:1606

Blood of the Revolutionary Martyrs Fertilizing the Earth (mural), 10:1339

Blue Collar World of Joe Wong, The (painting), 5:609

Blues (painting), 6:739

Blues Singer, The (painting), 6:732

Bonne Parole, La (painting), 10:1425

Booster (painting), 6:849

Boy Fishing (watercolor), 10:1320

Boy with a Snowball (painting), 3:345

Bread (painting), 1:98

Bride, A (painting), 12:1645

Bridges in Winter (painting), 1:124

Brooklyn Crucifixion (painting), 9:1275

Buffalo Nickel (painting), 7:938

Bustling City (painting), 11:1479

Café Francis, The (painting), 3:391

Caffe Florian (painting), 11:1556

Can Fire in the Park (painting), 1:109

Cannery, 1931, The (painting), 11:1465

Cape Cod Morning (painting), 5:605

Cathedral Forest (painting), 11:1533

Celestial Atlas, A (Jamieson), 9:1292

Cena Capitalista, La (mural), 10:1437

Ceremonial at Black Lake (painting), 7:1003

Chain Gang (painting), 12:1702

Child and Her Mother, Wapato, Yakima Valley, Washington (photograph), 8:1081

Chilmark Hay (painting), 4:566

Chinese Patron of the Arts (still life), 2:231

Church on Lenox Avenue (painting), 1:106

Chute d'Icare, La (painting), 12:1725

Coffee Shop (painting), 10:1308

Coiffeur, The (watercolor), 12:1609

Colorful Landscape with Aquatic Birds (painting), 11:1484

Comiendo, Platicando (painting), 9:1190

Concert Singer, The (painting), 3:351

Coney Island (watercolor), 10:1412

Confederate soldier surrender (painting), 4:488

Connecticut Autumn (painting), 1:15

Conversation (painting), 7:928

Conversion (painting), 4:452

Cornice (painting), 2:285

Corrida, Death of a Torero (painting), 5:680

Cortés Enters Mexico (painting), 7:900

Cottage Garden, The (painting), 4:449

Cotton Pickers, Georgia (painting), 12:1594

Cotton Picking, Pulaski County, Arkansas (photograph), 8:1053

Cotton Plantation on the Mississippi, A (lithograph), 3:415, 4:495

Couple Descending Stairs (painting), 4:525

Couple, The (painting), 2:202

Crapshooters, The (painting), 6:757

"Crops Left to Dry and Rot" (painting), 4:453

Cross, The (mixed-media piece), 9:1187

Crossing (artwork), 10:1373

Crowd in a Landscape (painting), 12:1680

Crowd XX (painting), 11:1548

Crucifixion (wood carving), 6:743

Cummings self-portrait (painting), 3:321

Dancer in White Before the Footlights (painting), **4**:*510*

Daniel Boone Escorting Settlers Through the Cumberland Gap (painting), **2**:*153*

Dash for the Timber, A (painting), **10**:*1350*

Daydreaming (painting), **12**:*1625*

Dean's Roll Call, The (painting), **2**:*229*

Death as a Bride (watercolor), **1**:*92*

Descent (painting), **7**:*907*

Destiny 1 (painting), **11**:*1550*

Dogs Resting, Greenland (painting), **7**:*886*

Domino's Futurity (painting), **1**:*56*

Double Portrait of the Artist in Time (painting), **8**:*1079*

Dragons (mural), **8**:*1036*

Dream of Consciousness (painting), **4**:*484*

Dream of the Poet, The (painting), **8**:*1124*

Drifter (painting), **7**:*969*

Drought Stricken Area (painting), **1**:*18*

Early Spring, Pleasant Valley, Lyme, Connecticut (painting), **6**:*804*

Early Sunday Morning (painting), **6**:*853*

Edith Wharton's chateau (watercolor), **12**:*1627*

Educacion de Maria, La (painting), **9**:*1184*

E. E. Cummings (painting), **3**:*312*

Empire of Lights, The (painting), **2**:*249*

En Barque sur la Marne (painting), **3**:*385*

Equality (art work), **5**:*644*

Ernest J. Gaines (photograph), **5**:*582*

escaping slaves crossing the Rappahannock River (photograph), **4**:*487*

Espace, L' (painting), **10**:*1336*

Eva Green (painting), **8**:*1050*

Eve (painting), **7**:*906*

Eviction/Lower East Side (painting), **7**:*882*

Factory at Horta de Ebro (painting), **11**:*1474*

Fallen Warrior (Burnt Man) (painting), **5**:*686*

Family, The (collage), **6**:*741*

Faux Miroir, Le (painting), **2**:*251*

Fence Mending (painting), **9**:*1237*

Fétiches, Les (painting), **6**:*754*

Fiesta Pig (artwork), **12**:*1723*

Fifth of November, The (engraving), **4**:*456*

Fire (painting), **9**:*1251*

Firefly (painting), **5**:*712*

Firestone tire shop (photograph), **4**:*545*

Five Girls from Quaratingueta (painting), **1**:*38*

Flame Emerging from Water (painting), **12**:*1699*

Flower of the Flock, The (painting), **11**:*1554*

Fog, Amagansett (painting), **4**:*523*

Folk Family (painting), **5**:*583*

Foresight (painting), **9**:*1167*

Forked Road, The (watercolor), **4**:*565*

42nd Street Nocturne (painting), **10**:*1305*

Forward Retreat (painting), **5**:*675*

400 Years of Our People (painting), **1**:*121*

Fragmented (painting), **12**:*1605*

Friday Evening (painting), **10**:*1408*

Friends (painting), **1**:*86*

Funeral, The (painting), **7**:*946*

Georgia Jungle (painting), **7**:*980*

Gertrude Stein (painting), **10**:*1428*

Glance in the Mirror, A (painting), **12**:*1601*

Gloucester (painting), **4**:*444*

Gore Vidal (photographic portrait), **6**:*810*

Gospel Singer, Study #3 (painting), **5**:*655*

Grace (painting), **10**:*1316*

Grandfather Clock with Blue Wing (painting), **3**:*340*

Great Ideas of Western Men series (paintings), **7**:*917*

Green Leaf and the Sere, The (painting), **11**:*1538*

Grosstadt-Big Town (painting), **12**:*1681*

Group (painting), **10**:*1304*

Happy Is the Bride the Sun Shines On (painting), **10**:*1318*

Harlem (painting), **1**:*103*

Harper Lee (photograph), **6**:*834*

Harvest Time (painting), **8**:*1088*

Hasidim in Israel (photograph), **10**:*1402*

Haymaker, The (painting), **11**:*1568*

Her Shadow II (painting), **9**:*1226*

Her Shadow III (painting), **3**:*308*

History of Barbie, A (painting), **9**:*1206*

Hoeing (painting), **4**:*465*

Hollywood Study #2 (print), **4**:*529*

Holy Mountain III (painting), **8**:*1140*

Horse in the Landscape (painting), **11**:*1577*

Hotel Lucerne (painting), **3**:*368*

I Baptize Thee (painting), **1**:*115*

Ice Floes on the Seine at Bougival (painting), **12**:*1623*

Immaculate Conception (painting), **3**:*346*

Immigrant, The (painting), **9**:*1186*

Impedimenta (painting), **8**:*1083*

In the Cottonfields (painting), **3**:*414*

Invincible Soldier, The (painting), **3**:*299*

Italian Landscape II: Europa (painting), **5**:*685*

It Must Be Love (painting), **9**:*1250*

Jackie (artwork), **2**:*241*

Jefferson Thomas (photograph), **1**:*119*

Jitterbugs (painting), **2**:*206*

Job (painting), **7**:*903*

John Brown Going to His Hanging (painting), **2**:*151*

John Gardner (photograph), **5**:*596*

Jonah (painting), **6**:*760*

June Teenth (painting), **4**:*471*

King Cophetua and the Beggar Maid (painting), **8**:*1082*

Kitchen, The (painting), **3**:*341*

Lady and Sinister Figure (watercolor), **1**:*92*

Landscape (painting), **3**:*369*

Landscape with Characters and a Boy in Red (painting), **10**:*1307*

Langston Hughes, Poet (pastel), **6**:*738*

Lawdy Mama (painting), **5**:*643*

Library, The (painting), **5**:*653*

Life of a Hunter, The: A Tight Fix (painting), **4**:*496*

Lift Up Thy Voice and Sing (painting), **1**:*75*

Light and Shadow (painting), **1**:*50*

Li'l Sis (painting), **8**:*1065*

Little Sweet (painting), **1**:*79*

Long-Distance Information (painting), **5**:*623*

Lord Is My Shepherd, The (painting), **3**:*407*

Lost Button Owner Identification Calendar (mixed-media artwork), **5**:*704*

Lotto: American Dream (painting), **9**:*1193*

Lower East Side (painting), **1**:*39*

Lucky Dragon, The (painting), **5**:*695*

Lullaby (painting), **5**:*640*

Lynching (painting), **12**:*1706*

Madame Severine (painting), **10**:*1370*

Madonna of 1847 (painting), **6**:*826*

Maimonides (painting), **9**:*1273*

Manitoba prairie (photograph), **6**:*821*

Man on Top of the World (painting), **7**:*902*

Mano Poderosa, La (painting), **1**:*36*

Margaret Atwood with Mug (painting), **1**:*83*

Margaret Garner and the slave catchers (engraving), **8**:*1059*

Men Exist for the Sake of One Another. Teach Them Then or Bear with Them (painting), **1**:*109*

Migration (painting), **4**:*549*

Migration Gained in Momentum, The (painting), **4**:*467*

Migration of the Negro, The (painting series), **4**:*453, 467*

Miranda in Springtime (painting), **5**:*705*

Missouri family on Highway 99 (photograph), **11**:*1463*

Missouri Spring (painting), **7**:*955*

mockingbird (lithograph), **6**:*837*

Monte Cristo Cottage (photograph), **9**:*1158*

Moodie and the Wilderness (collage), **1**:*95*

Moonlight Lovers (painting), **2**:*204*

Moon over Harlem (painting), **12**:*1708*

Morehouse (painting), **3**:*322*

Mother and Child (painting), **4**:*511*, **6**:*831*

Mother and Child before a Washstand with Jar and Bowl (illustration), **3**:*387*

Mother and Son (painting), **1**:*58*

Mother Courage (painting), **5**:*628*

Mountain Lake (painting), **11**:*1486*

Mount Chocorua (painting), **3**:*331*

Mr. Prejudice (painting), **5**:*641*

Mysteries (collage), **4**:*468*

Nat Turner (painting), **11**:*1499*

Nebraska Farmstead (painting), **2**:*276*

Necklace, The (painting), **3**:*390*

New Frontier, The (painting), **2**:*156*

Night (painting), **9**:*1208*

Nighthawks (painting), **2**:*262*

Nuit Espagnole, La (painting), **1**:*30*

Nun with Girl, New Orleans (photograph), **8**:*1069*

Office at Night (painting), **6**:*856*

Old Kentucky Home—Life in the South (painting), **3**:*409*

Olmec carved head, **9**:*1257*

One Mystery Figure (painting), **3**:*304*

Ontario Farmhouse (painting), **3**:*309*

Operatic Duet (painting), **7**:*930*

Orthodox Jewish man (photograph), **9**:*1264*

Our Lady of Poetry (painting), **2**:*260*

Outside Looking In (painting), **8**:*1076*

Overcoats (painting), **7**:*934*

Panel number 13, "Crops Left to Dry and Rot" (painting), **4**:*453*

Paraded American Prisoner (watercolor), **8**:*1125*

Parkville, Main Street (Missouri) (painting), **1**:*53*

Passion of Sacco and Vanzetti, The (painting), **9**:*1234*

Pastoral Family (painting), **2**:*186*

Patchwork Quilt (painting), **8**:*1057*

Pathetic Song, The (painting), **2**:*272*

Paul Dunbar (photograph), **3**:*398*

Paul's Magic (painting), **5**:*608*

Peaceable Kingdom, The (painting), **9**:*1204*

Pemaquid, Spring Snow (painting), **9**:*1222*

People, People - -Plus (painting), **10**:*1433*

Perpetual Care (painting), **7**:*957*

Pigeon's Egg Head, Going To and Returning From Washington (painting), **7**:*999*

Pinar del Rio (painting), **5**:*666*

Pioneers of the West (painting), **2**:*282*

Pogrome (painting), **10**:*1407*

Point Lobos, Carmel (painting), **6**:*786*

Portrait (In Middle Age), **11**:*1553*

Portrait of Frederick Douglass (painting), **3**:*403*

Portrait of Madame Cézanne (Cézanne), **10**:*1429*

Portrait of Mr. and Mrs. Philip Wase (painting), **9**:*1235*

Portrait of Pearl Buck (painting), **2**:*216*

post office scene (mural), **4**:*508*

Powerful Hand, The (painting), **1**:*36*

Priest at the Altar (painting), **2**:*280*

Prison Baths, The (painting), **3**:*324*

Puzzle Bottle (painting), **7**:*942*

Quattro Generazioni (painting), **11**:*1547*

Rabbi, The (painting), **9**:*1271*, **10**:*1410*

Rabbinic Dispute (painting), **10**:*1415*

Race Trace, The (Death on a Pale Horse) (painting), **9**:*1238*

Radha and Krishna Seated in a Grove (painting), **10**:*1309*

Railroad Sunset (painting), **6**:*801*

Rainbow Bronto (painting), **12**:*1716*

Ray's Ghost Fish (painting), **2**:*260*

Rebecca Cummings (painting), **3**:*317*

Red Cover Breadbox (artwork), **9**:*1211*

Red Stairway, The (painting), **5**:*689*

Reflections (painting), **2**:*253*

Return Home, The (ink-and-paint scroll), **2**:*219*

Revival (painting), **11**:*1497*

Revolutionists (artwork), **9**:*1241*

Road Side: Lamy (painting), **9**:*1201*

Road to Mt. Vernaunt, The (painting), **12**:*1600*

Roots that Never Die (painting), **5**:*632*

Round Table Indeed!, A (painting), **4**:*502*

Sacco and Vanzetti (painting), **1**:*131*

Salmon Trawlers (painting), **6**:*800*

Santa Margarita Grade (watercolor), **8**:*1091*

Sarah A. Stevens (watercolor), **4**:*509*

Sarah Weather Hill (painting), **9**:*1219*

Saturday Night (painting), **8**:*1055*

Scale, L' (painting), **10**:*1330*

Scene from Shakespeare's "Tempest" (painting), **3**:*349*

Schoolchildren Struggle Against Illiteracy (painting), **10**:*1314*

School's Out (painting), **1**:*73*

Scorpio or Scorpion, Signs of the Zodiac (artwork), **8**:*1367*

Sea, The (painting), **2**:*161*

Sea of Time, The (painting), **11**:*1485*

Self-Portrait with Rita (painting), **11**:*1502*

Separation (painting), **9**:*1220*

Shadow and Sunlight (painting), **5**:*646*

Sharecropper (linocut), **2**:*192*

Sharecroppers (illustration), **2**:*207*

Shotgun, Third Ward #1 (painting), **12**:*1688*

Sir Philip Sassoon (painting), **3**:*393*

Sky Simulated by Red Flamingoes (painting), **11**:*1473*

Slave with Her Mistress (watercolor), **11**:*1574*

Snow Shovellers (painting), **5**:*650*

Sob, The (drawing), **1**:*137*

soldier with rocket launcher (photograph), **8**:*1131*

Sol y Mariposas (painting), **1**:*35*

Sommers: Kettleburn (painting), **8**:*1144*

Spanish Night, The (painting), **1**:*30*

Spring Outing, A (painting), **3**:*329*

Spring Sale at Bendel's (painting), **4**:*521*

Springtime Angel (painting), **11**:*1559*

Starry Night (painting), **10**:*1363, 1364*

Still Life (painting), **7**:*899*

Still Life; Bust, Bowl and Pallette (painting), **10**:*1435*

Stone City (painting), **7**:*953*

Story Teller (painting), **7**:*1000*

Stranger, The (painting), **5**:*603*

Strike (painting), **8**:*1045*

Study or The Schoolgirl (painting), **8**:*1072*

Subway, The (painting), **4**:*443*

Summer Night on the Beach, A (painting), **8**:*1117*

Sun and Butterflies (painting), **1**:*35*

Sunday Morning (painting), **4**:*493*

Sunlight (painting), **2**:*283*

Sunny Day with Gentle Breeze, A (painting), **11**:*1511*

Swing (painting), **4**:*464*

Talmudists, The (painting), **10**:*1404*

Tenant Farmer (painting), **1**:*22*

tenant farmer and child (photograph), **4**:*485*

Tenement Flats (Family Flats) (painting), **7**:*910*

Tenor Sermon (painting), **1**:*117*

Thankful Poor, The (painting), **3**:*405*

That Terrible Stone Wall (photograph), **10**:*1337*

This Is Harlem (painting), **6**:*740*

Thoughts of a Hungry Man (painting), **3**:*376*

Three A.M. (painting), **3**:*379*

Times Square (painting), **1**:*27*

Toussaint L'Ouverture series (silk screen-on-paper), **2**:*191*

Trade (Gifts for Trading Land with White People) (painting), **7**:*998*

Tragic Prelude (mural), **2**:*158*

Trapper, The (painting), **7**:*889*

Traveller Woman (painting), **6**:*828*

Trees in March, Millbrook (painting), **7**:*897*

Tribute to the American Working People (painting), **4**:*506*, **12**:*1603*

Trinita dei Monti and Villa Medici, Rome (painting), **12**:*1635*

Tuskegee Airmen, **4**:*473*

Twelve Planes and a Single Egg (painting), **1**:*55*

Two Girls (painting), **8**:*1077*

Two Heads (painting), **1**:*87*

Two Men (painting), **1**:*141*

Two Women on a Wall (painting), **9**:*1290*

Ulysses and His Companions on the Island of Cyclops (painting), **11**:*1515*

Unemployment (painting), **11**:*1526*

Unloading Coal (painting), **12**:*1648*

Valley Farms (painting), **7**:*974*

View in Chambers Street (painting), **12**:*1689*

Visit from the Old Mistress, A (painting), **2**:*189*

Voice of the City of New York Interpreted, The: The Bridge (painting), **8**:*1030*

Waiting (painting), **3**:*382*

Walter's Shoes (painting), **5**:*606*

Wandering Acrobats (painting), **7**:*893*

Wanted, Poster Series No. 17 (painting), **8**:*1067*

War, The (painting), **12**:*1690*

Ward for Irritable Patients at San Bonifacio (painting), **10**:*1374*

Watching (art work), **5**:*638*

Wedding, The (painting), **1**:*135*, **3**:*348*

Western Tourist Camp (watercolor), **4**:*546*

Westward the Course of Empire Takes Its Way (painting), **3**:*354*

Whispers from the Walls (installation), **5**:*587, 657*

Winter Games (painting), **5**:*600*

With Jack London Aboard the Snark— *Christmas Morning in Mid-Ocean* (painting), **7**:*872*

Woman/Fire (painting), **9**:*1287*

Woman with a Dog (painting), **9**:*1242*

Woman with Child (painting), **12**:*1595*

WPA Artists (painting), **8**:*1044*

Young Girl Sewing in a Garden (painting), **12**:*1665*

Young Man in Blue Suit (painting), **11**:*1578*

Zora Neale Hurston (photograph), **6**:*747*

Index of Visual Artists

Appleton, J. M.
    photograph of young Dunbar, **3**:*398*
Ar, Giuseppe
    Desk, The, **2**:*197*
Arrequin, Alfredo
    Our Lady of Poetry, **2**:*260*
    Ray's Ghost Fish, **2**:*260*
    *Sol y Mariposas (Sun and
        Butterflies),* **1**:*35*
Ascencios, Natalie
    Round Table Indeed!, A, **4**:*502*
Auerbach-Levy, William
    Lewis caricature, **6**:*852*
Avedon, Richard, **1**:*110*

Backus, Stan
    Santa Margarita Grade, **8**:*1091*
Bailey, Radcliffe
    Roots That Never Die, **5**:*632*
Bard, James
    Sarah A. Stevens, **4**:*509*
Barile, Xavier J.
    42nd Street Nocturne, **10**:*1305*
Bartlett, Bo
    Firefly, **5**:*712*
Basquiat, Jean-Michel, **1**:*68*
Bates, Dewey
    Daydreaming, **12**:*1625*
Bauer, Jerry
    photo portrait of Gore Vidal, **6**:*810*
Bearden, Romare
    Family, The, **6**:*741*
    Patchwork Quilt, **8**:*1057*
    Tenor Sermon, **1**:*117*
Beardon, Romare
    Mysteries, **4**:*468*
Beckman, William
    Overcoats, **7**:*934*
Bellows, George
    Club Night, **8**:*1109*
    as Oates subject, **8**:*1109,* *1111*
    *Portrait of Mr. and Mrs. Philip
        Wase,* **9**:*1235*
Beltrame, A.
    *Schoolchildren Struggle Against
        Illiteracy,* **10**:*1314*Benn, Nathan
    Orthodox Jewish man, **9**:*1264*

Benson, Frank W.
    Sunlight, **2**:*283*
Benton, Thomas Hart
    Achelous and Hercules, **7**:*959*
    Arts of the South, **8**:*1146*
    Chilmark Hay, **4**:*566*
    Cotton Pickers, Georgia, **12**:*1594*
    Self-Portrait with Rita, **11**:*1502*
    Sunday Morning, **4**:*493*
    Twelve Planes and a Single Egg,
        1:*55*
    Western Tourist Camp, **4**:*546*
Bierstadt, Albert
    Cathedral Forest, **11**:*1533*
Biggers, John T.
    Sharecroppers, **2**:*207*
    Shotgun, Third Ward #1, **12**:*1688*
Bingham, George Caleb
    *Daniel Boone Escorting Settlers
        Through the Cumberland Gap,*
        2:*153*
Bishop, Isabel
    Waiting, **3**:*382*
Black, LaVerne Nelson
    Ceremonial at Black Lake, **7**:*1003*
Blaine, Nell, **9**:*1205*
Bosch, Hieronymus, **7**:*970*
Brancusi, Constantin, **3**:*318*
Braque, Georges, **10**:*1429,* *1431,*
    1432, *1434*
Brook, Alexander
    Georgia Jungle, **7**:*980*
Brown, John George
    Boy with a Snowball, **3**:*345*
Brunelli, Anthony
    Walter's Shoes, **5**:*606*
Bunker, John S.
    Springtime Angel, **11**:*1559*
Burne-Jones, Edward, **8**:*1082*
Burra, Edward
    Harlem, **1**:*103*
Burrows, Larry
    soldier with rocket launcher,
        8:*1131*

Campigli, Massimo
    Amazons, The, **11**:*1580*

Capote, Truman
    Harper Lee photograph, **6**:*834*
Carter, Dwight
    Maya Angelou photograph, **1**:*71*
Cassatt, Mary
    Mother and Child, **3**:*387,* **4**:*511*
    Young Girl Sewing in a Garden,
        12:*1665*
Catlett, Elizabeth
    Sharecropper, **2**:*192*
Catlin, George
    *Pigeon's Egg Head, Going to and
        Returning from Washington,* **7**:*999*
Cerbakov, B. V.
    Invincible Soldier, The, **3**:*299*
Cézanne, Paul, **3**:*318,* **10**:*1419,*
    1427, 1429
Chagall, Marc
    Chute d'Icare, La, **12**:*1725*
    *Grandfather Clock with Blue
        Wing,* **3**:*340*
    Rabbi, The, **9**:*1271,* **10**:*1410*
    Wedding, The, **1**:*135*
Chery, Jean
    Pastoral Family, **2**:*186*
Chintreuil, Antoine
    L'espace, **10**:*1336*
Ch'i Pai-Shih
    Return Home, The, **2**:*219*
Cienfuegos, Gonzalo
    *Landscape with Characters and a
        Boy in Red,* **10**:*1307*
Clark, Christopher
    Crapshooters, The, **6**:*757*
Clark, Ed
    rural burial photograph, **4**:*491*
Clark, Joseph
    Flower of the Flock, The, **11**:*1554*
Cohen, Helen
    Red Cover Breadbox, **9**:*1211*
Colclough, Jim
    Crucifixion, **6**:*743*
Condon, Julia
    Flame Emerging from Water,
        12:*1699*
Cook, James
    Fence Mending, **9**:*1237*

Crite, Allan Rohan
    School's Out, **1**:73
    Shadow and Sunlight, **5**:646
Crocker, Will
    envelope image, **1**:134
Cruz Azaceta, Luis
    Immigrant, The, **9**:1186
    Lotto: American Dream, **9**:1193
Cudworth, Nick
    Long-Distance Information (paint-
        ing), **5**:623
Cummings, E. E.
    Morehouse painting, **3**:322
    self-portrait, **3**:321
    untitled painting, **3**:326
    view of Mount Chocorua, **3**:331
Currier & Ives
    Plantation on the Mississippi, A,
        3:415, **4**:495
Curry, John Steuart
    Tragic Prelude, **2**:158

Dali, Salvador
    Mountain Lake, **11**:1486
Davenport, Rebecca
    Sommers: Kettleburn, **8**:1144
Davies, Arthur B.
    *Beach Scene with Female Bather
        Holding an Umbrella: Morning*,
        10:1319
De Carava, Roy, **6**:737
Deineka, Alexander
    Road to Mt. Vernaunt, The,
        12:1600
Delacroix, Eugene, **10**:1429
Delaney, Beauford
    Can Fire in the Park, **1**:109
Demuth, Charles, **12**:1676
Dewey, David
    Pemaquid, Spring Snow, **9**:1222
Dewing, Thomas Wilmer
    Necklace, The, **3**:390
    Walt Whitman chalk sketch,
        6:731
Dickinson, Ross
    Valley Farms, **7**:974
Dighton, Robert
    watercolor of Prospero, **3**:335
Dinnerstein, Simon
    Birthday Dress, The, **7**:981
    Night, **9**:1208
Dix, Otto
    Grosstadt-Big Town, **12**:1681
    Woman with Child, **12**:1595
du Bois, Guy Pène
    Fog, Amagansett, **4**:523

Duchamp, Marcel, **10**:1429
Duesberry, Joellyn
    Trees in March, Millbrook, **7**:897
Dunton, W. Herbert
    *With Jack London Aboard the
        Snark—Christmas Morning in
        Mid-Ocean*, **7**:872

Eakins, Thomas
    Concert Singer, The, **3**:351
    Dean's Roll Call, The, **2**:229
    Pathetic Song, The, **2**:272
Eckel, Julia
    Revival, **11**:1497
Edwards, Mary Ellen
    Green Leaf and the Sere, The,
        11:1538
Escoffery, Michael
    400 Years of Our People, **1**:121
    June Teenth, **4**:471
    Moonlight Lovers, **2**:204
    Mother and Son, **1**:58
Estes, Richard
    Hotel Lucerne, **3**:368
Evans, Walker, **1**:11, 13, 15, 17, 21
Eyerman, J. R.
    Hersey photograph, **5**:684

Farbman, Nat
    photograph of Jeffers, **6**:789
    photograph of Jeffers as baby
        with mother, **6**:784
Farrar, John
    Couple, The, **2**:202
Fellig, Arthur. *See* Weegee
Ferguson, Max
    Coffee Shop, **10**:1308
Fishchl, Eric
    Funeral, The, **7**:946
Fisher, Vernon
    Bikini, **5**:693
Forbes, Stanhope Alexander
    Boy Fishing, **10**:1320
Frank, Mary
    Woman/Fire, **9**:1287

Gauguin, Paul, **10**:1427
Giovanopoulos, Paul
    Buffalo Nickel, **7**:938
Gipstein, Todd
    Monte Cristo Cottage, **9**:1158
Giraud, Eugene
    Flaubert portrait, **2**:243
Giusti, George
    Great Ideas of Western Men se-
        ries, **7**:917

Goldthwaite, Anne
    Coiffeur, The, **12**:1609
Golub, Leon
    Fallen Warrior (Burnt Man),
        5:686
Gonzalez, Juan
    Cortés Enters Mexico, **7**:900
    Educacion de Maria, La, **9**:1184
Goodenough, Clifford
    It Must Be Love, **9**:1250
    Still Life, **7**:899
Gotfryd, Bernard
    Davies photograph, **3**:334
Gould, Philip
    Ash Wednesday photograph, **4**:455
    Ernest J. Gaines, **5**:582
Graham-Stewart, Michael
    Slave with Her Mistress, **11**:1574
Granet, François Marius
    Priest at the Altar, **2**:280
    *Trinita dei Monti and Villa Medici,
        Rome*, **12**:1635
Grant, Duncan
    Kitchen, The, **3**:341
Greve, Gerrit
    Her Shadow II, **9**:1226
    Her Shadow III, **3**:308
    image of an angel, **5**:614
    One Mystery Figure, **3**:304
Gris, Juan, **10**:1429, 1434
Gropper, William
    Automobile Industry, **11**:1537
    Migration, **4**:549
Grosz, George, **10**:1412
Grummaire, Marcel
    War, The, **12**:1690
Guglielmi, O. Louis
    Connecticut Autumn, **1**:15
    View in Chambers Street, **12**:1689
Gwathmey, Robert
    Belle, **8**:1141
    Hoeing, **4**:465
    Lullaby, **5**:640
    Reflections, **2**:253

Hahn, William
    Harvest Time, **8**:1088
Hannah, Duncan
    Adrift in Soho, **9**:1217
    Betrayal, **5**:715
Hansen, Armin Carl
    Salmon Trawlers, **6**:800
Hartley, Marsden
    New Mexico landscape, **2**:279
Hassam, Childe
    Point Lobos, Carmel, **6**:786

Hawkins, Louis-Welden
    Madame Severine, **10**:*1370*
Hayden, Palmer
    Blues Singer, The, **6**:*732*
Hayllar, James
    *Happy Is the Bride the Sun Shines
        On*, **10**:*1318*
Hempel, Wes
    American Rudder, **7**:*937*
Hendricks, Barkley
    Lawdy Mama, **5**:*643*
Henri, Robert
    Eva Green, **8**:*1050*
Herrera, Velino Shije
    Story Teller, **7**:*1000*
Hewitt, Charles
    Arthur Miller, **8**:*1017*
Hicks, Edward
    Peaceable Kingdom, The, **9**:*1204*,
        1205
Hirsch, Joseph
    Death of a Salesman poster,
        8:*1015*
Hodalic, Arne
    Phillips Exeter Academy photo-
        graph, **6**:*813*
Hodges, Elizabeth Barakah
    Africa, **11**:*1581*
Hogarth, William
    *Scene from Shakespeare's
        "Tempest"*, **3**:*349*
Hogue, Alexandre
    Drought Stricken Area, **1**:*18*
Holmes, Robert
    Manitoba prairie, **6**:*821*
Homer, Winslow
    Visit from the Old Mistress, A,
        2:*189*
Hopkinson, Charles
    portrait of Rebecca Cummings,
        3:*317*
    portrait of young E. E.
        Cummings, **3**:*312*
Hopper, Edward
    American Village, **6**:*846*
    Cape Cod Morning, **5**:*605*
    Early Sunday Morning, **6**:*853*
    Forked Road, The, **4**:*565*
    Nighthawks, **2**:*262*
    Office at Night, **6**:*856*
    Railroad Sunset, **6**:*801*
Hughes, Lenore
    As Seen on TV, **9**:*1210*
    Foresight, **9**:*1167*
Hull, John
    Road Side: Lamy, **9**:*1201*

Hull, Marie Atchison
    Tenant Farmer, **1**:*22*

Jacobi, Kathryn
    Between the Wars #3, **5**:*624*
    Gospel Singer, Study #3, **5**:*655*
    Miranda in Springtime, **5**:*705*
    Operatic Duet, **7**:*930*
Jarboe, Charles S.
    *Blue Collar World of Joe Wong,
        The*, **5**:*609*
Johnson, Eastman
    Lord Is My Shepherd, The, **3**:*407*
    *Old Kentucky Home—Life in the
        South*, **3**:*409*
Johnson, William H.
    Chain Gang, **12**:*1702*
    Church on Lenox Avenue, **1**:*106*
    Folk Family, **5**:*583*
    I Baptize Thee, **1**:*115*
    Jitterbugs, **2**:*206*
    Lift Up Thy Voice and Sing, **1**:*75*
    Li'l Sis, **8**:*1065*
    Little Sweet, **1**:*79*
    Moon over Harlem, **12**:*1708*
    Nat Turner, **11**:*1499*
    untitled painting, **6**:*735*
Jones, Lois Mailou
    Fétiches, Les, **6**:*754*
Jordan, Robert
    Missouri Spring, **7**:*955*

Kantor, Morris
    Baseball at Night, **7**:*923*
Karsh, Yousuf
    Davies photograph, **3**:*337*
Kaufmann, Isador
    Friday Evening, **10**:*1408*
Kennington, Dale
    Caffe Florian, **11**:*1556*
Kent, Rockwell
    Dogs Resting, Greenland, **7**:*886*
    Trapper, The, **7**:*889*
Knight, Charles
    Fifth of November, The, **4**:*456*

Lange, Dorothea, **9**:*1252*
    *Child and Her Mother, Wapato,
        Yakima Valley, Washington*, **8**:*1081*
    Missouri family on Highway 99,
        11:*1463*
Lankes, J.J.
    New England rural scene, **4**:*563*
Lawrence, Jacob
    "Crops Left to Dry and Rot,"
        4:*453*

Hughes collaboration, **6**:*729*
    Library, The, **5**:*653*
    *Men Exist for the Sake of One
        Another. Teach Them Then or
        Bear with Them*, **1**:*109*
    *Migration Gained in Momentum,
        The*, **4**:*467*
    Migration of the Negro, The,
        4:*453*, 467
    Strike, **8**:*1045*
    This Is Harlem, **6**:*740*
    Toussaint L'Ouverture series,
        2:*191*
Lebasque, Henri
    En Barque sur la Marne, **3**:*385*
Lee, Anna Belle
    Baptism, **11**:*1503*
Lee, Doris
    post office scene, **4**:*508*
Lee, Russell
    Firestone tire shop, **4**:*545*
Lee-Smith, Hughie
    Impedimenta, **8**:*1083*
    The Stranger, **5**:*603*
    Two Girls, **8**:*1077*
Lemmers, Georges
    After Tea, **11**:*1472*
Leutze, Emanuel
    *Westward the Course of Empire
        Takes Its Way*, **3**:*354*
Levinthal, David
    untitled image, **5**:*714*
Levitt, Helen
    Agee photograph, **1**:*13*
Levy-Dhurmer, Lucien
    Eve, **7**:*906*
Leyendecker, J. C.
    Couple Descending Stairs, **4**:*525*
Lhote, Andre
    L'escale, **10**:*1330*
Longoni, Emilio
    Thoughts of a Hungary Man,
        3:*376*
Lovell, Whitfield
    Whispers from the Walls, **5**:*587*,
        657
Lozowick, Louis
    Lynching, **12**:*1706*
Luks, George
    Café Francis, The, **3**:*391*
Lundeberg, Helen
    *Double Portrait of the Artist in
        Time*, **8**:*1079*
    Pioneers of the West, **2**:*282*
Lynch, James
    Outside Looking In, **8**:*1076*

Magritte, René
    Blank Signature, The, **3:**328
    Bonne Parole, La, **10:**1425
    Empire of Lights, The, **2:**249
    Faux Miroir, Le, **2:**251
Manning-Carner, Hyacinth
    Fragmented, **12:**1605
Marc, Franz
    Horse in the Landscape, **11:**1577
Martin, Donald
    Portrait (In Middle Age), **11:**1553
Mashkov, Illya
    Bread, **1:**98
Matisse, Henri, **10:**1419, 1422,
    1423, 1424, 1429,
    1431
Maurer, Henry
    Two Heads, **1:**87
Mayers, Gil
    Swing, **4:**464
McFadden, Regina
    Pinar del Rio, **5:**666
McLeary, Kindred
    Lower East Side scene, **1:**39
McManaway, David
    Cross, The, **9:**1187
Metzinger, Jean
    *Colorful Landscape with Aquatic
      Birds,* **11:**1484
Midjau-Midjawu
    Birem, Iguana of the Rocks,
      12:1673
Miller, Evylena Nunn
    Chinese Patron of the Arts, **2:**231
Miller, Wayne F.
    Chicago South Side pho-
      tographs, **2:**201
Mocialskij, D. K.
    Quattro Generazioni, **11:**1547
Monet, Claude
    Ice Floes on the Seine at Bougival,
      12:1623
    Unloading Coal, **12:**1648
Mori, C.
    Traveller Woman, **6:**828
Motley, Archibald
    Blues, **6:**739
    Saturday Night, **8:**1055
Moyse, Edouard
    Rabbinic Dispute, **10:**1415
Munch, Edvard
    Anxiety, **4:**442
    Ballo della Vita, Il, **11:**1483
    Separation, **9:**1220
    Summer Night on the Beach, A,
      8:1117

    Two Girls with Blue Aprons,
      12:1691

Nast, Bernhard
    Best of Simple illustration, **6:**734
    Best of Simple title page, **6:**733
Nast, Thomas
    political cartoon, **8:**1097
Nevins, Daniel
    Crossing, **10:**1373
Nguyen Duc Tho
    Paraded American Prisoner,
      8:1125
Nobel, Thomas
    Margaret Garner scene, **8:**1059
Norton, John Warner
    Light and Shadow, **1:**50
Norton, Robert
    Edith Wharton's chateau,
      12:1627
Nowitz, Richard T.
    photograph of Hasidim,
      10:1402

Okamoto, Naoki
    untitled painting, **11:**1512
O'Keeffe, Georgia
    Didion essay on, **3:**371
    Landscape, **3:**369
Ong, Diana
    America, **11:**1524
    Conversion, **4:**452
    Crowd XX, **11:**1548
    Destiny 1, **11:**1550
    Group, **10:**1304
    People, People - -Plus, **10:**1433
Orozco, José Clemente
    Revolutionists, **9:**1241
    Sob, The, **1:**137
Ortega, Tony
    Comiendo, Platicando, **9:**1190
Osborne, Brett
    Sarah Weather Hill, **9:**1219
O'Sullivan, Timothy
    escaping slaves crossing the
      Rappahannock River, **4:**487

Pachter, Charles, **1:**83, 85
    Margaret Atwood with Mug, **1:**83
Parker, Olivia
    History of Barbie, A, **9:**1206
Patterson, Leslie
    *Lost Button Owner Identification
      Calendar,* **5:**704
Perez, Santiago
    Drifter, **7:**969

Picabia, Francis
    *Nuit Espagnole, La (The Spanish
      Night),* **1:**30
Picasso, Pablo, **7:**894, **9:**1274
    Corrida, Death of a Torrero,
      5:680
    as Cummings influence, **3:**318
    Factory at Horta de Ebro,
      11:1474
    Gertrude Stein portrait, **10:**1428
    as Stein influence, **10:**1419,
      1422, 1423, 1424, 1426,
      1427, 1429, 1431, 1434,
      1435
    as Stevens influence, **11:**1474
    Still Life; Bust, Bowl and Pallette,
      10:1435
    Wandering Acrobats, **7:**893
Pierre, Christian
    Rainbow Bronto, **12:**1716
Pippin, Horace
    Holy Mountain III, **8:**1140
    John Brown Going to His Hanging,
      2:151
    Mr. Prejudice, **5:**641
Plattner, Phyllis
    Bare Bones #34/Constellation,
      9:1192
Potok, Chaim
    Brooklyn Crucifixion (painting),
      9:1275
Prater, Leland J.
    Smokey the Bear photograph,
      6:781
Puy, Jean
    Study or The Schoolgirl, **8:**1072

Qian, Zifen
    Sunny Day with Gentle Breeze, A,
      11:1511
Quick-to-See-Smile, Juane
    *Trade (Gifts for Trading Land with
      White People),* **7:**998

Ray, Charles
    Puzzle Bottle, **7:**942
Reece, Jane
    Matilda Dunbar photograph,
      3:404
Reiss, Winold
    Langston Hughes, Poet, **6:**738
Remington, Frederic
    Dash for the Timber, A, **10:**1350
Renoir, Pierre, **10:**1427
Ribera, Jusepe de
    Job, **7:**903

Rivera, Diego
  Blood of the Revolutionary Martyrs Fertilizing the Earth, **10:**1339
  Cena Capitalista, La, **10:**1437
Robinson, Michael Mortimer
  Grace, **10:**1316
Rodulfo, Peter
  Crowd in a Landscape, **12:**1680
Rousseau, Henri, **10:**1429
Ruscha, Ed
  Hollywood Study #2, **4:**529
Russell, Captain
  That Terrible Stone Wall, **10:**1337
Ryder, Albert Pinkham
  Jonah, **6:**760
  Race Track, The (Death on a Pale Horse), **9:**1238

Saar, Betye
  Equality, **5:**644
  Watching, **5:**638
Sadler, Walter
  Wedding, The, **3:**348
St. Laurent, Louis
  Dreiser photograph, **3:**378
Sargent, John Singer
  Sir Philip Sassoon, **3:**393
Savinio, Alberto
  Dream of the Poet, The, **8:**1124
Schaefer, Carl
  Ontario Farmhouse, **3:**309
Schuenke, Susanne
  Sea of Time, The, **11:**1485
Schuman, Wade
  Conversation, **7:**928
Scott, Julian
  surrendering Confederate soldier, **4:**488
See, Imogene
  Nebraska Farmstead, **2:**276
Severini, Gino
  Acrobats, or Masks and Ruins, **3:**342
Shahn, Ben
  Cotton Picking, Pulaski County, Arkansas, **8:**1053
  Italian Landscape II: Europa, **5:**685
  Lucky Dragon, The, **5:**695
  Maimonides, **9:**1273
  Passion of Sacco and Vanzetti, The, **9:**1234
  Red Stairway, The, **5:**689
  Sacco and Vanzetti, **1:**131
  Unemployment, **11:**1526
  untitled painting, **1:**128

Sharrer, Honore Desmond
  Tribute to the American Working People, **4:**506, **12:**1603
Sheets, Millard
  Tenement Flats (Family Flats), **7:**910
Shinn, Everett
  Dancer in White Before the Footlights, **4:**510
  Dreiser and, **3:**395
  Eviction/Lower East Side, **7:**882
Sholties, Robert
  Fire, **9:**1251
  impending hurricane, **9:**1253
  Winter Games, **5:**600
Sickles, Peter
  Bustling City, **11:**1479
Signorini, Telemaco
  Prison Baths, The, **3:**324
  Ward for Irritable Patients at San Bonifacio, **10:**1374
Simon, Peter
  photograph of Blume, **2:**165
Sloan, John
  Three A.M., **3:**379
Smith, Jacob Getlar
  Snow Shovellers, **5:**650
Smythe, Lionel Percy
  Spring Outing, A, **3:**329
Solomon, Vita Petrosky
  Portrait of Pearl Buck, **2:**216
Soyer, Moses
  Two Men, **1:**141
  WPA Artists, **8:**1044
Spare, Austin Osman
  Dream of Consciousness, **4:**484
Stannard, Theresa
  Cottage Garden, The, **4:**449
Steichen, Edward, **10:**1325, 1331, 1338
Stella, Joseph
  Voice of the City of New York Interpreted, The: The Bridge, **8:**1030
Stettheimer, Florine
  Spring Sale at Bendel's, **4:**521
Stockwell, Gale
  Parkville, Main Street (Missouri), **1:**53
Stoddard, Alice Kent
  Young Man in Blue Suit, **11:**1578
Straus, Adam
  Descent, **7:**907
  Man on Top of the World, **7:**902
Stull, Henry
  Domino's Futurity, **1:**56

Tait, Arthur Fitzwilliam
  Life of a Hunter, The: A Tight Fix, **4:**496

Tanner, Henry Ossawa
  Thankful Poor, The, **3:**405
Tansey, Mark
  Forward Retreat, **5:**675
Tchelitchew, Pavel
  Alice B. Toklas, **10:**1431
Teasdel, Mary
  Mother and Child, **6:**831
Teichert, Minerva
  Madonna of 1847, **6:**826
Thayer, Abbott Henderson
  Bride, A, **12:**1645
  Sky Simulated by Red Flamingoes, **11:**1473
Tibaldi, Pellegrino
  Ulysses and His Companions on the Island of Cyclops, **11:**1515
Tiepolo, Giambattista
  Immaculate Conception, **3:**346
Tissot, James Jacques Joseph
  Ball, The, **12:**1621
Tooker, George
  Cornice, **2:**285
  Subway, The, **4:**443
Torres-Garcia, Joaquin
  Apple Harvest, The, **6:**805
Toulouse-Lautrec, Henri, **10:**1429

Valerio, James
  Paul's Magic, **5:**608
Van Gogh, Vincent
  Starry Night, **10:**1363, 1364
Van Vechten, Carl
  Baldwin photograph, **1:**111
  Zora Neale Hurston photograph, **6:**747
Van Velde, Henry de
  Haymaker, The, **11:**1568
Vonnoh, Robert
  Early Spring, Pleasant Valley, Lyme, Connecticut, **6:**804

Walker, Wiilliam Aiken
  In the Cottonfields, **3:**414
Warhol, Andy
  Capote portrait, **2:**241
  Fiesta Pig, **12:**1723
  Jackie, 241, **2:**241
Weber, Max
  Talmudists, The, **10:**1404
Weegee (Arthur Fellig)
  segregated theater photograph, **3:**412
Welliver, Neil
  Birches, **4:**570

Wenger, John
  Coney Island, **10**:*1412*
Whistler, James Abbot McNeil
  Sea, **2**:*161*
White, Charles
  Mother Courage, **5**:*628*
  Wanted, Poster Series No. 17,
    8:*1067*
Wolcott, Marion Post
  tenant farmer and child, **4**:*485*

Wood, Grant
  Arnold Comes of Age, **1**:*52*
  Booster, **6**:*849*
  Stone City, **7**:*953*
Wyeth, Andrew
  Perpetual Care, **7**:*957*

Zaborov, Boris
  Woman with a Dog, **9**:*1242*
Zeldis, Malcah

  Times Square, **1**:*27*
Ziroli, Nicola Victor
  Bridges in Winter, **1**:*124*
Zrzavy, Jan
  Friends, **1**:*86*

Index of Films

Aaron's Magic Village, **10**:1401
About Last Night..., **7**:932
Abraham Lincoln, **2**:153, 155
Accidental Tourist, The, **11**:1541, 1545
Advance to the Rear, **10**:1349
Adventure, **7**:875
African Queen, The, **1**:11, 13, 14, 17
Age of Innocence, The (1924, 1934, 1993), **12**:1617
Ah, Wilderness!, **9**:1161
Ah, Wilderness! (television), **9**:1161
All My Sons, **8**:1021
All That Money Can Buy, **2**:153, 155
All the Pretty Horses, **7**:965, 970
American Buffalo, **7**:932, 935
American Tragedy, An, **3**:383
Angel Levine, The, **7**:914, 924
Anna Christie (1923; 1930), **9**:1161
Ann Vickers, **6**:855, 861
Arrowsmith, **6**:855, 858
As I Lay Dying (television), **4**:478, 479, 481, 486, 490-92
Assassination Bureau, The, **7**:875
Assistant, The, **7**:914
Autobiography of Miss Jane Pittman, The (television), **5**:584, 585, 586, 589, 590
Autumn of the Leaves, **2**:261

Babbitt (1924; 1934), **6**:855
Babes in Toyland (television), **12**:1717, 1722
Baby Doll, **12**:1663, 1664
Baby, the Rain Must Fall, **4**:541, 544, 547
Ballad of the Sad Café, The, **7**:983, 984
Barricade, **7**:875
Battler, The, **5**:673
Battler, The (television), **5**:673
Beat the Devil, **2**:235, 238, 242
Bell for Adano, A, **5**:685, 691
Bell Jar, The, **9**:1223
Beloved, **8**:1052, 1054, 1063
Bernice Bobs Her Hair (television), **4**:519

Beyond the Horizon (television), **9**:1161
Big Sleep, The, **4**:479, 486
Big Wave, The, **2**:214, 217
Black Widow, **7**:934
Boom!, **12**:1663
Bourbon Street Blues (film), **12**:1663
Breakfast at Tiffany's, **2**:244
Breaking Point, The, **5**:673
Breathing Lessons (television), **11**:1545
Bridge of San Luis Rey, The (1929, 1944), **12**:1631
Bridge of San Luis Rey, The (television), **12**:1631
Brooch, The (television), **4**:479
Buccaneers, The (television), **12**:1617
Bumblebee Flies Anyway, The, **3**:296, 298
Burning Bright (television), **11**:1449
Burning Daylight: The Adventures of Burning Daylight in Civilization, **7**:875

Cafeteria, The, **10**:1401
Call of the Wild, The, **7**:875, 884
Cannery Row, **11**:1449
Carrie, **3**:383
Cass Timberlane, **6**:855
Cat on a Hot Tin Roof, **12**:1663, 1669
Cat on a Hot Tin Roof (television), **12**:1663
Chase, The, **4**:541
Chechako, The (film), **7**:875
Cheers for Miss Bishop (film), **2**:153, 155
Cheers for Miss Bishop, **2**:153, 155
China Sky, **2**:217
Chocolate War, The, **3**:296, 298
Chorus Girl's Romance, The, **4**:519
Chosen, The, **9**:1263, 1265, 1267, 1268
Cider House Rules, The, **6**:767, 768, 773, 774, 775
Cimarron, **4**:501
Classified, **4**:501

Cobweb, The, **5**:613, 615, 619
Color Purple, The, **11**:1561, 1565, 1566, 1568, 1570, *1571*, 1572-73
Come and Get It, **4**:501
Conflict, **7**:875
Connecticut Yankee in King Arthur's Court, A (television), **12**:1717, 1722
Convicts, **4**:547
Corner in Wheat, A, **8**:1090
Courtship, **4**:547
Crucible, The, **8**:1023

Death of a Salesman, **8**:1026
Desert Gold, **8**:1090
Desire Under the Elms, **9**:1161
Dinner at Eight, **4**:501
Dinner at Eight (television), **4**:501
Dodsworth, **6**:855, 860
Don't Look Back, **3**:422
Dragon Seed, **2**:217
Drift, The, **12**:1663

Earthly Possessions (television), **11**:1545
East of Eden, **11**:1448, 1449, 1466
Eat the Document, **3**:422
Eccentricities of a Nightingale, The (television), **12**:1663
Edge, The, **7**:932, 935
Effect of Gamma Rays on Man-in-the-Moon Marigolds, The, **12**:1717, 1720
Effect of Gamma Rays on Man-in-the-Moon Marigolds, The (television), **12**:1713, 1717
Eight Men Out, **11**:1521, 1527
Elmer Gantry, **6**:859
Emperor Jones, The, **9**:1161
Enemies: A Love Story, **10**:1401, 1405, 1406
Ethan Frome, **12**:1617
Ethan Frome (television), **12**:1617
Expert, The, **4**:501

Farewell to Arms, A, **5**:663, 672, 673

Farewell to Arms, A (television), **5**:673
Feathers, **2**:261
Festival, **3**:422
Fifth Column, The (television), **5**:673
Fifty Grand, **5**:673
Fifty Grand (television), **5**:673
Fighter, The, **7**:875
First Seven Years, The, **7**:914
Fixer, The, **7**:914, *921*
Flight, **11**:1449
Forgotten Village, The, **11**:1453, 1454
For Love of Gold, **7**:875
For Whom the Bell Tolls, **5**:673
For Whom the Bell Tolls (television), **5**:673
Foxfire, **8**:1106
Free Air, **6**:855
Fugitive Kind, The, **12**:1663, 1664
Fun and Fancy Free, **6**:855

Gambler, the Nun, and the Radio, The (television), **5**:673
Gardner's Son, The, **7**:970
Gardner's Son, The (television), **7**:963, 965, 970
Gathering of Old Men, A (television), **5**:584, 586
Gay Old Dog, A, **4**:501
"Getting to Know You", **8**:1106
Giant, **4**:501
Gigolo, **4**:501
Glamour, **4**:501
Glass Menagerie, The (1950, 1987), **12**:1653, 1663, 1664
Glass Menagerie, The (television; 1966, 1963, 1987), **12**:1663
Glengarry Glen Ross, **7**:930, 932, 935, *940*
Glimpses of the Moon, The, **12**:1617
Good Earth, The, **2**:217, 219-22
Good Earth, The (film), **2**:217, 219-22, *220, 222*
Grapes of Wrath, The, **11**:1449, 1455-56, *1457*, 1458
Grapes of Wrath, The (television), **11**:1449
Grass Harp, The, **2**:246
Great Gatsby, The, **4**:519, 526-29, *530*
Greed, **8**:1090, *1094, 1096*
Green Magic, **1**:17
Grit, **4**:519
Guide, The, **2**:217
Gun Runners, The (television), **5**:673

Hairy Ape, The, **9**:1161
Hard to Get, **4**:501

Harness, The (television), **11**:1449
Heart Is a Lonely Hunter, The, **7**:983
Hearts of Fire, **3**:422
Hello, Dolly!, **12**:1631
Hemingway's Adventures of a Young Man, **5**:673
Hills Like White Elephants (television), **5**:673
Hoffa, **7**:932, 935
Homicide, **7**:929, 930, 932, 934, 935
Hook, The, **8**:1015
Hotel New Hampshire, The, **6**:768, 773, 776
House of Games, **7**:929, 930, 931, 932, 934, 935, 941
House of Mirth, The (1918, 2000), **12**:1617
House of Mirth, The (television), **12**:1617
Hughie (television), **9**:1161
Hurry Sundown, **4**:544, 546-47
Husband Hunter, The, **4**:519

I Am the Cheese, **3**:296, 298
Iceman Cometh, The, **9**:1161
Ice Palace, **4**:501
I Married a Doctor, **6**:855
In Cold Blood, **2**:245, *250*
In Love and War, **5**:673
Innocents, The, **2**:237, 238, 242
Islands in the Stream, **5**:673

Jennie Gerhardt, **3**:383
John Barleycorn, **7**:875
Joy Luck Club, The, **11**:*1506*, 1508, 1509, 1510, *1513*

Killers, The (1946; 1964), **5**:673, 679
Killers, The (television), **5**:673
Klondike Fever, **7**:875

Lapse of Memory, **3**:298
Last of the Mobile Hot Shots, **12**:1663
Last Time I Saw Paris, The, **4**:519
Last Tycoon, The, **4**:519, 537
Last Waltz, The, **3**:422
Lesson Before Dying, A (television), **5**:584, 586, 589, *592*
Let Me Hear You Whisper (television), **12**:1717, 1722
Lies of the Twins (television), **8**:1106
Lifeboat, **11**:1449, 1453, 1454
Life in the Theater, A (television), **7**:932, 934, 935

Life's Whirlpool (film), **8**:1090
Lip Service (television), **7**:934, 935
Long Day's Journey into Night (1962; 1996), **9**:1161
Long Day's Journey into Night (television; 1973; 1987), **9**:1161
Long Hot Summer, The, **4**:479
Long Voyage Home, The, **9**:1161
Lost Lady, A, **2**:273
Love, Honor, and Behave, **2**:153
Long Hot Summer, The (television), **4**:479

Macomber Affair, The, **5**:673
Magician of Lublin, The, **10**:1401, *1405*
Main Street, **6**:855
Mame, **12**:1717, 1722
Man of the House, The, **4**:547
Mantrap, **6**:855
Maria's Lovers, **12**:1717, 1722
Marriage Playground, The, **12**:1617
Martin Eden, **7**:875
Matchmaker, The, **12**:1631
Member of the Family (television), **4**:547
Member of the Wedding, The (1953; 1996), **7**:983
Member of the Wedding, The (television), **7**:983
Migrants, The (television), **12**:1663
Miracle Worker, The, **5**:613, 615, 619
Miracle Worker, The (television), **5**:611, 613, 615, 619
Misfits, The, **8**:1016, 1019, *1020*, 1025
Monte Walsh, **10**:1349, 1352
Moon for the Misbegotten, A (television), **9**:1161
Moon Is Down, The, **11**:1449
Moran of the Lady Letty, **8**:1090
Mother Knows Best, **4**:501
Mourning Becomes Electra, **9**:1161
Moveable Feast, A, **5**:673
Mr. North, **12**:1631
Murder by Death, **2**:237
My Antonia (television), **2**:273
My Gal Sal, **3**:383
My Old Man (television), **5**:673

Native Son, **12**:1696, 1697, 1703, 1705
Natural, The, **7**:914, *915*, 923
Necessary Evil, The, **2**:153
Newly Rich, **6**:855
Night of the Hunter, The, **1**:11, 13, 14, 17

Night of the Iguana, **12**:1663
1918, **4**:547
Noa Noa, **1**:17
No Place to Go, **4**:501
Norman and the Killer (film), **8**:1106
Norwood, **9**:1249
No Woman Knows, **4**:501

Odyssey of the North, An, **7**:875
Offshore Pirate, The, **4**:519
Of Mice and Men (1939; 1992), **4**:547, **11**:1449, 1456, 1462
Of Mice and Men (television), **11**:1449
Old Maid, The, **12**:1617
Old Man (television), **4**:479
Old Man and the Sea, The (1958; 1999), **5**:673
Old Man and the Sea, The (television), **5**:673
Oleanna, **7**:929, 930, 931, 932, 934, 935
On Valentine's Day, **4**:541
O Pioneers! (television), **2**:273
Orpheus Descending (television), **12**:1663
Our Mrs. McChesney, **4**:501
Our Town (1940, 1955, 1977), **12**:1631, 1647
Our Town (television), **12**:1631
Outsiders, The, **5**:700, 701, _701_, 702, 703, 711

Passion's Way, **12**:1617
Pastor's Son, **4**:547
Pat Garrett and Billy the Kid, **3**:422
Paul's Case, **2**:273
Pearl, The, **11**:1449, 1453, 1454
Period of Adjustment, **12**:1663
Pit, The, **8**:1090
Place in the Sun, A, **3**:383
Play It as It Lays, **3**:355, 357, 358, _360, 363, 364_
Postman Always Rings Twice, The, **7**:929, 931, 932, 935
Prince Who Was a Thief, The, **3**:383

Queen of the Yukon, **7**:875
Quiet One, The, **1**:14, 16

Rachel, Rachel, **6**:821, 823
Ragtime, **11**:1530
Raisin in the Sun, A, **5**:648, 649, 651-52, 654
Raisin in the Sun, A (television), **5**:652

Red Badge of Courage, The, **1**:17
Red Pony, The, **11**:1449, 1453, 1454
Red Pony, The (television), **11**:1449
Reef, The, **12**:1617
Reflections in a Golden Eye, **7**:983, _991_
Reivers, The (film), **4**:479
Renaldo and Clara, **3**:421, 422
Road to Glory, The, **4**:486
Roman Spring of Mrs. Stone, The, **12**:1663
Ronin, **7**:932, 935
Rose for Emily, A (television), **4**:479
Rose Tattoo, The, **12**:1653, 1663, 1664
Royal Family, The (television), **4**:501, _514_
Rumble Fish, **5**:700, 702, 703, 707, 708, 717
Runaway Train, **12**:1722

Saint Maybe (television), **11**:1545
Sanctuary, **4**:479
Sanford Meisner: The American Theatre's Best Kept Secret, **7**:934
Saratoga Trunk, **4**:501
Satan Never Sleeps, **2**:217
Saving Private Ryan, **11**:1538
Sea-Wolf, The (1913, 1920, 1941, 1997), **7**:875
Senso, **12**:1663
Separate Peace, A, **6**:806, 808, _809_, 812, _816_
Seven Brides for Seven Brothers, **2**:153
Shadow of a Doubt (1943), **12**:1632, 1634, 1639, _1640_, 1641, 1647, 1650
Shadow of a Doubt (1991), **12**:1631
Shane (television), **10**:1349
Shane, **10**:1348, 1349, _1353_, 1354
Ship of Fools, **9**:1232, 1241
Short Cuts, **2**:259, 261
Show Boat, **4**:501
Show Boat (television), **4**:501
Silver Whip, The, **10**:1349
Simon Birch, **6**:768, 773, _780_
Skin of Our Teeth, The (television; 1955, 1983), **12**:1631
Sky Is Gray, The (television), **5**:584, 586, 587
Slave Ship, **4**:486
Slipping-Down Life, A, **11**:1545
Smooth Talk, **8**:1106
Snows of Kilimanjaro, The, **5**:673
Snowbird, **1**:90
Snows of Kilimanjaro, The (television), **5**:673

Snowbird (television), **1**:84
So Big, **4**:501
Son of the Wolf, The, **7**:875
Sophie's Choice, **11**:1493
Sound and the Fury, The, **4**:479
Southerner, The, **4**:486
Spanish Prisoner, The, **7**:930, 932, 934, 935, 940-42
Spring Awakening (television), **2**:273
Stage Door, **4**:501
Stalking Moon, The, **4**:547
Star Is Born, A, **3**:358, 363
Star Rover, The, **7**:875
State and Main, **7**:932, 934, 935
Story of a Marriage, The, **4**:547
Story of Temple Drake, The, **4**:479
Strange Interlude, **9**:1161
Strange Wives (film), **12**:1617
Strange Interlude (television), **9**:1161
Streetcar Named Desire, A, **12**:1653, 1655, 1663, 1664
Streetcar Named Desire, A (television; 1984, 1995, 1998), **12**:1663
Stubby Pringle's Christmas (television), **10**:1349
Suddenly Last Summer, **12**:1663, 1664
Suddenly Last Summer (television), **12**:1663
Summer (television), **12**:1617
Summer and Smoke, **12**:1663, _1671_
Summer Holiday, **9**:1161
Sun Also Rises, The, **5**:673, 677
Sun Also Rises, The (television), **5**:673
Sweet Bird of Youth, **12**:1663
Sweet Bird of Youth (television), **12**:1663

Tarnished Angels, The, **4**:479
Ten Blocks on the Camino Real, **12**:1663
Tender Is the Night, **4**:519, 533
Tender Is the Night (television), **4**:519
Tender Mercies, **4**:541
Tex, **5**:700, _700_, 702, 703, 709
Texan, **7**:932
That Was Then, This Is Now, **5**:702, 703
Things Change, **7**:929, 932, 934, 935
Thin Red Line, The, **11**:1538
This Property Is Condemned, **12**:1663
This Property Is Condemned (television), **12**:1663
Today We Live, **4**:479, 486

To Have and Have Not, **4**:479, 486, **5**:673

To Have and Have Not (television), **5**:673

To Kill a Mockingbird, **4**:539, 542, 543, 546, 547, 550-52, **6**:835, 838, 839, *840*

Tom and Viv, **4**:441

Tomorrow, **4**:547

Tomorrow (television), **4**:542, 547

Tortilla Flat, **11**:1449

Touch of the Poet, A (television), **9**:1161

Tribute to a Bad Man (film), **10**:1349

Trip to Bountiful, The, **4**:541, 543, 546, 547, 554

Trip to Bountiful, The (television), **4**:542, 547, 554

Trooper Hook, **10**:1349

Tropical Nights, **7**:875

True Confessions, **3**:357, 363

True Grit, **9**:1248, 1249, *1255*

Two for the Seesaw, **5**:614, 615

Under My Skin, **5**:673

Unpainted Woman, The, **6**:855

Untamed, **6**:855

Untouchables, The, **7**:929, 932, 935

Up Close and Personal, **3**:357, 363

Up the Sandbox, **12**:1717, 1722

Valley of the Moon, The, **7**:875

Vanya on 42nd Street, **7**:929, 932, 935

Verdict, The, **7**:929, 931, 932, 935

Viva Zapata!, **11**:1453, 1454

Wag the Dog, **7**:932, 935

Warrior Marks, **11**:1566, 1575

Wayward Bus, The, **11**:1449

Welcome Home, **4**:501

We're No Angels, **7**:932, 935

White Fang (1925, 1991), **7**:875

White Mane, **1**:17

Winter of Our Discontent, The (television), **11**:1449

Wonder Boys, **3**:421

World According to Garp, The, **6**:768, 772, 773

World of Nick Adams, The (television), **5**:673

Yentl, **10**:1401, 1406

Yiddish Cinema, **7**:934

Young Bess, **9**:1231

Zorba the Greek, **11**:1530

Index of Literary Characters

Note: Character names are listed uninverted

Aaron Greidinger (*Meshugah*), 10:1413

Aaron Greidinger (*Shosha*), 10:1399, 1412-13

Aaronow (*Glengarry Glen Ross*), 7:940

Abbie Cabot (*Desire Under the Elms*), 9:1164, 1170

Abigail (*Crucible*), 8:1023

Abioseh Matoseh (*Nègres*), 5:657

Abraham Gordon (*Promise*), 9:1265, 1272, 1273

Abraham Lincoln (portrayed in "Hannah Armstrong"), 7:958

Abraham Lincoln (portrayed in *Manassaas*), 10:1384

Abram Shapiro (*Family Moskat*), 10:1402, 1409, 1410

Ada Jordan (*Lives of Girls and Women*), 8:1077, 1079

Adam (*Pale Horse, Pale Rider*), 9:1239

Adam (*Songs for Eve*), 7:906

Adam Brant (*Mourning Becomes Electra*), 9:1179

Adam Farmer (*I Am the Cheese*), 3:299, 306, 307

Adam Patch (*Beautiful and the Damned*), 4:536

Adam Pell (*Wind from an Enemy Sky*), 7:999, 1004, 1005

Adam Pell's son (*Wind from an Enemy Sky*), 7:1004, 1005

Adam Trask (*East of Eden*), 11:1466

Addie Bundren (*As I Lay Dying*), 4:490, 491, 492

Adele Landau (*Family Moskat*), 10:1410

Adolf Hitler (portrayed in Lanny Budd series), 10:1396

Adriance Hilgarde ("Death in the Desert"), 2:275

Aegisthus (*Oresteia*), 9:1179

Agamemnon (*Oresteia*), 9:1179

Agathon (*Wreckage of Agathon*), 5:598, 609-10

Ahab (*Moby Dick*), 5:608

Aharon Bendiger (*Certificate*), 10:1407

Aileen (*Financier*), 3:392, 394

Albert Corde (*The Dean's December*), 1:140

Alcmena Hungerfield ("Hungerfield"), 6:795, 796

Alejandra (*All the Pretty Horses*), 7:969

Alex (*Cocktail Party*), 4:448

Alexander (*Accidental Tourist*), 11:1552

Alexander Eppes (*Confessions of Nat Turner*), 11:1498

Alexander Levine ("Angel Levine"), 7:924

Alexandra Bergson (*O Pioneers!*), 2:275, 278, 279, 281-82, 283, 284

Alexandra Del Lago (*Sweet Bird of Youth*), 12:1672-73

Alfieri (*View from the Bridge*), 8:1031

Alice Hindman (*Winesburg, Ohio*), 1:52

Alison Langdon (*Reflections in a Golden Eye*), 7:982, 991

Allan Montague (father; *Manassas*), 10:1383

Allan Montague (son; *Metropolis*), 10:1383-84

Allan Montague (son; *Moneychangers*), 10:1383-84

Allie Caulfield (*Catcher in the Rye*), 10:1315

Alma Winemiller (*Summer and Smoke*), 12:1656, 1671

Alphonso (*Color Purple*), 11:1574-75

Alvaro Mangiacavallo (*Rose Tattoo*), 12:1672

Alvin Dewey (*In Cold Blood*), 2:248

Amanda Wingfield (*Glass Menagerie*), 12:1656, 1664, 1665, 1666

Amasa Dempster (*Fifth Business*), 3:345

Amelia Evans (*Ballad of the Sad Café*), 7:981, 982, 984-85, 986, 989

Amory ("Six of One —"), 4:523

Amory Blaine (*This Side of Paradise*), 4:534-35

Amy (*Beloved*), 8:1056

Amy ("Home Burial"), 4:563, 569

Amy (*I Am the Cheese*), 3:306

Amy Wustrin (*The Actual*), 1:133

Anacleto (*Reflections in a Golden Eye*), 7:991

Andres (*For Whom the Bell Tolls*), 5:676

Andrew Beard (*Spanish Bayonet*), 2:161

Angel (baby) (*Cider House Rules*), 6:775

Angela (nurse) (*Cider House Rules*), 6:774

Angela Blue ("*Genius*"), 3:395

Angelé's child (*Octopus*), 8:1093

Angelé Varian (*Octopus*), 8:1093

Angel Harper (*Mrs. Reynolds*), 10:1437

Angie Miglione (*Then Again, Maybe I Won't*), 2:179

Anita ("Home to El Building"), 9:1190

Ann (*This Music Crept by Me Upon the Waters*), 7:907

Anna ("Good Anna"), 10:1437-38

Anna Christie (*Anna Christie*), 9:*1169*

Anna Leath (*Reef*), 12:1618, 1626

Ann Deever (*All My Sons*), 8:1022

Anne Rutledge ("Anne Rutledge"), 7:958

Anne Shakespeare (portrayed in *Cry of Players*), 5:616, 621

Anne Sullivan (*Miracle Worker*), 5:613, 615, 616-17, 618, 619, 620, 621

Annie Allen (*Annie Allen*), 2:197, 204-5

Annie Sullivan (portrayed in *Miracle Worker*), 5:611, 613, 614, 615

Annixter (*Octopus*), 8:1098

Ann Vickers (*Ann Vickers*), 6:852, 861

Anse Bundren (*As I Lay Dying*), **4**:490, 491, 492

Anselmo (*For Whom the Bell Tolls*), **5**:676

Anshel ("Yentl, the Yeshiva Boy"), **10**:1405

Antanas Jurgis (grandfather; *Jungle*), **10**:1391-92, 1393

Antanas Jurgis (grandson; *Jungle*), **10**:1393

Anthony Patch (*Beautiful and the Damned*), **4**:536

Antonia Shimerda (*My Antonia*), **2**:275-76

Antrobus family (*Skin of Our Teeth*), **12**:1637, 1639, 1641, 1646

Apostle Alexandre (*Tender Is the Night*), **4**:534

Arab Hungerfield ("Hungerfield"), **6**:795

Archie Costello (*Beyond the Chocolate War*), **3**:304

Archie Costello (*Chocolate War*), **3**:302, 303, 304

Archilde Leon (*Surrounded*), **7**:999, 1002, 1003

Arlene Miller ("Neighbors"), **2**:265

Aron Trask (*East of Eden*), **11**:1466

Arrowsmith (*Arrowsmith*), **6**:852, 857, 858

Arthur (*Lady Oracle*), **1**:95, 96

Arthur ("Something I've Been Meaning to Tell You"), **8**:1084

Arthur Gordon Pym (*Narrative of Arthur Gordon Pym*), **5**:608

Arthur Keller (*Miracle Worker*), **5**:616, 618-19

Arthur Morse (*Martin Eden*), **7**:885

Arturo ("Arturo's Flight"), **9**:1188, 1190

Arturo ("Hour with Abuelo"), **9**:1190

Aryeh Lev (*Gift of Asher Lev*), **9**:1274

Aryeh Lev (*My Name Is Asher Lev*), **9**:1259, 1270, 1272

Asa Hawks (*Wise Blood*), **8**:1147

Asa Heshel Bannet (*Family Moskat*), **10**:1399, 1402, 1404, 1409, 1410-11

Asher Lev (*Gift of Asher Lev*), **9**:1259, 1265, 1267, 1274

Asher Lev (*My Name Is Asher Lev*), **9**:1259, 1267, 1270, 1272

Asher Lev's mythic ancestor (*My Name is Asher Lev*), **9**:1270, 1272

Asher Lev's uncle (*My Name Is Asher Lev*), **9**:1270

Ashley family (*Eighth Day*), **12**:1649

A. T. (Toby) Rafferty (*Wind from an Enemy Sky*), **7**:999, 1004

Ather Ownby (*Orchard Keeper*), **7**:973

Atticus Finch (*To Kill a Mockingbird*), **4**:550, 551, **6**:834, 835, 837, 838, 839, 840, 841

Aunt (*I Am the Cheese*, **3**:306

Aunt Hannah (*Death in the Family, A*), **1**:18, 19

Aunt Helen ("Tamar"), **6**:798, 799

Aunt Jenny ("Tamar"), **6**:798, 799

Aunt Lou (*Lady Oracle*), **1**:96

Aunt Stella ("Tamar"), **6**:798, 799

"Avenger, the" (*We All Fall Down*), **3**:310

Avigdor ("Yentl, the Yeshiva Boy"), **10**:1405

Avis Cunningham (*Iron Heel*), **7**:888, 889

Avrumel Lev (*Gift of Asher Lev*), **9**:1274

Babbitt's son (*Babbitt*), **6**:857

Baby Suggs (*Beloved*), **8**:1056, 1062

Banner Club (*Sport of Gods*), **3**:410

Baptiste ("Ax-Helve"), **4**:563

Barbara Fishelson (*Family Moskat*), **10**:1410, 1411

Barnaby (*Matchmaker*), **12**:1649

Barnaby Gaitlin (*Patchwork Planet*), **11**:1558-59

Barnaby Gaitlin's brother (*Patchwork Planet*), **11**:1558

Barnaby Gaitlin's father (*Patchwork Planet*), **11**:1558

Barney Glasgow (*Come and Get It*), **4**:504, 505

Barney Hainsfeather (*Spoon River Anthology*), **7**:957

Barry Rudd (*Child Buyer*), **5**:696, 697

Bashele Berman (*Family Moskat*), **10**:1409

Basque woodcarver (*Ship of Fools*), **9**:1239

Bayard Sartoris (*Flags in Dust*), **4**:484

Bayard Sartoris (*Unvanquished*), **4**:488-89

Bea (*Main Street*), **6**:854

Bea Carbone (*View from the Bridge*), **8**:1031

bear (*Hotel New Hampshire*), **6**:777

Beatrice Blaine (*This Side of Paradise*), **4**:534, 535

Beatrice Hunsdorfer (*Effect of Gamma Rays on Man-in-the-Moon Marigolds*), **12**:1719, 1720

Beau Boutan (*Gathering of Old Men*), **5**:592

Beaumont (*Townsman*), **2**:228

Beauty Smith (*White Fang*), **7**:887

Beaver (*Great Gatsby*), **4**:531

Beck Tull (*Dinner at the Homesick Restaurant*), **11**:1555, 1557

Bella (*Certificate*), **10**:1407

Beloved (*Beloved*), **8**:1058, 1063-64

Ben (*Black Thunder*), **2**:190

Beneatha Younger (*Raisin in Sun*), **5**:653, 654

Benedict Arnold (portrayed in "Devil and Daniel Webster"), **2**:157

Benedict Domdaniel (*Mixture of Frailties*), **3**:351

Benjy Compson (*Sound and Fury*), **4**:484, 493-94, 495

Ben Loman (*Death of a Salesman*), **8**:1025, *1026*, 1028

Benn Crader (*More Die of Heartbreak*), **1**:140, 141

Benny (*Rumble Fish*), **5**:702

Ben Raymond ("Viney's Free Papers"), **3**:411

Ben Redmond (*Unvanquished*), **4**:488, 489

Beowulf (*Grendel*), **5**:604

Berenice (*Member of the Wedding*), **7**:988, 989

Berenice Fleming (*Stoic*), **3**:395

Bergson family (*O Pioneers!*), **2**:275, 278, 281, 282, 284

Bernal Díaz del Castillo (portrayed in *Conquistador*), **7**:900

Bernard (*Death of a Salesman*), **8**:1019, 1027

Bernard Glasgow (*Come and Get It*), **4**:505

Bernice (*Gone to Soldiers*), **9**:1209

Berry family (*Hotel New Hampshire*), **6**:766, 771, 777, 778

Berry Hamilton (*Sport of Gods*), **3**:410

Bertha Dorset (*House of Mirth*), **12**:1626

Bessie (*Native Son*), **12**:1704, 1705

Beth (*Small Changes*), **9**:1210, 1211

Betty (*Boston*), **10**:1390-91

Betty (*them*), **8**:1114

Betty Slonim (*Shosha*), **10**:1413

Betty's mother (*Boston*), **10**:1391

Beulah (*Losing Battles*), **12**:1602

Beulah's husband (*Losing Battles*), **12**:1602

Bibikov (*Fixer*), **7**:921

Biff Brannon (*Heart Is a Lonely Hunter*), **7**:987, 989

Biff Loman (*Death of a Salesman*), **8**:1019, 1026, 1027, 1028

Big Boy ("Big Boy Leaves Home"), **12**:1698, 1699, 1706

Big Daddy Pollitt (*Cat on a Hot Tin Roof*), **12**:1669, 1670

Big Dan (*Gringos*), **9**:1256

Bigger Thomas (*Native Son*), **3**:410, **12**:1698, 1704, 1705

Bildad (*J.B.*), **7**:904

Bill Dillon (*Democracy*), **3**:361

Bill Gorton (*Sun Also Rises*), **5**:677

Billie (*Taming Star Runner*), **5**:715

Bill Kidder (*Young Man from Atlanta*), **4**:552, 553

Bill Miller ("Neighbors"), **2**:265

Billy (*The Robber Bride*), **1**:99

Billy Boy Watkins (*Going After Cacciato*), **8**:1129

Billy Brown (*Great God Brown*), **9**:1164

Billy Buck ("Gift"), **11**:1464-65

Billy Parham (*Crossing*), **7**:967

Billy Rose (*Bellarosa Connection*), **1**:139

Bishop Rayber (*Violent Bear It Away*), **8**:1144, 1145

Blaikie Noble ("Something I've Been Meaning to Tell You"), **8**:1084

Blanche DuBois (*Streetcar Named Desire*), **12**:1656, 1657, 1666, 1668

Bledsoe (*Invisible Man*), **4**:466, 469

Bob (*Outsiders*), **5**:706, 711

Bobbi Cowling (*Nuclear Age*), **8**:1133

Bobby (*American Buffalo*), **7**:936, 937, 938

Bob Ewell (*To Kill a Mockingbird*), **6**:840, 841

Bobo ("Big Boy Leaves Home"), **12**:1706

Bobo (*Raisin in Sun*), **5**:654

Bob Quinn ("Handcarved Coffins"), **2**:252

Bob Starrett (*Shane*), **10**:1349, 1354

Boo (Arthur) Radley (*To Kill a Mockingbird*), **4**:551, **6**:837, 840, 841, 842

Boo Boo Glass Tannenbaum ("Down at the Dinghy"), **10**:1321

Boo Boo Glass Tannenbaum (Glass family stories), **10**:1303

Boo Boo Glass Tannenbaum ("Raise High the Roof Beam, Carpenters"), **10**:1317

Booper ("Teddy"), **10**:1321

Boris Max (*Native Son*), **12**:1704-5

boss (*Of Mice and Men*), **11**:1461

Boss Finley (*Sweet Bird of Youth*), **12**:1672, 1673

Braddock Washington ("Diamond as Big as Ritz"), **4**:522

Braggioni ("Flowering Judas"), **9**:1241

Brander Matthews (*Jennie Gerhardt*), **3**:388

Breckinridge Lansing (*Eighth Day*), **12**:1649

Brendan Lucas (*Spreading Fires*), **6**:818

Br'er Rabbit (*Uncle Remus*), **8**:1057, 1058, 1070

Brett Ashley (*Sun Also Rises*), **5**:668, 677, 678

Brewsie (*Brewsie and Willie*), **10**:1436

Brian (*Celestial Navigation*), **11**:1558

Brick Pollitt (*Cat on a Hot Tin Roof*), **12**:1657, *1669*, 1670

Bridgetower family (*Leaves of Malice*), **3**:348

Bridgetower family (*Mixture of Frailties*), **3**:351

Brinis family (*Boston*), **10**:1390

Brinker Hadley (*Separate Peace*), **6**:810, 812, 815, 816

Brint (*I Am the Cheese*), **3**:306

Bronya Gritzenhendler Moskat (*Family Moskat*), **10**:1409

Brook Skelton (*Diviners*), **6**:826-27

Brother Andre (*Pavilion of Women*), **2**:229, 230

Brother Boxer (*Amen Corner*), **1**:111, 113

Brotherhood, the (*Invisible Man*), **4**:466, 469, 470

Brother Jack (*Invisible Man*), **4**:466

Brother Juniper (*Bridge of San Luis Rey*), **12**:1643, 1644

Brother Leon (*Chocolate War*), **3**:302, 303

Brother Tarp (*Invisible Man*), **4**:466

Bru (*Summer Sisters*), **2**:178, 179

Brutus Jones (*Emperor Jones*), **9**:1164-65, 1169

Bryon (*That Was Then, This Is Now*), **5**:716, 718

Bubber Kelly (*Heart Is a Lonely Hunter*), **7**:982

Buck (dog) (*Call of the Wild*), **7**:876, 877, 884-85

Buddy (*Bell Jar*), **9**:1223

Buddy Glass (Glass family stories), **10**:1303, 1304, 1307, 1308, 1309, 1317-18

Buddy Glass ("Hapworth 16, 1924"), **10**:1304

Buddy Glass ("Raise High the Roof Beam, Carpenters"), **10**:1317, *1318*

Buddy Glass ("Seymour: An Introduction), 10:1317-18, **10**:1319, 1321

Buddy Glass ("Zooey"), **10**:1316

Buddy Walker (*We All Fall Down*), **3**:310

bull ("Greenleaf"), **8**:1150

Bull (*Wind from an Enemy Sky*), **7**:1004

Bull's grandson (*Wind from an Enemy Sky*), **7**:1004, 1005

Bundren family (*As I Lay Dying*), **4**:490, 492

Byron Bunch (*Light in August*), **4**:497

BZ (*Play It as It Lays*), **3**:365, 366

Cacciato (*Going After Cacciato*), **8**:1128, 1129

Caddy (*Sound and Fury*), **4**:494, 495

Caitlin (*Summer Sisters*), **2**:178-79

Caleb Peck (*Searching for Caleb*), **11**:1559, 1560

Caleb Trask (*East of Eden*), **11**:1466

California (character) ("Roan Stallion"), **6**:796, 797-98

Caligula (*Lazarus Laughed*), **9**:1165

Callie Wells (*Nickel Mountain*), **5**:608

Calvin Cohn (*God's Grace*), **7**:924

Camila Perichole (*Bridge of San Luis Rey*), **12**:1643-44

canary (*McTeague*), **8**:1095

Candy (*Of Mice and Men*), **11**:1461

Candy Kendall (*Cider House Rules*), **6**:775

Candy Marshall (*Gathering of Old Men*), **5**:592

Captain Ahab (*Moby Dick*), **5**:608

Captain Andy Hawkes (*Show Boat*), **4**:510

Captain Flint ("King's Indian"), **5**:608

Captain Johanson (*If I Die in a Combat Zone, Box Me Up and Ship Me Home*), **8**:1133

Captain Wendell Penderton (*Reflections in a Golden Eye*), **7**:991

Carl Linstrum (*O Pioneers!*), **2**:284

Carl Luce (*Catcher in the Rye*), **10**:1309

Carlos Among the Candles (Stevens), **11**:1475

Carmella (Carol) Miglione (*Then Again, Maybe I Won't*), **2**:179

Carol (*Oleanna*), **7**:943

Carol Kennicott (*Main Street*), **6**:846, 852, 853-54, 858, 861

Carrie Meeber (*Sister Carrie*), **3**:380, 386, 388, 389, *390*, 391-92

Carrie Watts (*Trip to Bountiful*), **4**:554

Carter Lang (*Play It as It Lays*), **3**:361, 365, 366

Casey Kencaide (*Taming Star Runner*), **5**:713, 715-16

Cash Bundren (*As I Lay Dying*), **4**:490, 491, 492

Cass (*Another Country*), **1**:120

Cassie Morrison ("June Recital"), **12**:1602

Caterina (*Spanish Bayonet*), **2**:161

Catherine (*View from the Bridge*), **8**:1031

Catherine Barkley (*Farewell to Arms*), **5**:672, 673, 674

Catherine Cormier (*Catherine Cormier*), **5**:593-94

Catherine Creek (*Grass Harp*), **2**:246, 247

Catherine Le Loup (*Surrounded*), **7**:999, 1002, 1003

Catherine "Peter" Bourne (*Garden of Eden*), **5**:671

Cathy Ames (*East of Eden*), **11**:1466

Cathy Carlson (*That Was Then, This Is Now*), **5**:717

Catlips (*Great Gatsby*), **4**:531

Caulfield family (*Catcher in the Rye*), **10**:1302, 1303, 1305, 1307, 1308, 1309, 1314-15

Cecelia Brady (*Last Tycoon*), **4**:536

Celia Chentshiner (*Shosha*), **10**:1413

Celie (*Color Purple*), **11**:*1570*, 1571, 1572, 1574-76, 1581

Central American dictator (*Book of Common Prayer*), **3**:372

Chaim Menzies (*Oil!*), **10**:1394

Champ Perry (*Main Street*), **6**:854

Chance Wayne (*Sweet Bird of Youth*), **12**:1672, 1673

Char ("Something I've Been Meaning to Tell You"), **8**:1084

Charis (*The Robber Bride*), **1**:99

Charles Baker "Dill" Harris (*To Kill a Mockingbird*). *See* Dill (*To Kill a Mockingbird*)

Charles Drouet (*Sister Carrie*), **3**:389, 391

Charles Rigaud (*Into Valley*), **5**:697

Charley (*Death of a Salesman*), **8**:1019, 1027, 1028

Charlie (*That Was Then, This Is Now*), **5**:717

Charlie Chan (Charlie Chan mystery series), **9**:1178

Charlie Citrine (*Humboldt's Gift*), **1**:133, 136-37

Charlie Hughes (*Hughie*), **9**:1178

Charlotte Douglas (*Book of Common Prayer*), **3**:359-60, 361, 372

Charlotte Emory (*Earthly Possessions*), **11**:1548-49, 1558

Charlotte Emory's father (*Earthly Possessions*), **11**:1549

Charlotte Mills (*Paragon*), **6**:817

Charlotte Newton (*Shadow of a Doubt*). *See* Young Charlie

Charlotte Thrift (*Girls*), **4**:513

Charly Kemp (*Girls*), **4**:513

Chet Rollins (*Monte Walsh*), **10**:1351, 1352

Chick Lorimer ("Gone"), **10**:1339

Chief Fred Clumly (*Sunlight Dialogues*), **5**:600, 606-7

child genius (*Revenge of the Space Pandas*), **7**:944

Ch'iuming (*Pavilion of Women*), **2**:230

Cholly Breedlove (*Bluest Eye*), **8**:1065

Chorus of the Women of Canterbury (*Murder in Cathedral*), **4**:445

Chris (*Shane*), **10**:1354

Chris Keller (*All My Sons*), **8**:1019, 1022

Christiane de Treymes (*Madame de Treymes*), **12**:1618

Christie Logan (*Diviners*), **6**:826, 827

Christine (*Mourning Becomes Electra*), **9**:1170

Christine ("Roan Stallion"), **6**:796

Christine Mannon (*Mourning Becomes Electra*), **9**:1179

Chrysis (*Woman of Andros*), **12**:1650

Church Withour Christ (*Wise Blood*), **8**:1147

Civet (*Great Gatsby*), **4**:531

Clara Butterworth (*Poor White*), **1**:49, 51

Clara Page (*This Side of Paradise*), **4**:523

Claud Antle (*New Spoon River*), **7**:956

Claudia MacTeer (*Bluest Eye*), **8**:1065, 1066

Clay Wingate (*John Brown's Body*), **2**:159

Cleet Kinsolving (*Indian Summer*), **6**:809-10, 811, 817

Clement Lewy ("kitchenette folks"), **2**:207

Clio Dulain (*Saratoga Trunk*), **4**:504

Clutter family (*In Cold Blood*), **2**:248, 249

Clyde Griffith (*American Tragedy*), **3**:380, 385-86

Clytemnestra (*Oresteia*), **9**:1179

Cody Tull (*Dinner at the Homesick Restaurant*), **11**:1555, 1556-57

Cody Tull's son (*Dinner at the Homesick Restaurant*), **11**:1557

Cole Collins (*Tex*), **5**:710, 713

Collin Fenwick (*Grass Harp*), **2**:246, 247

Colonel Dick (*Unvanquished*), **4**:488

Colonel John Sartoris (*Flags in the Dust*), **4**:483

Colonel John Sartoris (*Unvanquished*), **4**:488, 489

Colossus (*Colossus and Other Poems*), **9**:1225

columnist ("Yearning Heifer"), **10**:1414

Comforters (*J.B.*), **7**:904, 905

Commander (*The Handmaid's Tale*), **1**:91, 94

Compson family (*Sound and Fury*), **4**:490, 493, 495

Connie Ramos (*Woman on the Edge of Time*), **9**:1207-9

Connor (*Jungle*), **10**:1393

Conquistador (MacLeish), **7**:891, 894, 895, 900, 901

Cordelia (*Cat's Eye*), **1**:97

Corky's stepdaughter (*What I Lived For*), **8**:1116

Cormiers (*Catherine Cormier*), 5:593-94

Cornelia Thornwell (*Boston*), 10:1390-91

Cornelius (*Matchmaker*), 12:1638, 1649

Cornelius Suttree (*Suttree*), 7:967, 971, 972

Corporal Brown (*Autobiography of Miss Jane Pittman*), 5:590

Corporate State (*It Can't Happen Here*), 6:861, 862

Cotton Blossom (boat) (*Show Boat*), 4:510

Count Greffi (*Farewell to Arms*), 5:674

Cousin Vit (*Annie Allen*), 2:204

Cressler (*Pit*), 8:1099, 1100

Cross Damon (*Outsider*), 12:1709

Culla Home (*Outer Dark*), 7:973-74

Curley (*Of Mice and Men*), 11:1461

Curley's wife (*Of Mice and Men*), 11:1461

Curtis Jadwin (*Pit*), 8:1093, 1099, 1100

Dacha (*Family Moskat*), 10:1410

Dacha Moskat (*Family Moskat*), 10:1409

Daisy Buchanan (*Great Gatsby*), 4:521, 526, 527, 528, 529, 530, 531, 532

Dallas ("Dally") Winston (*Outsiders*), 5:702, 710, 711

Daniel (*Gone to Soldiers*), 9:1209

Daniel Boone (portrayed in *Book of Americans*), 2:153, 154

Daniel Peck (*Searching for Caleb*), 11:1559, 1560

Daniel Webster (portrayed in "Devil and Daniel Webster"), 2:157

Danny (*Tortilla Flat*), 11:1453, 1459-60

Danny Saunders (*Chosen*), 9:1259, 1264, 1268-69

Danny Saunders (*Promise*), 9:1264, 1272, 1273

Danny's grandfather (*Tortilla Flat*), 11:1460

Darcy (*Celestial Navigation*), 11:1557

Darl Bundren (*As I Lay Dying*), 4:490, 491-92

Darrel ("Darry") Curtis (*Outsiders*), 5:711

Daughter ("Yearning Heifer"), 10:1414

Dave ("Man Who Was Almost a Man"), 12:1707

Dave's mother ("Man Who Was Almost a Man"), 12:1707

David (*The Amen Corner*), 1:111, 113

David Bannet (*Family Moskat*), 10:1410

David Bendiger (*Certificate*), 10:1407-9

David Bendiger's father (*Certificate*), 10:1409

David Bourne (*Garden of Eden*), 5:671

David Cauldwell ("Tamar"), 6:798

David Frieber (*Man Who Had All the Luck*), 8:1017

David Lurie (*In the Beginning*), 9:1266

David Staunton (*Manticore*), 3:350

Dawson Ryder (*This Side of Paradise*), 4:535

Days gang (*Song of Solomon*), 8:1067, 1068

D. B. Caulfield (*Catcher in the Rye*), 10:1307

Deacon Swift ("Mess of Pottage"), 3:412-13

Deborah Grimes (*Go Tell It on the Mountain*), 1:115, 116

Dee ("Everyday Use"), 11:1579

Deenie (*Deenie*), 2:176, 178

Del (*Cryptogram*), 7:942, 943

Delia Grinstead (*Ladder of Years*), 11:1548

Del Jordan (*Lives of Girls and Women*), 8:1073, 1078, 1079-80, 1082

Demodokos (Peeker) (*Wreckage of Agathon*), 5:609-10

Dempster family (*Fifth Business*), 3:345-47

Dennis (*My Darling, My Hamburger*), 12:1725

Denver (*Beloved*), 8:1058, 1063, 1064

Devorah Lev (*Gift of Asher Lev*), 9:1274

Dewey Dell Bundren (*As I Lay Dying*), 4:490, 491, 492

Dick Caramel (*Beautiful and Damned*), 4:536

Dick Diver (*Tender Is the Night*), 4:521, 525, 533, 534

Dick Hickock (*In Cold Blood*), 2:240, 248, 249

Dick McMahon (*Last Thing He Wanted*), 3:372-73

Dill (*To Kill a Mockingbird*), 4:551, 6:834, 837, 838, 841

Dilsey Gibson (*Sound and Fury*), 4:484, 493, 494, 495

Dion Anthony (*Great God Brown*), 9:1164

Dippold the Optician (*Spoon River Anthology*), 7:953

Dirk ("So Big") DeJong (*So Big*), 4:511, 512

Distant Voice (*J.B.*), 7:903, 905

Dixie Scott (*Tender Mercies*), 4:549

Doc (*Cannery Row*), 11:1452, 1465

doctor ("Jilting of Granny Weatherall"), 9:1243

Doctor Parcival (*Winesburg, Ohio*), 1:52

Doctor Reefy (*Winesburg, Ohio*), 1:52

Doctor Schumann (*Ship of Fools*), 9:1234

Dolek Berson (*Wall*), 5:696

Dolly (*Woman on the Edge of Time*), 9:1207

Dolly Bonner (*Lie Down in Darkness*), 11:1502, 1503

Dolly Levi (*Matchmaker*), 12:1649

Dolly Talbo (*Grass Harp*), 2:246, 247

Dona Corazon ("Corazon's Café"), 9:1192

Don Dubro (*American Buffalo*), 7:936-37, 938

Don Hector (*All the Pretty Horses*), 7:969

Donny (*Cryptogram*), 7:942, 943

Donny March (Mamet), 7:935

Don Parritt (*Iceman Cometh*), 9:1173, 1174, 1175

Dora Stolnitz (*Shosha*), 10:1413

Dorcas (*Jazz*), 8:1068

Doremus Jessup (*It Can't Happen Here*), 6:861-62

Dr. Adler (*Seize the Day*), 1:137-38

drawing teacher ("Paul's Case"), 2:285

Dr. Benedict Mady Copeland (*Heart Is a Lonely Hunter*, 7:987

Dr. Buchanan (father) (*Summer and Smoke*), 12:1671

Dr. Duer (*Arrowsmith*), 6:857

Dr. Holabird (*Arrowsmith*), 6:858

Dr. John Buchanan (son) (*Summer and Smoke*), 12:1671

Dr. Magoon ("Hundred Collars"), **4**:563

Dr. Pickerbaugh (*Arrowsmith*), **6**:857

Dr. Reo Symes (*Dog of the South*), **9**:1250, 1254, 1255

Drusilla Hawk Sartoris (*Unvanquished*), **4**:489

Dubin's wife (*Dubin's Lives*), **7**:924

Duna (bear) ("Pension Grillparzer"), **6**:781

Duncan Peck (*Searching for Caleb*), **11**:1559-60

Dunstaable (Dunstan) Ramsay (*Fifth Business*), **3**:345, 346, **5**:347

Dura (*Possessing the Secret of Joy*), **11**:1581, 1582

Duvey (*Gone to Soldiers*), **9**:1210

dying man (*Grapes of Wrath*), **11**:1463

Easter ("Moon Lake"), **12**:1601

Eben Cabot (*Desire Under the Elms*), **9**:1164, 1170

Eddie Carbone (*View from the Bridge*), **8**:1031

Eddie Cassavant (*Tunes for Bears to Dance To*), **3**:309

Eddie Kulanski (*In the Beginning*), **9**:1266, 1267

Edith Cortright (*Dodsworth*), **6**:860

Edmund Tyrone (*Long Day's Journey into Night*), **9**:1172, 1175, 1176, 1177

Edna (*Pardon Me, You're Stepping on My Eyeball!*), **12**:1715

Edusha (woman) (*Certificate*), **10**:1407, 1408

Edward (dog) (*Accidental Tourist*), **11**:1552

effeminate young man (*Violent Bear It Away*), **8**:1145

Egg Berry (*Hotel New Hampshire*), **6**:777

Elaine Risley (*Cat's Eye*), **1**:97

El Building (*Island Like You*), **9**:1187, 1188, 1189, 1190

El Building (*Latin Deli*), **9**:1187, 1188, 1191, 1192

elderly aunts ("Peace of Utrecht"), **8**:1083

elderly black man ("To Hell with Dying"), **11**:1575

Eleanor Savage (*This Side of Paradise*), **4**:535

Electra (*Oresteia*), **9**:1179

Elena McMahon (*Last Thing He Wanted*), **3**:361, 372-74

Eliphaz (*J.B.*), **7**:904

Elisha (*Go Tell It on the Mountain*), **1**:116

Elizabeth (*This Music Crept by Me Upon the Waters*), **7**:907

Elizabeth Abbott (*Clock Winder*), **11**:1550

Elizabeth Grimes (*Go Tell It on the Mountain*), **1**:115, 116

Elizabeth Proctor (*Crucible*), **8**:1023

Elizabeth Vaughn Robedaux (*Orphans' Home cycle*), **4**:553, 554

Ellen James Society (*World According to Garp*), **6**:778

Ellen Olenska (*Age of Innocence*), **12**:1618, *1620*, 1621-22

Ellgee Williams (*Reflections in a Golden Eye*), **7**:991

Ellyat, Jack (portrayed in *John Brown's Body*), **2**:159

El Mago (*Gringos*), **9**:1256

Elmer Gantry (*Elmer Gantry*), **6**:859, 860

Elwin (Leper) Lepellier (*Separate Peace*), **6**:812, 815, 816

Emerson family (*Clock Winder*), **11**:1548

Emil Bergson (*O Pioneers!*), **2**:278, 281, 282

Emily Webb (*Our Town*), **12**:*1636*, 1637, 1639, 1641, *1642*, 1644, 1645, 1650

Emma McChesney (*Emma McChesney and Co.*), **4**:513

Emma McChesney (*Our Mrs. McChesney*), **4**:504, 514

Emma McChesney (*Personality Plus*), **4**:513

Emma McChesney ("Representing T. A. Buck"), **4**:501

Emma McChesney ("Roast Beef Medium"), **4**:501

Emma McChesney (*Roast Beef Medium*), **4**:513

English teacher (*them*), **8**:1114

En-lan (*Patriot*), **2**:229

Enoch Emery (*Wise Blood*), **8**:1147

Ephraim (*Matchmaker*), **12**:1649

Ephraim Cabot (*Desire Under the Elms*), **9**:1164, 1170

Eric (*Another Country*), **1**:120

Eric ("Just Before the War with the Eskimos"), **10**:1321

Eric Matoseh (*Nègres*), **5**:657

Eric Poole (*Tenderness*), **3**:308

Erie Smith (*Hughie*), **9**:1178

Erik Valborg (*Main Street*), **6**:854

Ernest Everhart (*Iron Heel*), **7**:876, 888, 889

Esteban (*Bridge of San Luis Rey*), **12**:1643

Estelle ("Housekeeper"), **4**:563

Esther Clumly (*Sunlight Dialogues*), **5**:607

Esther Greenwood (*Bell Jar*), **9**:1223-24

Et Desmond ("Something I've Been Meaning to Tell You"), **8**:1084

Ethan Frome (*Ethan Frome*), **12**:1618, 1624, 1628

Ethan Leary (*Accidental Tourist*), **11**:1550, 1552

Ethan Page (*October Light*), **5**:606

Ethel (*Overlaid*), **3**:341

Eugene Henderson (*Henderson the Rain King*), **1**:140

Eugene Tennyson Witla ("*Genius*"), **3**:395

Eumenides, the (*Family Reunion*), **4**:446

Eva (*Sula*), **8**:1069

Evan (*Townsman*), **2**:228

Eve (*Songs for Eve*), **7**:906

Everett Hilgarde ("Death in the Desert"), **2**:275

Everett McClellan (*Run River*), **3**:360, 361

Ezra Mannon (*Mourning Becomes Electra*), **9**:1179

Ezra Tull (*Dinner at the Homesick Restaurant*), **11**:1555, 1556, 1557

Faith Matheny (*Spoon River Anthology*), **7**:958

Fanny Bick (*Dubin's Lives*), **7**:924

Fanny Hamilton (*Sport of Gods*), **3**:410

Farrokh Daruwalla (*Son of the Circus*), **6**:771, 781

Fate Turner (*Child of God*), **7**:973

Father (*All the Pretty Horses*), **7**:969

Father ("Boys and Girls"), **8**:1082, 1083

Father ("Child Who Favored Daughter"), **11**:1580

Father (*Chocolate War*), **3**:302

Father (*Fade*), **3**:305

Father (*I Am the Cheese*), **3**:306, 307

Father (*Member of the Wedding*), **7**:988, 989

Father (*Rumble Fish*), 5:702

Father Grepilloux (*Surrounded*), 7:1003

Father Lucero (*Death Comes for the Archbishop*), 2:277, 280

Father Martinez (*Death Comes for the Archbishop*), 2:280

Fay McKelva (*Optimist's Daughter*), 12:1604, *1605*

Feather Boy bundle (*Wind from an Enemy Sky*), 7:1004, 1005

Fern Mullins (*Main Street*), 6:854

Ferret (*Great Gatsby*), 4:531

fiancé (*Frog Prince*), 7:974

financial advisor (*What I Lived For*), 8:1116

Fiona Moran (*Breathing Lessons*), 11:1554

First Corinthians Dead (*Song of Solomon*), 8:1068

First Lieutenant Jimmy Cross ("Things They Carried"), 8:1132

Fishel Kutner (*Family Moskat*), 10:1410, 1411

"F. Jasmine" (*Member of the Wedding*), 7:988

Fletcher (*Shane*), 10:1353, 1354

Fletcher McGee (*Spoon River Anthology*), 7:956-57

Flo (*Who Do You Think You Are?*), 8:1081, 1082

Flora (horse) ("Boys and Girls"), 8:1083

Florence Grimes (*Go Tell It on the Mountain*), 1:115-16

Flossie Stecher (*White Mule*), 12:*1691*

Fonny (*If Beale Street Could Talk*), 1:121

Foolish Magistrate (*Chinese Siamese Cat*), 11:1517

Foreman (*Beloved*), 8:1062

Fort Yukon (*White Fang*), 7:887

Four Knights (*Murder in Cathedral*), 4:445

Four Tempters (*Murder in Cathedral*), 4:445

"Frances" (*Member of the Wedding*), 7:989

Francis Macomber ("Short Happy Life of Francis Macomber"), 5:678, 679

Francis Oakley (*Sport of Gods*), 3:410

François (*Call of the Wild*), 7:884

Fran Dodsworth (*Dodsworth*), 6:*851*, 860

Frank ("Home to El Building"), 9:1190

Frank (*If Beale Street Could Talk*), 1:122

Frank (*O Pioneers!*), 2:284

Frank Algernon Cowperwood (*Financier*), 3:380, 392, 393

Frank Algernon Cowperwood (*Stoic*), 3:394-95

Frank Algernon Cowperwood (*Titan*), 3:392, 393, 394

Frank Alpine (*Assistant*), 7:917, 919-20

Frank Berry (*Hotel New Hampshire*), 6:777

Frankie Addams (*Member of the Wedding*), 7:980, 981, 982, 985, 988-89

Franklin Graff ("Just Before the War with the Eskimos"), 10:1321

Frank Tarwater (*Violent Bear It Away*), 8:1141, 1144, 1145

Franny Berry (*Hotel New Hampshire*), 6:771, 777, 778

Franny Glass ("Franny"), 10:1315-16

Franny Glass (Glass family stories), 10:1303, 1308, 1309

Franny Glass ("Raise High the Roof Beam, Carpenters"), 10:1318

Franny Glass ("Zooey"), 10:1316

Franz (*Price*), 8:1029

fraudulent minister ("Wild Swans"), 8:1076

Fred "Bogus" Trumper (*Water-Method Man*), 6:782

Fred Brent (*Uncalled*), 3:415, 416

Fred Daniels ("Man Who Lived Underground"), 12:1699, 1708

Frederic Henry (*Farewell to Arms*), 5:672-74, 675

Frederick Douglass (portrayed in *Manassas*), 10:1384

Freud (fictional) (*Hotel New Hampshire*), 6:777, 778

Frieda MacTeer (*Bluest Eye*), 8:1065, 1066

friend (*Revenge of the Space Pandas*), 7:944

Furies (*Oresteia*), 9:1179

Fuzzy Stone (*Cider House Rules*), 6:780

Gabriel Grimes (*Go Tell It on the Mountain*), 1:115, 116

Gabriel Prosser (portrayed in *Black Thunder*), 2:188, 190

Gail Hightower (*Light in August*), 4:497

Gaitlin family (*Patchwork Planet*), 11:1558-59

game warden (*Surrounded*), 7:1003

García sisters (*How the García Girls Lost Their Accents*), 1:31, 32

Garners (*Beloved*), 8:1060

Garnet French (*Lives of Girls and Women*), 8:1080

Garp (*World According to Garp*), 6:764, 771, 772, 778-79, 781

Gaylord Ravenal (*Show Boat*), 4:510

Gene Forrester (*Separate Peace*), 6:812, 814, 815-17

Gene Harrogate (*Suttree*), 7:972

General Cape (*Hundred Secret Senses*), 11:1517

General Golz (*For Whom the Bell Tolls*), 5:676

General Marvin (*Bell for Adano*), 5:688, 692

Gentleman Caller (*Glass Menagerie*), 12:*1661*, 1666

George ("Jilting of Granny Weatherall"), 9:1243

George Antrobus (*Skin of Our Teeth*), 12:1641, 1646

George Babbitt (*Babbitt*), 6:849, 855, 856, 857, 858, 9:1178

George Darrow (*Reef*), 12:1626

George Gibbs (*Our Town*), 12:1636, 1637, 1639, 1644, 1645

George Hurstwood (*Sister Carrie*), 3:379, 386, 389, 391, 392

George Milton (*Of Mice and Men*), 11:1450, 1460-61, 1462

George Murchison (*Raisin in Sun*), 5:654

George O'Kelly ("Sensible Thing"), 4:521

George Rayber (*Violent Bear It Away*), 8:1144, 1145

George Willard (*Winesburg, Ohio*), 1:52-53

George Wilson (*Great Gatsby*), 4:526, 531, 532

Geraldo (*Woman on the Edge of Time*), 9:1207

Gerhardt family (*Jennie Gerhardt*), 3:380, 386, *387*, 388

Gerty Farrish (*House of Mirth*), 12:1618

Ghost (ship) (*Sea-Wolf*), 7:889, 890

Gibbs family (*Our Town*), 12:*1636*, 1637, 1639, 1644, 1645

Gideon ("Strength of Gideon"), 3:411, 412

Gildina (*Woman on the Edge of Time*), 9:1208

Giles Revelstoke (*Mixture of Frailties*), 3:351

Ginnie Mannox ("Just Before the War with the Eskimos"), 10:1319, 1321

Gittel Mosca (*Two for the Seesaw*), 5:613, 621, 622, 623, 624

Gladys Antrobus (*Skin of Our Teeth*), 12:1639, 1641, 1646

Glass family (Glass family stories), 10:1303, 1304, 1305, 1308, 1315-18, 1319, 1321

Gloria (*Gone to Soldiers*), 9:1210

Gloria Gilbert (*Beautiful and Damned*), 4:536

Gloria Patch (*Beautiful and Damned*), 4:536

Gloster Ridley (*Leaven of Malice*), 3:347, 348

Gnomen Society (*Masters of Atlantis*), 9:1258

God (portrayed in *J.B.*), 7:903, 904, 905

God (portrayed in *Masque of Reason*), 4:573

Golda Meir (portrayed in *Golda*), 5:614, 615, 621, 624-26

Gooper Pollitt (*Cat on a Hot Tin Roof*), 12:1670

Gordon (*Paragon*), 6:817

Governor Dale ("Devil and Daniel Webster"), 2:157

Grace ("Sonny's Blues"), 1:118

Grace Liang (*Three Daughters of Madame Liang*), 2:231, 232

Grace Smeath (*Cat's Eye*), 1:97

Grace Strassner-Mendana (*Book of Common Prayer*), 3:372

Grady Fring (*Norwood*), 9:1258

Gramma and Grampa Joad (*Grapes of Wrath*), 11:1463

Granddaughter ("Witch's Husband"), 9:1191

Grandfather (*All the Pretty Horses*), 7:969

Grandfather (*Invisible Man*), 4:469

Grandfather ("Witch's Husband"), 9:1191

Grandfather's wife ("Witch's Husband"), 9:1191

Grandmother ("Boys and Girls"), 8:1082

Grandmother ("Good Man Is Hard to Find"), 8:1142, 1149-50

Grandmother ("Save the Reaper"), 8:1078

Granny Ellen Weatherall ("Jilting of Granny Weatherall"), 9:1236, 1242, 1243

Granny Rosa Millard (*Unvanquished*), 4:488, 489

Granny Vaughn (*Losing Battles*), 12:1602

Grant Wiggins (*Lesson Before Dying*), 5:593

Grendel (*Grendel*), 5:603-4

Gretchen (*Are You There God? It's Me, Margaret*), 2:172

Grey (*I Am the Cheese*), 3:306

Grimes Family (*Go Tell It on the Mountain*), 1:115, 116

Griselda Webster (*Tempest-Tost*), 3:350

Growltiger (*Old Possum's Book of Practical Cats*), 4:443

Grumby (*Unvanquished*), 4:488, 489

Guitar (*Song of Solomon*), 8:1066, 1067, 1068

Gus Trenor (*House of Mirth*), 12:1626

Guy Dupree (*Dog of the South*), 9:1249, 1254

Guy Pollack (*Main Street*), 6:854

Guzman (*Line of the Sun*), 9:1193

Hadass ("Yentl, the Yeshiva Boy"), 10:1405

Hadassah Moskat (*Family Moskat*), 10:1409, 1410

Hagar (*Song of Solomon*), 8:1066, 1067

Hagar Shipley (*Stone Angel*), 6:831

Haiml Chentshiner (*Shosha*), 10:1413

Halle (*Beloved*), 8:1056

Halliday ("One Man's Fortune"), 3:412

Hama Moskat Shapiro (*Family Moskat*), 10:1409

Hamilton family (*Sport of Gods*), 3:410

Hamlet (*Hamlet*), 7:905, 9:1256

Hannah Armstrong ("Hannah Armstrong"), 7:957

Hannah Jelkes (*Night of the Iguana*), 12:1657, 1673

Hannes Graff (*Setting Free the Bears*), 6:781

Hanratty, Ontario (*Who Do You Think You Are?*), 8:1077, 1081, 1082

Happy Loman (*Death of a Salesman*), 8:1019, 1026, 1027, 1028

Hapsy ("Jilting of Granny Weatherall"), 9:1243

Harcourt-Reilly (*Cocktail Party*), 4:448

Harold Vilitzer (*More Die of Heartbreak*), 1:140

Harpo (*Color Purple*), 11:1574

Harran Derrick (*Octopus*), 8:1098

Harriet Stone ("Neighbors"), 2:265

Harry (*Harry and Hortense at Hormone High*), 12:1724

Harry (*Lie Down in Darkness*), 11:1503

Harry (*Snows of Kilimanjaro*), 5:679

Harry Hope (*Iceman Cometh*), 9:1173, 1174

Harry Lesser (*Tenants*), 7:925

Hatsuyo Nakamura (*Hiroshima*), 5:693

Hattie Downlier (*Elmer Gantry*), 6:859

Hattie Sterling (*Sport of Gods*), 3:410

Hawl Hungerfield ("Hungerfield"), 6:795, 796

Hazel Motes (*Wise Blood*), 8:1141, 1145, 1146-47

Hazel Motes's grandfather (*Wise Blood*), 8:1146

Hazel Motes's mother (*Wise Blood*), 8:1147

Heart's Haven (*Cider House Rules*), 6:775

Heart's Rock (*Cider House Rules*), 6:775

Heavenly Finley (*Sweet Bird of Youth*), 12:1672, 1673

Heckler (*Sweet Bird of Youth*), 12:1673

Heck Tate (*To Kill a Mockingbird*), 6:838, 840, 841

Hector Mackilwraith (*Tempest-Tost*), 3:349-50

Hedda Gabler (*Hedda Gabler*), 9:1165

heifer ("Yearning Heifer"), 10:1414

Helen (*Lie Down in Darkness*), 11:1502, 1503

Helen ("Peace of Utrecht"), 8:1083

Helen (*Snows of Kilimanjaro*), 5:679

Helen (*World According to Garp*), 6:778, 779

Helen Bober (*Assistant*), **7**:920

Helene (*Play It as It Lays*), **3**:365, 366

Helen Keller (portrayed in *Miracle Worker*), **5**:611, 613, 614, 615, 616-17, 618, 619-20

Henri Philippe Pétain (portrayed in Lanny Budd series), **10**:1396

Henry and Sarah Shephard (*Poor White*), **1**:49-50

Henry Antrobus (*Skin of Our Teeth*), **12**:1646

Henry Cassavant (*Tunes for Bears to Dance To*), **3**:309

Henry Fleming (*Red Badge of Courage*), **8**:1124

Henry Jim (*Wind from an Enemy Sky*), **7**:999, 1004

Henry L. Palmetto (*Great Gatsby*), **4**:531

Henry Ossawa Tanner, *Banjo Lesson, The*, **2**:182

Henry Soames (*Nickel Mountain*), **5**:608

Henry Van Weyden (*Se-Wolf*), **7**:889, 890

Henry Victor (*Democracy*), **3**:372

Herb Clutter (*In Cold Blood*), **2**:237, 248

Hernán Cortés (portrayed in *Conquistador*), **7**:900

Heroes (Cormier), **3**:299, 301

Herr Freytag (*Ship of Fools*), **9**:1239

Herr Rieber (*Ship of Fools*), **9**:1240

Hertz Grein (*Shadows on the Hudson*), **10**:1399, 1404

Hertz Yanovar (*Family Moskat*), **10**:1412

Hester (*Uncalled*), **3**:415

Hickey (*Iceman Cometh*), **9**:1171, 1173-74, 1175

High Prairie (*So Big*), **4**:511, 512

hired man ("Boys and Girls"), **8**:1083

Hirsch College (*Chosen*), **9**:1269

Hirsch University (*Promise*), **9**:1272

Hochschwinder (*Peace Breaks Out*), **6**:813, 814

Hodel ("Gentleman from Cracow"), **10**:1414

Hodge family (*Sunlight Dialogues*), **5**:607

Holden Caulfield (*Catcher in the Rye*), **10**:1302, 1305, 1307, 1308, 1309, 1314-15

Holden Caulfield ("I'm Crazy"), **10**:1303

Holden Caulfield ("Slight Rebellion off Madison"), **10**:1303

Holga (*After the Fall*), **8**:1028

Holly Golightly (*Breakfast at Tiffany's*), **2**:237, 239, 244

Homer Wells (*Cider House Rules*), **6**:771, 774, 775, 782

Homesick Restaurant (*Dinner at the Homesick Restaurant*), **11**:1556

Hooven (*Octopus*), **8**:1098

Hoover Shoats (*Wise Blood*), **8**:1141, 1147

Horace Robedaux (Orphans' Home cycle), **4**:553

Hornbeams (*Great Gatsby*), **4**:531

Hortense (*Harry and Hortense at Hormone High*), **12**:1724

Howard (*Death of a Salesman*), **8**:1026, 1027

Hrothgar (*Grendel*), **5**:603, 604

Hugh McVey (*Poor White*), **1**:49-51

Humphrey Cobbler (*Leaven of Malice*), **3**:348

Hungerfield's son ("Hungerfield"), **6**:795

Hurstwood's wife (*Sister Carrie*), **3**:389

Husband ("Home Burial"), **4**:563

Husband ("Long Black Song"), **12**:1707

Husband ("Yearning Heifer"), **10**:1414

Hwangs (*Good Earth*), **2**:224

Icy (*Bad Girls*), **8**:1117

Ida (*Another Country*), **1**:120

Ida ("Previous Condition"), **1**:122

Ida M'Toy (Welty), **12**:1596

Ilana Davita Chandal (*Davita's Harp*), **9**:1267

Inez Victor (*Democracy*), **3**:361, 372

Ingrid Boone (*Man Crazy*), **8**:1109

Ira Moran (*Breathing Lessons*), **11**:1554, 1555

Iris Brustein (*Sign in Sidney Brustein's Window*), **5**:656

Iris Lemon (*Natural*), **7**:922, 923

Isabel (Simple columns), **6**:736

Isabelle Borgé (*This Side of Paradise*), **4**:535

Jabez Stone ("Devil and Daniel Webster"), **2**:157

Jack Duane (*Jungle*), **10**:1393

Jack Lovett (*Democracy*), **3**:372

Jack Pepper ("Handcarved Coffins"), **2**:252

Jack Renfro (*Losing Battles*), **12**:1602, 1603

Jackson (*Catherine Cormier*), **5**:593, 594

Jack Wilkie (*Dog of the South*), **9**:1254

Jacob Kahn (*Gift of Asher Lev*), **9**:1267, 1274

Jacob Kahn (*My Name Is Asher Lev*), **9**:1267, 1270, 1272

Jacob Levine (*Tunes for Bears to Dance To*), **3**:309

Jacob Stein ("Jacob and the Indians"), **2**:160-61

Jacqueline (*Gone to Soldiers*), **9**:1210

Jadine (*Tar Baby*), **8**:1070

Jaime (*Bridge of San Luis Rey*), **12**:1643-44

Jake Barnes (*Sun Also Rises*), **5**:668, 675, 677, 678

Jake Blount (*Heart Is a Lonely Hunter*), **7**:982, 987

Jake Hanlon (*Mavericks*), **10**:1349, 1355-56

Jake Simms (*Earthly Possessions*), **11**:1558

J. Alfred Prufrock ("Love Song of J. Alfred Prufrock"), **4**:442

James Chandler (*Resurrection*), **5**:609

James (Jamie) Tyrone, Jr. (*Long Day's Journey into Night*), **9**:1172, 1175, 1176, 1177

James McDermott (*Alias Grace*), **1**:91

James Page (*October Light*), **5**:604, 605, 606

James Tyrone (*Long Day's Journey into Night*), **9**:1172, 1175, 1176-77

Jamie Collins (*Tex*), **5**:702, 713

Jane Brown (*Autobiography of Miss Jane Pittman*), **5**:590

Jane Eyre (*Jane Eyre*), **6**:775

Jane Gallagher (*Catcher in the Rye*), **10**:1314

Jane Jerome (*We All Fall Down*), **3**:309, 310

Jane Pittman (*Autobiography of Miss Jane Pittman*), **5**:588, 590-91

Janice Evans (*Member of the Wedding*), **7**:988

Janie Crawford (*Their Eyes Were Watching God*), **6**:750-51, 752, 756-57, 758, 759

Janie's grandmother (*Their Eyes Were Watching God*), **6**:751, 756, 758

Jared Heath (*Company of Cowards*), **10**:1349, 1355

J. Arnold (Bunny) Ross, Jr. (*Oil!*), **10**:1394-95

J. Arnold (Dad) Ross (*Oil!*), **10**:1394, 1395

Jarvis Addams (*Member of the Wedding*), **7**:988

Jason (*Medea*), **6**:801

Jason Compson (*Sound and Fury*), **4**:483, 493, 494, 495

Jason Rohr (*Harry and Hortense at Hormone High*), **12**:1724, 1725

Jason Rohr's aunt (*Harry and Hortense at Hormone High*), **12**:1724

Jay (*Death in the Family, A*), **1**:18-19, 20

Jay Gatsby (Jay Gatz) (*Great Gatsby*), **4**:523, 526, 527, 528, 529, 530, 531, 532, 534

J.B. (*J.B.*), **7**:903-5

Jean Louise (Scout) Finch (*To Kill a Mockingbird*). *See* Scout Finch

Jean Marie Latour (*Death Comes for the Archbishop*), **2**:276-77, 278, 279, 280-81

Jeannot (*Morning in Antibes*), **6**:810, 811

Jeff (*Gone to Soldiers*), **9**:1210

Jeff Campbell ("Melanctha"), **10**:1438

Jefferson (*Lesson Before Dying*), **5**:592-93

Jefferson Davis (portrayed in *Manassas*), **10**:1384

Jeff Patton ("Summer Tragedy, A"), **2**:193-94

Jellicles (*Old Possum's Book of Practical Cats*), **4**:443

Jem (Jeremy) Finch (*To Kill a Mockingbird*), **6**:837, 838, 839, 840

Jem (*To Kill a Mockingbird*), **4**:551

Jennie Patton ("Summer Tragedy, A"), **2**:193-94

Jennie Gerhardt (*Jennie Gerhardt*), **3**:380, 386, 387, 388

Jenny Brown (*Ship of Fools*), **9**:1239, 1240

Jenny Fields (*World According to Garp*), **6**:778, 779

Jenny Tull (*Dinner at the Homesick Restaurant*), **11**:1555, 1557

Jeremiah (*Alias Grace*), **1**:91

Jeremiah Cobb (*Confessions of Nat Turner*), **11**:1498

Jeremy Pauling (*Celestial Navigation*), **11**:1557, 1558

Jeremy Pauling's mother (*Celestial Navigation*), **11**:1557

Jerome "Corky" Corcoran (*What I Lived For*), **8**:1115, 1116

Jerry Benson (*New Spoon River*), **7**:956

Jerry Renault (*Chocolate War*), **3**:302, 303, 304

Jerry Ryan (*Two for the Seesaw*), **5**:613, 621-22, 623

Jesse Bel (*Masque of Mercy*), **4**:572

Jesse B. Semple. *See* Simple

Jesse James (portrayed in *Book of Americans*), **2**:154

Jesse Moran (*Breathing Lessons*), **11**:1554, 1555

Jessie Victor (*Democracy*), **3**:360

Jester (*Clock Without Hands*), **7**:990

Jesus Fever (*Other Voices, Other Rooms*), **2**:252

Jesus Maria (*Tortilla Flat*), **11**:1460

Jethro (*Moses, Man of the Mountain*), **6**:761

Jevon Knapp (*Leaven of Malice*), **3**:347

Jewel Bundren (*As I Lay Dying*), **4**:490, 491

Jill Brenner (*Blubber*), **2**:173, 174

Jim ("Jimsella"), **3**:415

Jim (*Small Changes*), **9**:1210-11

Jim Casy (*Grapes of Wrath*), **11**:1455, 1463, 1464

Jimmie Burns (*Gringos*), **9**:1250, 1251, 1256-57

Jimmie Dunn (Schaefer fictional horse), **10**:1355

Jimmy (*Nickel Mountain*), **5**:608

Jimmy Aaron (*Autobiography of Miss Jane Pittman*), **5**:591

Jim O'Connor (the Gentleman Caller) (*Glass Menagerie*), **12**:*1661*, 1666

Jimsella ("Jimsella"), **3**:415

Jim Stone ("Neighbors"), **2**:265

Jing-mei (June) Woo (*Joy Luck Club*), **11**:1511, 1514

Joad family (*Grapes of Wrath*), **11**:1450, 1453, 1462, 1463

Joan Foster (*Lady Oracle*), **1**:95

Joanna Burden (*Light in August*), **4**:497

Joaquin ("Dear Joaquin"), **9**:1191-92

Job (*Masque of Reason*), **4**:573

Jock (*Roast Beef Medium*), **4**:513

Jody Tiflin ("Gift"), **11**:1464, 1465

Jody Tiflin ("Great Mountains"), **11**:1465

Jody Tiflin ("Promise"), **11**:1465

Jody Tiflin (*Red Pony*), **11**:1453

Joe (*East of Eden*), **11**:1466

Joe (*Taming Star Runner*), **5**:715

Joe Christmas (*Light in August*), **4**:484, 497

Joe Hamilton (*Sport of Gods*), **3**:410

Joe Keller (*All My Sons*), **8**:1017, 1019, 1021-22

Joel Harrison Knox (*Other Voices, Other Rooms*), **2**:252

Joel Hoober (*Then Again, Maybe I Won't*), **2**:179-80

Joel Moskat (*Family Moskat*), **10**:1409

Joe Mott (*Iceman Cometh*), **9**:1173

Joe Pittman (*Autobiography of Miss Jane Pittman*), **5**:591

Joe Randall (*Boston*), **10**:1391

Joe Ross (*Spanish Prisoner*), **7**:941, 942

Joe Starks (*Their Eyes Were Watching God*), **6**:750, 756, 758

Joe Starrett (*Shane*), **10**:1353-54

Joe Trace (*Jazz*), **8**:1068

Johanna von Haller (*Manticore*), **3**:350

John (*Cryptogram*), **7**:942, 943

John ("Housekeeper"), **4**:563

John (*Mules and Men*), **6**:753

John (*Oleanna*), **7**:943

John (*Pigman*), **12**:1721, 1722-23, 1724

John Allen (*Spoon River Anthology*), **7**:957

John Ashley (*Eighth Day*), **12**:1649

John Bergson (*O Pioneers!*), **2**:275, 281, 282

John Berry (*Hotel New Hampshire*), **6**:777, 778

John Brown (portrayed in *John Brown's Body*), **2**:153-54, 158-59

John Brown (portrayed in *Manassas*), **10**:1084

John Cunningham (*Iron Heel*), **7**:888, 889

John Dorman (*Gift of Asher Lev*), **9**:1274

John Grady Cole (*All the Pretty Horses*), **7**:969

John Grimes (*Go Tell It on the Mountain*), **1**:*115*, 116

John Henry (*Member of the Wedding*), **7**:988, 989

John Horne (*Resurrection*), **5**:609

John James Audubon (portrayed in *Book of Americans*), **2**:154

John M. Church (*Spoon River Anthology*), **7**:958

Johnnie Kestoe (*This Side Jordan*), **6**:829, 830

Johnny ("Roan Stallion"), **6**:796, 797

Johnny Cade (*Outsiders*), **5**:706, 710, 711

Johnny Collins (*Tex*), **5**:702, 713

John Pearson (*Jonah's Gourd Vine*), **6**:760, 761

John Proctor (*Crucible*), **8**:1023-24

John Selmer Dix (*Dog of the South*), **9**:1254

John Singer (*Heart Is a Lonely Hunter*), **7**:982, 986-87

John Smeet ("Devil and Daniel Webster"), **2**:157

John Sung (*Three Daughters of Madame Liang*), **2**:231, 232

John Thornton (*Call of the Wild*), **7**:884, 885

John Vilas (*John Brown's Body*), **2**:159

John Wade (*In the Lake of the Woods*), **8**:1130, 1131, 1133

John Weatherall ("Jilting of Granny Weatherall"), **9**:1243

John Webster (*Many Marriages*), **1**:55-56

John Wesley Rattner (*Orchard Keeper*), **7**:973

Jolly Seventeen (*Main Street*), **6**:854

Jonas Dove (*Masque of Mercy*), **4**:572

Jonathan (*Townsman*), **2**:228

Jonathan Upchurch ("King's Indian"), **5**:608

Jonathan Upchurch (*King's Indian Stories and Tales*), **5**:601

Jonquil Cary ("Sensible Thing"), **4**:521

Jordan Baker (*Great Gatsby*), **4**:526, 531, 532

Joseph (*Butterfingers Angel, Mary and Joseph...*), **5**:626

Joseph Asagai (*Raisin in Sun*), **5**:651, 654

Joseph Lane (*Mrs. Reynolds*), **10**:1437

Joseph Vaillant (*Death Comes for the Archbishop*), **2**:277, 278, 280

Joshua Leckler ("Ingrate"), **3**:411, 413

Josiah Thornwell (*Boston*), **10**:1390

Josie Hogan (*Moon for the Misbegotten*), **9**:1172, *1178*, *1179*

Joyce (Simple columns), **6**:736

Joyce Lanyon (*Arrowsmith*), **6**:858

Joy Liang (*Three Daughters of Madame Liang*), **2**:231-32

J. T. Malone (*Clock Without Hands*), **7**:990, 991

Juanita (*Blues for Mr. Charlie*), **1**:114

Juan Villegas ("María Concepción"), **9**:1243

Judge Barney Dolphin (*Ann Vickers*), **6**:861

Judge Cool (*Grass Harp*), **2**:245, 246, 247

Judge Fox Clane (*Clock Without Hands*), **7**:990-91

Judge Hathorne ("Devil and Daniel Webster"), **2**:157

Judge Holden (*Blood Meridian*), **7**:970, 971

Judge McKelva (*Optimist's Daughter*), **12**:1598, 1604

Judge Moody (*Losing Battles*), **12**:1598, 1602, 1603

Judge Moody's wife (*Losing Battles*), **12**:1603

Judge Parker (*True Grit*), **9**:1255

Judy (*Townsman*), **2**:228

Jules ("Previous Condition"), **1**:122

Jules Wendell (*them*), **8**:1114

Julian Chestny ("Everything That Rises Must Converge"), **8**:1148, 1149

Julia Shuttlethwaite (*Cocktail Party*), **4**:448

Julie Dozier (*Show Boat*), **4**:511

June (*This Proud Heart*), **2**:230

June Herzog (*Herzog*), **1**:135

junk dealer (*Price*), **8**:*1029*, 1031

Jurgis Rudkus (*Jungle*), **10**:1379, 1391-92, 1393, 1396

Justine Peck (*Searching for Caleb*), **11**:1559, 1560

Justin Peck (*Searching for Caleb*), **11**:1559

Karen Newman (*It's Not the End of the World*), **2**:178

Kate (*Play It as It Lays*), **3**:365

Kate Keller (*All My Sons*), **8**:1022

Kate Keller (*Miracle Worker*), **5**:618, 619

Katharine Gaylord ("Death in the Desert"), **2**:275

Katherine Danziger (*Forever...*), **2**:174, 176

Kathleen Moore (*Last Tycoon*), **4**:536

Kathy Wade (*In the Lake of the Woods*), **8**:1126, 1129, 1130, 1131

Katie (*Townsman*), **2**:228

Keeper (*Masque of Mercy*), **4**:572

Kelly Kelleher (*Black Water*), **8**:1117, 1118

Ken (*Indian Summer*), **6**:817

Kenneth Trachtenberg (*More Die of Heartbreak*), **1**:140, 141

Kenny Matoa ("Matoa's Mirror"), **9**:1190

Ketey Miri ("Gentleman from Cracow"), **10**:1414

Kid, the (*Blood Meridian*), **7**:970, 971

Kim Ravenal (*Show Boat*), **4**:510

king (*Medea*), **6**:801

King MacLain (*Golden Apples*), **12**:1601, 1602

King MacLain's twin boys (*Golden Apples*), **12**:1601, 1602

King Philip (portrayed in "Devil and Daniel Webster"), **2**:157

Kino (*Pearl*), **11**:1465-66

Kino's son (*Pearl*), **11**:1465

Kiowa ("Things They Carried"), **8**:1132

Kit Brandon (*Kit Brandon*), **1**:55

Kitty Hamilton (*Sport of Gods*), **3**:410

Kiyoshi Tanimoto (*Hiroshima*), **5**:693

Knowlt Hoheimer (*Spoon River Anthology*), **7**:957

Koppel Berman (*Family Moskat*), **10**:1409, 1410

Kubachin (*Marco Millions*), **9**:1178

Kwan (*Hundred Secret Senses*), **11**:1511, 1512, 1515, 1517

La Condesa (*Ship of Fools*), **9**:1239, 1240

Ladover Hasidim (*My Name Is Asher Lev*), **9**:1270

Lady Caroline Sibley-Biers (*Tender Is the Night*), **4**:534

Lafayette Resnick (*Ann Vickers*), **6**:861

Lafe ("Hundred Collars"), **4**:563

Lamar Jimmerson (*Masters of Atlantis*), **9**:1250, 1257-58

Lane Coutell ("Franny"), **10**:1315, 1316

Lanny Budd (Lanny Budd series), **10**:1395-96

Lansing family (*Eighth Day*), **12**:1649

large black woman ("Everything That Rises Must Converge"), **8**:1148

large black woman's young son ("Everything That Rises Must Converge"), **8**:1148

Larry (*The Robber Bride*), **1**:99

Larry Keller (*All My Sons*), **8**:1017, 1019, 1022

Larry Slade (*Iceman Cometh*), **9**:1173, 1174, 1175

Laura ("Flowering Judas"), **9**:1236, 1241

Laura (*Townsman*), **2**:228

Laura ("What We Talk About When We Talk About Love"), **2**:266

Laura Danker (*Are You There God? It's Me, Margaret*), **2**:171-72

Laura Dearborn (*Pit*), **8**:1098-1101

Laura Pottinger (*Mixture of Frailties*), **3**:351

Laura Wingfield (*Glass Menagerie*), **12**:1656, *1661*, 1664, 1666

Laurel McKelva Hand (*Optimist's Daughter*), **12**:1598, 1604, 1607

Lavinia Mannon (*Mourning Becomes Electra*), **9**:1179

Lawrence Selden (*House of Mirth*), **12**:1626

Lawyer Royall (*Summer*), **12**:1628

Lazarus (*Lazarus Laughed*), **9**:1165

Leah Moskat Margolis Berman (*Family Moskat*), **10**:1409, 1410

Leary family (*Accidental Tourist*), **11**:1548

LeBoeuf (*True Grit*), **9**:1255

Lee Cauldwell ("Tamar"), **6**:798, 799

Legwater (*Orchard Keeper*), **7**:973

Lem (*Tex*), **5**:713

Lena ("Gentle Lena"), **10**:1438

Lena Grove (*Light in August*), **4**:497

Lena's aunt ("Gentle Lena"), **10**:1438

Lena Younger (*Raisin in Sun*), **5**:653, 654, 655

Lennie Small (*Of Mice and Men*), **11**:1450, 1460-61, 1462

Leonard Westerfield (*Tide of Time*), **7**:959

Leonora Penderton (*Reflections in a Golden Eye*), **7**:991

Leopold Bloom (*Ulysses*), **7**:971

Leora Arrowsmith (*Arrowsmith*), **6**:858

Leota ("Petrified Man"), **12**:1608, 1609

Leroy Moran (*Breathing Lessons*), **11**:1554, 1555

Leslie Lynton (*Giant*), **4**:512, 513

Lester Ballard (*Child of God*), **7**:973

Lester Kane (*Jennie Gerhardt*), **3**:388

Letty (*Jennie Gerhardt*), **3**:388

Levene (*Glengarry Glen Ross*), **7**:940

Lieutenant Sidney Martin (*Going After Cacciato*), **8**:1129

Lillian Semple (*Financier*), **3**:392

Lillian Semple (*Titan*), **3**:392

Lily Bart (*House of Mirth*), **12**:1618, 1622-23, 1625-26

Lily Bart's aunt (*House of Mirth*), **12**:1625, 1626

Lily Berry (*Hotel New Hampshire*), **6**:777, 778

Lily Dale Kidder (*Young Man from Atlanta*), **4**:553

Lily McClellan (*Run River*), **3**:361

Lincoln West ("Life of Lincoln West"), **2**:207

Linda ("Lives of the Dead"), **8**:1132

Linda Fischer (*Blubber*), **2**:173-74

Linda Loman (*Death of a Salesman*), **8**:1026, 1027, 1028

Lindo Jong (*Joy Luck Club*), **11**:1511

Lindo Jong ("Red Candle"), **11**:1514

Lionel Tannenbaum ("Down at the Dinghy"), **10**:*1320*, 1321

Lionel Tannenbaum's father ("Down at the Dinghy"), **10**:*1320*, 1321

listener ("Idea of Order at Key West"), **11**:1483

Little Augie (*God Sends Sunday*), **2**:193

Little Bear (*Canyon*), **10**:1348, 1349, 1355

little brother ("Boys and Girls"), **8**:1082, 1083

Little Elk people (*Wind from an Enemy Sky*), **7**:999, 1004, 1005

Little Sunshine (*Other Voices, Other Rooms*), **2**:252

"Livvie" (Welty), **12**:1592

Liz (*My Darling, My Hamburger*), **12**:1725

Liz's mother (*My Darling, My Hamburger*), **12**:1725

Liz's stepfather (*My Darling, My Hamburger*), **12**:1725

Lloyd Searight (*Man's Woman*), **8**:1093, 1101, 1102

Loch Morrison ("Moon Lake"), **12**:1601

Logan Killicks (*Their Eyes Were Watching God*), **6**:756

Loman family (*Death of a Salesman*), **8**:*1015*, 1019, 1025-28

Loren ("Blueberries"), **4**:563

Loretta Wendell (*them*), **8**:1114

Loretta Wendell's brother (*them*), **8**:1114

Loretta Wendell's second husband (*them*), **8**:1114

Lori Cranston (*Tenderness*), **3**:308

Lorna Sue (*Tomcat in Love*), **8**:1134

Lorraine (*Pigman*), **12**:1721, 1722-23, 1724

Lorraine's mother (*Pigman*), **12**:1723

Lottie (*Girls*), **4**:513

Lottie Stecher (*White Mule*), **12**:*1691*

Lotus (*Good Earth*), **2**:220, 222, 224

Lou and Oscar Bergson (*O Pioneers!*), **2**:275, 278, 281, 282, 284

Lou Colfax (*Paragon*), **6**:810, 811, 817-18

Louise (*After the Fall*), **8**:1028

Louise (*Gone to Soldiers*), **9**:1209-10

Louise Kurle (*Gringos*), **9**:1257

Louis Leon (*Surrounded*), **7**:1003

Lucas Beauchamp (*Intruder in Dust*), **4**:484

Lucas Burch (*Light in August*), **4**:497

Lucien Lacamp (*Gift of Asher Lev*), **9**:1274

Luciente (*Woman on the Edge of Time*), **9**:1207, 1208, 1209

Lucille Lusk (*New Spoon River*), **7**:956

Lucius Atherton (*Spoon River Anthology*), **7**:956

Lucius Harney (*Summer*), **12**:1628

Lucy Potts (*Jonah's Gourd Vine*), **6**:761

Lucy Weatherby (*John Brown's Body*), **2**:159

Ludie Brooks (Foote; teleplay), **4**:547

Luke (*Amen Corner*), **1**:111, 113

Luster (*Sound and Fury*), **4**:494

Luz (*Giant*), **4**:512-13

Lycurgus (*American Tragedy*), **3**:386

Lykourgos (*Wreckage of Agathon*), **5**:609

Lyle Britten (*Blues for Mr. Charlie*), **1**:114

Lyman Derrick (*Octopus*), **8**:1093, 1098

Lymon Willis (*Ballad of the Sad Café*), **7**:981, 984, 985, 986

M&M (*That Was Then, This Is Now*), **5**:717

Macavity (*Old Possum's Book of Practical Cats*), **4**:443

Macbeth (*Macbeth*), **10**:1371

Macduff (*Macbeth*), **10**:1371

MacLain house ("June Recital"), **12**:1602

Macon Dead (grandfather) (*Song of Solomon*), **8**:1068

Macon Dead (grandson) (*Song of Solomon*), **8**:1066, 1067, 1068

Macon Leary (*Accidental Tourist*), **11**:1550, 1551, 1552

Mac Sledge (*Tender Mercies*), **4**:549, 550

Madame Bovary (*Madame Bovary*), **10**:1406

Maddy ("Peace of Utrecht"), **8**:1083, 1084

Madeleine Herzog (*Herzog*), **1**:134, 135

"Mad Mark" (*If I Die in a Combat Zone, Box Me Up and Ship Me Home*), **8**:1133

Mae Pollitt (*Cat on a Hot Tin Roof*), **12**:1670

Magdalena Dead (*Song of Solomon*), **8**:1068

Maggie (*After the Fall*), **8**:1028

Maggie ("Everyday Use"), **11**:1579

Maggie (*My Darling, My Hamburger*), **12**:1725

Maggie Antrobus (*Skin of Our Teeth*), **12**:1641, 1646

Maggie Moran (*Breathing Lessons*), **11**:1554-55

Maggie Pollitt (*Cat on a Hot Tin Roof*), **12**:1669, 1670

Magician (*Magician of Lublin*) (film), **10**:1405

Magnolia Hawkes Ravenal (*Show Boat*), **4**:509, 510

Magnus Derrick (*Octopus*), **8**:1093, 1098

Magnus Eisengrim (*Manticore*), **3**:350

Ma Joad (*Grapes of Wrath*), **11**:1455

Major Callicles (*If I Die in a Combat Zone, Box Me Up and Ship Me Home*), **8**:1133

Major Con Melody (*Tale of Possessors Self-Dispossessed* cycle), **9**:1166

Major Morris Langdon (*Reflections in a Golden Eye*), **7**:991

Major Victor Joppolo (*Bell for Adano*), **5**:688, 691, 692, 695, 696

Malachi the waiter (*Matchmaker*), **12**:1649

Mame ("Blueberries"), **4**:563

Mandy ("Jimsella"), **3**:415

Manischevitz ("Angel Levine"), **7**:924

Manuel (*Bridge of San Luis Rey*), **12**:1643

Manyek Berman (*Family Moskat*), **10**:1409

"Many Hats" (Sandburg), **10**:1339

Mao Zedong (portrayed in Lanny Budd series), **10**:1396

Marco (*Marco Millions*), **9**:1178

Marco (*View from the Bridge*), **8**:1031

Marcus Schouler (*McTeague*), **8**:1095, 1096

Margaret Rose (*Searching for Caleb*), **11**:1559

Margaret Simon (*Are You There God? It's Me, Margaret*), **2**:170, 171-72

Margaret Whitehead (*Confessions of Nat Turner*), **11**:1498, 1500

Margot Macomber ("Short Happy Life of Francis Macomber"), **5**:678, 679

Maria (*For Whom the Bell Tolls*), **5**:675, 676

María Concepción ("María Concepción"), **9**:1243

Maria Macapa (*McTeague*), **8**:1096

Marian ("Will You Please Be Quiet, Please?"), **2**:267-68

Marian Kestoe (*This Side Jordan*), **6**:830

María Rosa ("María Concepción"), **9**:1243

Maria Wyeth (*Play It as It Lays*), **3**:260, 359, 361, 364-66, 371

Maricela ("Job for Valentin"), **9**:1187

Marie (*O Pioneers!*), **2**:284

Marietta (*Bad Girls*), **8**:1116-17

Marija (*Jungle*), **10**:1393

Marion Sylder (*Orchard Keeper*), **7**:973

Marisol (*Line of the Sun*), **9**:1186, 1193

Marisol's mother (*Line of the Sun*), **9**:1193

Marita (*Garden of Eden*), **5**:671

Mark (*Paragon*), **6**:817

Mark Berquist (*Last Thing He Wanted*), **3**:373

Mark the "Lion" (*That Was Then, This Is Now*), **5**:716, 718

Marquesa de Montemayor (*Bridge of San Luis Rey*), **12**:1643

Marsh (*Pardon Me, You're Stepping on My Eyeball!*), **12**:1715

Marshall (*Gathering of Old Men*), **5**:592

Marsh's father (*Pardon Me, You're Stepping on My Eyeball!*), **12**:1715

Martha ("Strength of Gideon"), **3**:411

Martha Hersland (*Making of Americans*), **10**:1432

Martin Arrowsmith (*Arrowsmith*), **6**:852, 857, 858

Martine (*Patchwork Planet*), **11**:1559

Martin Eden (*Martin Eden*), **7**:877, 885, 886

Marvin Macy (*Ballad of the Sad Café*), **7**:982, 984, 985, 986

Mary (*Alias Grace*), **1**:91

Mary (*Butterfingers Angel, Mary and Joseph...*), **5**:614, 621, 626

Mary (*Death in the Family*), **1**:18-19

Mary ("Death of the Hired Man"), **4**:563, 569

Mary Abrams (*Tender Is the Night*), **4**:534

Marya Knauer (*Marya: A Life*), **8**:1109

Mary Bates (*Hotel New Hampshire*), **6**:777

Mary Dalton (*Native Son*), **12**:1704

Mary Dempster (*Fifth Business*), **3**:345-47

Mary Ellen/Maria Elenita (*Year of Our Revolution*), **9**:1194

Maryginia Washington ("kitchenette folks"), **2**:207

Mary North Minghetti (*Tender Is the Night*), **4**:534

Mary Tell (*Celestial Navigation*), **11**:1557, 1558

Mary Tyrone (*Long Day's Journey into Night*), **9**:1172, 1175, 1176, 1177

Masakazu Fujii (*Hiroshima*), **5**:693

Mason McCormick (*Tex*), **5**:702, 709, 710, 712, 713

Mason Tarwater (*Violent Bear It Away*), **8**:1144, 1145

Matilda Layamon (*More Die of Heartbreak*), **1**:140

matron of honor ("Raise High the Roof Beam, Carpenters"), **10**:1317

Matthew Snellgrove (*Leaven of Malice*), **3**:347

Mattie Ross (*True Grit*), **9**:1250, 1251, 1255-56

Mattie Silver (*Ethan Frome*), **12**:1624, 1628

Maud Brewster (*Sea-Wolf*), **7**:889

Maudie (*Lie Down in Darkness*), **11**:1502, 1503

Maud Martha (*Maud Martha*), **2**:207

Maureen (*them*), **8**:1114

Maurice Oakley (*Sport of Gods*), **3**:410

Max Epperson (*Last Thing He Wanted*), **3**:373

Max Gottlieb (*Arrowsmith*), **6**:857

Maxine Faulk (*Night of the Iguana*), **12**:1673

Max Leon (*Surrounded*), **7**:999, 1002

Max Lobe (*Gift of Asher Lev*), **9**:1274

Max Lurie (*In the Beginning*), **9**:1266

Mayella Ewell (*To Kill a Mockingbird*), **4**:551, **6**:838, 840

Mayella's father (*To Kill a Mockingbird*), **4**:551

May Welland (*Age of Innocence*), **12**:1621, 1622

McCampbell ("Jacob and the Indians"), **2**:160

McCaslin family (*Go Down, Moses*), **4**:497

McMahons (*Last Thing he Wanted*), **3**:372-73

McTeague (*McTeague*), **8**:1093, 1094-96, 1097, 1101

Medea (*Medea*), **6**:788, 801

Meg Peck (*Searching for Caleb*), **11**:1560

Mel ("What We Talk About When We Talk About Love"), **2**:266-67

Melanctha ("Melanctha"), **10**:1438

Melinda Cowling (*Nuclear Age*), **8**:1133

Melissa (*What I Lived For*), **8**:1116

Melody (*Black Thunder*), **2**:190

Melora Vilas (*John Brown's Body*), **2**:159

Memo Paris (*Natural*), **7**:922, 923

Mercy Sung (*Three Daughters of Madame Liang*), **2**:231, 232

Meridian Henry (*Blues for Mr. Charlie*), **1**:114

Meridian Hill (*Meridian*), **11**:1581

Meridian Hill's mother (*Meridian*), **11**:1581

Meyer Wolfsheim (*Great Gatsby*), **4**:526, 531

Michael Fane ("Romantic Egoist"), **4**:525

Michael Gordon (*Promise*), **9**:1265, 1272, 1273

Michael Wagner (*Forever...*), **2**:174, 176

Mick Kelly (*Heart Is a Lonely Hunter*), **7**:980, 981, 982, 985, 986, 987, 988

Miglione family (*Then Again, Maybe I Won't*), **2**:179-80

Mike (*Taming Star Runner*), **5**:715

Mike Campbell (*Sun Also Rises*), **5**:677, 678

Miles Bjornstam (*Main Street*), **6**:854

Milkmaid (*Frog Prince*), **7**:944

Milkman Dead (*Song of Solomon*), **8**:1066-68

Miller family ("Neighbors"), **2**:265

Millie Hodge (*Sunlight Dialogues*), **5**:607

Milton (*Lie Down in Darkness*), **11**:1502, 1503

Mindy (*Earthly Possessions*), **11**:1558

Minghetti (*Tender Is the Night*), **4**:534

Mingo (*Black Thunder*), **2**:190

minister (*Lie Down in Darkness*), **11**:1502, 1503

minister-husband (*Possessing the Secret of Joy*), **11**:1581

Minna Ahronson (*Certificate*), **10**:1407, 1408

Minnie (Simple columns), **6**:736

Mirabal sisters (*In the Time of the Butterflies*), **1**:30, 31, 34-36

Miranda (*Tempest*), **3**:349

Miranda Gay ("Grave"), **9**:1242-43

Miranda Gay (Miranda stories), **9**:1235-36

Miranda Gay (*Old Mortality*), **9**:1236

Miranda Gay (*Old Order*), **9**:1236

Miranda Gay (*Pale Horse, Pale Rider*), **9**:1236, 1238, 1239

Miriam (*Small Changes*), **9**:1210, 1211

Miriam Lucas (*Spreading Fires*), **6**:818

Misfit (serial killer) ("Good Man Is Hard to Find"), **8**:1149, 1150

Miss Baker (*McTeague*), **8**:1096

Miss Banner (*Hundred Secret Senses*), **11**:1517

Miss Eckhart (*Golden Apples*), **12**:1601, 1602, 1606

Miss Glenn (*Lesson Before Dying*), **5**:592, 593

Miss Julia Mortimer (*Losing Battles*), **12**:1603, 1606

Miss Julie (*Miss Julie*), **9**:1165

Miss Quentin (*Sound and Fury*), **4**:494, 495

Mister (Albert) (*Color Purple*), **11**:1572, 1574, 1575

Mitch (*Streetcar Named Desire*), **12**:1668

M'Lissa (*Possessing the Secret of Joy*), **11**:1582

Modeste (*Surrounded*), **7**:1003

Moira (*A Handmaid's Tale*), **1**:94

Moises Teubel (*Tender Is the Night*), **4**:534

Molly Bloom (*Ulysses*), **5**:598

Monica Gall (*Mixture of Frailties*), **3**:351

Monkey Face (horse) (Schaefer fictional), **10**:1352

Monroe Stahr (*Last Tycoon*), **4**:536, 537

Monsignor Thayer Darcy (*This Side of Paradise*), **4**:517

Monte Walsh (*Monte Walsh*), **10**:1351, 1352, 1355

Moon Lady (*Moon Lady*), **11**:1518

Morag Gunn (*Diviners*), **6**:825, 826-27

Moran (*Moran of the Lady Letty*), **8**:1093, 1101

Moreauxs (*Fade*), **3**:305

Morgan Gower (*Morgan's Passing*), **11**:1548

Morris Bober (*Assistant*), **7**:917, 919, 920

Morris Feitelzohn (*Shosha*), **10**:1412, 1413

Morris Ritz (*Grass Harp*), **2**:240, 246, 247

Moseley Sheppard (*Black Thunder*), **2**:190

Moses (*Moses, Man of the Mountain*), **6**:751

Moses Herzog (*Herzog*), 134-36, **1**:133

Moshe Gabriel Margolis (*Family Moskat*), **10**:1409

Moss (*Glengarry Glen Ross*), **7**:940

Mother (*All the Pretty Horses*), 7:969
Mother ("Boys and Girls"), 8:1082
Mother ("Everyday Use"), 11:1579
Mother (*I Am the Cheese*), 3:306, 307
Mother (*Jest of God*), 6:829
Mother ("Peace of Utrecht"), 8:1083, 1084
Mother Cat (*Chinese Siamese Cat*), 11:1517
Motorcycle Boy (*Rumble Fish*), 5:702, 706, 710, 716, *717*
Mr. and Mrs. Fonstein (*Bellarosa Connection*), 1:139-40
Mr. and Mrs. Henry van der Luyden (*Age of Innocence*), 12:1618, 1621
Mr. and Mrs. Whitestripe ("kitchenette folks"), 2:207
Mr. Chamberlain (*Lives of Girls and Women*), 8:1079
Mr. Dalton (*Native Son*), 12:1704
Mr. Dooley (Dunne character), 6:734
Mr. Eugenides (*Waste Land*), 4:442
Mr. Garner (*Beloved*), 8:1056
Mr. Gibbs (*Our Town*), 12:1645
Mr. Greenleaf ("Greenleaf"), 8:1150
Mr. Greenleaf's twin sons ("Greenleaf"), 8:1150
Mr. Hairston (*Tunes for Bears to Dance To*), 3:309
Mr. Hatch (*Noon Wine*), 9:1237
Mr. Head ("Artificial Nigger"), 8:1148
Mr. Helton (*Noon Wine*), 9:1237
Mr. Helton's mother (*Noon Wine*), 9:1237
Mr. Kincaide (*Tex*), 5:710
Mr. Lindner (*Raisin in Sun*), 5:653, 654
Mr. Miglione (*Then Again, Maybe I Won't*), 2:179
Mr. Mistoffeles (*Old Possum's Book of Practical Cats*), 4:443
Mr. Norton (*Invisible Man*), 4:466
Mr. Paterson (Dr. Paterson) (*Paterson*), 12:1687, 1688
Mr. Pignati (*Pigman*), 12:1721, 1722, 1723-24, *1725*
Mrs. Barnes (*Tex*), 5:702
Mrs. Breedlove (*Bluest Eye*), 8:1066
Mrs. Bridgetower (*Mixture of Frailties*), 3:351
Mrs. Bundren (*As I Lay Dying*), 4:492

Mrs. Chestny ("Everything That Rises Must Converge"), 8:1142, 1148-49
Mr. Scratch ("Devil and Daniel Webster"), 2:157
Mrs. Cressler (*Pit*), 8:1099-1100
Mrs. Dalton (*Native Son*), 12:1704, 1705
Mrs. Fielding (*Leaven of Malice*), 3:348
Mrs. Fletcher ("Petrified Man"), 12:1608
Mrs. Flood (*Wise Blood*), 8:1147
Mrs. Hale (*Ethan Frome*), 12:1624
Mrs. Liang (*Three Daughters of Madame Liang*), 2:231, 232
Mrs. Lucas (*Spreading Fires*), 6:818
Mrs. Manson Mingott (*Age of Innocence*), 12:1618
"Mrs. Manstey's View" (Wharton), 12:1614, 1615
Mrs. May ("Greenleaf"), 8:1142, 1150
Mrs. Pike ("Petrified Man"), 12:1608
Mrs. Reynolds (*Mrs. Reynolds*), 10:1437
Mrs. Reynolds' husband (*Mrs. Reynolds*), 10:1437
Mrs. Robert Kooshof (*Tomcat in Love*), 8:1134
Mrs. Ross (*Oil!*), 10:1395
Mrs. Snell ("Down at the Dinghy"), 10:1321
Mrs. Treadwell (*Ship of Fools*), 9:1240
Mrs. Turner (*Their Eyes Were Watching God*), 6:751
Mrs. Van Huysen (*Matchmaker*), 12:1649
Mrs. Wu (*Pavilion of Women*), 2:229, 230
Mr. Thompson (*Noon Wine*), 9:1237-38
Mr. Webb (*Our Town*), 12:*1642*
Mr. Wu (*Pavilion of Women*), 2:230
Mr. Zuss (*J.B.*), 7:903, *904*, 905
Ms. Dog (*Death Notebooks*), 10:1375
Mungojerrie (*Old Possum's Book of Practical Cats*), 4:443
Muraki (father) (*Patriot*), 2:229
Muriel Glass ("Perfect Day for Bananafish"), 10:1319
Muriel Glass ("Raise High the Roof Beam, Carpenters"), 10:1317
Muriel Glass's mother ("Perfect Day for Bananafish"), 10:1319

Muriel Pritchett (*Accidental Tourist*), 11:1545, 1551, 1552
Murray (*Gone to Soldiers*), 9:1210
Myra Babbitt (*Babbitt*), 6:857
Myrtle Wilson (*Great Gatsby*), 4:526, 531, 532

Nancy Montgomery (*Alias Grace*), 1:91
Nancy Wheeler (*Are You There God? It's Me, Margaret*), 2:170, 171
Nandine (*them*), 8:1114
Nang Er (*Good Earth*), 2:224
Nang Wan (*Good Earth*), 2:224
Naomi (*Gone to Soldiers*), 9:1210
Naomi (*Lives of Girls and Women*), 8:1079
narrator ("Diving into the Wreck"), 9:1288
narrator (*Eighth Day*), 12:1649
narrator (*Ethan Frome*), 12:1624
narrator ("I Don't Talk Service No More"), 9:1257
narrator (*Invisible Man*), 4:464, 466, 468, 469-70, 472, 473
narrator (Simple columns), 6:733, 734, 736
Natalie (*Patchwork Planet*), 11:1558
Nathan (*Sophie's Choice*), 11:1501, 1502
Nathaniel Amegbe (*This Side Jordan*), 6:829, 830
Nathan Moskat (*Family Moskat*), 10:1409
Nathan's brother (*Sophie's Choice*), 11:1501
Nat Turner (portrayed in *Confessions of Nat Turner*), 11:1492, 1494, 1497-98, *1499*, 1500
Natty Bumppo (Leatherstocking Tales), 2:160
Neap ("I Don't Talk Service No More"), 9:1257
Ned (*Autobiography of Miss Jane Pittman*), 5:590-91
Negrito (horse) (*Tex*), 5:702, 713
Neil (*Small Changes*), 9:1211
Neil Reardon (*Indian Summer*), 6:817
Nellie (*Summer and Smoke*), 12:1671
Nellie Clark (*Spoon River Anthology*), 7:956, 958
Nel's husband (*Sula*), 8:1069
Nelson ("Artificial Nigger"), 8:1148
Nel Wright (*Sula*), 8:1058, 1069
Nettie (*Color Purple*), 11:1574, 1575

Neville (*Spreading Fires*), **6**:818

Newland Archer (*Age of Innocence*), **12**:1618, *1620*, 1621-22

Newland Archer's son (*Age of Innocence*), **12**:1622

New York Knights (*Natural*), **7**:922

Nicholson ("Teddy"), **10**:1321

Nick Adams ("Battler"), **5**:668, 669, 679

Nick Adams ("Big Two-Hearted River"), **5**:663, 668, 669, 679

Nick Adams ("Fathers and Sons"), **5**:680

Nick Adams ("In Another Country"), **5**:679

Nick Adams ("Indian Camp"), **5**:668, 669, 679

Nick Adams ("Killers"), **5**:679

Nick Adams ("Light of the World"), **5**:680

Nick Adams ("Now I Lay Me"), **5**:679

Nick Adams ("Ten Indians"), **5**:679

Nick Adams ("Way You'll Never Be"), **5**:680

Nick Blackburn (*Peace Breaks Out*), **6**:814

Nick Carraway (*Great Gatsby*), **4**:523, 526, 527, 528-29, 530-31, 532

Nickles (*J.B.*), **7**:903, *904*, 905

Nicolai Lebedev (*Fixer*), **7**:921

Nicola Sacco (portrayed in *Boston*), **10**:1390, 1391

Nicole Warren Diver (*Tender Is the Night*), **4**:533, 534

Nina Leeds (*Strange Interlude*), **9**:1165, *1166*

Nina Leeds's family friend (*Strange Interlude*), **9**:1165

Nina Leeds's husband (*Strange Interlude*), **9**:1165, *1166*

Nina Leeds's lover (*Strange Interlude*), **9**:1165

Nina Leeds's son (*Strange Interlude*), **9**:1165, *1166*

Noach Levinson (*Wall*), **5**:695, 696

Nonno (*Night of the Iguana*), **12**:1673

Norma Midge (*Dog of the South*), **9**:1249, 1250, 1253, 1254, 1255

Norma's first husband (*Dog of the South*), **9**:1249

Norwood Pratt (*Norwood*), **9**:1247, 1248, 1250, 1251, 1258

Norwood Pratt's wife (*Norwood*), **9**:1258

Nunumu (*Hundred Secret Senses*), **11**:1517

nurse (*All the Pretty Horses*), **7**:969

Nyunie Moskat (*Family Moskat*), **10**:1409, 1410

Oakley brothers (*Sport of Gods*), **3**:410

Obie (*Beyond the Chocolate War*), **3**:304

Ocean View Orchard (*Cider House Rules*), **6**:774, 775

Offred (*A Handmaid's Tale*, **1**:91, 94-95

O-Lan (*Good Earth*), **2**:215, 219, 220, 222, 223-24

Old Grannis (*McTeague*), **8**:1096

old hermit (*What Use Are Flowers?*), **5**:658

old man ("Clean, Well-Lighted Place"), **5**:681

Old Pebble (*Single Pebble*), **5**:689, 698

Old Ramon (*Old Ramon*), **10**:1348

Olga ("Dear Joaquin"), **9**:1191-92

Olga ("Olga"), **9**:1191

Olga Knipper ("Errand"), **2**:264

Oliver Twist (*Oliver Twist*), **6**:772, 775

Olivia (*Color Purple*), **11**:1581

Olivia (*Hundred Secret Senses*), **11**:1511, 1515, 1517

Ollie McGee (*Spoon River Anthology*), **7**:956-57

Ona Lukoszaite Jurgis (*Jungle*), **10**:1391, 1392-93

"Ondie" Olszak (*American Beauty*), **4**:504

Ondine (*Tar Baby*), **8**:1070

One-Eye (wolf) (*White Fang*), **7**:886

Opal (*Patchwork Planet*), **11**:1558

Orestes (*Oresteia*), **9**:1179

Orin Mannon (*Mourning Becomes Electra*), **9**:1179

Orson (*Taming Star Runner*), **5**:715

Oscar Johnson (*Going After Cacciato*), **8**:1129

Oscar Slattery (*What I Lived For*), **8**:1115

Osterman (*Octopus*), **8**:1098

Owen Meany (*Prayer for Owen Meany*), **6**:780

Ozzie (*Fade*), **3**:305

Pablo (*For Whom the Bell Tolls*), **5**:676

Pablo (*Tortilla Flat*), **11**:1460

Paco ("Beauty Lessons"), **9**:1190

Paddy's Bar (Simple columns), **6**:736

Page family (*October Light*), **5**:604, 605, 606

Papa Gonzales (*Summer and Smoke*), **12**:1671

Parnell (*Blues for Mr. Charlie*), **1**:114

Parthenia Hawkes (*Show Boat*), **4**:509, 510

Pat Brady (*Last Tycoon*), **4**:536

Patrick (*Who Do You Think You Are*), **8**:1082

Patty (*Rumble Fish*), **5**:716

Paul ("Grave"), **9**:1242, 1243

Paul (*Lady Oracle*), **1**:96

Paul (*Masque of Mercy*), **4**:572

Paul (*Maud Martha*), **2**:207

Paul ("Paul's Case"), **2**:275, 285-86

Paul Berlin (*Going After Cacciato*), **8**:1125, 1128, 1129

Paul Berlin's father (*Going After Cacciato*), **8**:1129

Paul Chabas, *Glance in the Mirror, A*, **12**:*1601*

Paul D (*Beloved*), **8**:1063, 1064

Paul Delmonte (*I Am the Cheese*), **3**:306

Paul Dempster (*Fifth Business*), **3**:345, 347

Paul Moreaux (*Fade*), **3**:304, 305

Paul Reisling (*Babbitt*), **6**:855-56

Paul Roget (*Fade*), **3**:305

Paul's father ("Paul's Case"), **2**:286

Paul Watkins (*Oil!*), **10**:1394, 1395

Pearl (*Kitchen God's Wife*), **11**:1511, 1512, 1516

Pearl Bridgetower (*Mixture of Frailties*), **3**:351

Pearl Moskat (*Family Moskat*), **10**:1409

Pearl Tull (*Dinner at the Homesick Restaurant*), **11**:1555-56, 1557

Pearl Veronica Vambrace (*Leaven of Malice*), **3**:347, 348

Peck family (*Searching for Caleb*), **11**:1559

Pecola Breedlove (*Bluest Eye*), **8**:1058, 1065-66

Pedro Romero (*Sun Also Rises*), **5**:678

Peeker (*Wreckage of Agathon*), **5**:609-10

Percy Boyd ("Boy") Staunton (*Fifth Business*), **3**:345, 347

Percy Boyd ("Boy") Staunton (*Manticore*), **3**:350

Percy Grimm (*Light in August*), **4**:497

Perdita (*Mysteries of Winterthurn*), **8**:1112, 1113

Perrault (*Call of the Wild*), **7**:884

Perry Smith (portrayed in *In Cold Blood*), **2**:239, 240, 245, 248, 249, *250*

Pervus DeJong (*So Big*), **4**:512

Pete Hallam (*Peace Breaks Out*), **6**:814

Peter ("Previous Condition"), **1**:122

Peter (*This Music Crept by Me Upon the Waters*), **7**:907

pet rabbit (*Effect of Gamma Rays on Man-in-the-Moon Marigolds*), **12**:1719, 1720

Peyton Loftis (*Lie Down in Darkness*), **11**:1502, 1503

"Phantasia for Elvira Shatayev" (Rich), **9**:1289, 1291

Pharaoh (*Black Thunder*), **2**:190

Pharaoh (*Moses, Man of the Mountain*), **6**:751

"Phenomenology of Anger, The" (Rich), **9**:1286

Phenomenon of Man, The (Teilhard), **8**:1148

Pheoby (*Their Eyes Were Watching God*), **6**:756, 758

Philip Martin (*In My Father's House*), **5**:594

Philomaths (group) (*Iron Heel*), **7**:888

Phoebe Caulfield (*Catcher in the Rye*), **10**:1314, 1315

Phoenix Jackson ("Worn Path"), **12**:1608

Phoenix Jackson's grandson ("Worn Path"), **12**:1608

Pilar (*For Whom the Bell Tolls*), **5**:676

Pilate (*Song of Solomon*), **8**:1066, 1067

Pilon (*Tortilla Flat*), **11**:1459, 1460

Pinnie Moskat (*Family Moskat*), **10**:1409

Pip (*Great Expectations*), **6**:772

Pique (*Diviners*), **6**:826, 827

Pirate (*Tortilla Flat*), **11**:1460

Pittman family (*Autobiography of Miss Jane Pittman*), **5**:588, 590-91

Poet (*Poet and the Rent*), **7**:944

pony (*Red Pony*), **11**:1463-64

Ponyboy Curtis (*Outsiders*), **5**:705, 706, 711

Pool family (*So Big*), **4**:511

Pop (*Overlaid*), **3**:341

Pop (*Tex*), **5**:712, 713

Pop Fisher (*Natural*), **7**:922, 923

postman ("Strong Horse Tea"), **11**:1579

Powderhead (homestead) (*Violent Bear It Away*), **8**:1144, 1145

Presley (*Octopus*), **8**:1097

Pre-Teen Sensations (*Are You There God? It's Me, Margaret*), **2**:171, 172

Prince (*Frog Prince*), **7**:944

Prin Logan (*Diviners*), **6**:826

Prospero (*Tempest*), **3**:335, 349, 350

Quentin (*After the Fall*), **8**:1028

Quentin Compson (*Absalom, Absalom!*), **4**:496, 497

Quentin Compson (*Sound and Fury*), **4**:484, 493, 494, 495

Rabbi Benish (*Satan in Goray*), **10**:1398

Rabbi Ozer ("Gentleman from Cracow"), **10**:1414

Rachel (*Go Tell It on the Mountain*), **1**:116

Rachel Apt (*Wall*), **5**:696

Rachel Cameron (*Jest of God*), **6**:828, 829, 831

Rachel Gordon (*Promise*), **9**:1273

Rachel Menzies (*Oil!*), **10**:1394, 1395

Rachel Robinson (*Here's to You, Rachel Robinson*), **2**:167

Rachel Robinson (*Just as Long as We're Together*), **2**:167

Rachel's friend (*Jest of God*), **6**:829

Rafael Viventa (*Line of the Sun*), **9**:1193

Ralph ("Will You Please Be Quiet, Please?"), **2**:267-68

Ralph Miglione (*Then Again, Maybe I Won't*), **2**:179

Ramona (*Herzog*), **1**:132, 135

Ramsays (*Fifth Business*), **3**:345, 346, **5**:347

Randolph (*Other Voices, Other Rooms*), **2**:252

Randy Carter (*Young Man from Atlanta*), **4**:553

Raoul Cormier (*Catherine Cormier*), **5**:593, 594

Raphael Sanchez ("Jacob and the Indians"), **2**:160

Ras the Destroyer (*Invisible Man*), **4**:466, 470

Rat Kiley ("Things They Carried"), **8**:1132

Rav Kalman (*Promise*), **9**:1272, 1273

Rawlins (*All the Pretty Horses*), **7**:969

Raymond Earl Midge (*Dog of the South*), **9**:1249, 1250, 1251, 1253, 1254-55

Reardon family (*Indian Summer*), **6**:817

Rebbe (Asher Lev novels), **9**:1267

Rebbe (*Gift of Asher Lev*), **9**:1274

Rebbe (*My Name Is Asher Lev*), **9**:1270

Rebbe Saunders (*Chosen*), **9**:1264, 1267, 1268, 1269

Rebbe Saunders (*Promise*), **9**:1264, 1265

Reb Dan Katzenellenbogen (*Family Moskat*), **10**:1409

Reb Jerachmiel Bannet (*Family Moskat*), **10**:1409

Reb Meshulam Moskat (*Family Moskat*), **10**:1402, 1409, 1410

Rechele (*Satan in Goray*), **10**:1398

Refugio (*Gringos*), **9**:1256

Renata (*Humboldt's Gift*), **1**:136, 137

Rent-a-Back (business) (*Patchwork Planet*), **11**:1558

retired Army major (*Bad Girls*), **8**:1117

Reuben ("Rooster") Cogburn (*True Grit*), **9**:1248, 1250, 1255, 1256

Reuven Malter (*Chosen*), **9**:1259, 1264, 1268-69

Reuven Malter (*Promise*), **9**:1264, 1265, 1272, 1273

Reuven Malter's father (*Chosen*), **9**:1264, 1268, 1269

Reuven Malter's father (*Promise*), **9**:1264, 1265

Revelation Motor Car Company (*Dodsworth*), **6**:860

Reverend Alonzo Hickman (*Juneteenth*), **4**:471, 472

Reverend Dan Taylor ("Fire and Cloud"), **12**:1707

Reverend Parris (*Crucible*), **8**:1023

Reverend Simpson (*Uncalled*), **3**:415

Reverend T. Lawrence Shannon (*Night of the Iguana*), **12**:1673

Reverend Whitfield (*As I Lay Dying*), **4**:490, 491

Ric and Rac (*Ship of Fools*), **9:**1239

Richard (*Another Country*), **1:**120

Richard (*Go Tell It on the Mountain*), **1:**115, 116

Richard (*Morning Watch, The*), **1:**23

Richard Henry (*Blues for Mr. Charlie*), **1:**114

Richard Miller (*Ah, Wilderness!*), **9:**1166

Richard Page (*October Light*), **5:**606

Riley Henderson (*Grass Harp*), **2:**246, 247

Rinaldo Cantabile (*Humboldt's Gift*), **1:**136

Ringo (*Unvanquished*), **4:**488

Rinthy Home (*Outer Dark*), **7:**973, **9:**974

Rita ("Bad Influence"), **9:**1186, 1189

Rita's grandfather ("Bad Influence"), **9:**1186, 1189

Rivka (*Gone to Soldiers*), **9:**1210

Rivkeh Lev (*Gift of Asher Lev*), **9:**1274

Rivkeh Lev (*My Name Is Asher Lev*), **9:**1270

R. J. Bowman ("Death of a Traveling Salesman"), **12:**1607

Robedaux family (*Orphans' Home* cycle), **4:**554

Roberta Alden (*American Tragedy*), **3:**386

Roberta Muldoon (*World According to Garp*), **6:**773, 778, 779, 780

Robert Cohn (*Sun Also Rises*), **5:**668, 677, 678

Robert E. Lee (portrayed in *John Brown's Body*), **2:**153, 158, 159

Robert Jordan (*For Whom the Bell Tolls*), **5:**671, 675, 676

Robert Wilson ("Short Happy Life of Francis Macomber"), **5:**678-79

Robert X (*In My Father's House*), **5:**594

Robin Hood (legendary), **2:**213

Rodopho (*View from the Bridge*), **8:**1031

Roelf Pool (*So Big*), **4:**512

Rogets (*Fade*), **3:**305

Roma (*Glengarry Glen Ross*), **7:**940

Rooster Cogburn (*True Grit*), **9:**1248, 1250

Rosa (*Summer and Smoke*), **12:**1671

Rosa Coldfield (*Absalom, Absalom!*), **4:**496

Rosa Frumet Landau (*Family Moskat*), **10:**1410

Rosa Lee (*Tender Mercies*), **4:**549, 550

Rosario (*Rose Tattoo*), **12:**1672

Rose (*Accidental Tourist*), **11:**1552

Rose (*Who Do You Think You Are?*), **8:**1081-82

Rose ("Wild Swans"), **8:**1076, 1077

Rosemary Connage (*This Side of Paradise*), **4:**535

Rosemary Hoyt (*Tender Is the Night*), **4:**534

Rose Moreaux (*Fade*), **3:**305

Rose of Sharon (*Grapes of Wrath*), **11:**1455, 1463, 1464

Rose's father (*Who Do You Think You Are?*), **8:**1081

Ross Hungerfield ("Hungerfield"), **6:**795

Ross Wilbur (*Moran of the Lady Letty*), **8:**1101

Rowan Oak (Faulkner home), **4:**478, 481

Royal Porcupine (*Lady Oracle*), **1:**96

Roy Grimes (*Go Tell It on the Mountain*), **1:**116

Roy Hobbs (*Natural*), **7:**915, 917, 922, 923

Roz (*The Robber Bride*), **1:**99

Rudy Kurle (*Gringos*), **9:**1256, 1257

Rufus (*Death in the Family*), **1:**18, 19, 20

Rumble Fish (*Rumble Fish*), **5:**706, 716

Rumpelteazer (*Old Possum's Book of Practical Cats*), **4:**443

Rum Tum Tugger (*Old Possum's Book of Practical Cats*), **4:**443

Running Wolf (*Surrounded*), **7:**999

Russell Spaulding (*Ann Vickers*), **6:**861

Rusty-James (*Rumble Fish*), **5:**702, 707, 716, 717

Ruth (*Dinner at the Homesick Restaurant*), **11:**1556

Ruth Dead (*Song of Solomon*), **8:**1066

Ruth Gordon (*Promise*), **9:**1273

Ruth Hunsdorfer (*Effect of Gamma Rays on Man-in-the-Moon Marigolds*), **12:**1719, 1720

Ruthie (*Gone to Soldiers*), **9:**1210

Ruth Mayo (*Beyond the Horizon*), **9:**1164

Ruth Morse (*Martin Eden*), **7:**885

Ruth Younger (*Raisin in Sun*), **5:**653, 654, 655

Sabbath Lilly Hawks (*Wise Blood*), **8:**1147

Sabina (*Skin of Our Teeth*), **12:**1641, 1646

Sabra Venable Cravat (*Cimarron*), **4:**506, 507-8

sailor ("June Recital"), **12:**1602

St. Cloud orphanage (*Cider House Rules*), **6:**774, 775-76

Sally (*Jonah's Gourd Vine*), **6:**761

Sally Dupre (portrayed in *John Brown's Body*), **2:**159

Sally Hayes (*Catcher in the Rye*), **10:**1309, 1314-15

Sally J. Freedman (*Starring Sally J. Freedman as Herself*), **2:**170

Sally Page Abbott (*October Light*), **5:**604, 605-6

Salt (character) (*Runner in the Sun*), **7:**999, 1001

Sam Dodsworth (*Dodsworth*), **6:**860

Sam Dreiman (*Shosha*), **10:**1413

Samuel (*Color Purple*), **11:**1574

Samuel Marchbanks (*Diary of Samuel Marchbanks*), **3:**335, 337, 338, 339, 341, 343

Samuel Marchbanks (*Table Talk of Samuel Marchbanks*), **3:**336, 337, 338, 339, 341, 343

Samuel Prescott (*Samuel the Seeker*), **10:**1384

Samuel Turner (*Confessions of Nat Turner*), **11:**1498

Sanders ("Code"), **4:**563

Sandi ("Beauty Lessons"), **9:**1190

Sandra ("Down at the Dinghy"), **10:**1321

Sarah (*J.B.*), **7:**903, 904, 905

Sarah (*Nuclear Age*), **8:**1133

Sarkin Aung Wan (*Going After Cacciato*), **8:**1129

Sartoris family (*Flags in the Dust*), **4:**483, 489

Sartoris family (*Unvanquished*), **4:**487, 488, 489

Satan (*J.B.*), **7:**903, *904*

Satan (*Masque of Reason*), **4:**573

Satin Leg Smith ("Sundays of Satin Legs Smith"), **2:**197, 205-6

Saul Emory (*Earthly Possessions*), **11:**1558

S. Behrman (*Octopus*), **8:**1097-98

Scheherazade (*Arabian Nights*), **1:**28

school official (*My Name Is Asher Lev*), **9:**1272

Schoolteacher (*Beloved*), **8:**1056, 1064

science teacher (*Effect of Gamma*

Rays on Man-in-the-Moon Marigolds), **12**:1719

Scout Finch (*To Kill a Mockingbird*), **4**:550, 551, **6**:834, 837, 838, 839, 840, 841

Sean (*My Darling, My Hamburger*), **12**:1725

Sean's father (*My Darling, My Hamburger*), **12**:1725

Selena Graff ("Just Before the War with the Eskimos"), **10**:1319, 1321

Selina Peake (*So Big*), **4**:511-12

Senator Adam ("Bliss") Sunraider (*Juneteenth*), **4**:466, 471, 472

Senator Berzelius ("Buzz") Windrip (*It Can't Happen Here*), **6**:861, 862

Senator Mansfield (*Child Buyer*), **5**:696

Senator Skypack (*Child Buyer*), **5**:696

Senator Voyoko (*Child Buyer*), **5**:696

Serafina delle Rose (*Rose Tattoo*), **12**:1672

Seraphim Tullio (*Tender Is the Night*), **4**:534

Serena Joy (*A Handmaid's Tale*), **1**:94

Sergeant ("On the Road"), **6**:743

Serpent (*Songs for Eve*), **7**:906

Servingman (*Frog Prince*), **7**:944

Sethe (*Beloved*), **8**:1056, 1058, 1060, 1062, 1063, 1064

Sethe's mother (*Beloved*), **8**:1062, 1064

Seymour Glass ("Franny"), **10**:1316

Seymour Glass (Glass family stories), **10**:1303, 1308, 1309, 1315, 1317, 1321

Seymour Glass ("Hapworth 16, 1924"), **10**:1304

Seymour Glass ("Perfect Day for Bananafish"), **10**:1319

Seymour Glass ("Raise High the Roof Beam, Carpenters"), **10**:1317, 1318

Seymour Glass ("Seymour: An Introduction"), **10**:1317, 1318

Seymour Glass ("Zooey"), **10**:1316

Shack Dye (*Spoon River Anthology*), **7**:958

Shane (*Shane*), **10**:1348, 1349, 1352, 1353-54

Shaper (*Grendel*), **5**:603, 604

Sharon Falconer (*Elmer Gantry*), **6**:859

Sheldon Corthell (*Pit*), **8**:1099

Shepard (gang) (*That Was Then, This Is Now*), **5**:717

sheriff (*Trip to Bountiful*), **4**:554

Sheriff Quigley (*Surrounded*), **7**:1003

Sherman Pew (*Clock Without Hands*), **7**:990

Shira (*He, She, and It*), **9**:1210

Shira's grandmother (*He, She, and It*), **9**:1210

Shosha (*Shosha*), **10**:1412, 1413

Shosha Berman (*Family Moskat*), **10**:1409

Shug (*Color Purple*), **11**:*1570*, 1571, 1572, 1575, 1576

Shug's father (*Color Purple*), **11**:1572

sick child ("Strong Horse Tea"), **11**:1579

Sidney Brustein (*Sign in Sidney Brustein's Window*), **5**:650-51, 656

Siegried "Siggy" Javotnick (*Setting Free the Bears*), **6**:781

Silas ("Death of the Hired Man"), **4**:563, 569

Simon (*Hundred Secret Senses*), **11**:1517

Simon Girty ("Devil and Daniel Webster"), **2**:157

Simon Jordan (*Alias Grace*), **1**:89, 91

Simon Rosedale (*House of Mirth*), **12**:1618

Simple (Jesse B. Semple) (Simple columns), **6**:729, 730, 733-36, 737, 743

singing woman ("Idea of Order at Key West"), **11**:1483

"Sir Rabbit" (Welty), **12**:1601

Sister ("Why I Live at the P.O."), **12**:1608

Sister Boxer (*The Amen Corner*), **1**:111

sister-in-law (*Member of the Wedding*), **7**:988

Sister Margaret (*The Amen Corner*), **1**:111, 113

Sister Moore (*The Amen Corner*), **1**:111

Sister's grandfather ("Why I Live at the P.O."), **12**:1608

Sister's mother ("Why I Live at the P.O."), **12**:1608

Sister's uncle ("Why I Live at the P.O."), **12**:1608

Skinner Tonnerre (*Diviners*), **6**:826, 827

Skipper (*Cat on a Hot Tin Roof*), **12**:1657, 1670

S. Levin (*New Life*), **7**:924, 925

Smokey (*Rumble Fish*), **5**:702, 716

Sneed (Irving character), **6**:771

Snopes family (*Hamlet*), **4**:483

Snopes family (Snopes trilogy), **4**:478

Soaphead Church (*Bluest Eye*), **8**:1065

Socs (gang) (*Outsiders*), **5**:711, 717

Sodapop (*Outsiders*), **5**:711

Sofia (*Color Purple*), **11**:1574

Solace Layfield (*Wise Blood*), **8**:*1141*, 1147

Solly Bridgetower (father) (*Leaven of Malice*), **3**:348

Solly Bridgetower (father) (*Mixture of Frailties*), **3**:351

Solomon Bridgetower (grandfather) (*Leaven of Malice*), **3**:347

Solomon Hansen Bridgetower (son) (*Mixture of Frailties*), **3**:351

Son (*Tar Baby*), **8**:1070

Son (*Trip to Bountiful*), **4**:554

Sondra Finchley (*American Tragedy*), **3**:386

Sonny ("Sonny's Blues"), **1**:117, 118

Sonny and pregnant wife ("Death of a Traveling Salesman"), **12**:1607

Sonya (*Certificate*), **10**:1408

Sophia Jane Rhea (Miranda stories), **9**:1235

Sophia Maynard (*Patchwork Planet*), **11**:1558-59

Sophia Maynard's aunt (*Patchwork Planet*), **11**:1559

Sophie (*Sophie's Choice*), **11**:1500, 1501-2

Sophie Viner (*Reef*), **12**:1626

Spanish dancers (*Ship of Fools*), **9**:1239, 1240

Sparta Gentian (*Spanish Bayonet*), **2**:161

Spiros Antonapolous (*Heart Is a Lonely Hunter*), **7**:986, 987

Spitz (dog) (*Call of the Wild*), **7**:884

Spotted Turtle (*Canyon*), **10**:1355

Stacey Cameron MacAindra (*Fire-Dwellers*), **6**:831

Stage Manager (*Our Town*), **12**:*1636*, 1638, 1645

Stan (*Taming Star Runner*), **5**:713

Stanley Kowalski (*Streetcar Named Desire*), **12**:1667, 1668

Stark Wilson (*Shane*), **10**:1354

Star Runner (horse) (*Taming Star Runner*), **5**:713, *714*, 715, 716

Steering School (*World According to Garp*), **6**:771

Stella Kowalski (*Streetcar Named Desire*), **12**:1668

Stella-Rondo ("Why I Live at the P.O."), **12**:1608

Stephen Dedalus (*Portrait of the Artist as a Young Man*), **9**:1266

Stephen Douglas (portrayed in *New Spoon River*), **7**:955-56

Stephen Welles (*Wind from an Enemy Sky*), **7**:999

Steve (*Rumble Fish*), **5**:716

Steve Baker (*Show Boat*), **4**:511

Steve Hunter (*Poor White*), **1**:50

Steve Randle (*Outsiders*), **5**:711

Stingo (*Sophie's Choice*), **11**:1500-1501

Stone family ("Neighbors), **2**:265

Stonewall Jackson (portrayed in *Great Gatsby*), **4**:531

Stradlater (*Catcher in the Rye*), **10**:1314

Sue Anne (*Tender Mercies*), **4**:549

Sula Peace (*Sula*), **8**:1058, 1069

Sunlight Man, the (*Sunlight Dialogues*), **5**:598, 600, 606-7

Susan (*Spanish Prisoner*), **7**:941

Susanna Jones ("When Sue Wears Red"), **6**:742

Susan Roget (*Fade*), **3**:305

Susie (*Hotel New Hampshire*), **6**:777

Suyuan Woo (*Joy Luck Club*), **11**:1511, 1512, *1513*, 1514

Sweeney (*Sweeney Agonistes*), **4**:442

Sweet Home plantation (*Beloved*), **8**:1060, 1062, 1063

Sybil ("Perfect Day for Bananafish"), **10**:1319

Sydney (*Tar Baby*), **8**:1070

talking sheep (*Revenge of the Space Pandas*), **7**:944

Tama Muraki (*Patriot*), **2**:229

Tamar Cauldwell ("Tamar"), **6**:798-99

Tamar's father ("Tamar"), **6**:798, 799

Tamkin (*Seize the Day*), **1**:138

Tanis Judique (*Babbitt*), **6**:856

Tan Man ("Anniad, The"), **2**:204, 207

Tante Lou (*Lesson Before Dying*), **5**:593

Tashi (Evelyn Johnson) (*Possessing the Secret of Joy*), **11**:1581-82

Tea Cake Woods (*Their Eyes Were Watching God*), **6**:751, 756-57, 758

Teach (*American Buffalo*), **7**:937, 938

teacher (*My Darling, My Hamburger*), **12**:1725

Teach the Pirate ("Devil and Daniel Webster"), **2**:157

Teddy ("Teddy"), **10**:1321

Teddy's father ("Teddy"), **10**:1321

Ted Lavinder ("Things They Carried"), **8**:1132

Teibele Berman (*Family Moskat*), **10**:1409

Tekla (*Shosha*), **10**:1413

Teresa ("Job for Valentin"), **9**:1190

Teresa ("What We Talk About When We Talk About Love"), **2**:266

Terry Wickett (*Arrowsmith*), **6**:858

Terufumi Sasaki (*Hiroshima*), **5**:693

Tex McCormick (*Tex*), **5**:702, *709*, 710, 712, 713

Thea Kronborg (*Song of the Lark, The*), **2**:272, 275

Thomas à Becket (*Murder in Cathedral*), **4**:442-43, 445, 446

Thomas Chippering (*Tomcat in Love*), **8**:1126, 1133-34

Thomas Cowling (*Nuclear Age*), **8**:1133

Thomas Gray (*Confessions of Nat Turner*), **11**:1498

Thomas Hudson ("At Sea"), **5**:671

Thomas Hudson ("Bimini"), **5**:670-71

Thomas Hudson ("Cuba"), **5**:671

Thomas Hudson (*Islands in the Stream*), **5**:670-71

Thomas Jefferson (portrayed in *Book of Americans*), **2**:154

Thomas Kinnear (*Alias Grace*), 89, 91

Thomas Moore (*Confessions of Nat Turner*), **11**:1498

Thomas Sutpen (*Absalom, Absalom!*), **4**:483, 495, 496-97

three daughters (*Boston*), **10**:1390

Thyatria (*Masque of Reason*), **4**:573

Tianjin, China, Hersey and, **5**:683, 684, 687

Tiberius (*Lazarus Laughed*), **9**:1165

Ticey (*Autobiography of Miss Jane Pittman*), **5**:590

Tilia (*Woman on the Edge of Time*), **9**:1209

Tillie Hunsdorfer (*Effect of Gamma Rays on Man-in-the-Moon Marigolds*), **12**:1719, 1720

Tilmon Fring (*Norwood*), **9**:1258

Timothy Emerson (*Clock Winder*), **11**:1550

Tiresias (*Waste Land*), **4**:442

Tish (*If Beale Street Could Talk*), **1**:121-22

Tituba (*Crucible*), **8**:1023

Todd Clifton (*Invisible Man*), **4**:466

Tom Buchanan (*Great Gatsby*), **4**:526, *527*, 528, *529*, 530, 531, 532

Tom Butterworth (*Poor White*), **1**:51

Tom Chaney (*True Grit*), **9**:1255, 1256

Tom Joad (*Grapes of Wrath*), **11**:1455, *1457*, 1462, 1463

Tommy Aronson (*Forever...*), **2**:174

Tommy Barban (*Tender Is the Night*), **4**:534

Tommy Wilhelm (*Seize the Day*), **1**:129, 133, 137-38

Tom Robinson (*To Kill a Mockingbird*), **4**:551, **6**:837, 838, 840, 841

Tom Swift ("Mess of Pottage"), **3**:412

Tom Wingfield (*Glass Menagerie*), **12**:1662, 1663, 1664, 1666

Tony (*The Robber Bride*), **1**:99

Tony Miglione (*Then Again, Maybe I Won't*), **2**:179-80

Toshiko Sasaki (*Hiroshima*), **5**:693

Toussaint-Louverture (portrayed in *Drums at Dusk*), **2**:191-92

Tracy Wu (*Blubber*), **2**:173

Travis Harris (*Taming Star Runner*), **5**:706, 710, 713, *714*, 715, 716

Travis Younger (*Raisin in Sun*), **5**:653

Treat Morrison (*Last Thing He Wanted*), **3**:373

Treckie (*More Die of Heartbreak*), **1**:141

Trina Sieppe McTeague (*McTeague*), **8**:1093, *1094*, 1095, 1101

T. S. Garp (*World According to Garp*), **6**:764, 771, 772, 778-79, 781

Tshembe Matoseh (*Nègres*), **5**:657

Two-Bit Matthews (*Outsiders*), **5**:711

Two Sleeps (*Wind from an Enemy Sky*), **7**:999

Tyrone family (*Long Day's Journey into Night*), **9**:1172, 1175, 1176, 1177

Ulysses S. Grant (portrayed in *John Brown's Body*), **2:**158

Ulysses Swett (*Great Gatsby*), **4:**531

Uncle Adelard (*Fade*), **3:**304-5

Uncle Charlie (*Shadow of a Doubt*), **12:**1639, *1640*, 1641

Uncle Ken (*Taming Star Runner*), **5:**710, 713, 715

Uncle Luke (*Our Town*), **12:**1645

Uncle Pio (*Bridge of San Luis Rey*), **12:**1643-44

Uncle Yitzchok (*My Name Is Asher Lev*), **9:**1270, 1274

Valentine Gersbach (*Herzog*), **1:**134, 135

Valentine Rich (*Tempest-Tost*), **3:**350

Valerian Street (*Tar Baby*), **8:**1070

Vanamee (*Octopus*), **8:**1093

Vandergelder (*Matchmaker*), **12:**1638, 1649

Vandover (*Vandover and the Brute*), **8:**1100-1101

Vandover's father (*Vandover and the Brute*), **8:**1100-1101

Vandover's mother (*Vandover and the Brute*), **8:**1100

Vanessa (*Bird in the House*), **6:**826, 830-31

Vardaman Bundren (*As I Lay Dying*), **4:**490, 491, 492

Vaughn family (*Orphans' Home cycle*), **4:**554

Vaughn-Renfro-Beecham clan (*Losing Battles*), **12:**1602

Verna Talbo (*Grass Harp*), **2:**246, 247

Vernell Pratt (*Norwood*), **9:**1258

Verne Roscoe (*Oil!*), **10:**1394, 1395

Vic Slattery (*What I Lived For*), **8:**1115, 1116

Victor (*Price*), **8:**1029, 1031

Victor family (*Democracy*), **3:**360, 361, 372

Vida Sherwin (*Main Street*), **6:**854

Vigils, the (*Chocolate War*), **3:**302, 304

village doctor (*Pearl*), **11:**1465, 1466

Viney Raymond ("Viney's Free Papers"), **3:**411

Viola (Vee) Tracy (*Oil!*), **10:**1394

Viola Staley (*Resurrection*), **5:**609

Violet Trace (*Jazz*), **8:**1068

Virgie Rainey (*Golden Apples*), **12:**1602

Virgie Rainey's mother (*Golden Apples*), **12:**1601

Vivaldo (*Another Country*), **1:**120

Vix (*Summer Sisters*), **2:**178, 179

Von (*Summer Sisters*), **2:**178

Von Humboldt Fleisher (*Humboldt's Gift*), **1:**129, 136-37

waiter (*Matchmaker*), **12:**1638

Waker Glass (Glass family stories), **10:**1303

Waker Glass ("Zooey"), **10:**1316

Wally Worthington (*Cider House Rules*), **6:**764, 771, 775

Walter (*Price*), **8:**1029, 1031

Walter Butler ("Devil and Daniel Webster"), **2:**157

Walter Cunningham (*To Kill a Mockingbird*), **6:**838

Walter Glass (Glass family stories), **10:**1303

Walter Vambrace (*Leaven of Malice*), **3:**347

Walter Younger (*Raisin in Sun*), **5:**650, 651, 653, 654-55

Wanda (*Small Changes*), **9:**1211

Wang Lung (*Good Earth*), **2:**219, 220, 222, 223, 224, 227

Ward Bennett (*Man's Woman*), **8:**1093, 1101-2

Warren ("Death of the Hired Man"), **4:**563, 569

Waverley Jong (*Joy Luck Club*), **11:**1511, 1513

Webb family (*Our Town*), **12:**1636, 1637, 1639, 1641, *1642*, 1644, 1645, 1650

Webster (*Great Gatsby*), **4:**531

Weedon Scott (*White Fang*), **7:**887

Weili (*Kitchen God's Wife*), **11:**1511-12, 1515, 1516

welfare worker ("Revenge of Hannah Kemhuff"), **11:**1579

Wellspring Methodist Church (*Elmer Gantry*), **6:**859

Wendy (*Blubber*), **2:**173, 174

Wen Fu (*Kitchen God's Wife*), **11:**1516

West (*The Robber Bride*), **1:**99

Western engineer (*Single Pebble*), **5:**698

Wexford (*Peace Breaks Out*), **6:**813-14

What Was in the Garden (Atwood), **1:**90

White Fang (wolf) (*White Fang*), **7:**877, 886-87

White Goddess, The: A Historical Grammar of Poetic Myth (Graves), **1:**83, 88

white traveling salesman ("Long Black Song"), **12:**1707

Wife (*Trip to Bountiful*), **4:**554

Wife ("Yearning Heifer"), **10:**1414

Wilbur Larch (*Cider House Rules*), **6:**764, 771, 774, 775, 776

Wilhelmina Vesta (*Jennie Gerhardt*), **3:**388

Wilhelm Kleinsorge (*Hiroshima*), **5:**693

Will (*Confessions of Nat Turner*), **11:**1498

Will Andrews ("Tamar"), **6:**799

Will Hodge (*Sunlight Dialogues*), **5:**607

William and Emily (*Spoon River Anthology*), **7:**953

William Cowling (*Nuclear Age*), **8:**1126

William Dubin (*Dubin's Lives*), **7:**924

William Gerhardt (*Jennie Gerhardt*), **3:**388

Williamson (*Glengarry Glen Ross*), **7:**940

William Sycamore ("Ballad of William Sycamore, 1790-1871"), **2:**160

Willie (*Brewsie and Willie*), **10:**1436

Willie Ramsay (*Fifth Business*), **3:**347

Willie Spearmint (*Tenants*), **7:**925

Will Kennicott (*Main Street*), **6:**853, 854

Will Kidder (*Young Man from Atlanta*), **4:**552, 553

Will Shakespeare (portrayed in *Cry of Players*), **5:**613, 615, 616, 621

Willy (*Raisin in Sun*), **5:**654

Willy Loman (*Death of a Salesman*), **8:***1015*, 1019, 1025-28

Win Berry (*Hotel New Hampshire*), **6:**777, 778

Windy McPherson (*Windy McPherson's Son*), **1:**46

Wing Biddlebaum (*Winesburg, Ohio*), **1:**52

Wingfield family (*Glass Menagerie*), **12:***1656*, 1662, 1663, 1664, 1665, 1666

Winterthurn (*Mysteries of Winterthurn*), **8:**1112, 1113

Wissey Jones (*Child Buyer*), **5:**696, 697

witch (*Frog Prince*), **7:**944

Wolf Larsen (*Sea-Wolf*), **7**:877, 889-90
woman ("Sunday Morning"),
 11:1473, 1481, 1482
"Wonderboy" (baseball bat)
 (*Natural*), **7**:915, 922, 923
writer ("Gambler, Nun, and Radio"),
 5:681

Xavier (*Spreading Fires*), **6**:818
Xavier Kilgarvan (*Mysteries of
 Winterthurn*), **8**:1112-13

Yakov Bok (*Fixer*), **7**:917, 920-21
Yancey Cravat (*Cimarron*), **4**:506,
 507
Yentl (*Yentl, the Yeshiva Boy*),
 10:1401, 1405, 1406, 1411
Yiban (*Hundred Secret Senses*),
 11:1517

Ying-ying (*Moon Lady*), **11**:1518
Yod (*He, She, and It*), **9**:1210
Yolanda García (*How the García Girls
 Lost Their Accents*), **1**:33
Yolanda García (*!Yo!*), **1**:36-37
Yonkel (*Gift of Asher Lev*), **9**:1274
young black mother ("Long Black
 Song"), **12**:1707
young boy (*Old Ramon*), **10**:1349
Young Charlie (Charlotte Newton)
 (*Shadow of a Doubt*), **12**:1639,
 1640, 1641, 1650
Young Charlie's mother (*Shadow of a
 Doubt*), **12**:1641
young girl ("Boys and Girls"),
 8:1082
young girl ("Child Who Favored
 Daughter"), **11**:1580
young princess (*Medea*), **6**:801

young woman ("Sir Rabbit"),
 12:1601
Yudel Krinsky (*My Name Is Asher
 Lev*), **9**:1270
Yves (*Another Country*), **1**:120

Zarita (Simple columns), **6**:736
Zbigniew Shapira (*Certificate*),
 10:1407, 1408
Zenia (*The Robber Bride*), **1**:99
Zenobia (Zeena) Frome (*Ethan
 Frome*), **12**:1624, 1628
Zerkow (*McTeague*), **8**:1093, 1096
Zilla Reisling (*Babbitt*), **6**:856
Zoo (*Other Voices, Other Rooms*), **2**:252
Zooey Glass (Glass family stories),
 10:1303, 1308, 1309
Zooey Glass (*Zooey*), **10**:1315, 1316
Zophar (*J.B.*), **7**:904

Geographical Index

Adano (Italy), as *Bell for Adano* setting, **5**:691-92

Adirondacks, **3**:385

Africa

Angelou and, **1**:60, 61, 73-74, 76, 80

Baldwin and, **1**:104

as Bellow novel setting, **1**:140

Brooks and, **2**:208

as *Color Purple* setting, **11**:1574, 1575

Giovanni tour, **5**:631, 632, 634

Hansberry and, **5**:657

Hemingway and, **5**:663, 664, 665

Hughes and, **6**:728, 730, 731, 738

Laurence and, **6**:820-21, 823, 824, 826, 831

Sexton and, **10**:1361

as *This Side Jordan* setting, **6**:821

as *Tomorrow-Tamer* settings, **6**:831

Walker and, **11**:1563, 1566

Wright and, **12**:1696, 1697

Alabama

Agee sharecropper documentary, **1**:13, 20

Baldwin and, **1**:106

Bontemps and, **2**:183, 184

Capote and, **2**:234

Hurston and, **6**:745, 746, 749

Lee and, **6**:833, 834, 835, 836, 838

Alaska

as *Call of the Wild* setting, **7**:884

as *Edge* setting, **7**:932

Ferber and, **4**:505

London and, **7**:876

McCarthy and, **7**:962

Albuquerque (N.M.), **7**:993, 997

Alexandria (La.), **2**:181, 182, 184

Allegheny (Pa.), **10**:1417, 1418, 1422

Alliston (Ontario, Canada), **1**:84

Andover (Mass.), **1**:28

Antigua (British West Indies), **7**:906-7

Antilles, as *This Music Crept by Me Upon the Waters* setting, **7**:907

Appalachian region, **7**:961, 966

Appleton (Wis.), **4**:500, 503, 508

Appomattox Courthouse (Va.), **2**:158

Arbuthnot-by-the-Sea (Irving fictional place), **6**:777

Arizona, Cather and, **2**:276, 280

Arkansas, **1**:*119*

Angelou and, **1**:58, 60, 65, 74, 75

Portis and, **9**:1245, 1246, 1247, 1249, *1252*, 1254

Atlanta (Ga.)

as "Artificial Nigger" setting, **8**:1148

Baldwin and1.104, **1**:106

as *Meridian* setting, **11**:1581

Atlantic City (N.J.)

as *Skin of Our Teeth* setting, **12**:1646

as *This Side of Paradise* setting, **4**:534

Augusta (Ga.)

Benét and, **2**:150, 152

Ortiz Cofer and, **9**:1182, 1185

Austin (Minn.), O'Brien and, **8**:1119, 1120, 1123

Austin (Tex.), as *Tender Mercies* setting, **4**:549

Austria

Davies and, **3**:339, 343

Irving and, **6**:764, 765, 771, 773, 776, 777, 778, 780, 781

Salinger and, **10**:1302

Stein and, **10**:1418, 1422

Back Creek Valley (Va.), **2**:269, 270, 274

Badenweiler (Germany), **2**:264

Baja California, Steinbeck and, **11**:1447, 1451

Baltimore (Md.)

as *Accidental Tourist* setting, **11**:1552

as *Breathing Lessons* setting, **11**:1554, 1555

as *Dinner at the Homesick Restaurant* setting, **11**:1555

as *Making of Americans* setting, **10**:1433-34

as *Patchwork Planet* setting, **11**:1558

Rich and, **9**:1277, 1278, 1281

as *Searching for Caleb* setting, **11**:1559, 1560

Stein and, **10**:1418, 1422

as *Three Lives* setting, **10**:1437, 1438

Tyler and, **11**:1543, 1544, 1545, 1546, 1548, 1549

Bataan peninsula (Philippines), **5**:685

Batavia (N.Y.), Gardner and, **5**:595, 596, 599, 600, 601, 606, 607, 609

Bayonne (La.), as *Lesson Before Dying* setting, **5**:588, 593

Bel-Air (Calif.), Capote and, **2**:233, 238

Belgium, Porter and, **9**:1232, 1233

Belignin (France), Stein and, **10**:1421, 1422, 1437

Bennington (Vt.)

Frost and, **4**:560

Malamud and, **7**:912, 914, 916

Berkeley (Calif.), **11**:1569

Berkshires, **1**:135

Berlin (Germany), **9**:1231

Bermuda

Capote and, **2**:234

Porter and, **9**:1231, 1235

Bethlehem, (Pa.), Benét, **2**:149, 150, 152

Bidwell, Ohio (Anderson fictional town), **1**:50, 51

Big Moose Lake (Dreiser fictional place), **3**:386

Big Sur (Calif.)

Jeffers and, **6**:785, 789, 790
Steinbeck and, **11**:1452
Bilgoray (Poland), Singer and,
    10:1398, 1399, 1403, 1408
Bixby (Okla.), **5**:712
Blacksburg (Va.), Giovanni and,
    5:632, 633
Boca Grande (Didion fictional
    place), **3**:359, 360, 361, 372
Boston (Mass.)
    Cormier and, **3**:296, 297
    as *Death of a Salesman* setting,
        8:1027, 1028
    Eliot and, **4**:438
    Frost and, **4**:555, 560
    MacLeish and, **7**:891, 896
    Norris and, **8**:1089
    O'Brien and, **8**:1123
    O'Neill and, **9**:1157, 1162, 1163
    Plath and, **9**:1213, 1218
    as "Weary Kingdom" setting,
        6:782
    as *World According to Garp* set-
        ting, **6**:778
Bottom (Morrison fictional neigh-
    borhood), **8**:1069-70
Bound Brook (N.J.), Sinclair and,
    10:1377, 1381
Bountiful (Tex.; Foote fictional
    place), **4**:554
Bowlegs (Ferber fictional place), **4**:508
Brazil
    Frost and, **4**:561
    Morrison and, **8**:1062
Briarcliff Manor (N.Y.), **5**:684
Britain. *See* Great Britain
British Columbia (Canada), **1**:82, 85
    as *Fire-Dwellers* setting, **6**:831
    Laurence and, **6**:821, 831
    Munro and, **8**:1074, 1075, 1077
    as *Who Do You Think You Are?* set-
        ting, **8**:1081, 1082
British Honduras, as *Dog of the South*
    setting, **9**:1253, 1254
British Isles. *See* Great Britain
British West Africa, as *This Side
    Jordan* setting, **6**:829
Bronx (N.Y.C.)
    as *In the Beginning* setting, **9**:1266
    Potok and, **9**:1259, 1260, 1263
    Terkel and, **11**:1519, 1520, 1523
Bronzeville (Brooks fictional place),
    2:197, 199, 203, 205-7
Brooklyn (N.Y.C.), **9**:1267
    as *Assistant* setting, **7**:919
    Capote and, 234

as *Chosen* setting, **9**:1267, 1268,
    1269
as *Death of a Salesman* setting,
    8:1025
as *Gift of Asher Lev* setting,
    9:1274
Malamud and, **7**:909, 910, 913
Miller and, **8**:1018, 1027
Moore and, **8**:1035, 1045-46,
    1047
as *My Name Is Asher Lev* setting,
    9:1270
Piercy and, **9**:1199
Potok and, **9**:1259, 1261, 1263,
    1264, 1266
as *Promise* setting, **9**:1265
Singer and, **10**:1397, 1403
as *Sophie's Choice* setting,
    11:1500-1501
Byhalia (Miss.), **4**:475

Cairo (Egypt), **1**:60, 61
California
    Angelou and, **1**:58-59, 62, 74,
        75, 76
    Benét and, **2**:150
    Bontemps and, **2**:182, 184, 191
    Capote and, **2**:233, 237, 238
    Carver and, **2**:256, 257, 258
    Didion and, **3**:353, 354, 356,
        357, 359, 361-62, 365, 366,
        368, 369, 371
    Foote and, **4**:541, 543
    Frost and, **4**:555, 556, 560, 562
    Gaines and, **5**:584, 593
    Giovanni and, **5**:629
    as *Grapes of Wrath* setting,
        11:1463
    Jeffers and, **6**:783, 785, 786,
        787, 789, 790, 791, 792,
        794, 796, 798
    as *Joy Luck Club* setting, **11**:1513
    London and, **7**:869, 870, 871,
        873, 874, 876, 877, 878, 883
    Norris and, **8**:1085, 1086, 1087,
        1088, 1089, 1090, 1094,
        1096, 1097, 1100
    O'Neill and, **9**:1162
    Rich and, **9**:1281, 1292, 1293
    Sinclair gubernatorial bid,
        10:1377, 1381, 1382, 1386-
        87, *1388*, 1389
    Stein and, **10**:1418, 1422, 1431
    Steinbeck and, **11**:1445, 1446,
        1447, 1448, 1449, 1450,
        1451, 1452, 1459, 1465

Tan and, **11**:1505, 1506, 1507,
    1509, 1513, 1514, 1515
Walker and, **11**:1564, 1566,
    1567, 1569, 1570
as *White Fang* setting, **7**:887
Wilder and, **12**:1641
Zindel and, **12**:1714, 1721
Cambodia, **8**:1127
Cambridge (Mass.)
    Cummings and, **3**:311, 312, 316
    Rich and, **9**:1281
    as *Sound and Fury* setting, **4**:492
Camden (Ohio), **1**:41, 42, 44
Canada
    Atwood and, **1**:81-100
    Bellow and, **1**:123, 124, 126
    Davies and, **3**:333-52
    Dreiser and, **3**:378, 389
    Dunbar and, **3**:404, 411
    Irving and, **6**:767
    Laurence and, **6**:819-32
    London (Jack) and, **7**:873, 874,
        876, 877, 880, 884, 885,
        886, 887, *889*, 890
    Munro and, **8**:1071-84
    Oates and, **8**:1105
    O'Brien and, **8**:1121, 1132
    seventeenth-century wilderness
        illustration, **2**:277
    Sinclair and, **10**:1378
    Tyler and, **11**:1543, 1546
Cape Cod (Mass.)
    O'Neill and, **9**:1160
    Piercy and, **9**:1199, 1202
Caribbean region
    as *Arrowsmith* setting, **6**:857, 858
    Bontemps and, **2**:183, 184
Carlisle (Pa.), **8**:1034, 1037
Carmel (Calif.)
    Jeffers and, **6**:783, 785, 786,
        787, 789, 791, 792, 794
    as "Tamar" setting, **6**:798
Catskills, **3**:402, **5**:608
Central America, **9**:*1257*
    Didion and, **3**:357, 359, 372,
        373
    as *Gringos* setting, **9**:1256
Chatham (N.J.), Moore and, **8**:1035,
    1037
Chicago (Ill.)
    as *American Buffalo* setting, **7**:936
    Anderson and, **1**:42, 44, 45, 46,
        47
    Bellow and, **1**:124-25, 126, 127,
        129, 134, 140
    Bontemps and, **2**:183, 184, 185

Brooks and, **2:**195, 196, 198, 199, 200, *201*, 202
as *Division Street* setting, **11:**1524
Dreiser and, **3:**376, 377, 384, 389, 392, 394, 395
Dunbar and, **3:**399, 402
Ferber and, **4:**500, 501, 502, 503
as *Girls* setting, **4:**513
Hansberry and, **5:**563, 645, 646, 649
as *Iron Heel* setting, **7:**889
as *Jungle* setting, **10:**1391, 1393
Mamet and, **7:**927, 928, 931
Masters and, **7:**947, 950
McCarthy and, **7:**962
as *Native Son* setting, **12:**1704
as *Natural* setting, **7:**922
Norris and, **8:**1085, 1086, 1089, 1090
as *Outsider* setting, **12:**1709
Piercy and, **9:**1197-98
as *Pit* setting, **8:**1091, 1098, 1099
Porter and, **9:**1230
as *Raisin in Sun* setting, **5:**653
Sandburg and, **10:**1323, 1325, 1326, 1328
as *Show Boat* setting, **4:**509, 510
Sinclair and, **10:**1377, 1379, 1384, 1385, 1391, 1392, 1393
as *So Big* setting, **4:**511, 512
South Side photographs, **2:***201*
as *Spoon River Anthology* setting, **7:**957
Terkel and, **11:**1520, *1522*, 1523, 1531
T. Williams and, **12:**1651, 1653, 1654
World's Columbian Exposition (1898), **3:**399, 402
Wright and, **12:**1694, *1695*, 1697, 1701, 1703
Chichester (England), **4:**445
China
    Buck and, **2:**209-12, 214, 215, 217, 223, 229
    Hemingway and, **5:**668
    Hersey and, **5:**684, 685, 686, 687, 689
    as *Joy Luck Club* setting, **11:**1513
    as *Kitchen God's Wife* setting, **11:**1515
    Miller and, **8:**1018, 1025
    Tan and, **11:**1508, 1509
    Wilder and, **12:**1630, 1634

Cincinnati (Ohio), **8:**1060
    as *Beloved* setting, **8:**1056, 1057, 1063
    Dunbar and, **3:**416
    Giovanni and, **5:**629, 631
Clarksdale (Miss.), **12:**1652
Clatskanie (Oregon), **2:**255, 256, 258
Cleveland (Ohio)
    Anderson and, **1:**44
    Dreiser and, **3:**386, 388
    Hughes and, **6:**727, 730
    Schaefer and, **10:**1343, 1347
Clinton (Ontario, Canada), **8:**1075
Club Night (painting), **8:***1109
Clyde (Ohio), **1:**42, 44
Coaltown (Ill.; Wilder fictional place), **12:**1648
College Park (Md.), **9:**1232
Colorado
    Cather and, **2:**276
    Didion and, **3:**372
    Dunbar and, **3:**401, 402
    Porter and, **9:**1230, 1233, 1238, 1239
Columbus (Miss.), T. Williams and, **12:**1651, 1652, 1654
Columbus (Ohio), **3:**386
Comax (British Columbia@ Canada), **8:**1075
Coney Island (N.Y.C.)
    as *Sophie's Choice* setting, **11:**1501, 1502
    in work of Singer, **10:***1412*, 1413
Connecticut
    Ferber and, **4:**502, 503
    as *Indian Summer* setting, **6:**817
    Lewis and, **6:**848
    O'Connor and, **8:**1136, 1137, 1138
    O'Neill and, **9:***1158*, 1159, 1166, 1175, 1176
    Schaefer and, **10:**1345, 1347
    Stevens and, **11:**1467, 1470, 1471, 1482
    Styron and, **11:**1492, 1493
    Wilder and, **12:**1629, 1633, 1634, 1637
Contra Costa County (Calif.), **9:**1162
Conway (Mass.), MacLeish and, **7:**894, 895, 896
Cornish (N.H.), Salinger and, **10:**1303, 1306, 1309, 1310, 1311
Corvallis (Ore.), Malamud and, **7:**911, 913, 925

Costa Rica, Didion and, **3:**373
Cuba
    Anderson and, **1:**42
    Capote and, **2:**234
    Hemingway and, **5:**664, 665, 668
    Norris and, **8:**1089, 1090
Cuernavaca (Mexico), **12:**1695
Cumberland Gap, **2:***153*
Czechoslovakia, **3:**430

Dallas (Tex.), Foote and, **4:**541
Danby (Vt.), **2:**209, 212
Danville (Ind.), **1:**45
Danville (Pa.), as *Song of Solomon* setting, **8:**1067
Dar es Salaam (Tanzania), **2:**208
Dayton (Ohio)
    Dreiser and, **3:**376
    Dunbar and, **3:**397, 398, 399, 401, 402, 404
Death Valley (Calif.), as *McTeague* setting, **8:**1094, 1096
Delaware, **1:**28
Denmark, **5:**603
Denver (Colo.)
    Didion and, **3:**372
    as *Pale Horse, Pale Rider* setting, **9:**1238, 1239
    Porter and, **9:**1230, 1233
Deptford (Ontario, Canada; Davies fictional place), **3:**335, 337, 338, 340, 343, 345-47, 350
Derry (N.H.), Frost and, **4:**557, 558, 560, 562, 565, 566, 567
Des Moines River, **4:**508
Detroit (Mich.)
    Hersey and, **5:**687
    Oates and, **8:**1104-5, 1108, 1109, 1110
    slums photograph, **8:***1108*
    as *Song of Solomon* setting, **8:**1066
    as *them* setting, **8:**1113, 1114
Devon (England), Plath and, **9:**1216, 1218
Devonshire (England), as "For Esmé—with Love and Squalor" setting, **10:**1303
Dexter (Dunbar fictional town), **3:**416
District of Columbia. *See* Washington (D.C.)
Dodge City (Kans.), as *Monte Walsh* setting, **10:**1351
Dominican Republic, Alvarez and, **1:**26-39

Duluth (Minn.)
  Dylan and, **3**:417, 418, 421
  Lewis and, **6**:848

East Egg (Long Island, N.Y.; Fitzgerald
    fictional place), **4**:531, 532
East End (London), **7**:873, 874,
    880, 882-83
Eatonton (Ga.), Walker and,
    11:1561, 1562, 1563, 1566
Eatonville (Fla.)
  Hurston and, **6**:746, 747, 751, 752, 760
  as *Their Eyes Were Watching God*
    setting, **6**:756, 757
Edinburgh (Scotland), Eliot and,
    4:446, 448
Egypt, **1**:60, 61, 80
El Dorado (Ark.), Portis and,
    9:1245, 1246, 1249
Elizabeth (N.J.), Blume and, **2**:164, 166
El Paso (Tex.), McCarthy and,
    7:963, 965
El Salvador, Didion and, **3**:360
Elyria (Ohio), **1**:43, 44
England. *See* Great Britain
Europe
  Capote and, **2**:234, 235
  Hughes and, **6**:728, 731
  Jeffers and, **6**:784, 787
  Knowles and, **6**:805, 808
  Laurence and, **6**:831
  Lewis and, **6**:848, 860
  Malamud and, **7**:912, 913
  McCarthy and, **7**:965
  Moore and, **8**:1035
  Norris and, **8**:1088, 1089
  Rich and, **9**:1279
  Sexton and, **10**:1361
  Steinbeck and, **11**:1451
  Styron and, **11**:1492, 1496
  Wharton and, **12**:1612, 1614,
    1615, 1616, 1619, 1620
  T. Williams and, **12**:1652
  W. C. Williams and, **12**:1676, 1679
  See also specific cities and countries
Evansville (Ill.), **3**:376
Everglades (Fla.), as *Their Eyes Were
    Watching God* setting, **6**:756,
    757, 758
Excelsior (N.J.; Wilder fictional
    place), **12**:1646
Exeter (N.H.), Irving and, **6**:763,
    764, 767

Fairmont (W. Va.), Knowles and,
    6:803, 804, 808

Fayetteville (N.C.), McCullers and,
    7:977, 979
Flat Rock (N.C.), Sandburg and,
    10:1323, 1327, 1328
Florida, **1**:65
  Benét and, **2**:261
  Blume and, **2**:164, 166, 170
  in Capote works, **2**:248
  as "Good Man Is Hard to Find"
    setting, **8**:1149
  Hemingway and, **5**:663, 665,
    666
  Hersey and, **5**:683, 687, 688
  Hurston and, **6**:745, 746, 747,
    749, 751, 752, 753, 755,
    756, 757, 758, 760
  Knowles and, **6**:807
  Rich and, **9**:1288
  Singer and, **10**:1397, 1400, 1403
  as Stevens influence, **11**:1470,
    1473, 1480, 1482, 1484
  T. Williams and, **12**:1653, 1654,
    1660
  Zindel and, **12**:1713
Fort Adams (R.I.), Wilder and,
    12:1630, 1634
Fort Benning (Ga.), McCullers and,
    7:976, 977, 985
Fort Lauderdale (Fla.), **6**:807
Fort Pierce (Fla.), **6**:745
Fort Smith (Ark.), as *True Grit* set-
    ting, **9**:1255
Frampol (Singer fictional town),
    10:1414
France
  Anderson and, **1**:45
  Baldwin in, **1**:101, 104, 105, 107
  Benét and, **2**:151, 152
  Cather and, **2**:276, 281
  Cummings and, **3**:314, 316, 318,
    324-25, 329
  Eliot and, **4**:439, 441
  Faulkner and, **4**:477, 485
  as *Gift of Asher Lev* setting,
    9:1265, 1274
  Hemingway and, **5**:661, 663,
    665, 666, 670, 676, 677
  Knowles and, **6**:07, 806
  MacLeish and, **7**:894, 895, 902
  Malamud and, **7**:913
  McCarthy and, **7**:963
  McCullers and, **7**:978
  McNickle and, **7**:994, 1004
  as *My Name Is Asher Lev* setting,
    9:1270
  Norris and, **8**:1089

O'Connor and, **8**:1138
  as *Spreading Fires* setting, **6**:818
  Stein and, **10**:1421, 1422, 1437
  as *Tender Is the Night* setting,
    4:533, 534
  Wharton and, **12**:1611, 1615,
    1616, 1622
  T. Williams and, **12**:1653
  W. C. Williams and, **12**:1676
  Wright and, **12**:1693, 1695,
    1696, 1697, 1708
  See also Paris; Riviera
Franconia (N.H.), Frost and, **4**:558,
    560
French Riviera. *See* Riviera
Frenchtown (Mass.; Cormier fic-
    tional place), **3**:294, 300

Galesburg (Ill.), Sandburg and,
    10:1323, 1324, 1325, 1328,
    1331, 1340
Galveston (Tex.), **4**:470
Garnett (Kans.), Masters and, **7**:945,
    946, 950
Geneva (Switzerland), W. C.
    Williams and, **12**:1676
Georgia, **8**:1135, 1136, 1137, 1138,
    1139, 1142, **9**:1266
  Baldwin and, **1**:105, 106
  Benét and, **2**:159
  as *Clock Without Hands* setting,
    7:990
  as *Color Purple* setting, **11**:1574
  McCullers and, **7**:976, 977, 985
  as *Member of the Wedding* setting,
    7:988
  O'Connor and, **4**:548, **8**:1135-
    39, 1142, **9**:1266
  Ortiz Cofer and, **9**:1182, 1185
  Walker and, **11**:1561, 1562,
    1563, 1566
Germany
  Eliot and, **4**:439, 441
  Ferber and, **4**:502
  Miller and, **8**:1016, 1019
  Porter and, **9**:1234, 1235, 1241
  W. C. Williams and, **12**:1677
Ghana
  Angelou and, **1**:60, 61, 72, 73-74
  Laurence and, **6**:829, 830, 832
Glencoe (Ill.), MacLeish and, **7**:891,
    895
Glen Ellen (Calif.), London and,
    7:869, 874
Gloucester (Mass.), Eliot and,
    4:438, 444

Gloucestershire (England), Frost and, **4**:560, 565

Good as I Been to You (Dylan; record album), **3**:421, 425

Gopher Prairie (Lewis fictional place), **6**:844, 849, 853-54

Grafton's saloon (Schaefer fictional place), **10**:1354

Great Britain
Davies and, **3**:336, 339, 343
Dunbar and, **3**:401, 402
Eliot and, **4**:437, 441, 444, 445, 446, 448
Faulkner and, **4**:477, 485
as *Four Quartets* settings, **4**:449
Frost and, **4**:558, 560, 565, 567
Jeffers and, **6**:786, 787
Laurence and, **6**:821, 823
Lewis and, **6**:844, 848
London (Jack) and, **7**:873, 874, 880, 882-83
Malamud and, **7**:913
McCarthy and, **7**:962, 963, 965
McNickle and, **7**:994, 997, 1004
Moore and, **8**:1035, 1037
Norris and, **8**:1087, 1089
Plath and, **9**:1213, 1215, 1216, 1218
Portis and, **9**:1247, 1249
Rich and, **9**:1279
Stein and, **10**:1419, 1420
Steinbeck and, **11**:1451
T. Williams and, **12**:1653
Wright and, **12**:1696

Great Dismal Swamp, **4**:557

Great Plains, **10**:1351

Greece
Capote and, **2**:235
Frost and, **4**:559, 561
Miller and, **8**:1013, 1016, 1018
as *Woman of Andros* setting, **12**:1636

Green Mountain (Vt.) town meeting, **6**:*811*

Greenwich Village
Baldwin and, **1**:105, 109
Cummings and, **3**:315
Foote and, **4**:544
Hansberry and, **5**:648
Malamud and, **7**:913
as *Masque of Mercy* setting, **4**:572
Masters and, **7**:949
Moore and, **8**:1035, 1037
O'Neill and, **9**:1160
Porter and, **9**:1230, 1233
as *Sign in Sidney Brustein's Window* setting, :655

Wright and, **12**:1695

Grover's Corners (N.H.; Wilder fictional place), **12**:1639, 1644, 1645, 1648

Guadalcanal Island
Hersey and, **5**:685, 688
as *Into Valley* setting, **5**:697

Guadarrama Mountains, **5**:675

Haight-Ashbury district (San Francisco), **3**:368, *370*

Haiti
Bontemps and, **2**:186, 188, 191-93
Hurston and, **6**:748, 749

Hamburg (Ark.), Portis and, **9**:1246, 1249

Hamden (Conn.), Wilder and, **12**:1629, 1633, 1634, 1637

Harlem, **1**:*64, 103, 106*
as "Angel Levine" setting, **7**:924
Baldwin and, **1**:102, 104, 105, 116, 121
Ellison and, **4**:459, 461, 463
Hughes and, **6**:729, 731, 733, 736, 738, 741
Hurston and, **6**:747, 752
as *Invisible Man* setting, **4**:460, 465, 468, 470
as *Jazz* setting, **8**:1054

Harpers Ferry raid, **6**:726

Harrison (Tex.), Orphans' Home cycle, **4**:545, 553, 554

Hartford (Conn.), Stevens and, **11**:1467, 1470, 1471, 1482

Hawaii, Didion and, **3**:369, 371

Hell's Kitchen (N.Y.C.), **12**:1677

Hibbing (Minn.), **3**:418, 424

Hillsboro (W. Va.), **2**:209, 210, 212

Hiroshima (Japan), **5**:686, 692

Holcomb (Kans.), **2**:248, 249

Hollywood
as Didion influence, **3**:362, 364
Dreiser and, **3**:375, 378, 384
Faulkner and, **4**:478, 479, 481, 485
Fitzgerald and, **4**:519, 520, 521, 522, 523, 29, 531, 536
Foote and, **4**:547, 550
Porter and, **9**:1231
Sandburg and, **10**:1335

Honduras, O'Neill and, **8**:1159, **9**:1163

Hong Kong, Wilder and, **12**:1630, 1634

Honolulu (Hawaii), as Didion influence, **3**:371

Hormigueros (Puerto Rico), Ortiz Cofer and, **9**:1181, 1182, 1185

Houston (Tex.)
as *Trip to Bountiful* setting, **4**:554
as *Young Man from Atlanta* setting, **4**:552

Huntsville (Ala.), Bontemps and, **2**:183, 184

Ibiza island, **7**:963

Idaho, Hemingway and, **5**:659, 664, 665, 668

Illinois
Bontemps and, **2**:183, 184
Dreiser and, **3**:376
Ferber and, **4**:500, 501, 502, 503
Hansberry and, **5**:645, 646, 649, 653
Hemingway and, **5**:659, 660, 665, 666
Hughes and, **6**:730
MacLeish and, **7**:891, 895
Mamet and, **7**:927, 928, 931
Masters and, **7**:943, 946, 947, 949, 950, 952, 953, 959
as *New Spoon River* setting, **7**:945
Norris and, **8**:1085, 1086, 1089, 1090
Poet Laureate, **2**:195, 198, 199
Sandburg and, **2**:195, 198, **10**:1323, 1324, 1325, 1326, 1328, 1331, 1340
as *Spoon River Anthology* setting, **7**:945
Terkel and, **11**:1520, *1522*, 1523, 1531
Wright and, **12**:1694, *1695*, 1697, 1701, 1703
See also Chicago

India
Buck and, **2**:214
as *Son of the Circus* setting, **6**:781

Indiana
Anderson and, **1**:45
Dreiser and, **3**:375, 376, 380, 384

Indian Creek (Tex.), Porter and, **9**:1229, 1232, 1233

Indian Territory, as *True Grit* setting, **9**:1255

Indonesia, Wright and, **12**:1696, 1697

Iran
as *Going After Cacciato* setting, **8**:1129
Tyler and, **11**:1543

Ireland, Jeffers and, **6**:786, 787, 791
Isle des Chevaliers (Morrison fictional place), **8**:1070
Israel, **1**:104, 130, 139
    Frost and, **4**:559, 561
    Potok and, **9**:1261, 1263, 1268
    as *Shosha* setting, **10**:1412, 1413
Italy
    as *Cabala* setting, **12**:1635, 1636
    as *Dubin's Lives* setting, **7**:924
    Ellison and, **4**:462
    as *Farewell to Arms* setting, **5**:672
    Faulkner and, **4**:477, 485
    Hemingway and, **5**:664, 665, 666, 672
    Hersey and, **5**:685, 688, 692
    Lewis and, **6**:843, 847, 848
    Malamud and, **7**:912, 913, 917
    McCarthy and, **7**:963
    Norris and, **8**:1087, 1089
    Porter and, **9**:1232
    Stein and, **10**:1419, 1422
    as *Tender Is the Night* setting, **4**:533
    Wharton and, **12**:1613, 1614, 1622
    Wilder and, **12**:1630
    T. Williams and, **12**:1653, 1660
    See also Rome

Jacinto, (Calif.), **2**:150
Jackson (Miss.)
    Walker and, **11**:1564, 1566
    Welty and, **4**:548, **12**:1589, 1590, 1591, 1592, 1593, 1596, 1597, 1606
Jacksonville (Fla.), **6**:746
Jaffrey (N.H.), **2**:274
Jakarta, **3**:372
Jamaica, Hurston and, **6**:748, 749
Japan
    Buck and, **2**:212, 214
    Hersey and, **5**:685, 686, 692
Jefferson (Faulkner fictional town), **4**:483, 489, 490, 491, 492, 494, 496, 497
Jersey City (N.J.), **2**:179
Jerusalem (Israel), **1**:139, **9**:1263
Jerusalem (Va.; Styron fictional place), **11**:1498
Jiangxi (China), **2**:*221*
Joplin (Mo.), Hughes and, **6**:725, 726, 730

Kalamazoo (Mich.), Ferber and, **4**:499, 500, 503

Kansas
    Benét and, **2**:*158*
    Brooks and, **2**:195, 196, 199
    in Capote work, **2**:248, 249
    Gibson and, **5**:612, 613, 615, 616
    Hughes and, **6**:725, 726, 738
    Masters and, **7**:945, 946, 950
Kansas City (Mo.)
    Dreiser and, **3**:385
    Hemingway and, **5**:666
    Hughes and, **6**:738, 739
Kenya, **2**:208
Ketchum (Idaho), Hemingway and, **5**:659, 664, 665, 668
Key West (Fla.)
    Hemingway and, **5**:663, 665, 666
    Hersey and, **5**:683, 687, 688
    Rich and, **9**:1288
    T. Williams and, **12**:1653, 1654, 1660
Kiev (Ukraine), as *Fixer* setting, **7**:920, 921
Kingston (Ontario, Canada), Davies and, **3**:334, 335, 338, 343
Kirkwood (Mo.), Moore and, **8**:1033, 1037
Klondike. *See* Yukon Territory
Knoxville (Tenn.)
    Agee and, **1**:11, 12, 14, 18
    Giovanni and, **5**:627, 628, 631
    McCarthy and, **7**:962, 965
    as *Suttree* setting, **7**:971, 972
Korea, **2**:214
Kyle (Tex.), **9**:1230

Lachine (Canada), Bellow and, **1**:123, 124, 126
Lakefield (Ontario, Canada), Laurence and, **6**:819, 822, 823
Lake Tahoe, **11**:1447, 1451
Lakewood (Ohio), **10**:1344
Las Vegas (Nev.), in Capote work, **2**:248
Lawrence (Kans.), Hughes and, **6**:725, 726, 738
Lawrence (Mass.), Frost and, **4**:556, 557, 560, 562
Leipzig (Germany), **12**:1677
Lenox (Mass.), Wharton and, **12**:1614, 1615, 1616
Leominster (Mass.), Cormier and, **3**:293, 294, 295, 296, 297, 300

Leoncin (Poland), Singer and, **10**:1397, 1398, 1403
Les Trois Sauvages (Mass.), **4**:438
Lewistown (Ill.), Masters and, **7**:946, 953, 959
Liberia, **1**:61
Lincoln (Ill.), Hughes and, **6**:730
Lincoln (Neb.), Cather and, **2**:270, 274, 278, 284
Little Rock (Ark.)
    as *Dog of the South* setting, **9**:1254
    Portis and, **9**:1249
Lockport (N.Y.), Oates and, **8**:1103, 1104, 1107
London (England)
    Anderson and, **1**:45
    Baldwin play productions, **1**:113, 114
    Davies and, **3**:336
    Eliot and, **4**:437, 441, 445, 446, 448
    London (Jack) and, **7**:873, 874, 880, 882-83
    Norris and, **8**:1087
    Plath and, **9**:1213, 1216, 1218
    Portis and, **9**:1247, 1249
    T. Williams and, **12**:1653
    Wright and, **12**:1696
Long Island (N.Y.)
    as *Great Gatsby* setting, **4**:526, 530
    Knowles and, **6**:807, 808
    Steinbeck and, **11**:1448, 1449
Lorain (Ohio)
    as *Bluest Eye* setting, **8**:1057, 1065
    Morrison and, **8**:1049, 1050, 1051, 1052
Los Angeles (Calif.)
    Angelou and, **1**:59
    Bontemps and, **2**:182, 184
    as Didion influence, **3**:358, 364, 366, 369
    Jeffers and, **6**:784, 787
    Sinclair and, **10**:1389
    as *Taming Star Runner* setting, **5**:713, 715
    Watts section, **2**:182, **5**:629
Los Gatos (Calif.), **11**:1448
Louisiana
    Bontemps and, **2**:188
    Capote and, **2**:233, 234, 238
    Faulkner and, **4**:477, 485, 486
    Ferber and, **4**:503
    Gaines and, **5**:581-93

Hurston and, **6**:753
  as *Searching for Caleb* setting,
    11:1560
  T. Williams and, **12**:1652, 1666,
    1668
Louisville (Ky.), as *Great Gatsby* set-
    ting, **4**:531
Louisville (Tenn.), McCarthy and,
    7:963, 965
Lourdes (France), **8**:1138
Lower East Side (N.Y.C.), **1**:39
Lynchburg (Va.), **2**:210, 212

Madison (Wis.), Wilder and,
    12:1629, 1630, 1634
Madrid (Spain)
  as *Fifth Column* setting, **5**:678
  Hemingway and, **5**:664
Maine
  as *Cider House Rules* setting,
    6:774
  as *Hotel New Hampshire* setting,
    6:776, 777, 778
Mallorca (Spain), Stein and,
    10:1420, 1422
Manhattan. *See* New York City
Manitoba (Canada), as *Jest of God*
    setting, **6**:829
Marion (Va.), Anderson and, **1**:44,
    45
Martha's Vineyard (Mass.)
  Blume and, **2**:*165*, 178
  Hersey and, **5**:688
  Styron and, **11**:1493
Maryland
  Porter and, **9**:1229, 1232, 1233
  Rich and, **9**:1277, 1278, 1281
  Schaefer and, **10**:1345
  Sinclair and, **10**:1377, 1378, 1382
  as *This Side of Paradise* setting,
    4:535
  Tyler and, **11**:1543, 1544, 1545,
    1546, 1548, 1549, 1552,
    1554, 1555, 1558
  See also Baltimore
Massachusetts, **1**:28, 135
  Blume and, **2**:*165*, 178
  Cormier and, **3**:293, 294, 295,
    296, 297, 300, 302-7
  Cummings and, **3**:311, 312, 316
  Eliot and, **4**:438, 444
  Ellison and, **4**:462, 463
  Frost and, **4**:555, 556, 557, 560,
    562
  Gibson and, **5**:613, 615, 617
  Hersey and, **5**:688

Irving and, **6**:782, 788
Lewis and, **6**:848
MacLeish and, **7**:891, 894, 895,
    896
Moore and, **8**:1035
Norris and, **8**:1089
O'Brien and, **8**:1123
O'Neill and, **9**:1160, 1169
Piercy and, **9**:1199, 1202
Plath and, **9**:1213, 1214, 1218,
    1222
Porter and, **9**:1231, 1234
Rich and, **9**:1281, 1293
Sexton and, **10**:1357, 1361
Sinclair and, **10**:1391
Styron and, **11**:1493
Wharton and, **12**:1614, 1615,
    1616
Maumee (Ohio), Dreiser and, **3**:377
Maycomb (Lee fictional town),
    6:838, 839, 840, 841
Medallion (Ohio; Morrison fictional
    setting), **8**:1069-70
Melrose Park (Pa.), Masters and,
    7:945, 949, 950
Memphis (Tenn.)
  as *Color Purple* setting, **11**:1575
  as *Suttree* setting, **7**:963
  T. Williams and, **12**:1652
  Wright and, **12**:1694, 1703
Mérida (Yucatán, Mexico), as
    Gringos setting, **9**:1256
Mexico
  as *All the Pretty Horses* setting,
    7:969
  as *Blood Meridian* setting, **7**:970
  Capote and, **2**:248
  Cather and, **2**:276, 280
  as *Dog of the South* setting,
    9:1250, 1253, 1254
  as *Gringos* setting, **9**:1256
  Hughes and, **6**:727
  McCarthy and, **7**:964
  as *Night of the Iguana* setting,
    12:1673
  Porter and, **9**:1229, 1231, 1233,
    1234, 1235
  Portis and, **9**:1249
  as *Runner in the Sun* setting,
    7:1001
  Wright and, **12**:1695
Mexico City
  as "Flowering Judas" setting,
    9:1241
  Porter and, **9**:1230
Miami (Fla.)

Hurston and, **6**:749
Zindel and, **12**:1713
Miami Beach (Fla.), Blume and,
    2:164, 166, 170
Michigan
  Ferber and, **4**:499, 500, 503
  Hemingway and, **5**:666
  Hersey and, **5**:687
  Oates and, **8**:1104-5, 1108,
    1109, 1110, 1113, 1114
  Piercy and, **9**:1195, 1199
  Sandburg and, **10**:1326, 1328
Middlebury (Vt.), **1**:28, 29
Middle East, Knowles and, **6**:805,
    808
Midwest, U.S., Anderson and, **1**:41,
    45, 47, 51, 52, 56
Milledgeville (Ga.), O'Connor and,
    8:1135-39, 1142, **9**:1266
Millennium Village (Walt Disney
    World), **1**:65
Milwaukee (Wis.)
  Eliot and, **4**:448
  Sandburg and, **10**:1325, 1328
Minneapolis (Minn.)
  Dylan and, **3**:421
  Tyler and, **11**:1541, 1542, 1546,
    1549
Minnesota
  Dylan and, **3**:417, 418, 421, 424
  Fitzgerald and, **4**:515, 516, 518,
    522, 531
  as *In the Lake of the Woods* setting,
    8:1129
  Lewis and, **6**:843, 844, 845, 847,
    848, 852, 853
  O'Brien and, **8**:1119, 1120, 1123
  Tyler and, **11**:1541, 1542, 1546,
    1549
Minorca, **2**:161
Mississippi
  Baldwin and, **1**:113, 114
  as *Cat on a Hot Tin Roof* setting,
    12:1669
  Faulkner and, **4**:475, 476, 477,
    478, 479, 480, 481, 485
  as *One Writer's Beginning* setting,
    12:1597
  Walker and, **11**:1564, 1566
  Welty and, **12**:1589, 1590, 1591,
    1592, 1593, 1596, 1597,
    1606
  T. Williams and, **12**:1651, 1652,
    1654
  Wright and, **12**:1693, 1694,
    1697

Mississippi River
Hughes and, **6**:742
as *Show Boat* setting, **4**:509, 510
Mississippi River Valley, **2**:193
Missoula (Montana), **7**:997
Missouri
Angelou and, **1**:57, 58, 60, 74
Dreiser and, **3**:377, 385
Eliot and, **4**:437, 438, 441, 444
Hemingway and, **5**:666
Hughes and, **6**:725, 726, 730, 738, 739
as *Indian Summer* setting, **6**:817
Moore and, **8**:1033, 1037
T. Williams and, **12**:1652, 1654, 1655, 1656, 1663, 1664
Mojave Desert, as *Old Ramon* setting, **10**:1356
Monroeville (Ala.)
Capote and, **2**:234
Lee and, **6**:833, 834, 835, 836, 838
Montana
McNickle and, **7**:997
as *Surrounded* setting, **7**:1002
as *Wind from an Enemy Sky* setting, **7**:1003
Monterey (Calif.)
as *Cannery Row* setting, **11**:1465
Steinbeck and, **11**:1446, 1447, 1450, 1451, 1452
as *Tortilla Flat* setting, **11**:1459
Montreal (Quebec, Canada)
Dreiser and, **3**:389
Tyler and, **11**:1543, 1546
Montreux (Switzerland), Tan and, **11**:1507, 1509
Monument (Mass.; Cormier fictional place) Cormier and, **3**:300, 304
Moscow (Russia), Hersey and, **5**:687, 688
Mottson (Faulkner fictional town), **4**:492
Mount Salus (Miss.; Welty fictional setting), **12**:1604, 1607

Nacogdoches (Tex.), as *Blood Meridian* setting, **7**:970
Nagasaki (Japan), **2**:211
Nairobi (Kenya), **2**:208
Nanking (China), Buck and, **2**:212, 220, 222, 224
Nashville (Tenn.)
Bontemps and, **2**:181, 183, 184, 185
Brooks and, **2**:199
Giovanni and, **5**:628, 631
T. Williams and, **12**:1652
Natchez (Miss.), Wright and, **12**:1693, 1694, 1697
Nebraska
Cather and, **2**:269, 270, 272, 274, 275, 276, 278, 279, 281, *282*, 284
Gibson and, **5**:621, 622
Neepawa (Ontario, Canada), Laurence and, **6**:819, 820, 822
Nevada, Didion and, **3**:364
New Albany (Miss.), Faulkner and, **4**:475, 481
New England
as *Bell Jar* setting, **9**:1222
Benét and, **2**:157
Bontemps and, **2**:192
Cummings and, **3**:312, 318
Eliot and, **4**:444
farmer (photograph), **4**:*564*
Frost and, **4**:555, 558, 559, 562, 563, 565, 568, 569, 570, 571
as *J.B.* setting, **7**:903
Knowles and, **6**:804, 805, 806, 809, 811
rural scene (woodcut), **4**:*563*
See also specific cities and states
New Hampshire
Benét and, **2**:157
Cather and, **2**:274, 281
Cummings and, **3**:311, 312, 316, 320
Foote and, **4**:543, 544
Frost and, **4**:557, 558, 560, 562, 565, 566, 567
as *Hotel New Hampshire* setting, **6**:776
Irving and, **6**:763, 764, 767, 776, 778
Knowles and, **6**:804, 805, 808, 810, 813, 815
Salinger and, **10**:1303, 1306, 1309, 1310, 1311
Wilder and, **12**:1639, 1644, 1645, 1648
as *World According to Garp* setting, **6**:778
New Haven (Conn.), Schaefer and, **10**:1345, 1347
New Jersey
Blume and, **2**:164, 166, 171, 174, 179
Buck and, **2**:211
Moore and, **8**:1035, 1037
Ortiz Cofer and, **9**:1182, 1185, 1187, 1189, 1191, 1193, 1194
Sinclair and, **10**:1377, 1381
W. C. Williams and, **12**:1675, 1677, 1679, 1685, 1686, 1687
New London (Conn.)
as *Ah, Wilderness* setting, **9**:1166
as *Long Day's Journey into Night* setting, **9**:1175, 1176
O'Neill and, **9**:*1158*, 1159
New Mexico
Blume and, **2**:166, 167
Cather and, **2**:274, 276, 277, 279-81
as *Company of Cowards* setting, **10**:1355
landscape painting, **2**:*279*
McNickle and, **7**:993, 997
as *Monte Walsh* setting, **10**:1351
Schaefer and, **10**:1343, 1346, 1347, 1350
New Orleans (La.)
Capote and, **2**:233, 234, 238
Faulkner and, **4**:477, 485, 486
Ferber and, **4**:503
Hurston and, **6**:753
as *Optimist's Daughter* setting, **12**:1604
as *Streetcar Named Desire* setting, **12**:1666, 1668
T. Williams and, **12**:1652
Newport (R.I.), Wharton and, **12**:1613, 1614
Newport News (Va.), Styron and, **11**:1489, 1490, 1496
Newton (Mass.), Sexton and, **10**:1357, 1361
New York (state)
Cather and, **2**:281
Dreiser and, **3**:385
Ellison and, **4**:462
Fitzgerald and, **4**:516
Foote and, **4**:543
Gardner and, **5**:595, 596, 599, 600, 601, 606, 607, 609
Hersey and, **5**:684
Knowles and, **6**:807, 808
McCullers and, **7**:975, 978, 979
Morrison and, **8**:1052, 1053
Oates and, **8**:1103, 1104, 1107, 1109, 1110, 1112
Steinbeck and, **11**:1448, 1449
New York City, **1**:*27*, *39*, **8**:1068

as *Age of Innocence* setting,
 12:1621
Alvarez and, **1**:25, 26, 28, 31, 38
Angelou and, **1**:59-60
as *Arrowsmith* setting, **6**:857
Baldwin and, **1**:101, 102-3, 104,
 105, 113-24
as *Bell Jar* setting, **9**:1222, 1223
Bellow and, **1**:124-25, 134, 138
Benét and, **2**:149, 150, 152, 161
Blume and, **2**:166, 171
Bontemps and, **2**:183, 184, 193
Buck and, **2**:211, 212
Capote and, **2**:234, 235, 238,
 240, 245
as *Catcher in the Rye* setting,
 10:1314, 1315
Cather and, **2**:269, 271, 274,
 275, 285, 286
Cummings and, **3**:313, 314, 315,
 324-25
Davies and, **3**:337, 341
as Didion influence, **3**:353, 355,
 356, 357, 358, 359, 362,
 366, *368*, 369
Dreiser and, **3**:377-78, 384, 386,
 389, 395
Dunbar and, **3**:401, 409, 410
Dylan and, **3**:419, 421
Eliot and, **4**:446, 448
Ellison and, **4**:461, 463
Faulkner and, **4**:485
Ferber and, **4**:499, 502, 503
Fitzgerald and, **4**:518
Foote and, **4**:541, 543, 544
as *Franny and Zooey* setting,
 10:1315
Frost and, **4**:560
Giovanni and, **5**:630, 631
as *Great Gatsby* setting, **4**:531, 532
Hansberry and, **5**:645, 648
as *House of Mirth* setting,
 12:1625
Hughes and, **6**:725, 730
as *Hughie* setting, **9**:1178
as *Iceman Cometh* setting, **9**:1173
as *Invisible Man* setting, **4**:469
Irving and, **6**:768
Knowles and, **6**:805, 808
Lee and, **6**:835, 836
Lewis and, **6**:845, 848
as *Lie Down in Darkness* setting,
 11:1494, 1502
London (Jack) and, **7**:880
Malamud and, **7**:909, 910, 913,
 914

Mamet and, **7**:928, 931
Masters and, **7**:949
McCullers and, **7**:976-77, 979
McNickle and, **7**:995, 997, 1005
Miller and, **8**:1013, 1014, 1017,
 1018
Moore and, **8**:1033, 1035, 1036,
 1037
Morrison and, **8**:1052, 1053
as *Natural* setting, **7**:922
Norris and, **8**:1090, 1092
as *Norwood* setting, **9**:1248
Oates and, **8**:1107
O'Connor and, **8**:1136, 1137
O'Neill and, **9**:1157, 1158, 1159,
 1160, 1163, 1176
Piercy and, **9**:1199
as *Pigman* setting, **12**:1722
Plath and, **9**:1215
Porter and, **9**:1230, 1233
Portis and, **9**:1247, 1249
Potok and, **9**:1259, 1260, 1261,
 1263, 1264, 1266
as *Price* setting, **8**:1029
as *Promise* setting, **9**:1272
as *Raise High the Roof Beam,
 Carpenter, and Seymour: An
 Introduction* settings, **10**:1317
Rich and, **9**:1280, 1281
Salinger and, **10**:1301, 1303,
 1305, 1306, 1309
Sandburg and, **10**:1324, 1331
Sinclair and, **10**:1378, 1382
Singer and, **10**:1397, 1403,
 1412, 1413, 1414
as *Spanish Prisoner* setting, **7**:940,
 941
Steinbeck and, **11**:1445, 1447,
 1448, 1449, 1451
Stevens and, **11**:1468, 1469,
 1471
Styron and, **11**:1491, 1492
Terkel and, **11**:1519, 1520, 1523
as *This Side of Paradise* setting,
 4:534, 535
as *Two for Seesaw* setting, **5**:621
Walker and, **11**:1563, 1564,
 1566, 1573
Welty and, **12**:1591, 1593
Wharton and, **12**:1611, 1612,
 1614, 1615, 1617, 1619,
 1621, 1622, 1625, 1626
T. Williams and, **12**:1651, 1653,
 1654, 1655
W. C. Williams and, **12**:1676,
 1677, 1678

as *Woman on the Edge of Time* set-
 ting, **9**:1207
Wright and, **12**:1695
Zindel and, **12**:1711, 1712,
 1714, 1721
See also Bronx; Brooklyn;
 Greenwich Village; Harlem
Nicaragua, Didion and, **3**:373
Noon City (Capote fictional place),
 2:252
Norfolk (Va.), **2**:190
Normandy (France), **12**:1696
North Africa, **2**:235, **11**:1451
North Carolina
 Angelou and, **1**:60, 61
 Baldwin and, **1**:106
 McCullers and, **7**:977, 979
 National Endowment for the Arts
  program, 29, **1**:28
 Sandburg and, **10**:1323, 1327,
  1328
 Tyler and, **11**:1542, 1546, 1549
North Conway (N.H.), Cummings
 and, **3**:311, 316
North Plymouth (Mass.; Sinclair fic-
 tional place), **10**:1390
Notasulga (Ala.), Hurston and,
 6:745, 746, 749
Nova Scotia (Canada), **1**:82
Nuremberg (Germany), **8**:1016,
 1019
Nyack (N.Y.)
 Foote and, **4**:543
 McCullers and, **7**:975, 978, 979

Oakland (Calif.)
 Didion and, **3**:369
 Giovanni and, **5**:637
 London (Jack) and, **7**:870, 871,
  873, 874, 876, 883
 Norris and, **8**:1086, 1089
 Stein and, **10**:1418, 1422, 1431
 Tan and, **11**:1505, 1506, 1509
Oak Park (Ill.), Hemingway and,
 5:659, 660, 665, 666
Oathe (Kans.), **2**:249
Ohio
 Anderson and, **1**:41, 42, 44, 46-
  47, 50, 51-53
 Dreiser and, **3**:376, 377, 386,
  388
 Dunbar and, **3**:397, 398, 399,
  401, 402, 404, 416
 Giovanni and, **5**:628, 629, 631
 Hughes and, **6**:727, 730
 Morrison and, **8**:1049, 1050,

1051, 1052, 1056, 1057, 1060, 1063, 1065

Schaefer and, **10**:1343, 1344, 1347

Oklahoma

as *Cimarron* setting, **4**:506, 507, 508, 509

Ellison and, **4**:459, 460, 461, 463, 464

Hinton and, **5**:699, 702, 703, 711, 717

Steinbeck and, **11**:1462, 1464

Oklahoma City (Okla.), Ellison and, **4**:459, 460, 461, 463

Ontario (Canada)

Atwood and, **1**:81, 82, 83, *84*, 85

Davies and, **3**:333, 334, *334*, 335, 337, 338, 343, 347, 349

as *Diviners* setting, **6**:825, 826

farmhouse (painting), **3**:*309*

Laurence and, **6**:819, 820, 822, 823

as *Lives of Girls and Women* setting, **8**:1079

Munro and, **8**:1071, 1073, 1075, 1077, 1079, 1080

Oates and, **8**:1105, 1106

as *Who Do You Think You Are?* setting, **8**:1081, 1082

Oregon

Carver and, **2**:255, 256, 258

Malamud and, **7**:911, 912, 913, 916, 924, 925

Orlando (Fla.), **1**:65

Oscar (La.), Gaines and, **5**:581, 585

Oswiecim (Poland), **11**:*1495*

Ottawa (Ontario, Canada), **1**:81, 82, 85

Oxford (Miss.), Faulkner and, **4**:476, 477, 478, 479, 480, 481, 485

Pacific Grove (Calif.), Steinbeck and, **11**:1447

Palm Springs (Calif.), Capote and, **2**:237

Palo Alto (Calif.), Carver and, **2**:257

Panama, Lewis and, **6**:844, 848

Panama Canal Zone, **1**:41, 44

Paradise (Calif.), Carver and, **2**:256, 258

Paris (France)

Anderson and, **1**:45

Baldwin and, **1**:104, 105

Benét and, **2**:151, 152

Cummings and, **3**:315, 317, 330-31

Hemingway and, **5**:661, 665, 666, 670

MacLeish and, **7**:894, 895, 897, 899

McCullers and, **7**:979

Moore and, **8**:1035

Norris and, **8**:1087

Stein and, **10**:1417, 1418, 1419, 1420, 1421, 1422, 1424, 1427, 1429, 1431

Styron and, **11**:1491

as *Sun Also Rises* setting, **5**:663, 676, 677

Wharton and, **12**:1615

T. Williams and, **12**:1653

W. C. Williams and, **12**:1676

Wright and, **12**:1693, 1696, 1697, 1708

Parris Island (S.C.), Styron and, **11**:1490-91, 1496

Pasadena (Calif.), Sinclair and, **10**:1379, 1382

Paterson (N.J.)

as *Island Like You* setting, **9**:1189

as *Latin Deli* setting, **9**:1191

as *Line of the Sun* setting, **9**:1193

Ortiz Cofer and, **9**:1182, 1185, 1187, 1194

W. C. Williams and, **12**:1685, 1686, 1687

Pearl Harbor (Hawaii)

Benét and, **2**:154

Didion and, **3**:354

Terkel and, **11**:1538, 1539

Pennsylvania

Benét and, **2**:149, 150, 152, 161

Cather and, **2**:270-71, 274, 275, 281, 285, 286

Dreiser and, **3**:377, 384, 392

Gardner and, **5**:595, 598, 599

Jeffers and, **6**:783, 784, 787

Knowles and, **6**:808

Masters and, **7**:945, 949, 950

Moore and, **8**:1034, 1037

Potok and, **9**:1263

as *Song of Solomon* setting, **8**:1067

Stein and, **10**:1417, 1418, 1422

Stevens and, **11**:1467, 1468, 1471, 1484

Peru, as *Bridge of San Luis Rey* setting, **12**:1636, 1643

Peterborough (Ontario, Canada)

Davies and, **3**:337, 338, 347, 349

Laurence and, **6**:823

Petersburg (Ill.)

Masters and, **7**:946, 949, 950, 953, 959

as *Spoon River Anthology* setting, **7**:957

Philadelphia (Pa.)

Benét and, **2**:161

Dreiser and, **3**:392

Knowles and, **6**:808

Philippines, **5**:685

Pittsburgh (Pa.)

Cather and, **2**:270-71, 274, 275, 285, 286

Dreiser and, **3**:377, 384

Jeffers and, **6**:783, 784, 787

Sandburg and, **10**:1324

Pittsburg Landing (Tenn.), **2**:159

Plainsfield (Mass.) Ellison and, **4**:463

Point Lobos (Calif.), Jeffers and, **6**:789, 792

Point Sur (Calif.), Jeffers and, **6**:789

Poland

Hersey and, **5**:686, 688, 694-96

Salinger and, **10**:1302

Singer and, **10**:1397, 1398, 1399, 1400, 1403, 1404, 1408, 1411, 1415

Port Angeles (Wash.), Carver and, **2**:255, 257, 258

Port Warwick (Va.; Styron fictional setting), **11**:1502

Prague (Czechoslovakia), **3**:430

Providence (R.I.), McCarthy and, **7**:961, 962, 965

Provincetown (Mass.), O'Neill and, **9**:1169

Puerto Rico

as *Island Like You* setting, **9**:1189

as *Latin Deli* setting, **9**:1191

Ortiz Cofer and, **9**:1181-94

Sandburg and, **10**:1324, 1328

Putney (Vt.), **6**:767

Quebec (Canada)

Atwood and, **1**:82

Bellow and, **1**:123, 124, 126

Cather and, **2**:272, 276, 277, 278

Dreiser and, **3**:389

seventeenth-century wilderness scene, **2**:277

Sinclair and, **10**:1378

Quebec City (Canada), Cather and, **2**:272, 274

Raleigh (N.C.), Tyler and, **11**:1542, 1546, 1549

Reading (Pa.), Stevens and,
    11:1467, 1468, 1471, 1484
Renfrew (Ontario, Canada), Davies
    and, **3**:334, 343
Rhode Island
    McCarthy and, **7**:961, 962, 965
    Wharton and, **12**:1613, 1614
    Wilder and, **12**:1630, 1634
Richmond (Va.), Bontemps and,
    2:189-90
Ridgefield (Conn.), O'Connor and,
    8:1136, 1137, 1138
Ripley (Miss.), **4**:476
Riviera (France)
    as *Garden of Eden* setting, **5**:671
    Knowles and, **6**:806
    as *Morning in Antibes* setting,
        6:807
    as *Tender Is the Night* setting,
        4:533
Rockford (Tenn.), McCarthy and,
    7:963, 965
Rockport (Mass.), **4**:438
Rome (Italy)
    as *Cabala* setting, **12**:1635, 1636
    Ellison and, **4**:462
    as *Lazarus Laughed* setting,
        9:1165
    Lewis and, **6**:843, 847, 848
    Malamud and, **7**:912, 913
    Wilder and, **12**:1630
    T. Williams and, **12**:1653, 1660
Rosemont (Long Island, N.Y.; Blume
    fictional place), **2**:179
Roxbury (Conn.), Styron and,
    11:1492, 1493
Ruby (Okla.), as *Paradise* setting,
    8:1069
Russia (formerly Soviet Union)
    Capote and, **2**:235, 238
    Cummings and, **3**:315, 316, 330
    Dreiser and, **3**:378, 384
    Frost and, **4**:559, 561
    Hersey and, **5**:687, 688
    Hughes and, **6**:728, 730
    Malamud and, **7**:913
    Miller and, **8**:1018, 1025
    Steinbeck and, **11**:1451
Rutherford (N.J.), W. C. Williams
    and, **12**:1675, 1677, 1679

Sacramento (Calif.)
    Carver and, **2**:257
    Didion and, **3**:353, 354, 358, 369
Sag Harbor (Long Island, N.Y.),
    Steinbeck and, **11**:1448, 1449

St.-Brice-sous-Forêt (France),
    Wharton and, **12**:1611,
    1615, 1616
St. Ignatius (Mont.), McNickle and,
    7:993, 994, 997
St. Louis (Mo.)
    Angelou and, **1**:57, 58, 60, 75
    Dreiser and, **3**:377
    Eliot and, **4**:437, 438, 441
    as *Glass Menagerie* setting,
        12:1663
    T. Williams and, **12**:1652, 1654,
        1655, 1656, 663, 1664
St. Nicholas' Cathedral (Davies fic-
    tional place), **3**:351
St. Paul (Minn.), Fitzgerald and,
    4:515, 516, 518, 522, 531
St. Paul-de-Vence (France), **1**:101,
    104, 107
Salem (Mass.)
    as *Crucible* setting, **8**:1019, 1022,
        1023, 1024
    Eliot and, **4**:438
    Porter and, **9**:1231, 1234
Salinas Valley (Calif.)
    as *East of Eden* setting, **11**:1466
    as *Of Mice and Men* setting,
        11:1460, 1461
    as *Red Pony* setting, **11**:1464
    Steinbeck and, **11**:1445, 1446,
        1449, 1451, 1452
Salterton (Ontario; Canada; Davies
    fictional place), **3**:337, 338,
    340-41, 347-50, 351
San Diego (Calif.), Angelou and,
    1:58-59
San Francisco (Calif.)
    Angelou and, **1**:58, 59, 60, 62,
        66, 67, 75
    as Didion influence, **3**:354, 360,
        366, 369
    Frost and, **4**:555, 556, 560, 562
    as *Hundred Secret Senses* setting,
        11:1517
    as *Joy Luck Club* setting, **11**:1513,
        1514
    London (Jack) and, **7**:869, 874,
        878
    as *McTeague* setting, **8**:1094
    as "Music from Spain" setting,
        12:1601, 1602
    Norris and, **8**:1085, 1086, 1087,
        1089
    as *Octopus* setting, **8**:1097
    as *Vandover and the Brute* setting,
        8:1100

Walker and, **11**:1564, 1566,
    1567, 1570
San Francisco Bay Area (Calif.)
    as *Kitchen God's Wife* setting,
        11:1515
    London (Jack) and, **7**:869, 871,
        874, 877
    as *Martin Eden* setting, **7**:885
    as *Sea-Wolf* setting, **7**:889
    Tan and, **11**:1506, 1507, 1509
Sangamon Valley, **7**:952, 953, 955,
    959
San Joaquin Valley (Calif.), as
    Octopus setting, **8**:1088, 1091,
    1097
San Miguel de Allende (Mexico)
    as *Dog of the South* setting,
        9:1254
    Portis and, **9**:1249
San Pedro (Calif.), **10**:1380
Santa Clara Valley (Calif.), as *Call of
    the Wild* setting, **7**:884, 885
Santa Cruz (Calif.), **9**:1281
Santa Fe (N.M.)
    Cather and, **2**:280, 281
    Schaefer and, **10**:1343, 1346,
        1347, 1350
Santa Rosa (Calif.), as *Shadow of a
    Doubt* setting, **12**:1641
Saratoga Springs (N.Y.), **1**:28
Sauk Centre (Minn.), Lewis and,
    6:843, 844, 845, 847, 848,
    852
Savannah (Ga.), O'Connor and,
    8:1135, 1136, 1139
Seattle (Wash.), as *Glengarry Glen
    Ross* setting, **7**:939
Sevier County (Tenn.), McCarthy
    and, **7**:962, 963
Shanghai (China)
    Buck and, **2**:210, 211, 212
    Wilder and, **12**:1630, 1634
Silver Lake (N.H.), **3**:312
Silver Spring (Md.), Porter and,
    9:1229, 1232, 1233
Skeena River (British Columbia),
    1:82
South, U.S.
    Dunbar and, **3**:407, 409, 410,
        411, 415
    Faulkner and, **4**:485
    Foote and, **4**:545, 554
    Hughes and, **6**:728, 730, 738
    Hurston and, **6**:747, 761
    as *Invisible Man* setting, **4**:465
    McCarthy and, **7**:961, 966, 971

McCullers and, 7:975-92
as *Meridian* setting, 11:1581
O'Connor and, 7:975, 8:1136,
1142, 1143, *1144*, 1148,
11:1495, 1512
Styron and, **11**:1489, 1490,
1492, 1494, 1495
Welty and, **12**:1589-1610
T. Williams and, **12**:1651-74
See also specific cities and states
South Africa, Norris and, **8**:1088,
1089
Southampton (Long Island, N.Y.)
Knowles and, **6**:807, 808
South Braintree (Mass.), **10**:1391
South Carolina, Styron and,
11:1490-91, 1496
Southern California
as *Oil!* setting, **10**:1394, 1395
Rich and, **9**:1293
South Side (Chicago), scene pho-
tographs, **2**:*201*
Southwest, U.S.
Cather and, **2**:272, 276, 281
as *Runner in the Sun* setting, **7**:1001
See also specific cities and states
Soviet Union. *See* Russia
Spain
Hemingway and, **5**:663, 664,
666, 675, 676, 677, 678
Hughes and, **6**:729, 730
Malamud and, **7**:913
McCarthy and, **7**:963
Plath and, **9**:1216
Porter and, **9**:1231, 1234
Stein and, **10**:1420, 1422
Wright and, **12**:1696, 1697
Stamps (Ark.), **1**:58, 60, 75
Staten Island (N.Y.C.)
as *Rats* setting, **12**:1715
Zindel and, **12**:1711, 1712, 1721
Stinson Beach (Calif.), **3**:354
Stockbridge (Mass.), Gibson and,
5:613, 615, 617
Stockholm (Sweden), **1**:114
O'Neill and, **9**:1163
Sandburg and, **10**:1326, 1328
Stockton (Calif.), **1**:59
Sullivan (Ind.), **3**:376
Surfside (Fla.), Singer and, **10**:1397,
1400, 1403
Susquehanna (Pa.), Gardner and,
5:595, 598, 599
Sweden
O'Neill and, **9**:1163
Sandburg and, **10**:1326, 1328

Switzerland
Baldwin and, 119-9
Davies and, **3**:339, 3431328
as *Farewell to Arms* setting,
5:672, 674
Porter and, **9**:1231
Tan and, **11**:1507, 1509
W. C. Williams and, **12**:1676
Sycamore Canyon (Calif.), **6**:790
Syracuse (N.Y.), Morrison and,
8:1052, 1053

Tacoma (Wash.), **6**:785
Tangier, **2**:235
Tanzania, **2**:208
Taormina, **2**:235
Tehran (Iran), as *Going After
Cacciato* setting, **8**:1129
Tennessee
Agee and, **1**:11, 12, 14, 18, 19,
21
Baldwin and, **1**:106
Benét, **2**:159
Bontemps and, **2**:181, 183, 184,
185
Brooks and, **2**:199
Giovanni and, **5**:627, 628, 631
McCarthy and, **7**:962, 963, 965,
971, 972
T. Williams and, **12**:1652
Wright and, **12**:1694, 1703
Tenochtitlán, as *Fall of the City* set-
ting, **7**:905
Terre Haute (Ind.), Dreiser and,
3:375, 376, 384
Texas
Foote and, **4**:541
McCarthy and, **7**:963, 965
as *Noon Wine* setting, **9**:1237
Oates and, **8**:1104
as "Old Order" setting, **9**:1235
Porter and, **9**:1230
Zindel and, **12**:1713, 1721
Thamesville (Ontario, Canada),
Davies and, **3**:333, 334, 337,
338, 343, 345
Toluca (Mexico), **6**:727
Topeka (Kans.)
Benét and, **2**:*158*
Brooks and, **2**:195, 196, 199
Gibson and, **5**:612, 613, 615, 616
Toronto (Ontario, Canada)
Atwood and, **1**:83, 84, 85, 87,
89, 96, 97, 99
Davies and, **3**:333, *334*, 335,
337, 338

Irving and, **6**:767
as *Who Do You Think You Are?* setting, **8**:1081
Tulsa (Okla.)
Hinton and, **5**:699, 703
as *Outsiders* setting, **5**:711
as *Tex* film setting, **5**:702
as *That Was Then, This Is Now* setting, **5**:717
Turkey, **1**:104

Unzen (Japan), **2**:212

Vancouver (British Columbia,
Canada)
as *Fire-Dwellers* setting, **6**:831
Laurence and, **6**:821
Munro and, **8**:1074, 1075
as *Who Do You Think You Are?* set-
ting, **8**:1081, 1082
Venice (Italy)
as *Across River and Into Trees* set-
ting, **5**:664
Hemingway and, **5**:666
as *Marco Millions* setting, **9**:1178
Ventana Mountains (Calif.), **6**:789
Vermont
Alvarez and, **1**:28, 29
as *Arrowsmith* setting, **6**:857, 858
Cormier and, **3**:306
as *Dubin's Lives* setting, **7**:924
Frost and, **4**:560
Gardner and, **5**:598, 604, 605
Irving, **6**:767
Lewis and, **6**:848
Malamud and, **7**:911, 912, 914,
916, 924
Mamet and, **7**:928, 930, 931
Rich and, **9**:1292, 1293
Vevey (Switzerland), **4**:534
Victoria (British Columbia, Canada),
8:1074
Vienna (Austria)
Davies and, **3**:339, 343
as *Hotel New Hampshire* setting,
6:776, 777
Irving and, **6**:764, 765, 771,
773, 776, 777, 778, 781
as *158-Pound Marriage* setting,
6:780
Stein and, **10**:1418, 1422
as *Tender Is the Night* setting, **4**:533
as *Water-Method Man* setting,
6:782
as *World According to Garp* setting, **6**:778

Vincennes (Ind.), Dreiser and, **3**:376
Vineyard Haven (Mass.), Styron
and, **11**:1493
Virginia
Anderson and, **1**:44, 45, 46, 55
Benét and, **2**:158, 159
Bontemps and, **2**:190
Buck and, **2**:210, 212
Cather and, **2**:269, 274
as *Confessions of Nat Turner* set-
ting, **11**:1497
Giovanni and, **5**:632, 633
Schaefer and, **10**:1345
Styron and, **11**:1489, 1490, 1496

Walden Pond, **3**:312
Wales, **3**:334
Walt Disney World (Orlando, Fla.),
1:*65*
Warsaw (Ind.), Dreiser and, **3**:376,
380, 384
Warsaw (Poland)
as *Certificate* setting, **10**:1407,
1409
as *Family Moskat* setting,
10:1409, 1410, **14**:1412
Hersey and, **5**:686, 688
as *Shosha* setting, **10**:1412, 1413
Singer and, **10**:1398, 1399,
1400, 1403, 1404, 1408,
1411, 1415
as *Wall* setting, **5**:694-96
Washington (D.C.)
Angelou and, **1**:60, *61*
Baldwin play productions, **1**:113
Dreiser and, **3**:386, 388
Dunbar and, **3**:401, 402, 411
Foote and, **4**:542, 543

as *Juneteenth* setting, **4**:470
Lewis and, **6**:848, 854
Malamud and, **7**:911, 913
Porter and, **9**:1232
Washington (state)
Carver and, **2**:255, 256, 257, 258
Jeffers and, **6**:784, 785
Watts section (Los Angeles), **2**:182,
5:629
Webster County (Neb.), Cather and,
2:270, 274, 281-84
Wellesley (Mass.), **9**:1214
West, U.S.
Bucks and, **2**:223
Carver and, **2**:256
McCarthy and, **7**:961, 964, 966,
969, 970
as Schaefer focus, **10**:1343,
1345, 1346, 1348, 1350,
1352, 1353, 1355, 1356
West Egg (Long Island, N.Y.;
Fitzgerald fictional place),
4:531
Weston (Mass.), **10**:1357
West Virginia
Buck and, **2**:209, 210, 212
Knowles and, **6**:803, 804, 808
Wharton (Tex.), Foote and, **4**:539,
540, *541*, 543, 544, 548
Wheatsylvania (N.D.); Sinclair fic-
tional place), **6**:857
Wichita (Kans.), as *Cimarron* setting,
4:506, 507
Wickburg (Mass.; Cormier fictional
place), **3**:308
Wilmington (Del.), **4**:518
Winesburg (Ohio); Anderson fic-
tional town), **1**:41, 42, 50

Wingham (Ontario, Canada), Munro
and, **8**:1071, 1073, 1075,
1079, 1080
Winthrop (Mass.), **9**:1214
Wisconsin
Eliot and, **4**:448
Ferber and, **4**:500, 503, 508
Sandburg and, **10**:1325, 1328
Welty and, **12**:1606
Worcester (Mass.), Cormier and,
3:294, 297
Worthington (Minn.), **8**:1120
Wyoming (Ohio), Giovanni and,
5:628, 631
Wyoming
Cather and, **2**:275
as *Shane* setting, **10**:1353

Yakima (Wash.), Carver and, **2**:256,
258
Yoknapatawpha county (Faulkner
fictional place), **4**:478, 487,
490, *493*, 495, 497, **6**:827
Yukon Territory (Canada)
as *Call of the Wild* setting, **7**:884,
885
London and, **7**:873, 874, 876,
877, 880
as "To Build a Fire" setting,
7:889, 890
as *White Fang* setting, **7**:886, 887

Zenith (Ohio; Lewis fictional place,
6:854, 855, 856, 859, 860,
861
Zurich (Switzerland), Davies and,
3:339